REVISION CHECKLIST Short Fiction

▶ Structure and Design

☐ Does your story begin at the moment of maximum tension and end in the most aesthetically satisfying place?

☐ Is the story's conflict immediately clear, and does that conflict generate some essential change in the characters or their situations?

▶ Creating Characters

☐ Have you clearly yet succinctly delineated each of your main characters and their primary goals?

☐ Have you eliminated unnecessary characters and combined those with redundant traits into a single character?

☐ If your characters are named, are their names fitting and believable?

☐ Is at least one of your main characters different at the end of the story than she or he was at the beginning?

▶ Writing Dialogue

☐ Is the nature and amount of dialogue appropriate to the characters and the action of your story?

☐ To avoid any confusion about who is saying what, have you clearly, and unobtrusively, tagged all speakers of dialogue?

▶ Setting the Scene

☐ Is the description of time and location believable, detailed, and relevant to your particular story?

▶ Deciding on Point of View, Developing Tone and Style

☐ Have you carefully weighed which point of view—first person, second person, or omniscient—and which verb tense—past or present—are most conducive to the telling of your story?

☐ Do the tone and style of your story suit its content?

Creative Writing
Four Genres in Brief

SECOND EDITION

David Starkey

Santa Barbara City College

Bedford/St. Martin's   Boston ◆ New York

For My Father

For Bedford/St. Martin's
Senior Executive Editor: Stephen A. Scipione
Production Editor: Kerri A. Cardone
Production Supervisors: Lisa Chow, Victoria Sharoyan
Senior Marketing Manager: Stacy Propps
Editorial Assistant: Alyssa Demirjian
Copy Editor: Beverly Miller
Indexer: Steve Csipke
Permissions Manager: Kalina K. Ingham
Senior Art Director: Anna Palchik
Cover Design and Art: Billy Boardman
Composition: Cenveo Publisher Services
Printing and Binding: RR Donnelley and Sons

President, Bedford/St. Martin's: Denise B. Wydra
Presidents, Macmillan Higher Education: Joan E. Feinberg and Tom Scotty
Editor in Chief: Karen S. Henry
Director of Marketing: Karen R. Soeltz
Production Director: Susan W. Brown
Associate Production Director: Elise S. Kaiser
Managing Editor: Elizabeth M. Schaaf

Library of Congress Control Number: 2012941691

Manufactured in the United States of America.
7 6 5 4
f e d

For information, write: Bedford/St. Martin's, 75 Arlington Street, Boston, MA 02116 (617-399-4000)

ISBN 978-1-4576-1156-8

Acknowledgments

PREFACE: A few words to instructors

After many years of teaching college creative writing classes, I prepared *Creative Writing: Four Genres in Brief* because I felt that the available textbooks, however excellent, didn't reflect some important realities of the course. One such reality is the lack of sufficient time. How can an instructor effectively teach writing in multiple genres over the course of only a semester or a quarter? Another reality is the variety of students. Although plenty of English majors hoping to become writers enroll, the course also attracts history and sociology and math and chemistry majors—students who only want to dip a toe in the pool of creative writing before deciding whether they want to jump in and take a swim.

Even though my students and I have learned much from the authors of other textbooks, we have found that the literary models in those books are usually much longer and far more complex than the work students in introductory courses can reasonably be expected to read and produce in the few weeks assigned to each literary genre. That's why this book is full of brief poems, short-short stories, short creative nonfiction, and ten-minute plays—works that students, whatever their commitment to creative writing, can realistically learn from and emulate in the short time an introductory course affords.

As much as I love Raymond Carver's frequently anthologized story "Cathedral," I'm doing my students a disservice if I hold up that carefully wrought, 6,000-word story as a model for their own work in the course. We creative writing instructors don't want our students to read bad models, but if we want them to write both briefly and well, then we need to give them readings that are as concise as the work we expect to see in their final portfolios. For that reason, rather than including "Cathedral" in this volume, I have selected Carver's equally deft short-short story "Popular Mechanics" instead.

Moreover, students tend to rush through each genre if they feel overwhelmed by the number of pages they have to produce. But when course goals are more realistic, student work often improves significantly. A student who has written only three pages of a four-page story feels considerably less distressed about starting over than when he is ten pages into a twelve-page story. And students are much more likely to thoroughly revise a shorter piece than a longer one.

Short forms also make it easier for instructors to engage their students in detailed analysis and discussion. Suddenly, a ninety-minute class meeting can allow for an extremely close reading of several professional works, or can provide feedback for four or five student works rather than just two. Outside of class, instructors can spend more time carefully commenting on student work if they have fewer pages to read.

But what of those students—the English majors, the creative writing majors—who aspire to have their work published and produced? They should realize that writing in short forms is not merely practice for longer work in later courses. Certainly students who work in short forms are learning fundamentals, but they are also creating potentially publishable pieces of writing. Short-short stories are now a staple of most literary magazines. Short essays are increasingly popular. And a ten-minute play is more likely to be produced (festivals for such plays are popping up all over) than a full-length piece.

In keeping with the short works of literature in the book, I have tried to keep my own instruction relatively brief. Because I have learned so much from other writers, I bring their voices in as much as possible, stepping aside to allow them to speak to students about the nature and process of creative writing and to offer advice and helpful hints.

How the book is organized

That's the "why" of *Creative Writing: Four Genres in Brief.* Here is how it's put together.

The book begins with a general introduction to the differences and similarities between creative writing and the expository writing done in most college classes. The introduction orients students by suggesting what they already know that might be useful, and what they can expect to learn.

Following the introduction are four chapters, each of which focuses on a specific genre: poetry, fiction, creative nonfiction, and drama. Each chapter begins with a brief opening section that sketches out the broad parameters of the genre. Then I analyze three model examples of work in the genre, focusing on their use of literary elements. After the discussion of each element, I summarize for students the main points about using the element in their own writing. Sprinkled throughout the chapter are key terms (called out in **boldface** the first time they appear and collected in a glossary at the end of the book). The chapters culminate with a series of "Kick-Starts"—exercises and strategies to help students generate ideas and begin the writing process.

After the "Kick-Starts" are short anthologies of work in each genre. Occasionally, I have included an important older work, but the focus is on excellent contemporary writers whom students probably have not encountered before. The selections range from the more traditional—with work by such writers as Roberta Allen, Ron Carlson, John Cheever, Edwidge Danticat, and Mary Oliver—to the experimental—including pieces by Rae Armantrout, Donald Barthelme, Dan Dietz, Joyce Carol Oates, and Matthew Zapruder.

Above all, *Creative Writing: Four Genres in Brief* is intended to be a pragmatic book. If money and time were no object, an introductory course might include four craft books on the four different genres, as well as four separate anthologies packed with representative examples of each genre. But because money and time are important considerations, this book attempts to combine all the resources students will need in a single, affordable package.

A few words about what's new in the second edition

Instructors who taught from the first edition suggested a number of changes, large and small. Accordingly I have incorporated many new examples of contemporary writing, added some necessary coverage of revision, and appended a new section for students who aspire to publish their writing or produce their plays.

▶ **Lots of new models of creative writing.** Half the anthologized literary works are new to the second edition, including poems by Marilyn Chin, Brenda Hillman, Ben Lerner, Molly Peacock, and Patricia Smith; stories by Margaret Atwood, Aimee Bender, Ursula Hegi, and Pam Houston; creative nonfiction by James Brown, Joan Didion, Pico Iyer, and Alice Walker; and drama by Adam Kraar and K. Alexa Mavromatis. The new selections introduce students to important voices in contemporary literature and should keep the book fresh and engaging for instructors who use it year after year.

▶ **Help with the revision process.** Because the book grew partially out of the notion that if students read and write short-short literary works, they'll have more time to revise, I've added advice to assist them in making the most of that time. A brief new section following the introduction lays out some proven strategies for revision, and students can turn to the endpapers to find checklists of tips for revising in each genre.

▶ **Advice for students on publishing their writing and producing their plays.** A new section at the back of the book offers students practical suggestions for getting their creative work out into the world. The recommendations are detailed and realistically scaled to what beginning writers can hope to achieve in their first attempts at bringing their poems, stories, essays, and plays to a larger public.

▶ **Available as an e-book.** *Creative Writing: Four Genres in Brief* is now available digitally. The second edition thus offers greater teaching flexibility for instructors and affordability for students. For more information about these electronic formats, visit bedfordstmartins.com/starkey/catalog.

Thanks

My thanks to the many readers, reviewers, and adopters of this book whose suggestions improved both editions: M. Lee Alexander, College of William and Mary; John Belk, Pennsylvania State University; Jenny Box, East Mississippi

Community College; Daryl W. Brown, University of North Alabama; Jeanne DeQuine, Miami-Dade College; Melvin Donalson, California State University, Los Angeles; Amie A. Doughty, SUNY-Oneonta; Laurie Lynn Drummond, University of Oregon; Marilyn Y. Ford, East Mississippi Community College; Pamela Gemin, University of Wisconsin, Oshkosh; Mary B. Graham, Cuyamaca College; Martha Greenwald, University of Louisville; Kevin Griffith, Capital University; Joseph D. Haske, South Texas College; Sonya Huber, Georgia Southern University; Claire Kageyama-Ramakrishnan, Houston Community College, Central Campus; Laura Kopchick, University of Texas at Arlington; Thomas Maltman, Normandale Community College; Michael Minassian, Broward Community College; Rebecca Mooney, Bakersfield College; Juan Morales, Colorado State University, Pueblo; Joyce Pesseroff, University of Massachusetts, Boston; Stuart Peterfreund, Northeastern University; Lauri Ramey, California State University, Los Angeles; Christopher Ransick, Arapahoe Community College; Brent Royster, Ball State University; Jeremy Schraffenberger, Binghamton University; Pat Tyrer, West Texas A & M University; Vallie Lynn Watson, Southeast Missouri State University; Theresa Welford, Georgia Southern University; Jerry Wemple, Bloomsburg University; Robert Wiley, Oakland Community College; Martha Witt, William Patterson University; and Angus Woodward, Our Lady of the Lake College.

Thanks also to the good folks at Bedford/St. Martin's: Maureen Tomlin, who suggested that I submit my proposal; Leasa Burton and Ellen Darion, who saw its potential; and Joan Feinberg, Denise Wydra, and Karen Henry, who gave the book the green light. I'd like to thank Margaret Gorenstein and Kalina Ingham for their work on permissions, and Alyssa Demirjian for the numberless editorial tasks she performed throughout the development process. Thanks to Stacey Propps for her marketing efforts. In the production department, I'm grateful to Elizabeth Schaaf and Elise Kaiser; to Beverly Miller for her sensitive and tactful copyediting; and especially to the book's friendly and efficient production editor, Kerri Cardone. Above all, I appreciate the editorial contributions of Steve Scipione, who was there from the initial concept to the final product—and every step in between.

Finally, I would like to thank my parents, Frank and Betty; my children and stepchildren, Elizabeth, Carly, Stephen, Miranda, Serena, Andrea, Julia, and John; and especially my lovely, patient, and brilliant wife, Sandy.

—David Starkey

You get more resources for *Creative Writing: Four Genres in Brief*

Creative Writing: Four Genres in Brief doesn't stop with a book. It's available in several digital formats, including CourseSmart e-book, PDF e-book, and as a Bedford e-Book to Go. Online, you'll find both free and affordable premium resources to help students get even more out of the book and your course. You'll also find convenient instructor resources. To learn more about or order any of the products below, contact your Bedford/St. Martin's sales representative, e-mail sales support (sales_support@bfwpub.com), or visit the Web site at **bedfordstmartins.com/starkey/catalog/.**

E-book Options **bedfordstmartins.com/starkey/catalog** Bedford/St. Martin's e-Books let students do more and pay less. For about half the price of a print book, the e-book for *Creative Writing; Four Genres in Brief*, Second Edition, offers the complete text of the print book combined with convenient digital tools such as highlighting, note-taking, and search. Both online and downloadable options are available.

Visit the Book Companion Site for *Creative Writing: Four Genres in Brief* **bedfordstmartins.com/starkey** The companion site offers instructors resources for teaching with the book, and students will find downloadable checklists for writing in each genre. In addition, you can supplement your print text with our free and open resources for literature (no codes required) and flexible premium content, including *VirtuaLit* tutorials for close reading (fiction, poetry, and drama); *AuthorLinks* and biographies for 800 authors; and a glossary of literary terms.

Access video interviews with today's writers. *VideoCentral: Literature*, our growing library of more than 50 video interviews with today's writers, includes Ha Jin on how he uses humor, Chitra Banerjee Divakaruni on how she writes from experience, and T. C. Boyle on how he works with language and style. Biographical notes and questions make each video an assignable module. See **bedfordstmartins.com/videolit/catalog**. This resource can be packaged with new student editions of this book. An activation code is required and must be purchased. To order *VideoCentral: Literature* with this print text, use **ISBN 978–1–4576–5417–6**.

Access Your Instructor Resources **bedfordstmartins.com/catalog/catalog** You have a lot to do in your course. Bedford/St. Martin's wants to make it easy for you to find the support you need—and to get it quickly.

Download your instructor's resources. *Resources for Teaching Creative Writing: Four Genres in Brief,* Second Edition, is written by David Starkey, who offers commentaries on all the poems, stories, essays, and plays in the book's anthologies, along with a bibliography of useful resources for teaching creative writing. For the PDF, go to **bedfordstmartins.com/starkeycatalog.**

Get teaching ideas you can use today. Are you looking for professional resources for teaching literature and writing? How about some help with planning classroom activities?

Teaching Central. We've gathered all of our print and online professional resources in one place. You'll find landmark reference works, sourcebooks on pedagogical issues, award-winning collections, and practical advice for the classroom—all free for instructors and available at **bedfordstmartins.com/teachingcentral**.

LitBits Blog: Ideas for Teaching Literature and Creative Writing. Our new *LitBits* blog—hosted by a growing team of instructors, poets, novelists, and scholars—offers a fresh, regularly updated collection of ideas and assignments. You'll find simple ways to teach with new media, excite your students with activities, and join an ongoing conversation about teaching. Go to **bedfordstmartins.com/litbits/catalog** and **bedfordstmartins.com/litbits**.

Package one of our best-selling brief handbooks at a discount. Do you need a pocket-sized handbook for your course? Package *Easy Writer* by Andrea Lunsford or *A Pocket Style Manual* by Diana Hacker and Nancy Sommers with this text at a 20 percent discount. For more information go to **bedfordstmartins.com/easywriter/catalog** or **bedfordstmartins.com/pocket/catalog**.

TradeUp and save 50 percent.

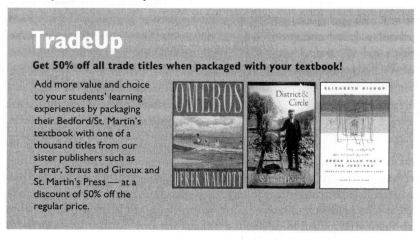

TradeUp

Get 50% off all trade titles when packaged with your textbook!

Add more value and choice to your students' learning experiences by packaging their Bedford/St. Martin's textbook with one of a thousand titles from our sister publishers such as Farrar, Straus and Giroux and St. Martin's Press — at a discount of 50% off the regular price.

CONTENTS

1 Writing Poetry 14

An Anthology of Short Poems 71

2 Writing the Short-Short Story 98

4 Writing the Ten-Minute Play 233

Playscript Format: A Model 297

An Anthology of Ten-Minute Plays 305

A Few Words about Getting Your Work Published and Produced 329

A Few Words of Farewell 337

A Few Things You Should Know about Creative Writing

The first thing I say to my students once they have settled in their seats on the first day of class is "Welcome to the best course in the college." I mean that, too. I can't imagine a better place to spend time as a student, or as a teacher, than in an introductory creative writing class.

The level of excitement and possibility in a class such as the one you're now part of is hard to match. You may already feel some of that exhilaration yourself as you begin reading this book. Are you the next great novelist? The next U.S. Poet Laureate? Is the memoir of your childhood destined to hit the best-seller lists? Is your play bound for Broadway? Of course, the chance of a fabulous success is always slim—especially in early-twenty-first-century America, where there are loads of writers and a lot of competition—but you never know. And even if your work doesn't receive wide critical acclaim, even if it's not published or performed, there is no satisfaction quite like the satisfaction writers get from knowing they have written something they can be proud of.

If this class truly is the best in your college or university, what makes it so different from the others? In order to enroll in introductory creative writing, you probably have taken at least one college writing, or composition, course as a prerequisite. "Composition" is a word students tend to dread seeing on their course enrollment forms. But is composition, or expository writing, really so different from creative writing? Not as much as you might think, and that's a good thing, believe it or not. In your composition classes, you acquired a repertoire of writerly skills and strategies that will serve you well in this class.

Creative writing builds on these abilities, although it's sometimes difficult to convince students of this fact. Do you recognize yourself in the description of a student who "found composition a dreary, teacher-imposed task and creative

1

writing something done to pass time, for fun"? This is how Wendy Bishop (one of the great creative writing teachers of the late twentieth century) described many of those who signed up for her courses. Another of Bishop's students said, "In creative writing, I feel that there are no set guidelines. It leaves room for experimentation, and you can go in any angle or direction. In expository prose [composition] you have set guidelines of what you must write and how you should write it."

Although experimentation is certainly a quality about creative writing that many writers find appealing, it is not true that the field has "no set guidelines." Once you begin thinking of publication, as most writers eventually do, more often than not you will find that there are particular editors and agents who handle specific **genres**—that is, particular categories of literary work. Poetry goes to the poetry editor, this agent only handles mysteries, another specializes in memoirs, and so on. Even within the broad outlines of a genre, editors have "set guidelines"—whether or not they are articulated—about what's good and what's not. Otherwise, how would they decide which work to accept or reject?

In her book *Released into Language: Options for Teaching Creative Writing*, Bishop made a number of innovative connections between the teaching of expository and creative writing. Most of her contentions were adaptations of ideas that theorists in composition and rhetoric had developed through decades of research and discussion. Many of these discipline-wide values were spelled out in November 2004, when the National Council of Teachers of English issued a position statement entitled "Beliefs about the Teaching of Writing." Looking more closely at these beliefs will be useful to you as a new creative writing student because

- ▶ these beliefs underlie the **pedagogy**, or theory of teaching, behind this book;

- ▶ your instructor—the person who will be awarding your final grade—probably shares many of these assumptions about the teaching of creative writing;

- ▶ knowing *how* we learn something is a necessary prelude to actually doing the learning; and

- ▶ even if you find yourself disagreeing with one or more of these beliefs, thinking about *why* can be a critical stage in your development as a creative writer.

"Beliefs about the teaching of writing" ▶

1. Everyone has the capacity to write, writing can be taught, and teachers can help students become better writers. This may sound like an obvious statement. After all, if your college or university didn't believe it, why would they be offering this course? But for a long time, creative writers themselves disagreed about whether creative writing *could* be taught. Some famous writers, who also happened to be teachers, contended that the ability to write well was a gift passed down from the gods. Either you had it or you didn't, and there wasn't much your teacher could do about it if you were in the "have-not" camp.

Fortunately, in recent years these writers have tended to leave teaching to those people who truly love doing it. And even though some students arrive in the class with more talent and experience than others, in general everyone in a creative writing class can learn quite a bit—not only from the teacher but also from one another.

2. People learn to write by writing. It's great to think about writing and to talk about it. It's wonderful to read the work of other writers. But the only way you will ever become a better writer is to sit down and write. "The first and most important thing you have to know about writing," according to Walter Mosley, "is that it is something you must do every day. Every morning or every night, whatever time it is you have. Hopefully, the time you decide on is when you do your best work."

For some people, finding that time can be a real problem. They have busy schedules—jobs, family obligations, other classes—that keep them from writing. Time management and sheer willpower are their allies. Other people have time but find they have difficulty focusing; they have enrolled in this class to force themselves onto a writing schedule. Fear of receiving a poor grade is a motivating factor for this group.

Even if you're not disorganized or in a perpetual time crunch, you may find that all those ideas that have been swirling around in your head for weeks or months or years have suddenly vanished now that you have been assigned to sit down and actually write something.

Don't panic. Listen to Mosley: Keep trying to write. Keep reading. Keep talking to people about what you're trying to do and why it suddenly seems so hard. Fortunately, writer's block is not fatal, and it doesn't last forever. In fact, it's a fairly common phenomenon. "Death and taxes. Writers and writer's block," Wendy Bishop said, suggesting that—like those other two inevitabilities—block is something no writer can avoid facing at one time or another. Writing theorist Robert Graves even argues that "blocking is a by-product of any creative endeavor." According to Graves, the problems and solutions represented by blocking allow us to grow as writers. If there weren't hurdles to overcome, our work would never get any better.

Writer's block usually comes when those writing hurdles are too great for our experience and skill to surmount. One of the rationales for beginning your creative writing experience with the very short forms featured in this book is that their parameters are more clearly defined, so your goal of completing each assignment will be more easily reached, than with longer forms.

3. Writing is a process. Again, this may seem self-evident, but too often students feel that their first draft, written at a moment of heightened inspiration, is all the writing they need to do. If this description of the writing process sounds like your own, you should—in this class, at least—try to modify it. While it's true that every creative writer remembers a moment when a piece of outstanding work just came pouring out, almost perfect from the start, that's a rarity for most of us. Chances are that the story, poem, play, or essay that looked "perfect" the night you wrote it will turn out to have more than a few flaws the next morning. "Did you ever notice," the playwright Melissa James Gibson asks, how "bits of middle of the night genius vanish without fail with the dawn?"

Researchers have found that writing done well is usually a recursive process rather than a one-time effort. We start with an idea, or an image, or a phrase. We talk about it with friends, or we begin to make notes, or we simply jump in and start writing. We breeze through the first draft, or we get stuck but keep returning to it until it is finished. We show the piece to another writer, or we put it in a drawer for a week. But we always come back to it, look it over, and work at it again. We may tweak a few sentences, or we may save only the final passage and delete everything else. We make more notes. We talk to friends. We go at it yet again.

Revision is crucial in the writing process. Most writers have a small but trusted group of friends or editors to whom they can show their drafts without worrying that the comments they receive will be overly negative. The more ambition you have for your work, the greater you want it to be, the more likely your work will need not only some major surgery but also plenty of tinkering and polishing.

Even professional journalists working on a deadline, who appear to produce flawless first drafts, have a process of some sort. If they're reporters, they have taken notes. And the rare writer who takes no notes at all will have been silently thinking about an idea, talking it over with colleagues or friends, rehearsing mentally and verbally for the task of facing the page.

4. Writing and reading are related. In *Reading like a Writer*, Francine Prose reminds those who want to be creative writers that there is no substitute for reading. She claims that is how it has always been:

> Long before the idea of a writer's conference was a glimmer in anyone's eye, writers learned by reading the work of their predecessors. They studied meter with Ovid, plot construction with Homer, comedy with Aristophanes; they honed their prose style by absorbing the lucid sentences of Montaigne and Samuel Johnson. And who could have asked for better teachers: generous, uncritical, blessed with wisdom and genius, as endlessly forgiving as only the dead can be?

Growing up in a home where reading is valued is a common experience for creative writers. Meg Wolitzer says, "Reading was always something given great importance in my family, and becoming a writer seems to be a natural progression." Nicholasa Mohr adds, "I am always glad to express gratitude to the library. I spent my youth there, reading."

Even if reading was not a central part of your own youth, you can still acquire the habit. Learning to write well in a genre requires reading extensively in that genre. Your instructor may not assign all the work in this book, but I urge you to read it anyway. And when you're finished, go to the library or the bookstore and check out or buy anthologies of recent work. Read *The Pushcart Prize* series, *Best American Poetry, Best American Short Stories,* and *Best American Essays.* Read the Actors Theatre of Louisville's ten-minute play collections. Visit literary clearinghouse Web sites such as the Council of Literary Magazine Publishers (clmp.org), Litline (litline.org), and Duotrope (duotrope.com). Read through sample issues of both print and online journals. What poems are being published in the *Kenyon Review*? What is the latest in avant-garde fiction according to the editors at *Conjunctions*? Who are the featured essayists in the latest issue of *Creative Nonfiction*?

The more committed you are to your own writing, the more likely you are to want to know what has been written before. Pulitzer Prize–winning poet Jorie Graham says, "Right from the beginning, I knew that I was going to be reading for the rest of my life, and I guess part of the act of writing poetry is involved with the enormous pleasures of reading a thousand years of poetry written in the English language and constantly feeling the people writing six, seven, eight hundred years ago are still bringing you the news."

Some students avoid reading because they worry about being overly influenced by another writer. Don't worry. Embrace the influence. *Try* to write the best Charles Bukowski imitation you can manage. You won't be able to pull it off, and sooner or later you will grow tired of sounding too much like the writer you adore. At that point, your own voice will begin to emerge.

Novelist Jeffrey Eugenides says it splendidly:

Influence isn't just a matter of copying someone or learning his or her tricks. You get influenced by writers whose work gives you hints about your own abilities and inclinations. Being influenced is largely a process of self-discovery. What you have to do is put all your influences into the blender and arrive at your own style and vision. That's the way it happens in music—you put a sitar in a rock song and you get a new sound. . . . Hybrid vigor. It operates in art, too. The idea that a writer is a born genius, endowed with blazing originality, is mostly a myth, I think. You have to work at your originality. You create it; it doesn't create you.

We learn from studying examples of good writing, but we also learn from the advice of other authors: those who have gone before us, faced similar struggles, and come up with strategies for overcoming the obstacles that are blocking our paths. Consequently, this book is liberally sprinkled with quotes from writers, both obscure and renowned.

5. Writing benefits from talking. Just about any introductory creative writing course will include a significant amount of in-class discussion. Most instructors will want to talk about both the model readings *and* the student work being produced for the class. Look at these discussions as a way to learn from your classmates as well as your instructor. If you're shy, try to participate at least once every class. If you're gregarious, look for ways not to dominate the conversation but to bring out those students who aren't lucky enough to have your confidence.

Talking about writing allows you to begin developing an **aesthetic**, a sense of what you want to see in a work of art. Becoming a creative writer means becoming articulate in your analysis and informed in your opinions of the writing of others. In fact, Brett Hall Jones believes that workshop participants grow "more by looking closely at another's work than they do when it is their turn to have their piece critiqued. The selfless attention to another writer's work is where the real learning takes place."

Moreover, as we noted earlier, if your own writing is suffering from block, talking about it can often help you see what you're doing wrong. Ideally, you can discuss your work with your instructor or another student in the class, but even if your conversation is with your mother, who knows nothing about creative writing, or your dog, Rusty, whose only qualifications as a listener are his big brown eyes, the act of dissecting your own work aloud is usually beneficial.

6. Writing and reading are part of a matrix of complicated social relationships. *How* you write depends on *who* your audience is. If, for instance, you are writing a story that only your best friend will read, you might include a number of **allusions**, or references, that only he or she would understand. That same story wouldn't work as well for a class of people who didn't already know the characters involved, and your classmates would probably recommend that you revise certain aspects of the story to make it more accessible. Your decision about whether to follow their advice might hinge on your ultimate goals for your story: Is it something personal and private, not meant to be shared after all? Or are you trying to reach a broader audience, which would mean that your responsibilities as a writer would change?

"If you want to write, or really create anything," Allegra Goodman says, "you have to risk falling on your face." Most writers would agree with Goodman, but do you really want to risk falling on your face when you're trying to get a good grade? Luckily, creative writing instructors tend to favor the portfolio method of assessment, which allows you to experiment and revise your work throughout the quarter or semester.

Writing is a social activity, and we don't all start writing from the same place. Some of us grew up in communities in which nonstandard English was spoken. Some of us come to English as our second language. The words you use and the way you use them depend largely on who you are and where you're from. In a traditional expository writing course, instructors sometimes try to minimize linguistic markers of class, race, gender, region, and so on. However, the same use of language that might worry a composition teacher can be the basis for outstanding creative writing. In her critically acclaimed work *Borderlands/ La Frontera: The New Mestiza*, Gloria Anzaldúa embraces "the borderland dialect that I grew up with, talking both Spanish and English." Anzaldúa wants her readers "to start thinking about the myth of a monocultural U.S." Multicultural and even multilingual writing celebrates the author's heritage; it reaches out to different groups and expands our ideas of creativity.

If in your class you read writing that describes experiences outside the boundaries of your own life and that doesn't initially resonate with you, come back to it later and give it a second chance. Whether this work is by a student or a professional writer, it's sure to have some merit, and one of the great benefits of taking a creative writing course is the way it deepens, enriches, and complicates our understanding of other people.

7. Conventions of finished and edited texts are important to readers and therefore to writers. When you turn in a paper for a standard academic course, whether it is for English or Communication or Psychology, your instructor is likely to expect a "clean" copy of that paper, one that has been edited to eliminate spelling, punctuation, and grammar errors. If you hand in an essay that hasn't been carefully proofread, you will probably get it back with lots of red ink.

Some students enroll in a creative writing class with the idea that the conventions of written English are no longer applicable. It's true that you can write sentence fragments here. If your characters have bad grammar, you can mimic their mistakes. However, it's not true that everything you have ever learned about "correct" writing goes out the window in creative writing. Just look at the models of professional writing in this book. Even the majority of the poets— who are typically the most relentless experimenters with language—write in carefully wrought sentences. The fiction and nonfiction writers are, if anything, *hyper*conscious of prose styles and conventions. And for all their attempts to capture the rhythms of ordinary speech, the playwrights do so with brevity and grace.

In short, don't turn in an unrevised first draft in the belief that all those mistakes won't really matter because your creativity will shine through. The best creative writers are the best *writers*. Period. Abstract painters know how to paint. Free jazz musicians know how to play. Language is your medium: use it with care.

8. Assessment of writing involves complex, informed human judgment. Like it or not, someone will grade your work, and that someone is your instructor. Evaluating writing does involve "human judgment." You can't feed a poem into a Scantron machine and get back a score. At least as of this moment, computers have serious difficulty in assessing expository writing, much less creative work. So, to a large extent, you have to trust your instructor's considered opinion about your work.

Some instructors provide a checklist or a rubric that details exactly what they want and don't want you to do. Other instructors allow their guidelines to develop from class discussion. If you're not clear what your instructor is looking for, just ask. Normally instructors feel they have already made their expectations clear, but they're happy to reiterate what they're looking for in a particular genre.

Sometimes students will find that an instructor doesn't have nearly as much enthusiasm for a piece as do the students in the class. The students *loved* it, but the instructor had a number of reservations. By all means, enjoy your classmates' compliments, but don't let them go to your head. The praise of one's peers, particularly when they are still in the process of finding their own voices, can be notoriously fickle. And the reservations of your instructor are likely based on his or her extensive experience in reading and assessing creative writing. What sounds like an incredibly innovative idea to a class of new writers—a story about a writer not being able to write a story, for instance—won't be nearly as fresh to your instructor, who will have read many versions of the same idea in the past.

And let's face it: your teacher may have a very different aesthetic than you do. Some of us are more sympathetic to experimental work. Others are quite traditional in their tastes. Not every piece you turn in is going to get a perfect reading from your instructor. Nevertheless, your teacher is quite likely a published author and, at the very least, has been reading and writing considerably longer than you have. Ultimately, for the duration of this academic term, you will have to trust his or her judgment of your work.

Words to Remember

Finally, here are a few simple words before you jump into this book:

- ▶ Read.
- ▶ Write.
- ▶ Listen.
- ▶ Don't give up.
- ▶ Have fun!

A Few Words about Revision

One of the reasons your instructor may have chosen *Creative Writing: Four Genres in Brief* is that the book's focus on short assignments encourages students to work hard on revising each piece. Although **revision**—the act of reconsidering and altering a piece of writing—may initially seem like a chore, most literary writers come to enjoy the process as much as, if not more than, the creation of the first draft. Indeed, finding yourself deep in a successful revision can become almost a mystical experience. "Revising makes a person aware of how vast imagination is," Baron Wormser writes. "One accesses something much larger than one's self."

While editing and proofreading may take place in the revision process, those tasks are not what most teachers mean by "revision." Editing means eliminating sentence-level errors. Proofreading is simply making a final pass through your draft to ensure that you haven't left in any silly mistakes ("loose" for "lose," "it's" for "its," and so on).

Revision in creative writing is a much larger process. It addresses global as much as local issues. A thorough revision of your story might mean reconceptualizing both the protagonist and the plot or deleting the first three paragraphs of your six-paragraph essay. According to Todd Lubart, "The revision process involves comparing an existing text to a writer's goals or ideal text, diagnosing the differences, and deciding how to reduce or remove these differences to bring the text as close as possible to the desired status." Georgia Heard likes to remind her students that "revision doesn't necessarily take place after they've finished a piece of writing, but instead . . . will most likely occur throughout the writing process."

In an essay comparing the composing strategies of student writers and experienced adult writers, Nancy Sommers notes that "experienced writers describe their primary objective when revising as finding the form or shape of their argument." Sommers goes on to remark that experienced writers believe that "their first drafts are usually scattered attempts to define their territory," while the goal of second drafts "is to begin observing general patterns of development and deciding what should be included and what should be excluded." Ultimately Sommers finds two general elements common to the revision process of most experienced writers: "the adoption of a holistic perspective and the perception that revision is a recursive process."

That word "recursive" comes up frequently when writing teachers discuss revision. It has different meanings in different contexts but usually refers to modifying a piece of writing repeatedly and in all stages of the composition process in order to discover the work's optimal form. Revision, as you probably already know, can be messy. Susan Osborn describes the composition process of fellow writer Florence Howe as "neither precise nor formulaic but rather ambiguous, complex, recursive, at times inefficient, bewildering." As Brock Dethier puts it, "Writing is almost never a linear process that starts with a title and marches directly to a conclusion, with never a backward glance. Instead, most writers take a few—or a few hundred—steps forward, then circle back and cut, expand, and revise."

If revision is such a challenging and unsystematic activity, you might ask yourself if it's even necessary. Aren't writers inspired by the Muses? Don't we know instinctively what to do? Doesn't the best writing just *happen*?

The answer to these questions is "Unfortunately not." While the white-hot process of unrevised composition may occasionally occur, every creative writer of any experience will acknowledge that redrafting nearly always comes into play before a work reaches its final state. As Donald Murray observed, "The published writer knows it takes a great deal of practice to be spontaneous." More often than not, that first draft turns out, on closer inspection, to be considerably less wonderful than you'd initially thought. Usually a word or image or phrase can be salvaged from even the least successful effort, but that's not always the case. Isaac Bashevis Singer once remarked, "The wastepaper basket is the writer's best friend," and any number of writers have made similar observations: it's better to dispose of material that simply isn't working rather than remaining stubbornly attached to it.

Let's say, though, that like Nancy Welch, you find yourself driven to the revision process because you are "getting restless . . . with familiar scripts in [your] writing, recognizing their limits." Something is wrong, and you want to make it right. How do you know what to revise?

Refer to your textbook ▶

The first place to turn is your textbook itself. Revision checklists punctuate every section of this book, and there are overall genre checklists on the inside covers. These are good places to look as you think about revising *specific* aspects of your work—making the dialogue in your story more believable, condensing the exposition in your play, trimming unnecessary words from your poem, restructuring your essay.

Work with your peers ▶

In *Acts of Revision*, Wendy Bishop writes, "You need others to revise wisely. You need to share your work with supportive readers (peers, friends, family) on the road to learning to share with more demanding critics. You need to learn to forgive yourself and play and to become your own most demanding reader." Much of the oral and written revision advice you receive in this class will be given in small peer groups and full-class workshops. To avoid sessions that amount to nothing more than an extended self-defense of the work, the author is normally asked not to speak while discussion of her manuscript is in progress. After the workshop, students return their marked copies to further guide the writer's revisions. The workshop model suggests that writing, like carpentry, *can* be both learned and taught. While the qualities that make a master carpenter—a feel for wood, a knowledge of the appropriate tools, precision, perceptiveness, and so on—may be as elusive as those that make a master writer, the assumption is that just about anyone can become functional in the craft.

The benefits of peer revision are obvious. Students working in small groups are able to share their work *before* it's graded with readers who are likely to be gentle in their assessment. You can talk through your goals and find out just where you succeeded—and where you went wrong. Some peer groups meet repeatedly throughout the academic term and become a support system for their members, encouraging everyone to stretch, to develop, to risk, to grow. As Yusef Komunyakaa notes, "Beginning [writers] will discover that their first like-minded community is often the workshop: this is where . . . exposure develops trust."

Consult your teacher or a tutor ▶

Receiving advice in the classroom is important, but what other avenues do you have if you find that particular venue daunting or just embarrassing? Individual conferences with your teacher are among the most valuable time you can spend while in the midst of the revision process. Your instructor knows you and your work, and she or he has a good deal of experience—as both a writer and a teacher—in negotiating the writing problems you are facing. Ask brief questions before or after class, and take advantage of your professor's posted office hours to look closely at your revised work together.

Your campus writing center is an important resource that many creative writing students forget to access. Granted, most tutors spend the majority of their time talking about academic prose, but many tutors are English majors and writers themselves, and they will jump at the chance to vary their workday and discuss poems and stories, creative nonfiction, and short plays. Even if your writing center tutor isn't a creative writer, she or he will be trained to point out places in your text that need further modification.

Be aware of your responses to revision advice. If you find yourself resistant to peer, instructor, and tutor feedback, you may have come into this class believing that the creative writing you do is "just for you" or the people it addresses. Your previous efforts may have dealt with extremely personal issues—the end of a relationship, say, or the loss of a loved one—and you have every right to feel that something written under those circumstances is not meant to be critiqued: You don't want to hear that your meter is off or your characters are flat when your grandmother has just passed away. However, if you carry that extreme sense of privacy into class, you're likely to have trouble. Think about why you are bringing in a piece for other people to read. Do you really want to make it as strong as it can be? Or do you simply want unqualified praise? Even if your work means a great deal to your personally, you probably wouldn't have signed up for this course if you didn't—at some level—want other people to read it. And presenting creative writing for your classmates and instructor to read necessarily makes that work public.

Read aloud, and read other writers ▶

What if your work was not selected for peer review, or what if you don't have time to visit your teacher or a tutor? Robert Graham notes, "A lot of writers swear by reading a work aloud—even better if it's to somebody else, because as you read you will see it through their eyes. In the absence of an audience, you will still find reading aloud to yourself an effective way of finding flaws in your writing. Read it to the wall." That may sound a bit odd, but generations of authors have found that simply hearing their work spoken makes it fresh and unfamiliar, allowing them to approach it from a new perspective.

Of course there is no substitute for reading other writers who have faced, and conquered, the very challenges confronting you. Reread the pieces in the book's mini-anthologies. Check out a new book from the library, or pick up an old favorite from your own shelves. Georgia Heard says, "Sometimes when I'm in the middle of writing, and I feel like I'm slogging through and the words just aren't flowing, I choose a book I like . . . that I know will sing with my own voice and help me write what I want to."

Take a break ▶

For millennia, writers have counseled putting away material and coming back to it later on. The Roman poet Horace suggested placing a piece of writing in a drawer for nine years before returning to it with fresh eyes. Poet Donald Hall revised that number down to nine months for contemporary writers, but students enrolled in a class that may be as short as ten weeks don't have the luxury of time. Nevertheless, you will find that most writing is, to use a culinary metaphor, tastier if it is allowed to simmer rather than if it is always cooked at a full boil. At the very least, it's worth setting something aside overnight before attempting another draft.

Clearly, though, there is no single revision strategy suitable for every writer. Far from it. In their study "Analyzing Revision," Lester Faigley and Stephen Witte "found extreme diversity in the ways expert writers revise." Among the "situational variables" Faigley and Witte discovered were "the reason why the text was being written, the format, the medium, the genre, the writer's familiarity with the writing task, the writer's familiarity with the subject, the writer's familiarity with the audience, the projected level of formality, and the length of the task and the projected text." In other words, the *context* of the situation dictates much of what can be done.

You already know that, though. You very likely have other classes, other responsibilities you need to address. Even if you hope to make creative writing your life's work, you can't devote every minute of your life to it. You may decide that revision can wait, or be avoided altogether. Don't make that mistake. While the revision process may be chaotic and frustrating at times, in the words of Naomi Shihab Nye, "*revision* is a beautiful word of hope. It's a new vision of something. It means you don't have to be perfect the first time. What a relief!"

Writing Poetry

▶ A few things you should know about poetry

A poem, according to the dry language of the dictionary, is "a composition in verse," and verse is "metrical writing," that is, writing concerned with the number and variety of accented and unaccented syllables.

Perhaps a few hundred years ago, this might have made a barely passable definition (or perhaps not), but it certainly doesn't work well in the twenty-first century. Even many traditionalists now acknowledge that **poetry** can be made in **free verse**, a composition *not* in metrical writing. The lines of free verse end where the poet feels they would be most effective ending, not when the required number of stressed and unstressed syllables are tallied up. Experimental writers push free verse so far that sometimes it almost seems to become a language other than English. And if many American poets are still uncertain about the issue, just about every French poet would acknowledge that there is something called a **prose poem**, a composition that looks very much like the paragraph you are now reading but has all the heightened, compressed, and figurative language found in poetry. (**Prose** is the ordinary language of writing and speaking.)

So in poetry does anything go? Not exactly. If it did, there would be no need for this chapter. In his poem "A Course in Creative Writing," William Stafford says that most students "want a wilderness with a map," a diagram of how to do things. As we have just seen, it can be difficult even to define poetry, yet it makes sense that creative writing textbooks should nevertheless attempt to sketch out the terrain. Consequently, in this chapter you will learn about everything from the basics of the poetic line to a few of the many poetic forms that have evolved over the centuries. Because short poems are significantly shorter than even very brief stories, essays, and plays, we have room to print quite a few examples in the anthology at the end of this chapter. For our model poems, we focus on three markedly different types of poetry: a sonnet by Gail White, a free verse poem by Ruth Stone, and an experimental piece by Rae Armantrout.

Although we'll be looking at poetry from various angles and breaking it down into its component parts, you should never lose sight of your ultimate goal for this chapter: to write good poems. Some of those poems may be generated by the creativity exercises in the "kick-starts" section at the end of this chapter, or by reading another poet's work, but be open to the possibility that your best poem of the semester may burst forth while you're in the middle of taking a shower or driving to class or eating dessert. Stafford's poem praises "errors that give a new start," and you may find that getting lost in the wilderness of poetry, and making your way without a map, can lead to some wonderful revelations.

Indeed, one of the pleasures of writing poetry is that it offers frequent surprises: you never know when you're going to say something you didn't know you knew, or say something you didn't think could be said. Even a master like Robert Frost found the process a constant adventure. "I have never started a poem yet whose end I knew," he said. "Writing a poem is discovering." Most good poems contain some element of the unexpected. A poem that's overdetermined from the start—one in which the poet can see the beginning, middle, and end before setting down a word on paper—will probably arrive dead on the page. And nothing kills a poem faster than a **cliché**, whether it's an overused phrase or a formulaic structure with a predictable conclusion. Novelists usually create an outline before they start to write, but poets rarely begin with more than an idea, a phrase, an image, or just a hunch. In fact, John Ashbery has said that "poetry is mostly hunches."

It may be that "hunch" is simply another word for "inspiration." John Keats famously wrote that "if poetry come not as naturally as the leaves to a tree, it had better not come at all." Ironically, poets frequently spend much more time working on a bad poem than on a good one, and in large measure that's because the stronger work tends to emerge more fully formed right from the start. Often the hunch turns out to be correct.

We may have to knock a while on the door of Poetry, but when we are finally let inside and are in the midst of what we feel to be a *real* poem, we know something special is happening. Charles Olson said that a poet caught up in the making of a genuine poem "can go by no other track than the one the poem under hand declares, for itself." Robert Frost believed that "like a piece of ice on a hot stove the poem must ride on its own melting." This sense that a poem is practically writing itself is one to which every experienced poet can attest, and even though the poem may ultimately need a fair amount of revision before it's finished, getting off to a good start is a significant advantage.

The problem with counting on the Muse, that Greek goddess presiding over the creation of poetry, is that she's notoriously fickle. The word "inspiration" refers to the sacred revelation visited upon a person by a god, and unfortunately that's not the sort of event that happens to most of us every day. Sometimes you'll find that the Muse is in the neighborhood, but you just don't know how to guide her to where you are: you may *want* to write a poem, but you don't have a wide enough repertoire of strategies to draw upon to get started. Or you may simply feel distant from the act of writing altogether (this condition often occurs the night before poems are due in class). In either case, the kick-start prompts will ease you into the writing process.

Another method of getting started when you're not sure where or how to begin is to write in fixed forms. For centuries, poets have been testing themselves not only against the "restrictions" imposed by elaborate rhyme and metrical schemes but also against poets who have come before them. Consider the sonnet, for instance. Among those who have entered its "field of play" (to quote Phillis Levin) are some of the greatest poets writing in English, everyone from canonical authors such as Shakespeare, Donne, Milton, Wordsworth, Keats, and Frost to contemporary masters such as Marilyn Hacker and Molly Peacock. The "Poetic Forms" section of this chapter looks at the sonnet, the villanelle, the cinquain, and several other types of poetry. You will also read about non-Western patterns, such as the ghazal and the pantoum, which have become staples for American poets.

For some students, entering the world of forms will be comforting. You may already be drawn to a certain type of "formalism," the regular metrical rhythm and perfect rhyme that many people associate with poetry. For much of the history of poetry written in English, meter and, to a lesser extent, rhyme were considered fundamental. Whether poets such as Gail White would consider themselves "new formalists"—a label given to those working in meter and rhyme in the 1980s—clearly they do value the traditional elements of verse. As the **etymology** (the derivation) of the word "poetry" suggests, a poet is one who arranges thoughts and images in an artful way. From this perspective, the poet is a kind of architect, an artisan. Like apprentice furniture makers, poets working in forms must study carefully, practice hard, and be prepared for their early efforts to be seriously flawed. A good chair, after all, is much harder to make than we might suspect—until we put our hands to the task.

Poetry can also be written in free verse, and poets such as Ruth Stone draw on a rich tradition. From the seventeenth-century translators of the King James

Bible, many of whom were poets, to the nineteenth-century American innovator Walt Whitman, an effort has long been under way to capture the power of poetry without having to adhere to strict metrical patterns and rhyme schemes. Drawing on the examples of writers such as T. S. Eliot and William Carlos Williams, twentieth-century poets turned more and more frequently to free verse, and in today's creative writing classes, poetry written in free verse is the norm rather than the exception. As one of my colleagues tells his new poetry students, "If it doesn't rhyme, and you think it's a poem but aren't sure what to call it, it's probably free verse."

Like poets working in forms and in free verse, experimental (or avant-garde or postmodern) poets such as Rae Armantrout are themselves part of a long tradition, although that tradition may not be as easy to pin down. Armantrout's "Duration" is in free verse; yet with its rhythms, repetitions, and rhymes, it also contains elements of traditional verse. What *is* explicitly avant-garde about "Duration" is the way it challenges conventional expectations of what a poem should do. For most readers, the poem will initially resist interpretation or will open itself to a myriad of possible readings. Those who want their poetry straight and simple may be frustrated by Armantrout. Unlike Gail White's "My Personal Recollections of Not Being Asked to the Prom," for instance, which works hard to convey a particular experience, Armantrout's poem seems to be a riddle with a number of equally plausible explanations.

Some beginning poetry students are drawn to experimental poetry because it seems to be an outsider's art: they imagine themselves as wild rebels like Allen Ginsberg, taunting the establishment, breaking all the rules, channeling the muse, and never *ever* revising their work. "First thought, best thought," Ginsberg often said; nevertheless, he frequently revised his work, as do most experimental writers. And as far as turning to poetry as a method of rebellion, it should be remembered that Ginsberg was a professor at both Brooklyn College and the Naropa Institute. Similarly, Rae Armantrout is a tenured professor at the University of California at San Diego. A glance at the résumé of most well-published experimental poets shows that they often make their living as professors. Moreover, one need only think of T. S. Eliot's *The Waste Land*, once the cutting edge of experimental poetry, to realize that today's avant-garde is tomorrow's assigned reading.

Naturally the varieties of poetry aren't limited to the three strands we have just discussed. If you have ever been to a poetry slam, you have been exposed to spoken-word or performance poetry. Although older audience members may sometimes feel they have wandered into a hip-hop show rather than a poetry reading, there's no doubt about the excitement generated by a talented performer and a ready, rowdy audience. However, because poetry intended primarily to be said aloud may differ drastically from poetry meant to be read on the page, some creative writing instructors have reservations about incorporating spoken-word poems into their curriculum.

Whatever the policy in your class, Pamela Gemin reminds us that "the poet and the lyricist are two different creatures, though some lyrics may be 'poetic.'" Gemin notes that "the poet is a one-man band," while "songwriters have the benefit of a full range of mood-enhancing instruments, formulas and automatic cues." Therefore, if you are writing a poem that you plan to read aloud, remember that your work should be able to stand on the merits of its language. If it's full of clichés on the page, it's still full of clichés when you are belting it out in front of a crowd—even if you are charismatic enough to convince your listeners that what you are saying is imaginative and new.

Perhaps it is sufficient to say that in a good poem, even a very long one, every syllable counts: every moment, every sound seems somehow necessary. This is where revision comes in. No matter how strong your first draft, a smart, thorough review of every poem you write is an essential part of the composition process. If you're lucky, you will become one of those poets who are excellent critics of their own work. They may compose in a fevered passion, but when they go back to reread their poetry, they look at it with the cold eye of a professional editor.

In the long run, the only real way to become a poet is to keep writing poems—lots of them, most of which you'll end up throwing away. Some of those you show to other people; others are never read by anyone but you. Sooner or later, something worthwhile is bound to appear on the page, and once you train yourself to write consistently, you will begin to distinguish the good poems from the bad. Students who turn in the best poems at the end of the semester tend to be those who have been writing constantly. Not only do they rework their better poems—revising and revising them—but they also write new poems whenever they can. Their best work, they believe, is always just around the corner.

However, no amount of revision can ever make your poem *perfect*. (What is "perfect" anyway?) As Paul Valéry said, "A poem is never finished, only abandoned." And poet and critic William Logan points out that "art is often in the flaws, in the sullen differences that allow a writer to evade the poetry of the age. (Sometimes what at first annoys us in a poet is just what we later appreciate.)" This is akin to Dylan Thomas's idea that the best poets "always leave holes and gaps in the works of the poem so that something that is *not* in the poem can creep, crawl, flush, or thunder in." Learning to appreciate those moments of odd insight and strange **imagery**—mental pictures or impressions that evoke one of the five senses—is a crucial step toward becoming a poet.

Of course, with so many contradictions inherent in the making of poetry, you may well wonder yet again, What is a poem? "If I read a book and it makes my whole body so cold no fire can ever warm me, I know that it is poetry," said

Emily Dickinson. "If I feel physically as if the top of my head were taken off, I know that is poetry." Poetry here sounds like a serious illness or a gunshot wound, but other poets have found it a more elusive quarry. "Poetry is a pheasant disappearing into the brush," said Wallace Stevens. And Naomi Shihab Nye writes: "Poems offer mystery. . . . [They] respect our ability to translate images and signs. Poems link seemingly disparate parts of experience." Coleridge's dictum that poetry is "the best words in the best order" makes sense, although one could obviously use that as a test for good prose and dramatic writing as well. Former U.S. Poet Laureate Robert Pinsky believes that "the medium of poetry is the human body: the column of air inside the chest, shaped into signifying sounds in the larynx and mouth. In this sense, poetry is just as physical or bodily an art as dancing."

A hunch, "errors that make a new start," melting ice, a life-changing physical experience, a disappearing pheasant, dancing breath: what poets come to learn is that a poem is all these things, and more. Poetry is intuition and hard work, tradition and innovation. It lifts the veil, to quote Shelley, "from the hidden beauty of the world, and makes familiar objects be as if they are not familiar." Poetry, in short, is what you make of it, but there's only one way to accomplish that goal: let the making begin.

The elements of poetry ▶

Poetry consists of a number of elements, which we discuss more fully later in the chapter:

- ▶ **Lines and Stanzas** When we write prose, the sentence is our basic unit of composition. In a poem, however, we think in terms of **lines**—those entities that begin on the left side of the page and end somewhere on the right. Like a line of computer code, a line of poetry contains one or more usually implicit commands on how it is to be read. (An exception to this rule—the prose poem—is covered in the "Poetic Forms" section.) **Stanzas** are made by grouping lines together.

- ▶ **Meter and Rhythm** **Meter** is a regular pattern of accented and unaccented syllables. **Rhythm** is a variable but nevertheless recognizable pattern of strong and weak elements in a poem. Because the term "rhythm" is more flexible than "meter," we often use it when referring to free verse or experimental poetry. Even if a poem is not strictly metered, it will still have a rhythm.

- ▶ **The Music of Poetry** Readers and listeners often comment on the "music" of a poem: the sounds words make when coming together. The section on the music of poetry focuses on rhyme and alliteration as devices for creating musical effects in poetry.

▶ **Images, Symbols, and Figurative Language** Using concrete images, as opposed to abstractions, is a cornerstone of most contemporary poetry. Poetry also relies on **symbols**—acts, sounds, or objects that signify something other than themselves. Much of the strangeness of poetry, as opposed to everyday conversation and writing, results from the dense use of figures of speech such as metaphor, simile, metonymy, synecdoche, personification, puns, and irony.

▶ **Diction, Syntax, and the Language of Poetry** **"Diction"** refers to the choice of the words themselves, while **"syntax"** refers to the way that words are put together to form phrases in a sentence. Together, these two elements ultimately result in the creation of each individual poet's "language of poetry."

▶ **Poetic Forms** One of the pleasures of writing poetry is working in the forms handed down to us from previous generations of poets. Many of these structures have strict rules that must be followed, although we will embrace a certain amount of play and experimentation in the forms we work with. In addition to the sonnet, we will look at the villanelle, the rondeau, the sestina, the cinquain, the pantoum, and the ghazal.

The short poem: Three models ▶

"What we term a long poem is, in fact, merely a succession of brief ones," Edgar Allan Poe writes in "The Philosophy of Composition," "that is to say, brief poetical effects. It is needless to demonstrate that a poem is such only inasmuch as it intensely excites, by elevating the soul; and all intense excitements are, through a pyschal [psychological] necessity, brief." Poe may be overstating the case, but in keeping with this book's focus on short work, the sections that follow—and the kick-starts and anthology at the end of the chapter—are designed to show you a variety of ways of "intensely exciting" your readers in brief poems.

M. H. Abrams defines the **lyric poem** as "any fairly short, non-narrative poem presenting a single speaker who expresses a state of mind or a process of thought and feeling." Some of the poems you write may indeed fit neatly into this category. Others, however, will contain elements of **narrative** (that is, storytelling) or will be told from multiple points of view. Your instructor may have specific restrictions on length, but in general, if your poem begins to creep onto a third page, it probably can benefit from paring down. Rare is the poem—lyric or otherwise—that cannot be strengthened by judicious editing. If it takes you three lines to say something, see if you can say it instead in two lines, or one line, or one word.

The three model poems take very different approaches to the art of poetry, and it will pay to reread each one several times. Gail White's sonnet "My Personal

Recollections of Not Being Asked to the Prom" foregrounds not just the meter and rhyme of formal verse but also the speaker's darkly comic voice. Ruth Stone's "Winter," written in densely imagistic free verse, uses the present to explore the power of memory. Rae Armantrout's elliptical "Duration" may be the least immediately accessible of the three; however, avant-garde poems like this one (and those in the anthology by Brenda Hillman, Ben Lerner, and Matthew Zapruder) represent an important strand in contemporary poetry and another potential source of inspiration for new poets looking to follow Ezra Pound's famous command to "make it new."

Gail White

My Personal Recollections of Not Being Asked to the Prom

Gail White lives in Breaux Bridge, Louisiana, and is a regular contributor to the *Formalist* and other journals specializing in traditional forms. White is known not only for her devotion to rhyme and meter but also for her dark sense of humor, a relative rarity in contemporary poetry. She is the author of two full-length collections, *The Price of Everything* and *Easy Marks*, as well as a number of **chapbooks** (a chapbook is a short book of poetry, usually fewer than thirty-two pages) and is coeditor, with Katherine McAlpine, of *The Muse Strikes Back: A Poetic Response by Women to Men*.

Of the admixture of light and darkness in White's poetry, Julie Kane has written: "By refusing to create a victimized female persona as the target of her own wit, White claims a new authority for the woman light-verse writer: the right to assert herself as a satirist, as a clear-eyed critic of the world around her—a role that men have occupied almost exclusively for more than two millennia." We see that strong sense of self very much on display in "My Personal Recollections of Not Being Asked to the Prom."

> I never minded my unpopularity
> in those days. Books were friends and poets (dead)
> were lovers. Brainy girls were still a rarity
> and boys preferred big bosoms to well-read
> and saucy wits. I look back now with pity
> on the young Me I didn't pity then.
> I didn't know that I was almost pretty
> and might have had a charm for older men.

And my poor mom, who never bought a fluffy
ball gown or showed me how to dress my hair—
she must have wondered where she got this stuffy
daughter. She didn't say it, but her stare
asked whether genes or nurture were to blame.
(But I got married, Mother, all the same.) ◀

Ruth Stone

Winter

Ruth Stone was born in Roanoke, Virginia, in 1915. Her husband, who may well be the man described in this poem, committed suicide in 1959. Widowed, with three daughters to support, Stone began teaching creative writing. According to critic Willis Barnstone, she worked "for nearly thirty years as a wandering professor at a new college or university almost each year, sometimes two in a year." Stone published her work widely but until recently was never given the credit her devoted readers believed she deserved. That began to change in 1999 when her book *Ordinary Words* received the National Book Critics Circle Award for Poetry. *In the Next Galaxy* won the National Book Award for Poetry in 2002 and *What Love Comes To: New and Selected Poems* was a finalist for the 2009 Pulitzer Prize. Stone died in 2011 at the age of ninety-six.

"Winter" is from Stone's book *Second-Hand Coat: Poems New and Selected* (1987). She returned again and again in her poetry to the loss of her husband, and here the speaker is someone who seems to be both on a train and yet waiting in a station; she is in the present, on an excursion to the city, but also in the past, remembering previous journeys with her late partner. With a tone as sharp as winter wind, the poem unrelentingly hurtles past an assortment of memorable images on the way to its astonishing conclusion.

The ten o-clock train to New York,
coaches like loaves of bread powdered with snow.
Steam wheezes between the couplings.
Stripped to plywood, the station's cement standing room
imitates a Russian novel. It is now that I remember you.
Your profile becomes the carved handle of a letter knife.
Your heavy-lidded eyes slip under the seal of my widowhood.
It is another raw winter. Stray cats are suffering.
Starlings crowd the edges of chimneys.

It is a drab misery that urges me to remember you.
I think about the subjugation of women and horses;
brutal exposure; weather that forces, that strips.
In our time we met in ornate stations
arching up with nineteenth-century optimism.
I remember you running beside the train waving good-bye.
I can produce a facsimile of you standing
behind a column of polished oak to surprise me.
Am I going toward you or away from you on this train?
Discarded junk of other minds is strewn beside the tracks:
mounds of rusting wire, grotesque pop art of dead motors,
senile warehouses. The train passes a station;
fresh people standing on the platform,
their faces expecting something.
I feel their entire histories ravish me. ◄

Rae Armantrout

Duration

A native Californian, Rae Armantrout earned her bachelor's degree at the University of California at Berkeley and her master's degree at San Francisco State. Frequently associated with the first generation of "language poets," she has served as a literature professor at the University of California at San Diego for two decades. Winner of the 2010 Pulitzer Prize and National Book Critics Circle Award for her poetry collection Versed, Armantrout has published ten other books of poems, including *Money Shot* (2011), from which "Duration" is taken. *Publisher's Weekly* notes that Armantrout builds her "wily, jumpy, intricately witty and wise poems from scraps of popular and high culture, overheard speech, and found text, as well as her own quirky observations."

We see this playful and "jumpy" eccentricity in "Duration." The poem transistions quickly and without comment from the speaker's memory of her mother's quick "leaky faucet" kisses to the afternoon sun on a power line outside her home to a heaven in which blackbirds "needle" the air all day with their songs. There is no easy answer for what these seemingly disparate scenes have in common, although we may find a clue in the title, which comes from two Latin roots—"to last" (*durare*) and "hard" (*durus*)—and in the final lines, which seem to insist that readers must pay careful attention to this "hard" poem if they are to appreciate it fully and tune in to the poet's airwaves.

Those flurries
of small pecks

my mother called
leaky faucet kisses.

Late sun winks
from a power line

beyond the neighbor's tree.
In heaven,

where repetition's
not boring—

Silver whistles
of blackbirds

needle
the daylong day.

We're still
on the air,

still on the air,
they say. ◄

Lines and stanzas ▶

The poetic line begins on the left side of the page (usually, but not always, at the left margin) and ends where the poet decides to "break" or wrap the line (usually, but not always, before the right margin). To illustrate (and to explain my parenthetical qualifications), here is the previous sentence broken into lines of poetry:

> The poetic line begins
> on the left side of the page (usually,
> > but not always,
> at the left margin)
> and ends where the poet decides to "break" or wrap the line
> > (usually, but not always, before the right margin).

The first line of this makeshift poem—"The poetic line begins"—is the way most lines of poetry look on the page. Sometimes, however, as in line 3, a line of poetry may be indented from the left margin and still be considered a line. Likewise, a very long line, like line 5, may continue *past* the right margin. To show the reader that the line continues, the poet flows some of the words to the next line and indents them five spaces. If you have read Walt Whitman, a devotee of long lines, you will recognize this convention. In his "A Song for Occupations," for example, Whitman writes the following single line:

> Coal-mines and all that is down there, the lamps in the darkness, echoes,
>   songs, what meditations, what vast native thoughts looking through
>   smutch'd faces.

It would take a book with wide pages, indeed, to accommodate a line such as that one, so Whitman simply indents the overflow five spaces at the left margin and stops his free verse line only at the point where he thinks it makes sense to do so.

Whether the lines of a poem are long or short, in traditional meter or in free verse, there should be some logic or intuition governing the placement of a line break. Whitman was a master of using line length to reflect a poem's content. Consider, for example, his poem "A Noiseless, Patient Spider":

> A noiseless, patient spider,
> I mark'd, where, on a little promontory, it stood, isolated;
> Mark'd how, to explore the vacant, vast surrounding,
> It launch'd forth filament, filament, filament, out of itself;
> Ever reeling them—ever tirelessly speeding them.
>
> And you, O my soul, where you stand,
> Surrounded, surrounded in measureless oceans of space,
> Ceaselessly musing, venturing, throwing,—seeking the spheres, to connect
>   them;
> Till the bridge you will need, be form'd—till the ductile anchor hold;
> Till the gossamer thread you fling, catch somewhere, O my soul.

The poem begins with a short four-word line announcing the presence of the spider; the subsequent longer lines seem to depict the spider spinning its web. In the second stanza, the lines become even longer, as Whitman imagines his soul engaged in the same process of sending out strands of filament, hoping that they too will latch onto something. The fact that a soul has to venture much farther than a spider to connect with a like-minded spirit makes these longer lines appropriate.

When you read, your eyes move back and forth across the page, and your sense of this forward and backward movement is often heightened in the process of reading a poem. Robert Pinsky reminds us that "*versus* in Latin, from which the word 'verse' derives, signifies the ploughman at the end of a furrow turning about to begin again, so that 'verse' and 'reverse' are closely related." If you haven't read many poems before this class, the experience can take a little getting used to. When we are reading prose, our eyes often skim across the surface, gleaning main ideas but not really pausing to linger over matters of style. However, that technique doesn't work well for readers of poetry, and it certainly won't work for you as a poet. Your reader expects more—word for word—from a poem. As you write and revise, you'll need to stop, think, slow down. Life might be hurtling around us faster and faster all the time, but poetry is an oasis in the midst of that rush.

In a poem properly written, every word receives its due, and every line begins and ends where it does for a reason. Fanny Howe has said that the rapid movement of prose across the page "indicates another thought process—one with a goal." Like drivers on a freeway, readers of prose usually want to get from one place to another as quickly as possible. Poetry, by contrast, puts up speed bumps. While poetry can also be said to have a "goal," that objective is often to make the reader pause, to reflect, to consider. According to Howe, the difference between prose and poetry is "the difference between taking a walk and sitting still."

Even the emptiness where a line ends and the so-called white space begins is important. Let's think for a moment about that white space. Suppose we were to take that last sentence and turn it into a three-line poem:

Let's think
for a moment
about that white space.

If you were to see this "poem" in a book, it might be the only thing on the page, and readers used to paragraphs and paragraphs of prose might well ask: "What's the point of all that emptiness when we normally try to cram as much content as possible into every nook and cranny? Why all that 'unused' space?"

The answer, of course, is that the white space isn't unused. The expanse of blank paper gives those nine words real importance. If the poet felt he could condense everything he wanted to say into a single short sentence, perhaps the expression of that thought deserves our attention. Similarly, because there are so few lines, each line takes on more weight, and a reader is likely to go back over the piece a number of times, looking hard for clues as to what it might be about. Consequently, the shorter a poem, the stronger it needs to be.

There is nothing more to find in our little "poem," so let's look at a real one by Barry Spacks:

Satie playing,
beloved cat on my lap—
    what more could be desired?

  Wait, wait . . .
        raspberries and cream?

If you know the piano music of the French composer Erik Satie—brief pieces with titles like "Jack in the Box" and "Le Flirt" that are by turns odd, warm, funny, and moody—you can imagine how those sounds inform the miniature world of this untitled poem. The notes in Satie's pieces are often soft and held until they almost diminish into silence. Spacks too seems to cherish empty space and quiet. After all, so much can happen in silence, just as so much can transpire in the white space of a poem. As Ted Kooser says, "The white space out there on the right is an opportunity, and you ought to take advantage of it." Spacks does this by including only the essentials of the experience he describes: the music, the cat, his feeling of near contentment, then the sudden desire for raspberries and cream. All the other wheres, whens, and whys of this moment are on the periphery; they have disappeared into the white space of the poem.

Because the last word of a poetic line—just before the white space—typically receives the most emphasis, poets delight in finding ways to exploit the line break. One way to do this is to let the end of the sentence coincide with the end of the line. A line that ends with any sort of punctuation (a period, semicolon, comma, or dash) is said to be **end-stopped**. Ruth Stone frequently employs this technique in "Winter":

> Your profile becomes the carved handle of a letter knife.
> Your heavy-lidded eyes slip under the seal of my widowhood.
> It is another raw winter. Stray cats are suffering.

In general, an end-stopped line slows the movement and rhythm of a poem; when many or all of its lines are end-stopped, readers pause and ponder during the act of reading. As Robert Wallace points out, "End-stopped free verse tends toward long lines because they permit internal pauses and greater internal rhythmic variation." The longish end-stopped lines in Stone's poem create the effect of a repeated halting, which emphasizes both the stop-and-start movement of a train and the finality of the speaker's loss: there is, after all, no more resounding "end-stop" than the one that Death insists on.

Unsure how to handle the freedom (or potential anarchy) represented by the line break, new poets often choose to end their lines on a mark of punctuation. That's a safe choice, but it can also be a boring one. The impact of this "chopped prose," Wallace says, "is about as arresting, in its lack of variety, as a stack of lumber." Ezra Pound similarly warns: "Don't make each line stop dead at the end, and then begin every next line with a heave. Let the beginning of the next line catch the rise of the rhythm wave, unless you want a definite longish pause." Be sure to have a reason for ending your line where you do, but if you always settle for a mark of punctuation, the movement of the poem may become too predictable.

The alternative to breaking a line at a mark of punctuation is to wrap it in the middle of a sentence so that related words are in different poetic lines: this is called **enjambment**. In contrast to a poem that is heavily end-stopped, a poem with run-on or enjambed lines tends to move more quickly down the page. Take a look at this short poem, "Foothill Road," by Paul Willis:

> It happens in the slow light
> of December dawn, the waking
> of clouds, the acknowledgement
> of a long presence. The road
>
> gathers under your feet, the roughness
> of it felt, not seen. Too cold
> for snakes, but a palm frond
> blown to the ground can rake
>
> your soles and spear your toes
> straight through with thorns.
> Crucifixion happens daily, just
> like that, on the heels of triumphal entry.

The images in "Foothill Road" are clearly drawn; the subject is weighty. Yet because of Willis's skillful use of enjambment, there's barely a pause here, even between stanzas, as we race down the road in morning light toward the marvelous and unforeseen ending.

In their essay "The Line/The Form/The Music," David Baker and Ann Townsend have this to say about enjambment: "The line argues with the sentence, it disrupts the momentum of the sentence, but it also can heighten the interior meanings of a sentence. The line focuses on and magnifies the phrase, the piece, the fragment." The simple act of breaking a line causes a reader to pause, if only for a microsecond, in preparation for the next line. We digest what we have just read and ask ourselves, "What's coming next?" Then we move our eyes down the page to learn if our expectations will be confirmed or confounded.

Look how the skillful enjambment in the second stanza of Gail White's sonnet accents meaning and highlights irony:

> And my poor mom, who never bought a fluffy
> ball gown or showed me how to dress my hair—
> she must have wondered where she got this stuffy
> daughter. She didn't say it, but her stare
> asked whether genes or nurture were to blame.
> (But I got married, Mother, all the same.)

Enjambment allows White a small moment of surprise; she makes us wonder what exactly is "fluffy" (a ball gown) and what is "stuffy" (herself). That slight pause—when our eyes are moving back to the left margin and we have yet to discover what noun the adjective is modifying—is essential to the experience of poetry. This is the *versus*, the turning and returning to which Pinsky alludes. Similarly, the break between "stare" and "asked" causes us to linger over it momentarily, to stare—like the speaker's mother—at her socially inept daughter.

Knowing when to break a line, how to take advantage of these gaps, and when not to is part of the learning curve of becoming a poet. The fact that there are no definitively right or wrong ways to enjamb lines of poetry makes that process all the more difficult, especially for students accustomed to classes in which there is only one correct answer. Practice, trial and error, conversations with peers and your instructor, reading lots and lots of other poems, and constant practice: these are the ways poets develop a sense of the integrity of their lines.

As you craft the lines of your poem, you will also want to think about how to group them into stanzas, a poem's equivalent to the paragraphs in prose. There are several ways to approach stanza formation. Poets who are drawn to symmetry may begin writing their poems and wait until the opening lines cohere into a single logical unit—five lines, for example. The poet then manipulates word choice and phrasing so that all subsequent stanzas are also five lines long. Other poets allow each stanza to develop organically, based on the poem's content. The opening stanza may be a single line long, the second stanza twenty lines, the third stanza five, and so on. Still other poets, especially those such as Gail White who are writing in forms, know beforehand the length of their stanzas; their efforts go toward writing lines that fit well into those preordained packages.

The important thing for you as a poet is to achieve the maximum impact from your stanzas. White space is both vertical and horizontal, and the pause between stanzas is even more pronounced than the one provided by a line break. If you want your reader to give extra weight to each grouping, you will, like Rae Armantrout in "Duration," want to have many stanzas with few lines. If, however, like Ruth Stone in "Winter," you want to present your poem as a single propulsive thought, one that will tolerate no interruption, you will avoid stanza breaks.

The word "stanza" is derived from the Italian word for "room," and like the many rooms in a mansion, the range of stanza forms is daunting. We will discuss a few of these in more detail in the section on poetic forms. However, in an introductory course like this one, you don't need to become a stanza expert. You simply need to know the names of the most common stanza forms:

A **couplet** is two lines of verse
that are connected in some way.

A **tercet**
is a group
of three lines.

A **quatrain**
is a group
of four lines
of poetry.

Beyond these, the most common patterns are stanzas with

five lines: **quintet**
six lines: **sestet**
seven lines: **septet**
eight lines: **octet**

CHECKLIST Lines and stanzas

☐ **Do your line endings make sense?** There are many rationales for when to end a line of poetry. As you'll see in the following sections, a certain meter may dictate line length, or end rhyme may be involved. Whatever your reasons, though, you should *intentionally* break your lines at an appropriate place. If your lines seem to stop without any reason (or rhyme), experienced readers will be skeptical of your command of the basics of poetry and may dismiss your poem without giving it a fair reading. Unless there is some compelling reason for doing so, stopping your line on relatively unimportant words such as articles ("a," "an," "the"), prepositions ("of," "on," "with"), or coordinating conjunctions ("but," "for," "so") will make your line breaks seem random and careless.

☐ **Do your line breaks surprise your reader?** When we're in the middle of a good book, we can't wait to turn the page to learn what will happen next. Similarly, effective line breaks create suspense for the reader: they make us want to discover what the next line will be. Enjambment is a useful tool for generating suspense. Of course, while you want to avoid entirely predictable line endings, you don't want to replace them with breaks that are merely baffling. A poem that begins "I can't / figure / out why / I'm breaking my lines here" will disrupt the reader's sense of rhythm before it can ever be established.

☐ **Do you vary your line breaks?** Although plenty of wonderful pre-twentieth-century poems end each line on a mark of punctuation, contemporary poems with nothing but end-stopped lines often feel predictable. Different poets will have different aesthetics, but most poets favor a *combination* of end-stopped and enjambed lines.

☐ **Are you effectively using the white space on the page?** Remember that the more white space you allow on the page, the more focus each word, line, and stanza receives. If you have only a few words per line, do those words merit all the space they are given? If, in contrast, your lines are long and crowded with ideas and images, do you leave your reader feeling overwhelmed? If you have frequent stanza breaks, do the pauses forced on the reader add to or detract from the method and message of your poem? No matter how your poem takes shape, try to take full advantage of the "silence" offered by the white space to increase the impact of your words.

☐ **If your lines are grouped into stanzas, do the groupings make sense?** Readers of poetry expect the poet to have given serious thought to stanza formation. A couplet requires a different sort of attention than a quatrain or a sestet does. Stanzas tend to end on a mark of punctuation, although that isn't always the case. If you do end a stanza mid-sentence, make sure there's a reason for that break: when your sentence continues in the beginning of the next stanza, your reader will expect a reason for the exaggerated pause.

Meter and rhythm ▶

In this section, we look at how meter and rhythm influence the poetic line. **Meter** is the arrangement of words in a poem based on the relative stress of their syllables. If you have written rhyming poems before, you probably composed in meter, even if you didn't realize it at the time. That da-DUM, da-DUM, da-DUM, da-DUM you were hearing in your head is actually called iambic tetrameter. Rhythm, which also refers to the recurrent alteration of pronounced and softer elements in a line, is generally a less specific term when applied to poetry. All poems have some kind of rhythm, although that rhythm may be closer to free jazz than to the classical precision suggested by meter. Even in metered poems, however, the rhythm of the line is likely to deviate from the meter the poet is using. In the words of Robert Pinsky, "Rhythm is the sound of an actual line, while meter is the abstract pattern behind the rhythm."

Later in this section, we look more closely at free verse—poetry in which the rhythm is metrically irregular. Although free verse now dominates contemporary poetry, metrical verse has had such a profound influence on poetry written in English that we begin by looking at it. In fact, for centuries, English-speaking poets and readers would have wondered how any writing that did *not* employ metrical regularity could possibly dare to claim the name of poetry. Conscious attention to the stressed and unstressed syllables in a line was simply part of what it meant to be a poet.

In her book *The Body of Poetry*, Annie Finch rhapsodizes on this very subject:

Meter is the gift that poetry gives me before words, through words, and after words. To hear meter is for me the most intimate part of reading and writing a poem, because it is impossible for it to be translated or told: it can only be experienced as the waving form of words and syllables carrying their own spine of metrical energy, the particular current of the rhythm, and everything that rhythm makes visible, audible, palpable.

That's a pretty amazing claim for the power of meter, but many poets who write metrically would probably agree with Finch that its force is hard to overestimate. For formalist poets, taking control of the rhythms of language by consciously manipulating the stressed and unstressed syllables of a line results in a far greater variety of effects than can be achieved otherwise. Meter allows these poets to help their readers more closely experience the same thoughts and emotions as the poets themselves.

Obviously, being able to name the meter that you're using is a big help. If in the past you have felt that something was off about a rhymed poem you wrote, chances are that the meter was irregular. Although **scansion**—the process of counting the number of stressed and unstressed syllables and analyzing their patterns—is a decidedly inexact science, it nevertheless brings some order and system to the language of poetry. As you begin to scan poems yourself, you will quickly notice that we are concerned with syllables rather than words. Each **foot**—the basic metrical unit in poetry—typically consists of one stressed and one or two unstressed syllables.

The ancient Greek plays were written in verse, and the labels we apply to meter come to us from those early comedies and tragedies. Following are the names of the most common types of poetic feet (the adjectival form is in parentheses). Here, an underscore (_) represents an unstressed syllable, while a slash (/) represents a stressed syllable:

> **iamb** (iambic): _ /
> **trochee** (trochaic): / _
> **anapest** (anapestic): _ _ /
> **dactyl** (dactylic): / _ _
> **spondee** (spondaic): / /
> **pyrrhic** (pyrrhic): _ _

The iamb is the most common foot in English poetry, and poets and critics have come up with various explanations for this phenomenon. Robert Pinsky thinks the iambic foot is "like a time signature" in music, guiding the reader "through the infinite, actual variety" of its sounds. Li-Young Lee believes that "meaning is born as the breath dies":

> As we inhale, our bones and muscles actually get very compacted, harder. When we exhale, on the other hand, our bodies become very soft. Ancient Daoists, so I'm told, believe that upon inhalation our ego-self becomes very inflated, while during exhalation our sense of ego and body diminishes and we become more open to a deeper, bigger presence.

That da-DUM may indeed represent the breathing body of the universe. Or it may echo our beating hearts, or the surging of ocean waves. Or there might be a more mundane explanation: the predominance of iambic feet in poetry written in English may simply be a tradition that has been passed down over the centuries. What's important to remember is that experienced readers of poetry, like your instructor, will be aware of the meter you choose—even if you aren't.

Line lengths are also given specific names. Earlier we mentioned iambic tetrameter (four iambic feet), and you may have heard of iambic pentameter (five iambic feet) while studying Shakespeare or other canonical poets. Line lengths are labeled as follows:

monometer: one foot

dimeter: two feet

trimeter: three feet

tetrameter: four feet

pentameter: five feet

hexameter: six feet

heptameter: seven feet

octameter: eight feet

With all these options laid out before you, you may want to jump in and try your hand at writing dactylic octameter or pyrrhic dimeter. However, a couple of words of warning are in order. Iambs are the prevailing foot in part because it is generally easier to write an iambic line. Certain feet, such as the pyrrhic and spondaic, are fairly rare in poetic lines because in a line of two or more feet, a pattern of stressed and unstressed syllables will reassert itself. Writing a poem in pyrrhic dimeter would be a remarkable feat indeed.

Moreover, very short lines like monometer can, as its name suggests, become monotonous rather quickly. At the other end of the spectrum, once you begin writing lines with more than six feet, it can be difficult to tell the difference between poetry and prose. Some meters are easier to master than others—for example, writing a poem in dactylic octameter wouldn't be quite as daunting as composing one in pyrrhic dimeter. However, if, as a new poet you tried to write either of these, most of your efforts would necessarily go into the technical effort of getting the meter correct. You probably wouldn't have much energy left over for the actual poem.

The line lengths of most poems fall somewhere in the middle of the very long and the very short lines just described. The longest line in our three model poems is this one from Ruth Stone's "Winter" (individual feet are separated by a vertical bar):

$$\_ \quad / \quad | \quad \_ / \quad | \quad \_ \quad / \quad | \quad / \quad / \quad | \quad \_ \quad \_ \quad / \quad | \quad \_ \quad \_ \quad / \quad | \quad \_ \quad /$$

Your heav | y-lid | ded eyes | slip un | der the seal | of my wid | ow hood.

Let's call this seven-foot line iambic heptameter, even though it has an irregular meter—that is, not all the feet are the same. We have marked the fourth foot as a spondee and the fifth and sixth feet as anapests. Nevertheless, the prevailing meter is iambic, so the line itself takes that adjective.

Now let's scan one of the short lines in Rae Armantrout's "Duration":

```
 _   /   _  /     _ /
be yond | the neigh | bor's tree
```

The line is perfect iambic trimeter, but only one other instance of this meter occurs in the poem. This isn't particularly surprising since neither Stone nor Armantrout employs a regular metrical pattern. It's important to note, therefore, that even though both of these poems are in free verse rather than in a strict meter, individual lines can still be scanned. In fact, you can scan almost any written work, including advertising jingles and prose. Scansion is simply a tool for seeing how the stresses in a line are put together.

All this information about meter may seem like a lot to handle, but it does get easier once you put it into practice. Let's give Gail White's "My Personal Recollections of Not Being Asked to the Prom" a full metrical scan:

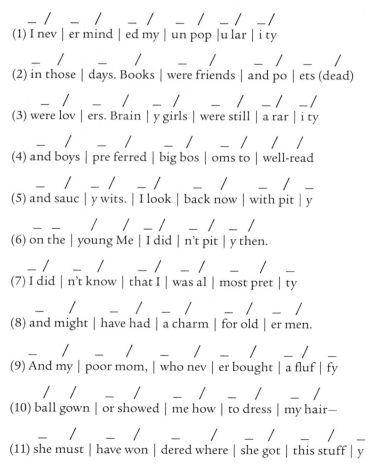

```
   _ /   _  /   _ /   _  /  _ /  _/
(1) I nev | er mind | ed my | un pop |u lar | i ty

   _    /    _    /     _    /     _  /   _   /
(2) in those | days. Books | were friends | and po | ets (dead)

    _  /   _   /   _ /   _   /  _ /  _/
(3) were lov | ers. Brain | y girls | were still | a rar | i ty

    _   /   _   /   _  /   _  /   /  /
(4) and boys | pre ferred | big bos | oms to | well-read

    _   /  _ /  _ /   _   /   _  /  _
(5) and sauc | y wits. | I look | back now | with pit | y

   _   _   /   /  _/  _ /  _ /
(6) on the | young Me | I did | n't pit | y then.

   _/   _   /    _ /  _ /  _  /   _
(7) I did | n't know | that I | was al | most pret | ty

   _    /   _   /  _ /   _  /  _  /
(8) and might | have had | a charm | for old | er men.

   _    /   _   /   _   /  _  /   _/  _
(9) And my | poor mom, | who nev | er bought | a fluf | fy

    /  /   _  /   _  /  _ /   _  /
(10) ball gown | or showed | me how | to dress | my hair—

    _   /   _   /   _   /   _ /   _  /   _
(11) she must | have won | dered where | she got | this stuff | y
```

```
        /   _    _  /   _ /  _  /   _   /
(12) daugh ter. | She did | n't say | it, but | her stare
```

```
      _      /   _  /   _ /   _  --  /   _   /
(13) asked wheth | er genes | or nur | ture were | to blame.
```

```
       _ /  _   /   _     /   _ /  _   /
(14) (But I | got mar | ried, Moth | er, all | the same.)
```

By scanning the fourteen lines of this sonnet, you can see how carefully attuned White is to metrical concerns. Because she is writing a sonnet, her lines are in iambic pentameter; the line lengths, within a few syllables' variation, are predetermined. Although there isn't as much metrical variation as in a free verse poem, "My Personal Recollections of Not Being Asked to the Prom" does contain a number of substituted feet. The use of several variations—the spondees at the end of line 4, in the second foot of line 6, and at the beginning of line 10; the trochee at the beginning of line 12; the extra unaccented syllables at the end of lines 5, 7, 9, and 11—keeps the poem from sounding like the ticktock of a metronome. Instead, this poem is livelier; it's closer to the way real people speak. This rhythmic variety is fairly common in metered poems. Absolute fidelity to a meter generally makes for wearisome reading, and the great masters of iambic pentameter—Shakespeare and Wordsworth, for instance—often employ variations in their lines.

If you have never scanned a poem before, you may feel overwhelmed by how much is going on. As one of my students once said, "Who would have thought that words had so many syllables?" And all these syllables hovering next to one another can make it difficult to tell which are stressed and which are unstressed. But don't become too "stressed" yourself: scansion allows for different ways of hearing a line; it is more like taking an educated guess than reaching a definitive answer. Another reader might scan White's sonnet differently, and that would be perfectly all right.

Maybe because all this business about **prosody**—the study of metrical structure—can sound so complicated, new creative writing students often gravitate toward free verse. Of course, students also write free verse because so many of the poets who first attract their attention also write extensively in nonmetered poetry. Allen Ginsberg, Gary Snyder, Jack Kerouac, Sharon Olds, Nikki Giovanni, and Billy Collins all make good use of free verse's flexible rhythms and line lengths.

In the early twentieth century, poets such as T. S. Eliot and William Carlos Williams mounted the first sustained and successful challenge to the primacy of metered poetry in English. Williams argued that we "must *listen* to the language for the discoveries we hope to make." He believed that a slavish adherence to a predetermined rhythmic pattern not only made for boring verse but also was in some sense downright un-American. (Williams preferred the flexibility of what he called the "variable foot," a concept that traditionalists found maddeningly paradoxical.)

Charles Olson, a slightly younger contemporary of Williams, uses the following formulation to describe the process a free verse poet goes through as his work moves from his mind to the page:

the HEAD, by way of the EAR, to the SYLLABLE

the HEART, by way of the BREATH, to the LINE

Like metrical poets referencing the beating of the heart or the breathing of the lungs, Olson's formulation suggests that writing free verse is not only a mental activity but also a physical one. Our heartbeat and breathing normally come with a steadiness and regularity, but they can also be heightened—when we're running or excited, for example—or slowed down—when we're relaxed or asleep. This open attitude toward line length, which could result in two feet in one line and eight in the next, is one of the chief ways of differentiating free verse from formal verse.

"Free verse is like . . ." Once you complete that sentence, your analogy will probably tell you something about your attitude toward poetry itself. In the past, my students have compared free verse to everything from skydiving to dancing at a Phish concert to cooking without a recipe. Literary critics frequently compare free verse to jazz, which wasn't always considered high art the way it is now. Originally, jazz was a daring urban and African American alternative to classical music. When asked to defend "jazz poems," Langston Hughes praised them because their rhythm pulsed with "the tom-tom of revolt against weariness in a white world, a world of subway trains, and work, work, work; the tom-tom of joy and laughter, and pain swallowed in a smile." Of course, if jazz was at one time a revolutionary musical form that inspired poets to break tradition, now it is largely considered boring by young people, who rarely listen to it. (Ironically, hip-hop, today's equivalent of jazz, is much closer to the older forms of strictly metered poetry.)

Mary Kinzie tells us that "the tradition of free verse has permitted two kinds of lineation: lines composed of broken phrases . . . as well as free verse lines organized in syntactically complete units, all the phrases set off and complete." The lines in Rae Armantrout's "Duration" are so brief that they inevitably take the form of "broken phrases," short bursts of energy that propel us from thought to thought and image to image down the page. "Duration" varies in the number of syllables per line, from two in the shortest line to six in the longest. Poets writing in free verse value this elasticity of language, and Armantrout uses it to excellent effect.

If your past efforts as a poet have been in free verse, then you are already aware of its virtues. However, if you're used to writing poems in meter and rhyme, it's helpful to remember that a poem composed in rhyming quatrains may actually be stronger if it's "translated" into free verse. When you are writing in meter and you realize your poem isn't what you had hoped it would be, allow yourself the freedom to explore other options. John Haines argues that even though a poet may begin by working in a prescribed form with a set meter, "when the spirit of things changes, and the inner substance of thought undergoes a transformation, it may turn out that the form is no longer adequate; it ceases to act for us in a vital way and becomes mere formality." A poet true to his or her poem must honor this transformation and alter the form to mirror the new idea:

> The true form thereafter would be one realized in the act of creation—the form in process, to be discovered in the language we speak, in which we express our thought and passion. This speech, carrying with it whatever elements of traditional form we might still feel to be useful and satisfying, would more nearly express for us the truth of our life and time.

Some poetry critics might call the "poems" that I created in the previous section "broken prose." W. H. Auden compared free verse poets to Robinson Crusoe on his desert island: "He must do all the cooking, laundry and darning for himself. In a few exceptional cases, this manly independence produces something original and impressive, but more often the result is squalor—dirty sheets on the unmade bed and empty bottles on the unswept floor." For poets like Auden and Robert Frost, meter provided the spine on which the body of their poems was created. Frost famously said that writing free verse is like "playing tennis with the net down," and one of the perils of writing in free verse is that your lines can become verbose and slack.

Of course, playing tennis without a net may not be the worst thing in the world if you're still having trouble getting your racket to make contact with the ball. Beginning poets who are trying to juggle the demands of meter and rhyme, as well as all the other elements of poetry (imagery, figurative language, tone, style, and so on), may simply be overtaxed. Every rule has its exceptions, but my experience over the years is that most students enrolled in an introductory creative writing class find it easier to write a good free verse poem than a good rhyming poem. Although T. S. Eliot's dictum may be true that no verse is free for the person who wants to do a good job, free verse generally provides a wider door for students who are still finding their way into the many-roomed house of Poetry.

CHECKLIST Meter and rhythm

☐ **If your poem is written in meter, have you scanned the meter to make sure it's doing what you want it to do?** Even if some student readers of your poem aren't aware of the presence or absence of meter, your instructor *will* recognize clumsy handling of regular metrical patterns. If you decide to write in a specific meter, take the time to do it right. Know the name of the meter you're using. Scan your lines repeatedly to determine when, where, and why you are deviating from the pattern you have chosen. Read model poems such as Gail White's to get a sense of how expert poets handle the challenges of meter. Rhyme normally emphasizes meter, so be particularly attentive to the placement of accented syllables if your poem rhymes.

☐ **If you're not writing in meter, does your poem still have a discernible rhythm?** The longer you write poetry, the easier it becomes to hear a poem's rhythm in your head, whether or not that rhythm is based on traditional meter. However, new creative writers sometimes feel that without the aid of meter, their poems' rhythms are too subtle to discern or may be altogether lacking. If you would like more regularity in your lines but don't want to use traditional meter, try creating lines with the same syllable count. Ten syllables doesn't always equal iambic pentameter, but it comes close. If all the lines of your poem contain basically the same number of syllables, a distinct rhythm often begins to emerge.

The music of poetry ▶

Denise Levertov says that "writing poetry is a process of discovery, revealing inherent music, the music of correspondences, the music of inscape." If you have never thought of written or spoken language as musical before, this statement initially may seem a bit baffling. What is the music of "correspondences" and "inscape"? And how can words make music if they aren't being sung?

First it's helpful to remember that music is the art of ordering sounds into combinations, and words, spoken aloud, do make sounds. We have also looked at the ways that poems use rhythm, another of the elements that poetry shares with music. Greek poetry was originally accompanied by the guitarlike lyre, from which we get the term "lyric poetry." English ballads like "Lord Randal" and "The Demon Lover" were passed from singer to singer long before they made their way to paper. More recently, Langston Hughes appropriated the blues form for his poetry, and one of the reasons many students sign up for a creative writing course is that they love listening to, analyzing, and writing song lyrics.

In short, making a direct connection between music and poetry isn't as farfetched as it might seem. Ideally, in a poem, phrases of words are like phrases of music; poets reading from their work are like musicians interpreting the notes on a page. To achieve this music in their poetry, poets use a range of devices. This section covers several of the most common tricks of the trade, beginning with the musical aspect of poetry you are probably most familiar with: **rhyme**, a correspondence of sound in two or more words.

Let's take another look at the one rhyming poem among our three models, "My Personal Recollections of Not Being Asked to the Prom":

I never minded my unpopularity
in those days. Books were friends and poets (dead)
were lovers. Brainy girls were still a rarity
and boys preferred big bosoms to well-read
and saucy wits. I look back now with pity
on the young Me I didn't pity then.
I didn't know that I was almost pretty
and might have had a charm for older men.

And my poor mom, who never bought a fluffy
ball gown or showed me how to dress my hair—
she must have wondered where she got this stuffy
daughter. She didn't say it, but her stare
asked whether genes or nurture were to blame.
(But I got married, Mother, all the same.)

As you read the poem, you can see that it has a rhyme scheme, a purposeful arrangement of rhyming words at the end of each line. A shorthand format has evolved over the years to aid us in discussing rhyme schemes. In this format, we give each rhyming word a letter and then put those letters in sequence. Each time a new rhyme occurs in a poem, it receives a new letter. White's sonnet rhymes as follows: *ababcdcd efefgg*. A rhyme scheme is important because it not only brings a sense of order to your work but also signals to your reader that you know what you're doing, that your rhyming is to some larger purpose. A rhyme scheme gives you authority.

White's sonnet employs the most common form of rhyme, **end rhyme**, which Mary Kinzie defines as "the agreement of two metrically accented syllables and their terminal consonants." Kinzie's precise definition tells us what end rhyme is, but it can't, of course, capture all of rhyme's **connotations**—the meanings a word *suggests* rather than specifically names or describes. Among the earliest rhymes we hear are nursery rhymes, which seem to evoke some deep-rooted human pleasure in similar sounds. Many of us take delight in the rhyme of song lyrics, and for poets who work mostly in rhyme, there is no question of its fundamental importance. Rhyme links words not only by sound but also, inevitably, by sense. Consequently, poets use rhyme to underscore the similarities between two words (and ideas) as well as to highlight their differences.

Of course, there is more than one way to rhyme. Consider the rhymes in the first four lines of White's poem: "unpopularity" and "rarity" in the first and third lines, and "dead" and "read" in the second and fourth lines. The no-nonsense single stressed syllables of "dead" and "read" used to be called "masculine rhymes." Not surprisingly, this terminology is now generally considered sexist, and we refer to a masculine rhyme as a **single rhyme**.

Rhymes such as those that end the first and third lines of the sonnet, "unpopularity" and "rarity," in which the rhyme is a stressed syllable followed by one or more unstressed syllables, used to be called "feminine rhymes" because they were considered "weak." Today, the preferred terminology is **falling rhyme**. "Rarity" and "unpopularity" are actually **triple rhymes**, since both contain the "ar-i-ty" sounds. Drawn-out **polysyllabic rhymes** (rhymes of more than one syllable) like these have long been considered a comic or satirical device in written poetry, and they are basically used for that purpose in White's poem. This particular rhyme, for instance, seems to accentuate the speaker's own awkwardness in social situations. The connection between "fluffy" and "stuffy," the **double rhyme** (with two rhyming syllables) in lines 9 and 11, is ironic, of course, since the stuffy teenager the speaker once was is anything but fluffy. Despite this long association with **light verse**—poetry, usually rhymed, that treats its subject in a comic or good-natured manner—polysyllabic rhymes may be more familiar to your ear from hip-hop, which frequently employs them. However, rap uses double, triple, and even quadruple rhymes as often for serious as for comic effect.

"Fluffy" and "stuffy," like "dead" and "read," are **perfect rhymes**: the correspondence between the two rhyme sounds is exact. The effect of perfect rhyme is a closure similar to Yeats's famous statement that "a poem comes right with a click like a closing box." Critic Julie Kane similarly believes that White's lines "snap shut like steel traps each time a rhyme is completed, imparting a sense of completeness to the preceding thought."

A perfect rhyme can indeed be sonorous, lifting readers into the realm of music. However, new poets are likely to overvalue perfect rhyme and ignore other musical effects. One of these variations is called the slant, imperfect, near, or off rhyme. In **slant rhymes**, the vowel sounds may be either similar or significantly dissimilar, and the rhymed consonants may be similar rather than identical. Rae Armantrout makes use of slant rhymes in "Duration," as in the connection between "heav<u>en</u>" and "repet<u>ition</u>'s" in lines 8 and 9.

Eye or **sight rhymes** are words that *look* as if they should rhyme, even though they don't when we say them aloud. Often these words *did* rhyme in the past, but as the language has evolved, the pronunciation of one of the formerly rhyming words has also changed. "Laughter" and "slaughter" are good examples of sight rhymes, as are "move" and "dove," "laid" and "said," "crow" and "brow," and so on.

Internal rhyme occurs within a single line of poetry: "I can't <u>wait</u> to be <u>late</u> for my <u>date</u>." Internal rhyme is used extensively in hip-hop, so much so that many writers of literary poetry have lately begun to shy away from it. Nevertheless, powerful poets, from Gwendolyn Brooks to Seamus Heaney, have made strong use of internal rhyme, and it can be an effective way to increase musicality in your poem.

Rhyming focuses on the ends of words, but that's not the only way to make connections between similar sounds. **Alliteration** normally refers to the repetition of initial consonant sounds. Gail White uses alliteration in lines 4 and 5 of her sonnet with "boys," "big bosoms," and "back." Ruth Stone uses it in lines 19 and 20 of "Winter" with "minds," "mounds," and "motors." And we can find alliteration in Armantrout's "Duration"; lines 5, 9, and 11 are linked by the *w* sound of "winks," "where," and "whistles."

The term "alliteration" can also be used as an umbrella to cover consonance and assonance. **Consonance**, as its name suggests, is the recurrence of consonant sounds, especially at the end of stressed syllables, but without the similar-sounding vowels. Armantrout employs consonance when she links the *l* sounds of "needle" and "still" in lines 13 and 15. Again, as is the case with rhyme, we can see how linking similar sounds is tied to the linking of similar ideas. The "needle" of the blackbirds' song is "still" on the air throughout the "daylong day." **Assonance** is the repetition of vowel sounds without the repetition of similar end consonants. Assonance is a form of slant or near rhyme, and the terms are often used interchangeably.

Despite its flat statements and "to be" verbs, Ruth Stone's "Winter," which might at first seem rather prosaic, in fact makes extensive use of musical devices. Take, for instance, the long *o* assonance in the opening lines of "Winter":

Steam wheezes between the couplings.

As we look at the many musical devices our three model poets employ, we begin to realize that the question of whether a poem should or should not rhyme is something of a false one. Gail White may be the only one of these poets writing in consistent end rhyme, but even without this device, good poets can make use of the music of language. To some extent, every poet who attempts to group similar-sounding words into a poem is a "rhyming" poet.

The ten o-clock train to New York,
coaches like loaves of bread powdered with snow.

(We can also appreciate the eye rhyme of "powdered" and "snow.") The next line contains both the assonance of the long *e* sound as well as the alliteration from closely repeated *w* sounds:

CHECKLIST The music of poetry

- ☐ **Does your rhyming poem need to rhyme?** Ask yourself whether the rhyme adds to or detracts from the poem's overall quality. Would the poem be more succinct and specific if it were in free verse rather than rhyme? Your main goal should be to write well, and a well-written poem doesn't have to rhyme.

☐ **If you're committed to keeping a rhyming poem in rhyme, are your rhyming words fresh and intelligent? Have you eliminated all "padding" rhymes?** Again, you should rhyme for a reason: to achieve a certain effect, to emphasize the sounds of certain words or because, in your opinion, your subject demands the special qualities of rhyme. In his satiric poem "A Fit of Rhyme against Rhyme," Ben Jonson warns that rhymes can be guilty of "wresting words from their true calling." That is, rhyme can force us to select an end word simply for its *sound*, when another word would make better overall *sense*. The result can be lines that are garbled and jumbled, with the poet going to elaborate lengths simply to make one word rhyme with another.

☐ **Would slant, internal, or eye rhyme give you more flexibility to say what you really want to say?** Perfect end rhyme too often leads to cliché because most of the perfect rhymes in English have been used so frequently that it's difficult to do anything very original with them. Slant rhymes, in contrast, offer more options and are more likely to allow you to "make it new."

☐ **Do you hear the "music" in your poetry?** Your response to this question may be based on subjective factors; nevertheless, your poem should "sing" to you. (Otherwise, why not just write in prose?) Listen carefully to how you have put your sounds together, and see if you can regroup them in ways that accent meaning. Remember that alliteration, including assonance and consonance, can add musicality to your poem, whether or not it rhymes.

Images, symbols, and figurative language ▶

Show, don't tell. Whether your creative writing class is being taught in Maine or Montana or Missouri, you will hear this piece of advice repeatedly from your instructor. The reason is that in nearly every culture, and for as long as we have had poetry, poets and their audiences have decided that imagery must play an integral part in the poetic experience.

C. Day Lewis called the image "a picture made out of words," although imagery may also refer to the other four senses: taste, touch, smell, and sound. That's a fairly straightforward description, but poets can become quasi-mystical when describing the power of imagery. Ezra Pound called an image "an intellectual and emotional complex in an instant of time." That's a trickier definition, but also a more provocative one. Pound seems to be suggesting that one of the key aspects of imagery is that it freezes time, a feat that our rational self tells us is impossible. Yet an image does make us linger. It "thingifies" the world long enough for us to consider it more carefully. Larry Levis focuses on the image's ability to temporarily halt the passage of time when he says, "The images we write hold still, and their stillness is curious because it reminds us that, someday, up ahead, at the end of the story, completion is inevitable but incomprehensible. Freud called it the 'riddle of death,' but a riddle is also an image, a stillness."

One of the most difficult things for new poets to do is to incorporate imagery into their poetry. Students often believe that if they use generalities rather than specific concrete examples, more readers will be able to "relate" to the poem. That argument makes sense from a distance, but it is rarely valid when applied to the actual experience of reading a poem.

For instance, you might think that simply saying, "She's beautiful," will automatically evoke for your readers a mental picture of someone they know who is beautiful. While that may happen occasionally, more often than not your readers will simply pass over those two words and not "see" the subject of your poem at all. Think back on the way you remember the important events in your own life. Do you think of those events in abstract terms? Or do you retain mental pictures of what happened? Humans tend to process stories in terms of pictures their minds create, and if you don't provide those pictures, your reader will probably tune you out. Images force readers to slow down—to see, hear, taste, touch, and smell the world that the poem creates.

Because we live in a world that is always rushing toward something else, a poem in which the only description is "She's beautiful" will call forth nothing but a blur. Contrast that statement with "Her hair was the orange of maple leaves in autumn; her eyes were as blue as the night sky in a painting by van Gogh." That second description requires some mental energy on the part of both the writer and the reader, but it pays off. We may not yet be able to see the face of the beautiful woman, but we are much closer to knowing the color of her hair and eyes. Ultimately, of course, words are too inexact a medium to convey precisely what *anyone* looks like, but the very fact of language's imprecision means that you owe it to your readers to make at least a gesture toward specificity.

Let's look at another example of how imagery works. One type of poem most often missing concrete imagery is the love poem. This is ironic, of course, given that we almost always claim to love someone because of his or her *specific* qualities. Yet creative writing teachers frequently receive poems like this one:

> My love, you fill my heart with bliss.
>   You give me so much peace,
> And bring me joy at the end of each long day.
>   Don't ever go away.
>
> Your eyes are as blue as the sky.
>   Your beauty cannot fade.
> Your hair is soft as silk.
>   With you, I'm never afraid.

You never leave my heart alone.
   You always show you care.
Your smile shines like the sun.
   You touched my soul forever.

I fell in love at first sight of you,
   Don't ask me why.
But something about you tells me that
   I'll love you till I die.

If you were given a poem like this from someone you cared about, you would probably be delighted. The poet—let's say it's a young man addressing a young woman—really seems to care about the person he is addressing. He remembers the color of her eyes (always a good sign), and he has even taken the trouble to rhyme! A love poem to a beloved doesn't have to be good; it just has to be sincere.

However, if you were reading this poem in a class, you might have a bit of a queasy feeling. Two abstractions you especially want to avoid are "heart" (short-hand for "romantic love") and "soul" (having to do with all things spiritual). Single words rarely become clichés, but "heart" and "soul" are exceptions. Scan your poems for these words. If you see them, look for ways to eliminate them and replace them with specific, concrete details.

Even though there *are* images in the poem, things we can touch and see, they are all clichés—trite expressions like "blue as the sky" "soft as silk," and "shines like the sun." Clichés persist for a reason: they have an essential truth to them. On clear days, a wide blue sky can make a big impression. Fine silk is indeed very soft. And nothing—in our solar system, at least—shines quite like the sun. But all of these images have been used so often and for so long that they no longer make the same impact they once did. Most readers will glide right over them, barely pausing to imagine what they are meant to convey.

Contrast "blue as the sky" with "blue as the night sky in a painting by van Gogh" or "blue as a bolt of lightning" or "blue as the feathers on a peacock's breast"—or simply "turquoise" or "ultramarine" or "robin's-egg blue." Not only do these revisions bring fresher language into the poem, but they also begin to give us a clearer sense of the *individuality* of the poet's beloved. Maybe she is as brooding and mysterious as van Gogh, or as fiery and explosive as lightning, or as proud as a peacock. The poet doesn't need to explicitly state, "She's mysterious" or "passionate" or "proud"; he can *suggest* those qualities by the images he uses.

Let's take it a step further. Look at the first stanza again:

My love, you fill my heart with bliss.
   You give me so much peace,
And bring me joy at the end of each long day.
   Don't ever go away.

These lines do little to distinguish this love affair from millions of others going on around the planet at this very moment. However, if we look for specifics, we see that there is potential for developing an image centered on the beloved bringing the speaker "joy at the end of each long day." How might that joy be brought? Perhaps the beloved gives the speaker a back rub or always has a lilac-scented candle lit in the evenings when he comes home from work. And what is the *nature* of the speaker's "long day"? Does he work construction in Tucson in the summertime? Or is he a mortgage broker in a Boston skyscraper?

The poem seems burdened by its rhymes, so let's see what happens if we drop them:

After a long day hammering nails
in the Arizona sun, I can't wait
to get home to a back rub and a bowl
of gazpacho, spicy and cold.

It's not great, but it's better. The *abcc* end rhyme has been replaced by the assonance of "nails" and "wait" and the slant rhyme of "bowl" and "cold." More important, we get a sense of who the speaker is and what his life is like when he returns to the person he loves. The image of gazpacho, a soup made from chopped raw vegetables, adds an unexpected twist. We tend to think of a love affair as spicy and *hot*, but maybe "after a long day hammering nails/in the Arizona sun," something cold would be all the more welcome.

All three of our model poems make use of imagery, but Ruth Stone's "Winter" clearly is the most imagistic. Here is the poem again, with each instance of an appeal to one or more of the five senses underscored:

The <u>ten o-clock train</u> to New York,
<u>coaches</u> like <u>loaves of bread powdered</u> with <u>snow</u>.
<u>Steam wheezes between the couplings</u>.
<u>Stripped to plywood, the station's cement standing room</u>
imitates a Russian novel. It is now that I remember you.
Your <u>profile becomes the carved handle of a letter knife.</u>
Your <u>heavy-lidded eyes slip under the seal of my widowhood</u>.
It is another <u>raw winter</u>. <u>Stray cats are suffering</u>.
<u>Starlings crowd the edges of chimneys</u>.
It is a drab misery that urges me to remember you.
I think about the subjugation of <u>women and horses</u>;
brutal exposure; <u>weather that forces, that strips</u>.
In our time we met in <u>ornate stations</u>
<u>arching up</u> with nineteenth-century optimism.
<u>I remember you running beside the train waving good-bye</u>.
I can produce a facsimile of <u>you standing</u>
<u>behind a column of polished oak to surprise me</u>.
Am I going toward you or away from you on this <u>train</u>?

Discarded junk of other minds is strewn beside the tracks:
mounds of rusting wire, grotesque pop art of dead motors,
senile warehouses. The train passes a station;
fresh people standing on the platform,
their faces expecting something.
I feel their entire histories ravish me.

Reading this poem is like watching a short film: with so much imagery, it's difficult *not* to feel as if you have just taken a ride on a train *and* been inside the speaker's mind as she relives selected memories. Even the final line—"I feel their entire histories ravish me"—though primarily composed of abstractions, nevertheless contains, in the word "ravish," a reference to the physical world. Although today "ravish" has the positive connotations of "to overcome with joy and delight," in earlier centuries it meant "to overcome by violence," and this etymological sucker punch brings home the full power of the poem. Stone leads us to the point where we can begin to feel some of her grief ourselves through her expert use of imagery.

J. A. Cuddon reminds us that "it is often the case that an image is not exclusively one thing or another; they overlap and intermingle and thus combine." Mentioning a freshly baked batch of chocolate chip cookies just being pulled from an oven appeals to our sense of taste, smell, and sight—maybe even touch if we imagine how hot and gooey they are. Some readers will go on to make associations with the sight and taste of a tall glass of cold milk. "Chocolate chip cookies" may further evoke fond memories of childhood, of certain family members, of the look and smell of a kitchen, and so on. In short, the image is a powerful triggering device, even though you can never dictate to your readers exactly what they will experience.

As you consider images for particular moments in your poem, it's important to realize that the *more specific* the image, the more likely it is to be remembered. Moreover, an image that is *unusual yet appropriate* is even more likely to make an impression on your readers. Look how Stone approaches one particular image toward the end of her poem. She first mentions "discarded junk," a rather generic phrase. But she is not content to leave it at that. Instead, we get specific instances of that junk as it is "strewn beside the tracks:/mounds of rusting wire, grotesque pop art of dead motors,/senile warehouses." We see not just wire but "mounds of rusting wire," not just dead motors but "grotesque pop art of dead motors." Even the warehouses are "senile." Like a painter going beyond her original sketch, Stone fills in the details, and she does so with just a few additional words.

Images have their own weight and power, but they have even more impact when they take on the resonance of symbols. Take the image of the rose as an example. Typically a rose stands for the fleeting nature of love and beauty. There is nothing quite as beautiful as a rose in full bloom, but that bloom doesn't last long, and the rose soon fades, its petals growing brown and discolored and dropping off one by one. Unfortunately, though, if you put a rose in your poem, this once terrific symbol will be sapped by its use in countless other poems. There might still be wonderful poems about roses yet to be written, but the poets who compose those poems will need to be exceptionally skillful in avoiding the many clichés now associated with this particular symbol.

If some symbols shout out their meanings, other symbols are so private that only the poet is likely to understand them. Say, for instance, that you associate telephone poles not with communication or height or a disruption of the natural world—associations that make sense because of the object's function in the world—but with the first thing you saw when you heard the news that your grandfather had passed away. If you place a telephone pole in your poem, alone and without any explanation—"My heart broke when I saw the telephone pole"— your readers will have no idea what associations that extremely personal symbol is supposed to evoke.

To help students avoid both of these pitfalls, authors of creative writing books generally warn against consciously using symbols. Symbols, they say, will emerge from your writing. There's some truth to that. Too much symbolism can ruin a piece of writing. As Umberto Eco says, "Where everything has a second sense, everything is irredeemably flat and dull." Nevertheless, as you grow more confident in your writing, you will often have the feeling that an image works both literally *and* symbolically. That certainly appears to be the case with Armantrout's blackbirds, which might be said to represent the persistence of small things in the face of endless time. (The blackbirds may also allude to Wallace Stevens's famous poem "Thirteen Ways of Looking at a Blackbird.") Similarly, Stone's discarded junk—the rusting wire, the dead motors, the senile warehouses—are not only objects one would be likely to see through a train window but also symbols of decay and ruin, images of a world that seems to have passed its prime.

One of the primary ways of bringing imagery and symbols into poetry is through the use of **figurative language**. In the words of M. H. Abrams, "Figurative language is a deviation from what speakers of a language apprehend as the ordinary, or standard, significance of words, in order to achieve some special meaning or effect." Much of the strangeness of poetry, as opposed to everyday conversation and writing, results from the dense use of figures of speech. There are far more of these rhetorical devices than we can cover in this book, so we'll look at only the most common examples.

Style in poetry usually refers to the author's selection and placement of words in a line, lines in a stanza, and stanzas in a poem. Aristotle said that the greatest element of style any writer could possess was "a command of metaphor." We'll include similes here also, for, as Aristotle said, the difference between the two "is but slight." A **metaphor** is a figure of speech in which a word or phrase that ordinarily denotes one thing is applied to something else in order to suggest an analogy or a likeness between the two things: "Your smile is a bouquet of daffodils." A **simile** is a figure of speech that states a likeness between two unlike things: "Your smile is *like* a bouquet of daffodils." I. A. Richards coined the terms **tenor** for the subject to which a metaphor is applied and **vehicle** for the metaphoric term itself. If we say, to borrow an example from Aristotle's *Rhetoric*, that a warrior was a lion in battle, the tenor of the metaphor is the warrior; the vehicle is the lion.

As Ted Kooser says, "If you think of a metaphor as being a bridge between two things, it's not the things that are of the most importance, but the grace and lift of the bridge between them, flying high over the surface." That bridge between the tenor and the vehicle is most fitting when the connection between the thing being described and what it is being compared to is both unexpected *and* somehow fitting. Consider the disappointing figurative language—"blue as the sky," "soft as silk," and "shines like the sun"—from "My Love," our awkward poem of clichés. Overuse has robbed these similes of all their power. In contrast, Ruth Stone's "coaches like loaves of bread powdered with snow" from "Winter" makes inventive use of simile.

Two common variations on metaphor are metonymy and synecdoche. In **metonymy**, the name of something is substituted with the name of something else closely associated with it. When reporters refer to "the White House," for instance, they mean the president of the United States. Similarly, when the president refers to "the press," he is talking about the news media, particularly print journalists. **Synecdoche** is sometimes considered a kind of metonymy, although the term is more often used when a part is used to describe the whole. When the captain of a ship cries out, "All *hands* on deck!" for instance, he wants more than just the hands of his crew members helping out: he wants the sailors themselves. Because metonymy and synecdoche rely heavily on long associations between two things, they are a species of cliché, and you should be wary of using either of them in your poetry.

Another figure of speech is **personification**, the awarding of human attributes to an abstraction or nonhuman thing. In Shakespeare's *Othello*, Iago uses personification when he refers to jealousy as "the green-ey'd monster which doth mock / The meat it feeds on." In his poem "To Autumn," John Keats personifies that season as a woman "sitting careless on a granary floor," her "hair soft-lifted by the winnowing wind." Personification can liven up a poem, but it can also quickly become ridiculous and is probably best used in moderation.

Similar advice goes for the use of the **pun**, a play on the multiple meanings of a word or its relation to other words that sound like it. (In the words of a famous pun, "A pun is its own reword.") There's a delayed pun in Rae Armantrout's "Duration," when she writes "We're still / on the air," as though she were a radio or TV announcer; the joke is that she has just been discussing blackbirds, who, when they take flight, are also "on the air." Finding puns is especially easy to do when reading Shakespeare, who was enamored of them. Shortly before Mercutio's death in *Romeo and Juliet*, the playwright has Mercutio say, "Ask for me tomorrow and you shall find me a *grave* man." Mercutio is suggesting not only that will he be in a somber frame of mind but also that he will very likely be dead. In a "Hymn to God the Father," John Donne writes, "at my death Thy *Son* / Shall shine as he shines now." Clearly, the pun here implies that Jesus in his glory is as bright as the sun. As the last two quotes indicate, punning has a long history in literature. Still, the value of puns is disputed. Some readers love the wit involved; others find punning a rather low form of comedy. Nevertheless, certain poets who make extensive and skillful use of puns—James Merrill and Stephen Yenser come to mind—focus our attention on the roots of words we have come to take for granted as well as the interconnectedness of all language.

Finally, we should mention one of the most frequent types of figurative language used in poetry: **irony**, the incongruity between the way things appear and the way they actually are. Irony comes from a Greek word meaning "affectation of ignorance," and it's a powerful rhetorical device not only in poetry but in every type of creative writing. We will discuss some specific forms in Chapter 4, but for now it's important to focus on the two types of irony that occur most often in poetry. **Verbal irony** results when someone says one thing but means another. For instance, when Gail White remarks that "poets (dead) / were lovers," we know she's not a necrophiliac; she is simply saying that the only "lovers" she had were the poets whose work she read in books. And of course Rae Armantrout is being ironic when she writes that "repetition's / not boring" in heaven, when heaven is, by definition, paradise—where nothing could possibly be boring.

Gail White's "My Personal Recollections of Not Being Asked to the Prom" is also an example of **situational irony**, in which the results of a situation are distinctly different from what one might reasonably expect. The central character in the poem—the speaker as a teenager—*should* be living a life full of parties and dances; in fact, she prefers books to boys and doesn't even attend her own prom. And Ruth Stone's "Winter" similarly relies on the situational irony that a train ride on a snowy day—which ought to be pleasant, if not downright romantic—evokes such a painful series of memories.

CHECKLIST Images, symbols, and figurative language

☐ **Do your poems have plenty of concrete, specific, and detailed images? Or are you relying on clichés and bland generalizations?** If the latter is the case, revise your work, looking for places where you can replace an abstraction with something that your reader can see, hear, smell, touch, or taste. According to Ezra Pound, "It is better to present one Image in a lifetime than to produce voluminous works." Pound was given to exaggerated pronouncements, but most beginning writers can benefit from his advice that poets should "go in fear of abstractions." Unless you have good reason to do otherwise, choose the image over the generalization every time.

☐ **Will the symbols in your poetry have resonance for both you and your readers?** Symbols that are too public and too obvious won't have much impact. If you use a cross to represent Christianity, for example, or a skeleton to represent death, or a fox to represent cunning, you might as well put up a neon sign announcing the meaning of your poem. However, you don't want your symbols to be so private and obscure that no one else will be able to understand them. Find a balance between the two extremes.

☐ **Are you making effective use of metaphors and similes?** Ted Kooser advises poets to consider "writing a poem around a metaphor" because it gives the poet "a head start toward poetry that has integral order and transcends the mere sum of its accumulated words." Try to write a poem built around a central, productive metaphor or simile. Or go back to a poem you have already written and see if you can replace flat and uninspiring language with metaphors and similes that bring your subject to life.

☐ **Is the irony in your poem intentional or unintentional?** Given the prevalence of irony in poetry, it will be difficult for you to write a poem that doesn't make some use of it. The key is for *you*, the poet, to be in control. Look at your poems carefully. Are you aware of potential absurdities in phrasing or situations? Are you handling your language and subject with assurance? Or can your poems be easily misread or misinterpreted? If so, your readers will quickly lose confidence in your poetic voice and authority.

Diction, syntax, and the language of poetry ▶

Words. They are our greatest delights as poets, but they also present us with our most difficult challenges. Learning how to say something with just the right words is one of the most rewarding achievements you can take away from a creative writing class. When the right words come, we feel as though we are channeling the universe; when we're blocked, those same words may seem incredibly elusive. However, especially in the revision process, you can increase your chances of writing a good poem by selecting strong, suitable words and placing them in a satisfying and effective order.

Writers using appropriate diction select words that are effective for their purposes. Mary Kinzie tells us that on one end of the spectrum is "plain style," which "employs concrete words, refers to things, objects and feelings, and tends to be monosyllabic." On the other end of the spectrum is "high style," which "employs elevated diction to suggest a refined mode of argument and description and a leisurely, sometimes involuted mode of thought."

Both Rae Armantrout and Ruth Stone use a fairly plain style in their poems. Granted, the absence of transitions from one image and idea to the next lends a certain mystery to "Duration," but we have no trouble understanding the individual sentences of the poem. Stone is more straightforward. "It is another raw winter," she writes. "Stray cats are suffering." Later, she asks the memory of her husband, "Am I going toward you or away from you on this train?" The fact that she uses a relatively matter-of-fact way of speaking in most of the poem highlights the elevated diction of the final line: "I feel their entire histories ravish me." The word "ravish" is not one we use in ordinary conversation, and its use here changes the **tone**—the style and manner of expression—of the poem.

As noted earlier, syntax refers to the way words are put together to form phrases in a sentence. The task of organizing a sentence for maximum effectiveness is made more complex by the fact that most poets consider the *line* the basic unit of a poem. When you are ordering the words of your poem, you need to be aware of both how they fit together as a sentence *and* how they appear as a line of poetry. Let's look once more at the first stanza of Gail White's sonnet:

> I never minded my unpopularity
> in those days. Books were friends and poets (dead)
> were lovers. Brainy girls were still a rarity
> and boys preferred big bosoms to well-read
> and saucy wits. I look back now with pity
> on the young Me I didn't pity then.
> I didn't know that I was almost pretty
> and might have had a charm for older men.

White must organize her sentences so that the last word in each line rhymes with the last word in another line. Obviously there is a real risk of writing sentences with syntax that is badly convoluted simply to ensure that the rhyming words appear at the correct places. Yet White manages to accomplish this difficult task without distorting her syntax. Here's the stanza as a paragraph of prose:

> I never minded my unpopularity in those days. Books were friends and poets (dead) were lovers. Brainy girls were still a rarity and boys preferred big bosoms to well-read and saucy wits. I look back now with pity on the young Me I didn't pity then. I didn't know that I was almost pretty and might have had a charm for older men.

We can still hear the rhymes, but the poet appears to be entirely in control of the syntax she uses.

This double awareness of line and syntax adds an exciting element to poetry. As readers, we are conscious of both when a line ends *and* when a sentence ends. When the endings of both lines and sentences correspond, there is an added emphasis on the closure of that thought. However, when the sentence ends in the middle of a line, or a line breaks in the middle of a sentence, we're left hanging.

That "unfinished" sense keeps us moving forward, or, as Robert Pinsky says, "The syntax is trying to speed up the line, and the line is trying to slow down the syntax."

Our three model poems—and, indeed, almost all the poems in this book—are closer to a plain style than to a truly high style that you might associate with someone like William Shakespeare. We selected plain-style poems for a good reason: unless you're an experienced and accomplished poet, any attempt to write in a high style might misfire. Why is that? Let's take a look at one of Shakespeare's sonnets to see what high style requires.

In Shakespeare's Sonnet XIX, the speaker claims that the beloved, even after death, will always remain alive in the poem:

> Devouring Time, blunt thou the lion's paws,
> And make the earth devour her own sweet brood;
> Pluck the keen teeth from the fierce tiger's jaws,
> And burn the long-liv'd phoenix, in her blood;
> Make glad and sorry seasons as thou fleet'st,
> And do whate'er thou wilt, swift-footed Time,
> To the wide world and all her fading sweets;
> But I forbid thee one most heinous crime:
> O! carve not with thy hours my love's fair brow,
> Nor draw no lines there with thine antique pen;
> Him in thy course untainted do allow
> For beauty's pattern to succeeding men.
> Yet, do thy worst old Time: despite thy wrong,
> My love shall in my verse ever live young.

Shakespeare's syntax in this sonnet is extremely complex. The first twelve lines constitute a single sentence containing seven commas, four semicolons, a colon, and an exclamation point: quite an impressive feat! Let's face it: the intricate phrasing of a sentence like this one would be extremely difficult for new creative writers to pull off. Moreover, words such as "thou," "thee," and "thine" and exclamations such as "O!" very clearly belong to the diction of Shakespeare's era. If you're tempted to dip into **archaic language**—that is, language that evokes an earlier time—remember that a poem making heavy use of deliberately old-fashioned words is more likely to sound like a bad King Arthur movie than a dazzling work of literature. Not surprisingly, therefore, most creative writing instructors advise students to start by writing in plain style rather than high style.

Particularly in the revision process, it's important to be aware of diction and syntax, but when you're actually in the middle of writing a poem, you will probably be more concerned with expressing the emotion or idea that inspired your poem in the first place. That's fine. Getting a rough approximation of what you want to say on the page is a necessary part of the process. But a good poem doesn't stop with the first draft. You must also revise your work, honing your choice of words. Richard Hugo called revision "probably the hardest thing about writing poems. . . . Somehow you must switch your allegiance from the triggering subject to the words." At first glance, this may not sound like an especially tricky task. After all, how else *are* you going to express yourself other than through the use of words? However, as Hugo goes on to remark, there is often a wide gap between the ideas or images that get a poem started and the way they are actually expressed.

And there, as Hamlet said, is the rub. Most poets take years to find their voices, so you probably won't be able to develop your own unique language of poetry in just one semester. What you can do is *begin* to get a sense of how poetry differs from everyday language and how you might infuse it with your own personality and habits of thinking. One of the best ways of doing this is to steer clear of some of the bad habits that many new poets develop.

First, remember that just because you are writing a poem, that doesn't mean you can throw all the rules of grammar out the window. Poetry allows you to write fragments, play around with punctuation, experiment with unusual phrasing, or scatter your words and lines across the page. However, to quote Ezra Pound again, "Poetry must be at least as well written as prose." One way to test this is to eliminate the line breaks from your poem (as we did with White's sonnet) and read it aloud. Does it sound awkward and forced, or eloquent and compelling? Even if you are experimenting with form and content, poetry doesn't give you the freedom to stop *thinking* clearly. Nor should you ignore a basic duty of every writer: carefully proofreading your work.

Avoid clichés—the old creative writing joke goes—like the plague. Clichés are a form of laziness: something comes into your head, and by virtue of its being there, you commit it to paper. The problem is that the phrase is in your head because you have heard it a thousand times before. That's not poetry; it's "received language." You can avoid most clichés by never settling for less than the most precise word or phrase. As Hugo says, look for "those words you can own and ways of putting them in phrases and lines that are yours by right of obsessive musical deed."

That's an interesting phrase: "obsessive musical deed." It hints at the way your own idiosyncratic ways of encountering the world can be a great strength as a poet. "A poet is materially estranging her language, all the time," Heather McHugh tells us. "Her own language must become strange to her." One of the great pleasures of poetry happens when you know that you're writing both inside and outside yourself, when you hear voices you didn't know were in your head.

It's useful to take the advice of McHugh and other creative writing instructors: *Compose toward clarity. Revise toward strangeness.* If in your early drafts you try to get your poem as close as possible to the way you want it, in your later drafts you will feel more comfortable about eliminating the verbiage and clichés and introducing elements that keep the poem from being merely average. Those later drafts are crucial: it's the rare poem that can't benefit from careful revision.

Remember, finally, that philosophy and poetry are different enterprises, especially for new poets. Some outstanding poetic works do in fact deal with complicated metaphysical issues, but these poems are nearly always written by highly experienced poets. You should master the fundamentals of poetry before you attempt to tackle questions about the meaning of the universe. "Great is the enemy of good," the writing theorist Donald Murray often said. Don't worry about earth-shaking profundity until you have written a decent poem.

CHECKLIST Diction, syntax, and the language of poetry

☐ **Do your diction and syntax reflect the goals of your poem?** As you reread your work, make sure you have selected the most accurate and powerful words and arranged them in the most powerful order. Of course, you can be flexible with your diction and syntax, but be wary of choosing highfalutin words like "morphophonemics" or "disestablishmentarianism" unless you have good reason to use them. And don't wrench your sentences around simply to sound different or to catch a rhyme: inverted syntax poetic is not.

☐ **Are you using archaic, antiquated language?** Stephen Minot reminds us in *Three Genres* that poetry written this year ought to sound as if it was written this year: "Every age has its own linguistic flavor, and like it or not, you're writing for the twenty-first century." That does not mean that all poets will have the same voice—far from it. But your poem should not sound as though it was composed using a quill pen in some long-ago world of dragons and damsels in distress.

☐ **Have you eliminated all the clichés from your poems?** As you reread your poetry, consider whether a phrase you're using is one you have heard many times before. If so, change it. Say something strange. Use an image or a metaphor or a simile that no one has ever tried before. When you start writing poetry, especially if you haven't read a lot in the past, you run the risk of repeating language previous writers have used. Finding a careful yet sympathetic reader for your early drafts is always helpful.

☐ **Are you seriously considering the revision advice of your instructor and peers?** Even if you have been writing for some time, you will never grow as a writer if you're not willing to learn from the advice of more experienced writers. Not all advice is good advice, but if you hear the same critique repeatedly, there may be some merit in your readers' recommendations.

Poetic forms ▶

Inspiration doesn't always arrive when you need it, and coming up with ideas for a new poem can be difficult. Fortunately, over the centuries, poets have developed hundreds of specific poetic forms. The Academy of American Poets lists some of these patterns on its Poetic Forms and Techniques Web page (poets .org), and Lewis Turco's *The Book of Forms*, now in its fourth edition, is another wonderful resource. The great number and variety of these forms *can* be a bit overwhelming, so for our purposes a few of the most common should suffice.

Sonnet

Many stanza patterns are organized around rhymes, with the sonnet being perhaps the most well-known example. A **sonnet** is fourteen lines of rhymed iambic pentameter, with varying rhyme schemes. Phillis Levin claims that the sonnet—"a meeting place of image and voice, passion and reason"—"has resulted in some of the greatest lyric poetry" by "almost every notable poet writing in a Western language."

When you write a sonnet, you become part of a long tradition, but the form continues to welcome newcomers. In part, that's because its rules help poets move from point to point, as though they were following road signs on a highway. Yet those guideposts allow a remarkable amount of freedom. Let's look at another sonnet by Shakespeare, the well-known Sonnet XVIII, as an example:

Shall I compare thee to a summer's day?
Thou art more lovely and more temperate:
Rough winds do shake the darling buds of May,
And summer's lease hath all too short a date:
Sometime too hot the eye of heaven shines,
And often is his gold complexion dimmed,
And every fair from fair sometime declines,
By chance, or nature's changing course untrimmed:
But thy eternal summer shall not fade,
Nor lose possession of that fair thou ow'st,
Nor shall death brag thou wander'st in his shade,
When in eternal lines to time thou grow'st.
So long as men can breathe, or eyes can see,
So long lives this, and this gives life to thee.

Sonnet XVIII is called an English sonnet, or more commonly a **Shakespearean sonnet**, which means that its three rhyming quatrains—*abab cdcd efef*—are followed by a final couplet that rhymes *gg*. Note that Gail White's sonnet also employs the rhyming couplet characteristic of a Shakespearean sonnet, but she breaks her poem into two stanzas—an opening **octave** of eight lines and a closing sestet of six. The octave and sestet give "My Personal Recollections of Not Being Asked to the Prom" elements of the Italian or **Petrarchan sonnet**, although that form traditionally rhymes *abbaabba cdecde*. This mixing and matching among the different sonnet rhyme schemes (there are many more we could name) is common and increases your flexibility as you scout out appropriate rhymes.

One feature common to both Shakespeare's and White's sonnets is the *volta* (Italian for "turn"). You will notice that after the eighth line, the poems change the direction of their "arguments": in Sonnet XVIII, Shakespeare begins to make the case that, unlike the short-lived pleasures of a summer day, his beloved will not grow old because he or she is being memorialized in poetry; White shifts to the disappointment her mother suffered over her daughter's lack of dating skills. Shakespeare uses a colon to signal this change, and White begins a new stanza altogether. Not all sonnets make this swerve after the eighth line, but every real sonnet does take a turn toward some unexpected place before it is finished.

Villanelle

Another popular form, this one with French origins, is the **villanelle**. A villanelle consists of five tercets and a final quatrain. Strictly speaking, all these lines should be in iambic pentameter, although that rule is often broken. The first and third lines of the first stanza alternately repeat as the third line in the subsequent tercets. (A repeating line or phrase is called a **refrain**.) In the quatrain, the first line of the first stanza is the next-to-last line, and the third line of the first stanza is the final line of the poem. The villanelle has only two rhymes. The first and third lines of every tercet rhyme with each other, and the second lines of every stanza have the same rhyme.

This sounds more complicated than it actually is. If we were to sketch out the rhyme scheme line by line, it would look like this, with the rhyming words in parentheses:

1. Refrain 1 (a)
2. (b)
3. Refrain 2 (a)

4. (a)
5. (b)
6. Refrain 1 (a)

7. (a)
8. (b)
9. Refrain 2 (a)

10. (a)
11. (b)
12. Refrain 1 (a)

13. (a)
14. (b)
15. Refrain 2 (a)

16. (a)
17. (b)
18. Refrain 1 (a)
19. Refrain 2 (b)

Initially, writing a villanelle might seem like a rather daunting task, but once you come up with a first and third line that are both powerful and flexible enough to be used in several different contexts, much of your work is already finished: you have written eight of the nineteen lines of your poem.

Two examples of villanelles follow. Both take a few liberties with the repeating lines. In "A Way of Healing," Perie Longo's poem about the grieving process, the refrain changes from "Only look to the outpouring of spring" to "Of looking to the outpouring of spring" in the final stanza. Chryss Yost's refrain mutates even more significantly. In her poem—which implies that leaving Los Angeles is as difficult as trying to escape from the Disneyland ride called Autopia—the line, "I, Miss Highway, I couldn't drive off track," becomes, "you have to stay. I couldn't drive off track," then, "And anyway, I couldn't drive off track," and finally, "and be okay. I couldn't drive off track." Nevertheless, the basic idea and pattern remain, and fudging the refrain is not uncommon among contemporary North American poets.

Here is Perie Longo's poem "A Way of Healing":

Only look to the outpouring of spring
To know how sitting in wait may open the heart,
How storm and bluster release a hidden thing

That first in stark silence set us reeling.
But as we listen, words like blossoms spark—
Only look to the outpouring of spring.

What seemed dead rises, begins the healing.
Little by little old thought comes apart.
How storm and bluster release a hidden thing.

Time is essential to grow wholeness of being.
Then weed what intrudes, tender caring remark,
Only look to the outpouring of spring,

The rush of river over rock to help us sing
And dance, beat the drum, decipher the dark.
How storm and bluster release a hidden thing.

Should those who seek soul's comfort cling
To what anchors change, offer the art

Of looking to the outpouring of spring.
See how storm and bluster release a hidden thing.

And now Chryss Yost's poem "Escaping from Autopia":

but even leaving, longing to be back,
to do again what I did yesterday—
I, Miss Highway, I couldn't drive off track

or crash. I joined the candy-coated pack
to follow yellow lines and concrete, gray
but even. Leaving. Longing to be back

beyond those lines, in other lines. Like smack
these flashback rides, E-ticket crack: You pay
you have to stay. I couldn't drive off track,

or spin to face my enemies' attack.
The road signs told me "NOW LEAVING L.A."
but even leaving, longing to be back

to go again. I knew I had a knack
for getting there and going. Child's play,
and anyway, I couldn't drive off track,

once safety-strapped onto that strip of black.
I couldn't lose or get lost on the way,
but even leaving, longing to be back
and be okay, I couldn't drive off track.

Rondeau

Another French form heavily reliant on repetition is the **rondeau**, which has fifteen lines in three stanzas: a quintet, a quatrain, and a sestet. Two rhyme sounds repeat themselves throughout the poem. The opening words of the first line reappear as a refrain at the end of the second and third stanzas. The pattern of the lines is as follows, with the rhyming words in parentheses:

1. (a)
2. (a)
3. (b)
4. (b)
5. (a)

6. (a)
7. (a)
8. (b)
9. Refrain

10. (a)
11. (a)
12. (b)
13. (b)
14. (a)
15. Refrain

Our two examples of a rondeau follow the pattern carefully. Each of these famous poems tackles an extremely serious subject: Paul Laurence Dunbar's "We Wear the Mask" is about racism experienced by African Americans; John McCrae's "In Flanders Field" memorializes the dead killed in a World War I battle. First, Dunbar's "We Wear the Mask":

> We wear the mask that grins and lies,
> It hides our cheeks and shades our eyes,—
> This debt we pay to human guile;
> With torn and bleeding hearts we smile,
> And mouth with myriad subtleties.
>
> Why should the world be overwise,
> In counting all our tears and sighs?
> Nay, let them only see us, while
> We wear the mask.
>
> We smile, but, O great Christ, our cries
> To thee from tortured souls arise.
> We sing, but oh the clay is vile
> Beneath our feet, and long the mile;
> But let the world dream otherwise,
> We wear the mask!

Now McCrae's "In Flanders Fields":

> In Flanders fields the poppies blow
> Between the crosses, row on row,
> That mark our place; and in the sky,
> The larks, still bravely singing, fly,
> Scarce heard amid the guns below.
>
> We are the dead; short days ago
> We lived, felt dawn, saw sunset glow,
> Loved and were loved, and now we lie
> In Flanders fields.
>
> Take up our quarrel with the foe:
> To you from failing hands we throw
> The torch; be yours to hold it high.
> If ye break faith with us who die
> We shall not sleep, though poppies grow
> In Flanders fields.

Sestina

The **sestina** was originally an Italian form. It consists of six sestets in iambic pentameter followed by a tercet, or, as it is commonly called, a triplet, which constitutes the envoi, the concluding remarks of the poem. The final words in each line (indicated by capital letters) repeat themselves as follows, with the envoi including all six words in its three lines:

Stanza 1: ABCDEF

Stanza 2: FAEBDC

Stanza 3: CFDABE

Stanza 4: ECBFAD

Stanza 5: DEACFB

Stanza 6: BDFECA

Envoi: Variable

The reason for the end words' arrangement is shrouded in mystery (although some critics believe it has to do with numerology), but the pattern is not *quite* as complex as it looks at first. As you can see, each new stanza repeats the final words of the previous stanza in the order 6–1–5–2–4–3; the only exception is the envoi.

"Sestina," a nineteenth-century poem by Edmund Gosse, imagines the medieval French troubador Arnault Daniel's first attempts at writing in the form:

In fair Provence, the land of lute and rose,
Arnaut, great master of the lore of love,
First wrought sestines to win his lady's heart,
For she was deaf when simpler staves he sang,
And for her sake he broke the bonds of rhyme,
And in this subtler measure hid his woe.

'Harsh be my lines,' cried Arnaut, 'harsh the woe
My lady, that enthorn'd and cruel rose,
Inflicts on him that made her live in rhyme!'
But through the metre spake the voice of Love,
And like a wild-wood nightingale he sang
Who thought in crabbed lays to ease his heart.

It is not told if her untoward heart
Was melted by her poet's lyric woe,
Or if in vain so amorously he sang;
Perchance through cloud of dark conceits he rose
To nobler heights of philosophic song,
And crowned his later years with sterner rhyme.

This thing alone we know: the triple rhyme
Of him who bared his vast and passionate heart
To all the crossing flames of hate and love,
Wears in the midst of all its storm of woe,—
As some loud morn of March may bear a rose,—
The impress of a song that Arnaut sang.

'Smith of his mother-tongue,' the Frenchman sang
Of Lancelot and of Galahad, the rhyme
That beat so bloodlike at its core of rose,
It stirred the sweet Francesca's gentle heart
To take that kiss that brought her so much woe
And sealed in fire her martyrdom of love.

And Dante, full of her immortal love,
Stayed his drear song, and softly, fondly sang
As though his voice broke with that weight of woe;
And to this day we think of Arnaut's rhyme
Whenever pity at the labouring heart
On fair Francesca's memory drops the rose.

Ah! sovereign Love, forgive this weaker rhyme!
The men of old who sang were great at heart,
Yet have we too known woe, and worn thy rose.

"You've got two basic tactics with those repeated end-words," Lewis Turco says. "You can try to hide them or you can use them as hammers." Barry Spacks's contemporary take on the form, "Sestina on Sestinas," leans toward the latter approach. The repeating words are "sestinas" and clever variations on the words "blur," "rush," "enter," "inside," and "build." Spacks mostly employs iambic pentameter, but many contemporary poets find that varying the meter, as well as modifying the repeating words, results in a stronger poem. Spacks's sestina has a decidedly humorous edge to it, which is often a characteristic of "these Seuss-y structures sadist poets build." (Incidentally, you can read dozens of examples of excellent contemporary sestinas on the Web site of *McSweeney's* literary magazine at mcsweeneys.net.) Here is Spacks's "Sestina on Sestinas":

Hard labor, pals, to push through most sestinas.
They'll natter on, repeating in a blur
like unremembered dreams, a madding rush
where meanings seldom dare to break and enter.
What battering-ram could sneak a thought inside
these Seuss-y structures sadist poets build?

Myself, I'd rather garden plants than build
such tottering, tumbling towers of words. Sestinas

we're liable to survive, once locked inside,
are those where proper warnings are not blurred:
"Abandon hope, all ye who choose to enter
here!" But some tout punchlines so we'll rush

toward absent consequence, a tourist crush
of scanning through the rooms of cunning buildings
where every stanza we expect to entertain us looks the same! Yet rare sestinas
sing. God bless the mark! I'd write a blurb
for any of that ilk: "One finds inside

this stream of sound, dear Reader, an Insider-
Spirit who will lift you from the rushes
(saved like Moses), clarify your blurry
Senses. . . ." Ha! We all know why the builders
place no exit doors in their sestinas:
so they can drive us bonkers once we enter

the long internment's torture. Fellow Enter-
tainers, Stand-Ups, Poets, deep inside
we should be wise enough to skip sestinas,
yet we endure them—hey, we even rush
to try our hands at tools intent to build
such insubstantial substance, one long blurt

of deadend clauses, high barbaric blurbles
over rooftops sense can't dent, er-
roneously passing as a sort of *Bild-*
ungsroman that plush lives are boxed in. Side
by side our gross sestinas pant like Russian
dancers kicking boots, boots, boots! Sestinas

claim we'll even live through most sestinas, blurs
of rushing time spring every trap we enter
insideout, such tricksy lives we build!

Cinquain

One final French form, the **cinquain** (from the French word *cinq,* meaning
"five"), is relatively easy to write. In the broadest sense, a cinquain is simply a
five-line stanza. However, the cinquain as it is now usually written has the following syllable count per line:

1. two syllables

2. four syllables

3. six syllables

4. eight syllables

5. two syllables

The American poet Adelaide Crapsey established this use of syllabic lines in cinquains. Here are three examples of the form by Glenna Luschei:

Writing
poems of five lines
is beautiful but hard.
Hail to pioneer Adelaide
Crapsey!
> ("Cinquain")

I pray
professors sign
my dissertation, leave me
free for my true work, writing
cinquains.
> ("Dissertation")

I buy
an amber watch
spider ensnared thirty
million years, a great way to spend
spare time.
> ("Amber")

Pantoum

The **pantoum** originated in Malaysia but has become another staple of American poetry. It consists of any number of quatrains that rhyme *abab*, with the second and fourth lines of one quatrain repeating as the first and third lines of the following quatrain. Like the villanelle, the pantoum requires strong repeating lines with flexible meanings, and in return it provides the poet with a clear structure. Because of the repeating lines, half of each new stanza is already written for you. New poets also appreciate the fact that the pantoum's end words, unlike the villanelle's, do not have to rhyme.

In her pantoum "Braids," which *does* rhyme, Lois Klein uses the repeating lines to emphasize the poignancy and loneliness of childhood, a time and place "both charmed and cruel":

The way Mother gripped my hair to wind in braids
her blue-veined hands cool and deft
as if remembering a shadow time:
her fault the man had left.

Her blue-veined hands cool and deft
against my forehead when I lay ill.
Her fault the man had left,
her old mistakes regretted still.

Against my forehead when I lay ill
striped sunlight through venetian blinds.
her old mistakes regretted still,
no defense could ease the pain.

Striped sunlight through venetian blinds
like prison bars enclosed my world.
No defense could ease the pain.
Braided hair bound tight my curls.

Prison bars enclosed my world.
Mother's hands that twirled and gripped
my hair tight against my head.
No strand escaped or ever slipped.

Mother's hands that gripped and twirled,
hands that seemed both charmed and cruel.
My hair tight against my head
yet she would place a ribbon there.

Her hands that seemed both charmed and cruel
as if remembering a shadow time,
yet she would place a ribbon there
despite the way she gripped my hair.

Ghazal

Another popular non-Western poem is the **ghazal**, derived from Persian and Urdu sources. Ghazals written in English often break at least one rule of the form; however, ghazals traditionally (1) consist of five to twelve loosely related but self-contained couplets of approximately the same length; (2) have a melancholy subject, often the hopelessness of an unsatisfied romantic attachment; and (3) repeat the final word or words of the second line at the end of all the second lines.

The ghazal became popular in the 1960s and 1970s when poets such as Jim Harrison began writing and publishing them. Many purists, then and now, derided these American versions of the form as watered down or off the mark altogether, but ghazals are now a familiar form in many creative writing classes.

In his ghazal "After the Holidays," John Ridland effectively evokes a mood of doomed love. However, unlike the poet of the traditional ghazal, who laments the absence of a lover, Ridland mourns the impending departure of children and grandchildren:

—*For Jenny and Sasha leaving after Christmas*

They are sorting and packing, picking up
Loose ends, toys, ribbons, bits and pieces of the heart.

I am father and grandfather, sitting by,
Letting the sorrow of parting wash into my heart.

Nonna is out doing errands, picking up more
Bits for attention, devotion, pumped along by her heart.

Each year this happens: together for a fortnight we build
A delicately balanced construction, learn it by heart,

Then dismantle it, leaving the floor of the mind flat
While the veins return their used blood to the heart.

Not sorrow, no: *fondness*. Fondness is all.
We all remember what absence does to the heart.

Prose poem

One final form to consider is poetry written in prose. Just about any reader of literature will acknowledge that there has been "poetic prose"—that is, prose that is rhythmic, imagistic, and condensed—for as long as there has been literature. Yet the term "prose poem" is relatively recent, dating to the work of nineteenth-century French poets such as Charles Baudelaire, Arthur Rimbaud, and Stéphane Mallarmé. As we suggested in the introduction to this chapter, some poets consider the very term "prose poem" an oxymoron. How, they ask, can poetry be prose?

For our purposes, a prose poem is any short, compact, "musical" piece of writing that does not have line breaks but which its author sees as a poem rather than a paragraph or paragraphs of fiction or nonfiction prose. Because this type of poem has no line breaks, prose poets pay attention to the sentence rather than the line, and the careful crafting of sentences is essential to the form's success. Among the other elements necessary for a well-written prose poem, anthologist Michael Benedikt lists "skill at managing metaphor"; "a keen ear for unusual, unconventional . . . sounds & music"; and "an especially keen ear for rhythm, and for the rhythms of natural speech in particular."

Prose poems are hybrids not only in form but also in content. They can be both lighthearted (one anthology of prose poems is called *The Party Train*) and ambitious (another anthology is called *Models of the Universe*). They are often surrealistic and experimental (see the work of Charles Simic, Russell Edson, and James Tate for American examples of this strain of the prose poem). The prose poem also has a freedom that allows what Brooks Horvath calls "fugitive content: a place where one may give voice to the otherwise no longer sayable, as well as to the yet-unsaid." David Soucy calls the prose poem "a flying trapeze act without a net," and it is this element of risk taking and exploration that draws many poets to the form.

The following five prose poems from Gertrude Stein's book *Tender Buttons* give a sense of the playfulness and resistance to easy interpretation characteristic of the experimental prose poem. Although the titles of the poems promise something straightforward, the sentences themselves at first seem to have only a tangential relation to their supposed subjects. Yet the longer one tries to match the title with the poem, the more possibilities open up, and it quickly becomes apparent that striving toward meaning, despite all the obstacles Gertrude Stein places in our way, is part of what these prose poems force us to do:

> A charm a single charm is doubtful. If the red is rose and there is a gate surrounding it, if inside is let in and there places change then certainly something is upright. It is earnest.
> ("Nothing Elegant")

> If lilies are lily white if they exhaust noise and distance and even dust, if they dusty will dirt a surface that has no extreme grace, if they do this and it is not necessary it is not at all necessary if they do this they need a catalogue.
> ("A Red Stamp")

> A blue coat is guided guided away, guided and guided away, that is the particular color that is used for that length and not any width not even more than a shadow.
> ("A Blue Coat")

> A purse was not green, it was not straw color, it was hardly seen and it had a use a long use and the chain, the chain was never missing, it was not misplaced, it showed that it was open, that is all that it showed.
> ("A Purse")

> A feather is trimmed, it is trimmed by the light and the bug and the post, it is trimmed by little leaning and by all sorts of mounted reserves and loud volumes. It is surely cohesive.
> ("A Feather")

Like Stein's pieces, "Hideous Towns" by David Case has a sense of humor. Yet Case's prose poem is both darker and closer to the world we know. It is an admission that we are all connected, no matter how much we might wish that wasn't the case:

> Turns out there's a song called "Hideous Towns," by The Sundays. I haven't heard it, I don't need to—I drove through Selma, Alabama, I've seen Needles, California. In hideous towns, there are real months of Sundays, the feeling at each sunset of crushing things to come, a doubtful tingling of

the fingers as all unreliably mapped space starts moving in: possums in the yard trailing naked tails through ill-clipped shrubs. Even the Dairy Queen shut down, the tiny Free Will churches packed—satellite dishes crying for remote possibilities.

They are, those in the hideous towns, cousins once removed, twice removed, a defeated people who open filling stations in Peach Springs, Arizona, with office door signs reading: Sorry, We're Open.

Jim Peterson's "The Empty Bowl," about the refusal of an old dog to eat its meals, is similar to Case's poem in that it discovers an element of strangeness, even dread, in our everyday life:

A man's dog was very old and crippled. Each morning she sniffed her food, giving it a few licks. Then she would drag herself over to an empty red bowl that had belonged to a previous dog. She would lick the empty bowl and shove it along the boards of the porch with her nose. The man would pick her up, crooning softly, "You must eat, Old Lady," and place her next to her own bowl of food. She would stand there and smack her lips a few times, then drag herself over to the empty bowl. The man tried different food, but that never worked. He tried putting the food in the red bowl, but she only reversed the process, sniffing the meaty morsels, then dragging herself resignedly to her own empty bowl. He tried removing one of the bowls, but then the old dog would haul herself around the porch, down the steps falling on her face at the bottom, then out into the yard and under every tree and bush looking for the empty bowl. So the man would put both bowls back on the porch to keep her happy. Every morning it was the same. The scruffy white hair of her muzzle, the raw floppy ears pestered by gnats and flies, that half-seeing gaze through cataracts. He couldn't understand how she survived without food. She looked so bad it embarrassed him for the neighbors to see her. "Maybe I should put her to sleep. That would be the merciful thing to do." All the way to the vet's office she lay on the front seat beside him with her head in his lap. If he took his hand away from her head, she would stare at him until he put it back. In the car there were no gnats or flies to nag her ears. No space demanding she drag herself here or there. When he arrived and lifted her from the seat, she was limp in his arms, pink tongue dangling lazily from her mouth.

CHECKLIST Poetic forms

☐ **Do you understand all the rules of the form in which you are working?** Some forms are fairly self-explanatory, but others have rather complex requirements. Breaking these rules can be part of the fun, but you should at least be aware of the rules you're ignoring. Get a feel for the form before trying to write in it. Reread the form's description; then try to match it up against several examples by other poets.

☐ **Does the form enhance your content rather than limit it?** When a form is working for your poem, it seems to propel what you have to say forward, sparking unexpected language and ideas. When the form is working against you, however, you will feel it dragging down your writing. Different forms fit different poems, so don't hesitate to try your idea in a pantoum rather than a sonnet, or a villanelle rather than a sestina. And an unsuccessful formal poem often opens up when it is recast in free verse.

Getting started writing poetry ▶

As Wendy Bishop tells us, "There is no single, best . . . invention technique that will get all writers drafting productively." Nor is there a "preferable sequencing system," with one type of exercise building on another. Instead, Bishop believes that "invention activities should provide students with exploratory moments and drafting options that develop flexibility and fluidity in a writer."

In short, not everything works for everyone, and you won't know what works for you until you try it. Moreover, you may find that a technique that inspires a poem one day won't yield much the next day, while an invention activity that seems useless this week will work for you next month. The brain remains a mysterious organ, and, as we have noted, poetic inspiration is unpredictable. Most poets will tell you that the more you experiment, try and fail and try again, the more likely you are to ultimately come up with a group of poems you will be proud to have written. So write, write, *write!*

Over the years, my students have found the following kick-starts quite useful. At least one of them should result in a poem you are proud to include in your final portfolio.

▶ KICK-STARTS Beginning your poems

▶ **1.** Keep a journal in which you write down *everything* that might become material for a poem: ideas, observations, images, words, phrases, lines, and stanzas. If in the process you feel a poem igniting, start writing the poem, but don't worry if you end up with fragments and false starts. The more material you collect, the more likely some of it will begin to cohere into a fully formed poem.

▶ **2.** Find a book full of interesting words. It could be this one, or an anthology of literature, an encyclopedia, or a dictionary. Open up the book at random, and skim the page until a word catches your eye. It might be an unusual word like "kleptomaniac," or it might be a common or evocative word such as "bruise" or "salt." Write it down quickly and move on. Try to avoid abstractions and instead seek out words that are concrete and specific. Put real *things* into your poem (peach preserves and wedding rings, dishwater and cobwebs), and look for strong, clear verbs ("slash," "punch," "stroke," "sneeze"). Go easy on the adverbs and adjectives. Once you have jotted down ten to fifteen good words, use as many of them as you can in a short poem. Try to keep your poem fairly serious (it's tempting to transform this word salad into a comic jumble), and see if you can finish it in fifteen to twenty minutes. You'll often be amazed at the results.

▶ **3.** Read published poems (in this book, in an anthology, or online) and respond to them with poems of your own. It doesn't matter whether you respond to the subject of the other person's poem or to just a single line or image. Generally it's most effective to find the moment of maximum energy or tension in the published poem. Identify what excites you about the poem; then make the same thing happen in your own work.

▶ **4.** A variation on exercise 3 is to write a poem beginning and/or ending with one or more lines by another poet. Choose a line that you find particularly marvelous and write from or toward it. Many poets ultimately transform or eliminate the model poet's line from their own poem. (If you choose not to, be sure to give the other poet credit for his or her work.)

▶ **5.** Respond to poems written by poets you know personally, such as fellow students or friends who write poetry. Exchange your poems by hand or through e-mail. If you know someone is waiting to read your poetry, you are much likelier to write it.

▶ **6.** Write a poem inspired by one of the other arts. For example, does a painting you love seem to want you to tell its story in words? If you haven't found that painting yet, the art section of your library will have plenty of books with full-color illustrations, or you can go online to a virtual gallery such as the WebMuseum (ibiblio.org/wm). Do more than simply describe the scene in front of you: set your imagination free and consider using what you see as a springboard for something more personal. You can also use music as an inspiration. For instance, write a poem that evokes a Chopin étude or a punk song by Extreme Noise Terror. Excellent poems have also been written about dance, theater, and even architecture.

▶ **7.** Everyone who has ever composed a poem for a special occasion such as a birthday or an anniversary knows this desire to connect with someone else. We want to please that person by showing that we have thought longer than we normally would about the event at hand. Write a poem that celebrates some special occasion, whether it be an **epithalamium** for a marriage; an **elegy** for someone who has passed away; or an **ode**, which can commemorate everything from a military victory, to the painting on a Grecian urn, to the song of a nightingale.

▶ **8.** Write a poem in a form not discussed in this chapter. (You can find descriptions in Lewis Turco's *The Book of Forms*, on the Academy of American Poets'

Web site, or simply by Googling "poetic forms and techniques.") Write a **ballad** (a narrative poem in quatrains rhyming *abcb*, with alternating four- and three-beat lines) or a **triolet** (an eight-line poem in iambic tetrameter, with two refrains—*A* and *B*—and with the rhyme scheme of *ABaAabAB*) or a poem in **terza rima** (a poem in three-line stanzas, in which the end words of the first and third lines rhyme, and the end word of the second line becomes the rhyming word in the following stanza). You can spend your lifetime as a writer working in the hundreds of patterns that previous poets have devised. If you are drawn to the challenge and boundaries of forms, experiment with as many of them as possible.

9. Write a poem that describes and focuses on an unusual object that is right in front of you. Students have written poems about everything from stuffed animals to old pocket watches to Christmas ornaments to bottle openers. In the best of these poems, careful depiction of the object merges with storytelling and the creation or re-creation of vivid memories.

10. Write the poem *behind* a news story that captures your attention. Your poem may stick to the facts as much as possible, or it may begin from a significant moment in the story and quickly become a pure creation of your imagination. Consider writing the poem from an unusual point of view. A poem about a kidnapping, for instance, might be told from the perspective of the kidnapper or the person who has been kidnapped, but it also might be seen from the vantage point of the kidnapper's neighbor or the kidnapped person's childhood friend. Note: Text-based sources—that is, newspapers and newsmagazines (in print or online)—tend to work better than television stories because the facts remain in front of you for easy perusal.

11. Write a poem in the form of a letter. Richard Hugo's book *31 Letters and 13 Dreams* is a great source for these types of poems. Hugo addresses poems to close old friends and to new friends he doesn't yet know well. He brings these people detailed news of his own life and asks for information about their world. However, because the letter is in the form of a poem, Hugo condenses what he has to say and presents the material as eloquently—and as imagistically—as possible.

12. Write a poem in the persona of someone other than yourself. In this type of poem, also called a **dramatic monologue**, you become a character from history or of your own invention. Usually set during a moment of crisis in the speaker's life, the dramatic monologue is addressed to an audience of one or more silent listeners and gives the inside story from the perspective of someone who, on the exterior, may not be an especially sympathetic character. The friction between how we are likely to see the speaker and how he or she sees himself or herself has resulted in some outstanding work. Among the master poets who have worked extensively from behind the mask of personae are the British Victorian poets Robert Browning and Alfred Tennyson and the contemporary American poets C. K. Williams, Richard Howard, Robert Hayden, and Ai.

An Anthology of Short Poems

Elizabeth Alexander

House Party Sonnet: '66

Small, still. Fit through the bannister slit.
Where did our love go? Where did our love go?
Scattered high heels and the carpet rolled back.
Where did our love go? Where did our love go?
My brother and I, tipping down from upstairs
Under the cover of "Where did our love go?"
Cat-eyed Supremes wearing siren-green gowns.
Pink curls of laughter and hips when they shake
Shake a tambourine *where did our love go?*
Where did our love go? Where did our love go?
Stale chips next morning, shoes under the couch,
Smoke-smelling draperies, water-paled Scotch.
Matches, stray earrings to find and to keep–
Hum of invisible dancers asleep. ◀

Sherman Alexie

Basketball

After a few beers here, every Indian is a hero of "unbroken horses." Someone always remembers I was the Reservation point guard with the Crazy Horse jump shot. Someone always wants to go one-on-one in the alley while Lester FallsApart balances on a garbage can, his arms forming the hoop. Someone always bets his ribbon shirt against mine, and we play, and I win. Someone always finishes the night bareback, like it should be, while I go home, hang another shirt in my closet, another Crazy Horse dream without a skeleton or skin. ◀

Agha Shahid Ali

Postcard from Kashmir

Kashmir shrinks into my mailbox,
my home a neat four by six inches.

I always loved neatness. Now I hold
the half-inch Himalayas in my hand.

This is home. And this the closest
I'll ever be to home. When I return,
the colours won't be so brilliant,
the Jhelum's waters so clean,
so ultramarine. My love
so overexposed.

And my memory will be a little
out of focus, in it
a giant negative, black
and white, still undeveloped.

for Pavan Sahgal ◄

Lorna Dee Cervantes

Poem for the Young White Man Who Asked Me How I, an Intelligent, Well-Read Person, Could Believe in the War between Races

In my land there are no distinctions.
The barbed wire politics of oppression
have been torn down long ago. The only reminder
of past battles, lost or won, is a slight
rutting in the fertile fields.

In my land
people write poems about love,

full of nothing but contented childlike syllables.
Everyone reads Russian short stories and weeps.
There are no boundaries.
There is no hunger, no
complicated famine or greed.

I am not a revolutionary.
I don't even like political poems.
Do you think I can believe in a war between races?
I can deny it. I can forget about it
when I'm safe,
living on my own continent of harmony
and home, but I am not
there.

I believe in revolution
because everywhere the crosses are burning,
sharp-shooting goose-steppers round every corner,
there are snipers in the schools . . .
(I know you don't believe this.
You think this is nothing
but faddish exaggeration. But they
are not shooting at you.)

I'm marked by the color of my skin.
The bullets are discrete and designed to kill slowly.
They are aiming at my children.
These are facts.
Let me show you my wounds: my stumbling mind, my
"excuse me" tongue, and this
nagging preoccupation
with the feeling of not being good enough.

These bullets bury deeper than logic.
Racism is not intellectual.
I can not reason these scars away.

Outside my door
there is a real enemy
who hates me.

I am a poet
who yearns to dance on rooftops,
to whisper delicate lines about joy
and the blessings of human understanding.

I try. I go to my land, my tower of words and
bolt the door, but the typewriter doesn't fade out
the sounds of blasting and muffled outrage.
My own days bring me slaps on the face.
Every day I am deluged with reminders
that this is not
my land
and this is my land.

I do not believe in the war between races.

but in this country
there is war. ◄

Marilyn Chin

Repulse Bay

Hong Kong, Summer 1980

1

Washed ashore
At Repulse Bay
Creatures that outgrew their shells—
I saw a mussel hang
On a shell's hinge: the sun
Turned its left side brown
What remained carried
Around the lips
Like a human tongue
Unfit for speech

Suddenly, the sea
Sweeps it up, with
A stub-necked bottle, bits of feces and the news
Printed in red and black
Bilingual editions for the Colonialists
And two-bit Japanese tourists
Seeking thrills

2

Back to Kowloon, in Granny's
One room apartment, her laundry waves

On her sun-filled balcony—
I recognize some of mine: blue jeans, bright T's
A black lace bra on a hook . . .
Two stories below, an old hawker
Selling abalone on a stick, chicken asses
Pig ears, tripe of all species burnt pink—
Looks up, shakes his fist

3

The rain over Hong Kong falls
Over all of us, Li Ching, though
This postcard will tell you nothing
About the country I have lost

Overhead, a building blinks
Of Rolex, Omega and yet
Another brand that ticks

4

Last night, drunk out of my mind
I promised everybody visas and a good time
(should they make it to America)
Autumn is here now, though
There are no rustling New England leaves
Or Oregon grapes tugging the vines

5

How the sun shines through the monsoon brightly
On the small men selling viscera
On the dead and swimming creatures of the sea ◀

Wanda Coleman

Brute Strength

last night blonde spitfire Angie Dickinson beat steel-eyed
Lee Marvin's impervious chest until she dropped to gangland's
floor exhausted *point blank*

aunt ora used to threaten us kids with whippings
if half bad, she used her hand
if real bad, we got the hard wood paddle
if monstrous, there was the horsewhip that hung above the door
in the den. one day my brother and i were half bad
she gave me the glad hand and i cried
she laid it to him and he laughed. so she got the paddle
and he laughed even harder
in consternation she abandoned his punishment
he was more daring after that

and then there was my geechie lover
i once went at him with a 2 × 4 as hard as i could
i clubbed his chest. he smiled at me
i dropped the 2 × 4 and ran

my first husband wasn't much. i could take
his best punch ◀

Billy Collins

Nostalgia

Remember the 1340s? We were doing a dance called the Catapult.
You always wore brown, the color craze of the decade,
and I was draped in one of those capes that were popular,
the ones with unicorns and pomegranates in needlework.
Everyone would pause for beer and onions in the afternoon,
and at night we would play a game called "Find the Cow."
Everything was hand-lettered then, not like today.

Where has the summer of 1572 gone? Brocade and sonnet
marathons were the rage. We used to dress up in the flags
of rival baronies and conquer one another in cold rooms of stone.
Out on the dance floor we were all doing the Struggle
while your sister practiced the Daphne all alone in her room.
We borrowed the jargon of farriers for our slang.
These days language seems transparent, a badly broken code.

The 1790s will never come again. Childhood was big.
People would take walks to the very tops of hills
and write down what they saw in their journals without speaking.

Our collars were high and our hats were extremely soft.
We would surprise each other with alphabets made of twigs.
It was a wonderful time to be alive, or even dead.

I am very fond of the period between 1815 and 1821.
Europe trembled while we sat still for our portraits.
And I would love to return to 1901 if only for a moment,
time enough to wind up a music box and do a few dance steps,
or shoot me back to 1922 or 1941, or at least let me
recapture the serenity of last month when we picked
berries and glided through afternoons in a canoe.

Even this morning would be an improvement over the present.
I was in the garden then, surrounded by the hum of bees
and the Latin names of flowers, watching the early light
flash off the slanted windows of the greenhouse
and silver the limbs on the rows of dark hemlocks.

As usual, I was thinking about the moments of the past,
letting my memory rush over them like water
rushing over the stones on the bottom of a stream.
I was even thinking a little about the future, that place
where people are doing a dance we cannot imagine,
a dance whose name we can only guess. ◄

Elaine Equi

A Quiet Poem

My father screamed whenever the phone rang.

My aunt often screamed when she opened the door.

Out back, the willows caterwauled.

In the kitchen, the faucet screamed
a drop at a time.

At school, they called screaming "recess"
or sometimes "music."

Our neighbors' daughter had a scream
more melodious than my own.

At first, Col. Parker had to pay girls
to get them to scream for Elvis.

I didn't want to scream when I saw The Beatles,
but I did. After that, I screamed for even
mediocre bands.

Late in his career, John Lennon
got into Primal Scream.

Many people find it relaxing to scream.

Just as crawling precedes walking, so screaming
precedes speech.

The roller coaster is just one of many
scream-inducing devices.

The ambulance tries, in its clumsy way, to emulate
the human scream, which in turn tries to emulate nature.

Wind is often said to shriek, but Sylvia Plath
also speaks of "the parched scream of the sun."

Jim Morrison wanted to hear the scream of the
butterfly.

With ultra-sensitive equipment, scientists measure
the screams of plants they've tortured.

It's proven that if you scream at a person
for years, then suddenly stop, he will hear even
the tenderest words of love as violent curses.

And to anyone who speaks above a whisper, he will say:
"Don't you dare. Don't you dare raise your voice to me." ◀

Joy Harjo

Santa Fe

The wind blows lilacs out of the east. And it isn't lilac season. And I am walking the street in front of St. Francis Cathedral in Santa Fe. Oh, and it's a few years earlier and more. That's how you tell real time. It is here, it is there. The lilacs have taken over everything: the sky, the narrow streets, my shoulders, my lips. I talk lilac. And there is nothing else until a woman the size of a fox breaks through the bushes, breaks the purple web. She is tall and black and gorgeous. She is the size of a fox on the arm of a white man who looks and tastes like cocaine. She lies for cocaine, dangles on the arm of cocaine. And lies to me now from a room in the DeVargas Hotel, where she has eaten her lover, white powder on her lips. That is true now; it is not true anymore. Eventually space curves, walks over and taps me on the shoulder. On the sidewalk I stand near St. Francis; he has been bronzed, a perpetual tan, with birds on his hand, his shoulder, deer at his feet. I am Indian and in this town I will never be a saint. I am seventeen and shy and wild. I have been up until three at a party, but there is no woman in the DeVargas Hotel for that story hasn't yet been invented. A man whose face I will never remember, and never did, drives up on a Harley Davidson. There are lilacs on his arm, they spill out from the spokes of his wheels. He wants me on his arm, on the back of his lilac bike touring the flower kingdom of San Francisco. And for a piece of time the size of a nickel, I think, maybe. But maybe is vapor, has no anchor here in the sun beneath St. Francis Cathedral. And space is as solid as the bronze statue of St. Francis, the fox breaking through the lilacs, my invention of this story, the wind blowing. ◄

Geoffrey Hill

September Song

born 19.6.32–deported 24.9.42

Undesirable you may have been, untouchable
you were not. Not forgotten
or passed over at the proper time.

As estimated, you died. Things marched,
sufficient, to that end.
Just so much Zyklon and leather, patented
terror, so many routine cries.

(I have made
an elegy for myself it
is true)

September fattens on vines. Roses
flake from the wall. The smoke
of harmless fires drifts to my eyes.

This is plenty. This is more than enough. ◄

Brenda Hillman

Shadows in Snow

When shadows are unhinged from bodies,
    they make chords with clouds
    impossible to hear.

In the end, there will be nothing wrong.
Tonight red ring surrounds the moon
like a hurt boy
following a married woman;

you hurry along, tried of your travels,

& the dense beauty from whose demands
    you never recover
stays beside you
as the orchid keeps the black stripe
of its personal winter— ◀

Allison Joseph

On Being Told I Don't Speak like a Black Person

Emphasize the "h," you hignorant ass,
was what my mother was told
when colonial-minded teachers
slapped her open palm with a ruler
in that Jamaican schoolroom.
Trained in England, they tried
to force their pupils to speak
like Eliza Doolittle after
her transformation, fancying themselves
British as Henry Higgins,
despite dark, sun-ripened skin.
Mother never lost her accent,

though, the music of her voice
charming everyone, an infectious lilt
I can imitate, not duplicate.
No one in the States told her
to eliminate the accent,
my high school friends adoring
the way her voice would lift
when she called me to the phone—
A-ll-i-son, it's friend Cathy.
Why don't you sound like her,
they'd ask. I didn't sound
like anyone or anything,
no grating New Yorker nasality,
no fastidious British mannerisms
like the ones my father affected
when he wanted to sell someone
something. And I didn't sound
like a Black American,
college acquaintances observed,
sure they knew what a black person
was supposed to sound like.
Was I supposed to sound lazy,
dropping syllables here and there
not finishing words but
slurring their final letters
so each sentence joined
the next, sliding past the listener?
Were certain words off limits,
too erudite for someone whose skin
came with a natural tan?
I asked them what they meant
and they stuttered, blushed,
said *you know, Black English,*
applying a term from that
semester's text. *Does everyone*
in your family speak alike,
I'd ask, and they'd say *don't*
take this the wrong way,
nothing personal.

Now I realize there's nothing
more personal than speech,
that I don't have to defend

how I speak, how any person,
black, white, chooses to speak.
Let us speak. Let us talk
with the sound of our mothers
and fathers still reverberating
in our minds, wherever our mothers
or fathers come from:
Arkansas, Belize, Alabama,
Brazil, Aruba, Arizona.
Let us simply speak
to one another,
listen and prize the inflections,
never assuming how any person will sound
until his mouth opens, until her
mouth opens, greetings welcome
in any language. ◄

Jane Kenyon

The Blue Bowl

Like primitives we buried the cat
with his bowl. Bare-handed
we scraped sand and gravel
back into the hole.
                    They fell with a hiss
and thud on his side,
on his long red fur, the white feathers
between his toes, and his
long, not to say aquiline, nose.

We stood and brushed each other off.
There are sorrows keener than these.

Silent the rest of the day, we worked,
ate, stared, and slept. It stormed
all night; now it clears, and a robin
burbles from a dripping bush
like the neighbor who means well
but always says the wrong thing. ◄

Galway Kinnell

That Silent Evening

I will go back to that silent evening
when we lay together and talked in low, silent voices,
while outside slow lumps of soft snow
fell, hushing as they got near the ground,
with a fire in the room, in which centuries
of tree went up in continuous ghost-giving-up,
without a crackle, into morning light.
Not until what hastens went slower did we sleep.
When we got home we turned and looked back
at our tracks twining out of the woods,
where the branches we brushed against let fall
puffs of sparkling snow, quickly, in silence,
like stolen kisses, and where the *scritch scritch scritch*
among the trees, which is the sound that dies
inside the sparks from the wedge when the sledge
hits it off center telling everything inside
it is fire, jumped to a black branch, puffed up
but without arms and so to our eyes lonesome,
and yet also—how could we know *this*?—*happy*!
in shape of chickadee. Lying still in snow,
not iron-willed, like railroad tracks, willing
not to meet until heaven, but here and there
making slubby kissing stops in the field,
our tracks wobble across the snow their long scratch.
Everything that happens here is really little more,
if even that, than a scratch, too. Words, in our mouths,
are almost ready, already, to bandage the one
whom the *scritch scritch scritch,* meaning *if how when*
we might lose each other, scratches scratches scratches
from this moment to that. Then I will go back
to that silent evening, when the past just managed
to overlap the future, if only by a trace,
and the light doubles and shines
through the dark the sparkling that heavens the earth. ◄

Ben Lerner

We have assembled

WE HAVE ASSEMBLED for the athletic contest in tiered seats. Once, we assembled in a central core with mobile spiral arms. Or, lying on our backs, we formed a radiating cluster, imposing animal figures and names upon the stars. Now we watch heavily armored professionals assume formations on a grid of artificial grass. Wishbone. Shotgun. Power I. ◀

D. Nurske

Left Field

Told I threw *like a girl*
I waited out in the shadows

while the infielders made spectacular leaps
—by luck or memory of the future?

Some threw like older girls,
some hurled streaks of evening,

all grew equally remote
as night fell and the voices
singing *no batter, no pitcher*
faded under crickets.

I pounded my glove,
spat, dug my cleats
savagely in the sod
and growled *swing.*

Secretly, I was proudest of my skill
at standing alone in darkness. ◀

Naomi Shihab Nye

I Feel Sorry for Jesus

People won't leave Him alone.
I know He said, *wherever two or more*
are gathered in my name . . .
but I'll bet some days He regrets it.

Cozily they tell you what He wants
and doesn't want
as if they just got an e-mail.
Remember "Telephone," that pass-it-on game

where the message changed dramatically
by the time it rounded the circle?
Well.
People blame terrible pieties on Jesus.

They want to be his special pet.
Jesus deserves better.
I think He's been exhausted
for a very long time.

He went *into the desert*, friends.
He didn't go into the pomp.
He didn't go into
the golden chandeliers

and say, *the truth tastes better here.*
See? I'm talking like I know.
It's dangerous talking for Jesus.
You get carried away almost immediately.

I stood in the spot where He was born.
I closed my eyes where He died and didn't die.
Every twist of the Via Dolorosa
was written on my skin.

And that makes me feel like being silent
for Him, you know? A secret pouch
of listening. You won't hear me
mention this again. ◀

Mary Oliver

Crossing the Swamp

Here is the endless
   wet thick
      cosmos, the center
         of everything—the nugget
of dense sap, branching
   vines, the dark burred
      faintly belching
         bogs. Here
is *swamp*, here
   is struggle,
      closure—
         pathless, seamless,
peerless mud. My bones
   knock together at the pale
      joints, trying
         for foothold, fingerhold,
mindhold over
   such slick crossings, deep
      hipholes, hummocks
         that sink silently
into the black, slack
   earthsoup. I feel
      not wet so much as
         painted and glittered
with the fat grassy
   mires, the rich
      and succulent marrows
         of earth—a poor
dry stick given
   one more chance by the whims
      of swamp water—a bough
         that still, after all these years,
could take root,
   sprout, branch out, bud—
      make of its life a breathing
         palace of leaves. ◀

David O'Meara

The Game

The trees skitter past, a rush of verticals
at the roadside, I'm fifteen
in the rear-view, off to play
the softball tournament at Golden Lake.

There's Tommy, Trevor, and me.
And Trevor's older brother, Kevin,
who shit-grins behind the steering wheel,
getting us there for the 10 a.m. pitch.

Somewhere down these back routes,
just for kicks, he guns the rusted chassis
at rising humps in the road,
full speed, trying to jimmy us

loose from gravity, and slip
a fat envelope of air
between our wheels and the earth.
Each time we land, our tailbones jab

the vinyl seats, and the stitched gloves
jostle in our laps, their punched palms
a darker tan than last summer.
Kevin's loving the morning breeze

forced through the rolled-down windows,
but especially the looks of panic
on his passengers' faces,
as if we were clean, plush cushions

he'd been itching to knock
the stuffing from. "Watch
this," he says, pushing the gas pedal
to the dusty mat, then charges

the wrong side of the next blind hill.
Our heads are numb; our stomachs roll
and clutch, I catch my own eye
in the side mirror, giddy with the look
of death, every bit as close as it might appear. ◀

Deborah Parédez

Bustillo Drive Grocery

On the corner of Bustillo Drive
in the years before the campaign
to widen the street so cars veered off
Roosevelt Avenue right into mailboxes
right into stray dogs and second cousins,
in the years before we found the cockroach
floating inside a bottle of R.C. Cola
and swore off sodas forever
our righteous boycotts lasting
only halfway through Lent,
in the years before the thieves
tore through the screen doors and cracked
open the cash registers and *Abuelito's*[1] head
with the butts of their guns, in the years
before I turned sour as *chamoy*[2]
coarse and tough as stale *chicharón*,[3]
I was in charge of *los dulces*.[4]
In those years, *Abuelita*[5] harnessed
me with my first job, setting me on a stool
behind the counter, setting me
like chocolate poured—quick—into the
candy mold before it hardens.
In the afternoons I fulfilled my duties
with a reverence for the expansive variations,
the countless shapes of sweetness:
aligning cylinders of Life Savers by flavor,
the Milky Ways near the Three Musketeers,
the dainty swirled straws of pixie sticks near
the prized plastic heads of Pez dispensers,
the packets of pop rocks in grape, cherry and orange.
I sat tall in my stool, a big girl, I was in charge

---

1. **Abuelito:** Grandpa
2. **chamoy:** savory sauce made from pickled fruit
3. **chicharón:** a dish made from fried pork rinds
4. **los dulces:** the sweets or candies
5. **Abuelita:** Granny

of *los dulces*. In the shelves above my reach
jars of Spanish olives, bottles of Bayer aspirin,
rolls of Charmin stood at attention,
awaiting their orders, but I could not be bothered
by the weight of such practical inventory.
I cared only for saccharine indulgence
so when on Friday nights the regular crowd
of relatives arrived for the gossip and the gambling,
I descended from my *dulce* throne
leaned coyly against the domino table
until Uncle Louis finished off his Falstaff
slapped his last domino down and with the same
triumphant hand, grabbed hold of me, swooped me up,
the fringes of my crocheted *poncho*[6] fanning out in radiant plume.
He would lower me into the cavernous
depths of the oldtime soda water cooler
that ran the length of the front wall, the length of a coffin
and twice as deep, my body plunged head first
into the cool humming darkness, arms outstretched,
hands grabbing hold of a slender bottleneck
and just then—catch complete—my plumed body
in pelican dive—I went soaring again—
Uncle Louis pulling me out from the depths,
poncho fringes fluttering, giggles spouting
from my mouth, syrupy bubbles erupting
from the opened bottle of my shaken Orange Crush.
In those years, my unwavering devotion to *los dulces*,
my faith in the choreography of return spurred
every harrowing descent, brought me back
every time—flushed and dizzy and eager for more. ◄

Linda Pastan

November

It is an old drama
this disappearance of the leaves,
this seeming death

---

6. **poncho:** a blanket-like outer garment

of the landscape.
In a later scene,
or earlier,
the trees like gnarled magicians
produce handkerchiefs
of leaves
out of empty branches.

And we watch.
We are like children
at this spectacle
of leaves,
as if one day we too
will open the wooden doors
of our coffins
and come out smiling
and bowing
all over again. ◀

Bradley Paul

Short Ends

I thought my dog would die for a while.
Her kidneys were gone for a while.
I paid to get them back for a while.
For a while my dog won't die.

They were shooting a movie at the state beach for a while.
The sea grapes popped underfoot for a while.
My dog insisted she swim for a while.
For a while I was next to the sea.

In the cooler it was cool for a while.
The flesh of the pear was cold for a while.
The Coke was not flat for a while.
For a while there was something to eat.

But where is my brother? He was here for a while.
Where is my mother? She was here for a while.
They were healthy as my dog for a while.
For a while we made quite a scene. ◀

Molly Peacock

Instead of Her Own

Instead of her own, my grandmother washed my hair.
The porcelain was cold at the back of my neck,
my fragile neck. Altogether it was cold there.

She did it so my hair would smell sweet.
What else is like the moist mouse straw
of a girl's head? Why, the feeling of complete

peace the smell brings to a room whose window
off oily Lake Erie is rimmed with snow.
Knuckles rasping at young temples know,

in the involuntary way a body knows,
that as old is, so young grows. Completion
drives us: substitution is our mission.

Thin little head below thin little head grown old.
Water almost warm in a room almost cold. ◀

Patricia Smith

Listening at the Door

Beneath the door, I could practically see
the wretched slither of tobacco and English Leather.
Hiding on the other side, I heard Mama giggle
through clenched teeth, which meant potential
husband sitting spitshined on our corduroy couch.
The needle hit that first groove and I wondered
why my mama had chosen the blues,
wrong, Friday-angled, when it was hope
she needed. I pressed my ear against the door,
heard dual damp panting, the Murphy bed squeal,
the occasional directive,
the sexless clink of jelly jar glasses.

What drove me to listen on those nights
when my mother let that fragrant man in,

banished me to the back of the apartment,
pretended she could shine above hurting?
I'd rest my ear against the cool wood all night
as she flipped through the 45s—
looking for Ray Charles, Stevie Wonder,
somebody blind this time,
somebody crawling on his knees toward love. ◄

Gary Snyder

I Went into the Maverick Bar

I went into the Maverick Bar
In Farmington, New Mexico.
And drank double shots of bourbon
                    backed with beer.
My long hair was tucked up under a cap
I'd left the earring in the car.

Two cowboys did horseplay
                    by the pool tables,
A waitress asked us
                    where are you from?
a country-and-western band began to play
"We don't smoke Marijuana in Muskokie"
And with the next song,
                    a couple began to dance.

They held each other like in High School dances
                    in the fifties;
I recalled when I worked in the woods
                    and the bars of Madras, Oregon.
That short-haired joy and roughness—
                    America—your stupidity.
I could almost love you again.

We left—onto the freeway shoulders—
                    under the tough old stars—
In the shadow of bluffs
                    I came back to myself,
To the real work, to
                    "What is to be done." ◄

Gary Soto

What Is Your Major?

One spring I thought that maybe archeology
Was better than mortuary studies,
That a person scanned the wreck of a pagan temple
And by intuition commanded, "This is where we dig."
I knew people died like minutes,
And that someone had to tie shoelaces one last time
And fiddle with the collars before the coffins,
Soft as pin cushions, were closed.
I knew they were similar, the ancient dead
Washed by the rise and fall of the Nile,
And the recent dead, like Mrs. White's husband,
Poor man whose head fit through the rollers
Of industrial machinery. I knew
Mr. White would go nowhere, even if his coffin rotted
And rain washed over his face,
Now narrow as a hatchet.
He wouldn't get up and scare me,
And the temples wouldn't litter
My back with goose bumps.
I had outgrown ghost stories,
And at night I was not in the least scared
Of petting my own flesh,
Eventual fodder for the carnivorous earth.
I was nineteen, in junior college,
Piling up units so that I could help the dead.
I wanted to use my hands,
Either by shoveling for pharaohs by the Nile,
Or, in the college basement under a twenty-watt bulb,
Patting rouge on a poor fellow,
Cooing, "Come on, friend, let's make a good show." ◀

James Tate

Teaching the Ape to Write Poems

They didn't have much trouble
teaching the ape to write poems:
first they strapped him into the chair,
then tied the pencil around his hand
(the paper had already been nailed down).
Then Dr. Bluespire leaned over his shoulder
and whispered into his ear:
"You look like a god sitting there.
Why don't you try writing something?" ◄

Gloria Vando

new shoes and an old flame

shopping today i see a pair of kinky
yves st. laurent
shoes and
think of you
now why do you
suppose my mind
not unlike bubble
gum pushed to its
very limits springs
back upon your image
sticking to the thought
of you wondering how
you'd feel about those
skinny call-girl heels cause
i'm still   coming on to you
you see   even though i
tell my-   self you're gone
now one   of those people we
speak   of with reverence or
a hint   of smile suggesting something
deeper   than we ever let on your name
still   makes me smile and think of
high-   heel shoes—the higher, the better ◄

Alma Luz Villanueva

bitch   bitch

bitch

bitch

I kind of like the sound
of bitch—   such a word,
seems to leap right
off the tongue:
      reminds me of a woman looking
         directly at a man
            (and he doesn't like it)
      of a woman fighting with her kids
            (but they need it)
      of a woman needing something real
         and swearing at the world
            (and the world doesn't have it)
      reminds me of when I have to
reach right down
inside me, right into
the fleshy hurt and let it
come inching out—then bursting out
by way of laugh/cry, and cry
being the best of all because then
the ocean that lives within
me shatters the seawall
of my reason
and washes over my sandyface and
I catch them on my tongue
and replenish the salt that evaporates
between tidal waves;
and maybe when I'm
reaching down to
fathoms of this sea
I never dreamed existed,
and the pull of the moon is
stronger than usual,
    maybe I look like a bitch, probably
because that's what
I am. ◄

David Wojahn

The Assassination of John Lennon as Depicted by the Madame Tussaud Wax Museum, Niagara Falls, Ontario, 1987

Smuggled human hair from Mexico
Falls radiant upon the waxy O

Of her scream. Shades on, leather coat and pants, Yoko
On her knees—like the famous Kent State photo

Where the girl can't shriek her boyfriend alive, her arms
Wind-milling Ohio sky.
                              A pump in John's chest heaves

To mimic death-throes. The blood is made of latex.
His glasses: broken on the plastic sidewalk.

A scowling David Chapman, his arms outstretched,
His pistol barrel spiraling fake smoke

In a siren's red wash, completes the composition,
And somewhere background music plays "Imagine"

Before the tableau darkens. We push a button
To renew the scream.
                              The chest starts up again. ◀

Matthew Zapruder

Automated Regret Machine

My friend and I were watching television
and laughing. Then we saw
white letters begin to crawl along
the bottom of the screen.
People were floating on doors and holding
large pieces of cardboard
with telephone numbers scrawled
in black fear up to the helicopters.

The storm had very suddenly
come and now it was gone.
I saw one aluminum rooftop flash
in sunlight, it would have burned
the feet of anyone trying to wait there.
My friend by then had managed
to will her face into that familiar living
detachment mask. I thought
of the very large yellow house
of the second half of my childhood, how through
my bedroom window I could reach my hand
out and upward and touch
the branch of an elm. At night
in the summer I heard the rasp
of a few errant cicadas whose timing
devices had for them tragically drifted.
And the hoarse glassy call
of the black American crow.
Though I am at least halfway through
my life, part of my spirit
still lives there, thinking very soon
I will go down to the room where my father
carefully places his fingers on the strings of the guitar
he bought a few years before I was born.
Picking his head up he smiles
and motions vaguely with his hand, communicating
many contradictory things. ◀

2

1̶8̶ ̶ ̶ ̶W̶r̶i̶t̶i̶n̶g̶ ̶t̶h̶e̶ ̶S̶h̶o̶r̶t̶-̶S̶h̶o̶r̶t̶ ̶S̶t̶o̶r̶y̶

Writing the Short-Short Story

▶ A few things you should know about the short-short story

What is **fiction**? In the largest sense, it is something that's made up. Of course, a story can be entirely fabricated, or just *not quite* true, although as literary critics have often said, it's hard to tell the truth even when we want to. The word "fiction" comes from a Latin root meaning "to shape or fashion," and whenever we recount some past event, even if it's only what we did yesterday, we inevitably include certain details and leave others out. We shape what we have to say to make a point or produce a desired effect. Through this process, raw material becomes fictionalized.

And fictions are everywhere, from the implied stories in magazine advertisements ("Using this product will make you more attractive to other people"), to politicians' speeches, to the extended stories, or **narratives**, found in films. Indeed, any form of communication that relies extensively on imagination might be labeled fiction, which brings us into potentially dangerous territory: a definition isn't worth much if it is all-inclusive.

However, even if we limit our discussion of fiction to creative writing, two of the other genres included in this book, **poetry** and **drama**, also fall into that category. Fortunately, we can distinguish what we generally call fiction from poetry because fiction is written in **prose**, the ordinary language of speaking and writing. Poetry—highly charged and rhythmic language—may be notoriously difficult to define, but it is relatively easy to identify on the page: prose moves in a straight line from the left to the right margin, while the right-hand margins of a poem are ragged, with each line ending where it does for added emphasis (the **prose poem** notwithstanding). And we can distinguish a story or a novel from a play because a play is written in the form of a script, a document intended primarily to be seen and heard, not read silently like a book.

The difference between fiction (and poetry and drama) and **creative nonfiction**—literary writing that claims to be true—is more striking. Writers of creative nonfiction are always accountable to the evidence. James Frey, for instance, found himself in hot water when it was revealed in 2006 that his Oprah Winfrey–endorsed, best-selling book *A Million Little Pieces*, which he called a memoir, actually included a number of incidents that either were exaggerated or hadn't occurred at all. Had the book been labeled a novel, no one would have blinked an eye: novelists, after all, are *supposed* to make things up.

We have a further sense of how liberating the word "fiction" can be when we look at what is called historical fiction, in which the author's perspective inevitably affects how the facts are presented. Although more fact finding may be involved in this enterprise than with other types of fiction writing, we still read a historical novel rather than a nonfiction book of history because we want to be caught up in the story. E. L. Doctorow, for example, carefully researched General William Tecumseh Sherman's advance through the South for his novel *The March* and adheres to the broad outlines of what really happened. However, his book is admired not primarily for its documentation of the Civil War but because readers enjoy being inside the minds and hearts of the characters he has created.

The March, written by a great American author, is clearly a literary novel, while a novel such as John Jakes's *North and South,* about the same time period, is likely to be labeled "genre fiction." What's the difference? **Genre fiction**, which includes romance, spy/thriller, horror, fantasy, science fiction, and the like, requires the writer to adhere to certain conventions, such as good triumphing over evil. In a romance novel, for instance, we know early on that a man and a woman will fall in love but will be prevented from coming together by a series of obstacles. Yet no matter how many plot complications ensue, just at the point when those barriers seem insurmountable, the conventions of a romance require that the two lovers ultimately unite. Fans of the genre know the basic story line by heart—indeed, they *demand* that the writer stick to it—and they receive pleasure from watching the author work variations on time-honored themes.

Unfortunately, genre stories do not work well in short-shorts. Fantasy and espionage require too much **backstory**, the narrative of events leading up to the current moment in a work of fiction. It takes pages and pages to create a convincing world of dragon slayers and elves, and the world of spies seems thin and unbelievable if it is not layered with insider details. Horror fiction relies on suspense, and there simply is not enough time to develop that anticipation in a short-short. Romances similarly require the gradual accretion of details and events: if a relationship's delayed climax is to have any impact on the reader, there must be many twists and turns before the two lovers finally come together.

In contrast, writers of literary fiction go in fear of adhering too closely to a standard set of expectations. Knowing that there are only a handful of basic plots on which to draw, literary writers look to evoke the specific, the individual, the original. They value character over plot, and they spend a great deal of time on the nuances of authorial voice and style. John Jakes may provide us with a great page turner, but E. L. Doctorow makes us want to slow down and savor each sentence of his prose, each moment of his narrative.

Literary fiction values ambiguity. Although they rarely occur in real life, happy endings are something we love, and writers of genre fiction cater to that desire. Many recreational readers savor a pleasant diversion that doesn't require much investment of mental energy, and they prefer all the questions and complications in a story to be resolved by the end. But writers and readers of literary fiction value uncertainty; they enjoy the possibility that a character or situation can be interpreted in more than a single way. Life is complex, their thinking goes; fiction should be too.

You may have enrolled in this course hoping to practice genre fiction, but your instructor will probably ask you to write literary fiction instead. Don't despair. Even if you are determined to write the next *Lord of the Rings*, you can still learn a great deal that will be useful for your novel. Every time you're in the midst of creating a piece of fiction and you face, and solve, a narrative problem, you will be that much better equipped to handle the issue the next time you encounter it. Every story you write makes you a better writer. And just as literary writers borrow from the conventions of genre fiction all the time, the best writers in the genres—J. R. R. Tolkien in fantasy, for instance—do their utmost to create works of literature.

The elements of fiction ▶

As with all the other genres discussed in this book, the similarities between the short and long forms are more pronounced than are the differences. Both the one-page short-short and the thousand-page novel make use of the same basic elements of fiction. Naturally, deciding which elements are basic and which aren't varies, depending on who is doing the deciding. The focus of this chapter is on the fundamentals that are most pertinent to the very short fiction you will be writing. Each of these elements will be discussed in more detail later in this section; for now, let's get acquainted with the terms.

▶ **Structure and Design**   Obviously novelists need a plan to carry them through their projects. But writers of short-shorts must also consider structure and design. With only a few pages of working room, there can be no digressions. Every piece of the story must interact effectively with the others.

▶ **Character**   The **characters**—the people in your story—should be recognizable as human beings, showing both their good and bad sides, and should be capable of changing, even if they don't ultimately rise to the challenges they face.

▶ **Dialogue**   The **dialogue** is what characters say to one another. The best dialogue not only reveals who the characters are but also moves the story along. Some stories have no dialogue at all, but most have at least some conversation, and learning how to write significant and selective dialogue is an essential skill.

▶ **Setting**   The **setting** is where and when the story takes place. Like good dialogue, deft use of detail and description illuminates character and propels a scene forward.

▶ **Point of View, Tone, and Style**   **Point of view** allows us into, or keeps us out of, the characters' minds; it dictates how much we learn of their internal, unspoken thinking. According to I. A. Richards, **tone** is a literary speaker's "attitude toward his listener." And **style** is how writers say what they have to say. Point of view, tone, and style are covered together because, especially in the short-short story, *who* is telling the story and *how* it's told are closely intertwined.

The short-short story: Three models ▶

We have said that fiction is imaginative writing in prose. It encompasses the novel, the novella, the short story, and the short-short story. How long *is* a short-short story? Different writers and critics give different answers, but most would agree that the short-short is at least 100 but no more than 2,000 words. Within the limits of the form, that turns out to be a fairly broad range, from less than one double-spaced page to seven or eight pages. Still, this is a relatively small canvas, and readers of short-shorts expect that every moment of a story will engage their interest. There can be no dead spots in a short-short. A writer may be able to get away with a bum paragraph in the middle of a strong twenty-page story, but that same paragraph in a three-page story can prove disastrous.

In the introduction to *Sudden Fiction*, the first anthology of contemporary American short-short stories, Robert Shapard notes that the popularity of the form began in the 1960s with the experimental and playful work of writers such as Robert Coover, Gordon Lish, and Donald Barthelme (Barthelme's work is featured in this section). Post–World War II readers enjoyed that brief blaze of mental energy that the short-short delivered. Yet the short-short story is hardly a late-twentieth-century invention; the list of nineteenth- and early-twentieth-century writers who wrote superbly in the very short form includes Leo Tolstoy, Franz Kafka, Anton Chekhov, James Joyce, and Isaac Babel (Babel's work is included in this chapter). Moreover, in its incarnation as "the tale," the short-short has been around for centuries. Aesop's fables and the fairy tales collected by Jacob and Wilhelm Grimm are just two examples.

Perhaps the most important thing to remember about the short-short story is that it is *not* a fragment. It is a complete work, with a beginning, a middle, and an end. Although parts of it may be drastically condensed, the art of fiction is, in part, the art of learning which things to include and which to omit. Writers and readers of the form often speak admiringly of its energy and density. According to Shapard, a good short-short is highly compressed and highly charged; it "confers form on a small corner of chaos" and "can do in a page what a novel does in two hundred."

Alice Turner, a former editor at *The New Yorker*, believes that "pacing has everything to do with it—and the snap at the end." Charles Baxter echoes this call for a sharp finish: "What we need is surprise, a quick turning of the wrist toward texture, or wisdom, something suddenly broken or quickly repaired." *Snap, quick turning, surprise*: the point is that readers must be left in a different place from where they began. In the introduction to his anthology *Short Shorts*, Irving Howe contends that "short shorts are indeed like most ordinary short stories, *only more so*." What Howe means is that short-shorts highlight the need for intensity, "one sweeping blow of perception." He argues that in the strongest short-shorts, "we see human figures in a momentary flash. . . . An extreme condition serves as emblem of the universal."

These grand descriptions may make short-shorts sound incredibly difficult to write—"like being asked to paint a landscape on a grain of rice," in the words of Jerome Stern—yet short-shorts are also a great deal of fun to work with, and more and more fiction writers are turning to them as a viable form of storytelling. Roberta Allen, whose story "Marzipan" is reprinted on p. 107, thinks that the reason the short-short has become so popular is obvious: "In our fast-paced age, as people have shorter and shorter attention spans and little time to read, the short-short is perfect. Some stories are brief enough to be read in the time it takes to watch a television commercial."

Of course, what you are doing in this class is far more important than making substitutes for commercials: you are making literature. But literature can, and probably *should*, be as pleasurable as it is demanding.

Even if your instructor has not yet given you your fiction-writing assignment, the moment you feel the urge to begin stringing words together into a story, *go for it*. Creative impulses don't necessarily arrive on a schedule, and whether you begin your story now or after reading every word in this chapter, any time that you feel like writing is a good time.

Assuming, however, that the Muse hasn't struck you while reading the first pages of this chapter, you'll probably want to become familiar with a few examples of the short-short before you start writing your own. The following three stories, all quite different from one another, give you a range of models. Isaac Babel's dark and descriptive "Crossing the River Zbrucz" shows war at its grimmest. In sharp contrast, Donald Barthelme's "The Baby" takes a potentially grim situation and turns it into comedy. Finally, Roberta Allen's "Marzipan" is both wry and poignant.

Together, these three stories provide material for a discussion of the elements of fiction. We will make frequent reference to the three stories, so it's worth reading each one at least twice. If you're still not ready to write after reading about the basics of fiction, you will want to turn to the kick-starts writing prompts in "Getting Started Writing the Short-Short Story." And because reading is so often a trigger for writing, the mini-anthology of short-shorts that concludes this chapter is another potential source of inspiration.

Isaac Babel

Crossing the River Zbrucz

The Russian writer Isaac Babel (1894–1940) is considered by many as one of the greatest writers of short fiction of the twentieth century. Francine Prose praises the way Babel typically introduces "some element of unease" so that his paragraphs "make us catch our breath in the final sentence." And Tom Teicholz writes: "He stands in the footsteps of the reader, alternately awed, impressed and horrified by [his] characters and their world."

Babel was a war correspondent for the Soviets during World War I, so he had firsthand knowledge of the conflict between Russia and Poland described in this story, which was first published in his 1926 collection, *The Red Cavalry Stories*. It is important to remember, however, that even though "Crossing the River Zbrucz" is written in the voice of a callous Russian army officer, Babel himself was Jewish, and his real sympathies are clearly with the Jewish family whose home has been invaded. Although Babel enjoyed considerable success while he was alive, his life was cut tragically short. Never one to mute his condemnation when he saw injustice, Babel ran afoul of the Soviet authorities and was arrested by the secret police and "disappeared" in 1939. It was later learned that not long after his arrest, he was executed and his body was thrown into a communal grave.

The commander of the Sixth Division reported that Novograd-Volynsk[1] was taken at dawn today. The staff is now withdrawing from Krapivno,[2] and our

---

1. **Novograd-Volynsk:** A city in the border region between Russia and Poland.
2. **Krapivno:** A town in that same region.

cavalry transport stretches in a noisy rear guard along the high road that goes from Brest to Warsaw, a high road built on the bones of muzhiks[3] by Czar Nicholas I.

Fields of purple poppies are blossoming around us, a noon breeze is frolicking in the yellowing rye, virginal buckwheat is standing on the horizon like the wall of a faraway monastery. Silent Volhynia[4] is turning away, Volhynia is leaving, heading into the pearly white fog of the birch groves, creeping through the flowery hillocks, and with weakened arms entangling itself in the underbrush of hops. The orange sun is rolling across the sky like a severed head, gentle light glimmers in the ravines among the clouds, the banners of the sunset are fluttering above our heads. The stench of yesterday's blood and slaughtered horses drips into the evening chill. The blackened Zbrucz roars and twists the foaming knots of its rapids. The bridges are destroyed, and we wade across the river. The majestic moon lies on the waves. The water comes up to the horses' backs, purling streams trickle between hundreds of horses' legs. Someone sinks, and loudly curses the Mother of God. The river is littered with the black squares of the carts and filled with humming, whistling, and singing that thunders above the glistening hollows and the snaking moon.

Late at night we arrive in Novograd. In the quarter to which I am assigned I find a pregnant woman and two red-haired Jews with thin necks, and a third Jew who is sleeping with his face to the wall and a blanket pulled over his head. In my room I find ransacked closets, torn pieces of women's fur coats on the floor, human excrement, and fragments of the holy Seder plate that the Jews use once a year for Passover.

"Clean up this mess!" I tell the woman. "How can you live like this?"

The two Jews get up from their chairs. They hop around on their felt soles and pick up the broken pieces of porcelain from the floor. They hop around in silence, like monkeys, like Japanese acrobats in a circus, their necks welling and twisting. They spread a ripped eiderdown[5] on the floor for me, and I lie down by the wall, next to the third, sleeping Jew. Timorous poverty descends over my bed.

Everything has been killed by the silence, and only the moon, clasping its round, shining, carefree head in its blue hands, loiters beneath my window.

I rub my numb feet, lie back on the ripped eiderdown, and fall asleep. I dream about the commander of the Sixth Division. He is chasing the brigade commander on his heavy stallion, and shoots two bullets into his eyes. The bullets pierce the brigade commander's head, and his eyes fall to the ground. "Why did you turn back the brigade?" Savitsky, the commander of the Sixth Division, shouts at the wounded man, and I wake up because the pregnant woman is tapping me on the face.

"Sir," she says to me, "you are shouting in your sleep, and tossing and turning. I'll put your bed in another corner, because you are kicking my papa."

---

3. **muzhiks:** Peasants.

4. **Volhynia:** The name of the area in which the story is set.

5. **eiderdown:** A comforter filled with the soft feathers of eider ducks.

She raises her thin legs and round belly from the floor and pulls the blanket off the sleeping man. An old man is lying there on his back, dead. His gullet has been ripped out, his face hacked in two, and dark blood is clinging to his beard like a clump of lead.

"Sir," the Jewess says, shaking out the eiderdown, "the Poles were hacking him to death and he kept begging them, 'Kill me in the backyard so my daughter won't see me die!' But they wouldn't inconvenience themselves. He died in this room, thinking of me. . . . And now I want you to tell me," the woman suddenly said with terrible force, "I want you to tell me where one could find another father like my father in all the world!" ◄

Donald Barthelme

The Baby

Donald Barthelme (1931–1989) was a founding member of the prestigious creative writing program at the University of Houston and one of the most widely respected writers of fiction in the twentieth century. Many of his stories appeared in *The New Yorker*, and Barthelme was partly responsible for bringing **postmodern** (an ironic, skeptical, and self-aware writing style) fiction into the mainstream. He is also a master of the short-short, as evidenced in collections such as *Sixty Stories* (1981) and *Flying to America* (2007).

Barthelme often wrote about family themes, though in wild and unlikely permutations, as in "The Baby," originally published as "The First Thing the Baby Did Wrong" in *Overnight to Many Distant Cities* (1983) and later reprinted with its current title in *Forty Stories* (1987). Playful and experimental in his writing, Barthelme can veer from philosophy to parody in an instant. Above all, he is a writer with a pronounced sense of humor and irony. He locates the comic in the absurd and in the horrifying—as in this story about parents who take childhood discipline to ridiculous lengths. A consummate craftsperson, Barthelme is particularly well suited to the short-short story, in which every sentence must be well made and every word matters.

The first thing the baby did wrong was to tear pages out of her books. So we made a rule that each time she tore a page out of a book she had to stay alone in her room for four hours, behind the closed door. She was tearing out about a page a day, in the beginning, and the rule worked fairly well, although the crying and screaming from behind the closed door were unnerving. We reasoned that that was the price you had to pay, or part of the price you had to pay. But then as her grip improved she got to tearing out two pages at a time, which meant eight hours alone in her room, behind the closed door, which just doubled the annoyance for everybody. But she wouldn't quit doing it. And then as time went on we began getting days when she tore out three or four pages, which put her alone in her room for as much as sixteen hours at a stretch, interfering with normal feeding and worrying my wife. But I felt that if you made a rule you had to stick to it, had to be consistent, otherwise they get the wrong idea. She was about fourteen months old or fifteen months old at that point. Often, of course, she'd go to sleep, after an hour or so of yelling, that was a mercy. Her room was very nice, with a nice wooden rocking horse and practically a hundred dolls and stuffed animals. Lots of things to do in that room if you used your time wisely, puzzles and things. Unfortunately sometimes when we opened the door we'd find that she'd torn more pages out of more books while she was inside, and these pages had to be added to the total, in fairness.

The baby's name was Born Dancin'. We gave the baby some of our wine, red, whites and blue, and spoke seriously to her. But it didn't do any good.

I must say she got real clever. You'd come up to her where she was playing on the floor, in those rare times when she was out of her room, and there'd be a book there, open beside her, and you'd inspect it and it would look perfectly all right. And then you'd look closely and you'd find a page that had one little corner torn, could easily pass for ordinary wear-and-tear but I knew what she'd done, she'd torn off this little corner and swallowed it. So that had to count and it did. They will go to any lengths to thwart you. My wife said that maybe we were being too rigid and that the baby was losing weight. But I pointed out to her that the baby had a long life to live and had to live in a world with others, had to live in a world where there were many, many rules, and if you couldn't learn to play by the rules you were going to be left out in the cold with no character, shunned and ostracized by everyone. The longest we ever kept her in her room consecutive was eighty-eight hours, and that ended when my wife took the door off its hinges with a crowbar even though the baby still owed us twelve hours because she was working off twenty-five pages. I put the door back on its hinges and added a big lock, one that opened only if you put a magnetic card in a slot, and I kept the card.

But things didn't improve. The baby would come out of her room like a bat out of hell and rush to the nearest book, *Goodnight Moon* or whatever, and begin tearing pages out of it hand over fist. I mean there'd be thirty-four pages of *Goodnight Moon* on the floor in ten seconds. Plus the covers. I began to get a little worried. When I added up her indebtedness, in terms of hours, I could see that she wasn't going to get out of her room until 1992, if then. Also, she was looking pretty wan. She hadn't been to the park in weeks. We had more or less of an ethical crisis on our hands.

I solved it by declaring that it was all right to tear pages out of books, and moreover, that it was *all right* to have torn pages out of books in the past. That is one of the satisfying things about being a parent—you've got a lot of moves, each one good as gold. The baby and I sit happily on the floor, side by side, tearing pages out of books, and sometimes, just for fun, we go out on the street and smash a windshield together. ◀

Roberta Allen

Marzipan

The *New York Times Book Review* calls Roberta Allen's short-short stories "quicksilver dreams." Writing in the *Village Voice*, Gary Indiana describes her fiction as "a quick read full of lightning-like emotional illuminations." And the *American Book Review* says her stories "exist somewhere between narrative fiction and prose poetry. Allen's writings could be said to stretch the boundaries of both or bridge the narrowing gap between them."

Clearly, Allen is a master of the short form, and, in fact, she is the author of a textbook on writing short-shorts, *Fast Fiction: Creating Fiction in Five Minutes* (1997). "Marzipan," from her collection of short-shorts, *Certain People* (1997), is perhaps the most traditional of our three model stories. Initially it seems to be about nothing more than a tipsy and slightly egotistical young man hitting on a pretty young woman at a party, but his conversation grows increasingly strange, and the narrative takes a sharp and unexpected turn at the end.

At a crowded party, a pretty girl closes her eyes and bites into a marzipan pear, a look of rapture on her face. "I just love marzipan!" she says to the tipsy young Englishman beside her.

The haughty young man, who seems to be posing, says with a mocking smile, "Balzac loved marzipan too." His bright blue eyes intrigue her. "There was once a rumor in Paris that he opened a candy store just to sell marzipan. But the truth was Balzac always bought marzipan from the same shop." There is a mischievous gleam in his eye. "For a while crowds swarmed to this store to sample the sweet."

"Did you just make that up?" asks the girl, her mouth full.

"It's a true story," the young man replies.

"What a silly story!" laughs the girl, taking another marzipan fruit from the dish on the table. She likes his curly hair, she wonders what's behind his mocking smile. "How do you know such a silly story?" she asks.

"I'm a poet and a food lover," the young man says, half-serious. "When I tire of poetry, I read the food encyclopedia just for fun."

As the girl laughs, licks her sticky fingers, and chooses another marzipan morsel, the poet glances at the other guests. After quickly appraising the girls, he turns back to the one beside him.

"How do you stay so thin?" he asks, as she toys with a marzipan apple.

"Metabolism I guess. I never gain weight," she lies. "What other silly stories can you tell me?" she says to change the subject.

He pauses for a moment, swaying slightly. His every move seems mannered, artificial; he plays a role, but knows he plays it well.

"I know so many stories," he smiles. "During the blockade of Malta by the English and the Neapolitans, the people had nothing to eat but domestic animals like dogs, cats, rats, and donkeys. In time they came to prefer donkey meat over beef and veal." He raises his brows and waits for her reaction.

"That's an awful tale!" she laughs, as she munches on another piece of marzipan. "Tell me another."

For a moment the poet seems to have lost his memory; his mind goes blank as he stares into the distance. His mocking smile disappears. Suddenly he blurts out, "My mother killed herself in 1978." The girl looks at him, surprised. The man turns a deep shade of pink and lowers his eyes; he wonders what came over him.

"I'm so sorry," says the girl, removing her hand from the candy dish.

"So am I," says the man, who knows he's ruined his performance; he feels the curtain falling on his stage. The scent of the almond-flavored sweet, however, stirs his memory; he suddenly recalls how much his mother loved marzipan. Angry at himself, he avoids the girl's eyes as he thinks about his hours wasted in the library searching for stories to use at parties, where he feels shy, where he rarely meets girls, where he's so afraid someone will see how much he's been hurt. As he turns to walk away, he tosses a piece of marzipan into his mouth, but its taste gives him no pleasure. ◄

Structure and design ▶

Story, according to E. M. Forster in his book *Aspects of the Novel*, is "a narrative of events arranged in their time-sequence. . . . The king died and then the queen died." A **plot** is also a narrative of events, but with the emphasis on causality: "The king died, and then the queen died of grief. If it is in a story, we say 'and then?'" Forster tells us. "If it is in a plot, we ask 'why?'"

Both story (the *what*) and plot (the *why*) have to do with events occurring in time. Dealing with time is one of the most challenging aspects of fiction writing because what is on the page rarely corresponds with the passage of real time. A character may have a memory that lasts for pages, although in life those pages would have passed in only a second or two. Conversely, fiction writers can make lifetimes disappear with just a wave of their typing fingers. "Centuries passed," we say, and, as far as the story or book is concerned, they have.

A **chronology** is an account of the way time actually moves, from past to present to future. In novels and longer stories, chronology may be all jumbled up. A story may begin just as the **protagonist**—the main character on whom our attention is centered—is about to die. The narrative then might return elsewhere in time via a **flashback**, the sudden intrusion of past events in the middle of a description of current action. The story might then **flash forward**—cutting to the future—after the protagonist has passed away and all his family are gathered at his funeral. We are accustomed to this jumping around in time from watching movies, in which filmmakers often cut to another scene just when something important is about to happen in order to increase **suspense**, that anxiety about the outcome of an event that audiences find so painfully delicious.

In a short-short, however, you should avoid a convoluted plot. Keep flashbacks and flash forwards to a minimum. If you do decide that it is briefly necessary for your narrative to provide information from the past or the future—as Roberta Allen does in "Marzipan"—it may help to graph your story as a timeline:

$----$ Past Events $-----$ |The Story| $-----$ Future Events $-----$

If you're conscious of when something occurred in relation to the main story that is "happening" as the reader reads it, you're less likely to get tripped up with chronology. Your protagonist may be bewildered about when something happened, but you shouldn't be.

Even if the information never makes it into the story itself, thinking about what comes before and after what is actually written on the page can be of real value to the writer. Ernest Hemingway's "iceberg theory" is especially relevant for writers of the short-short: "If it is any use to know it, I always try to write on the principle of the iceberg. There is seven-eighths of it underwater for every part that shows. Anything you know you can eliminate and it only strengthens your iceberg. . . . If a writer omits something because he does not know it then there is a hole in the story."

Screenwriters are told they must be able to summarize their movies in a **logline**, a one-sentence summary of twenty-five words or less. "A soldier encounters a chilling surprise in the home he occupies overnight." "A baby receives comically disproportionate punishments for tearing out the pages of books." "A young man inadvertently reveals a dark secret at a party." These three loglines don't do justice to our three model stories, but they do demonstrate that the basics of each story can be encapsulated in a few words. Readers of literary fiction normally don't demand a synopsis, but if you can't summarize your short-short in a few sentences, you may not yet know the story well enough to tell it properly.

Once you have decided on your story, you need to decide where on the time line of events to begin. Too often, students write about that moment in the story that first occurs to them, although the more intriguing conflict actually takes place at another point in the chronology of events. Say, for instance, that you want to write about a couple breaking up. It might seem logical to begin with the last fight between the two lovers; yet their very first fight two years earlier, long before the breakup occurred, may be the real crux of the story. Or perhaps the story you really want to tell only briefly references the breakup. What interests you is how, after the breakup, your protagonist wandered forlornly into a city park and got into a fight with an old acquaintance.

Just about every fiction writer will tell you to find the moment when your protagonist is close to a disaster of some sort. In the words of Lajos Egri, a story "must open with a crisis which is the sole point of attack—in the life or lives of one or more of the characters. A decision must be imminent and the characters must be ready to take action." The ancient Greeks called this technique of beginning a story in the midst of the main action **in medias res**: "in the middle of things." It was good advice for storytellers then, and it is even more valid now, when we have so little patience for entertainment that does not engage us immediately.

A short-short that begins with three pages of backstory about how Princess Palonia has spent years battling witches and dragons in her quest for the magic crown of Capel Tywynsoch won't hold the attention of most readers. **Exposition**—the history leading up to the present moment in the story—may be provided quickly at the beginning, or in a sentence or two at a time over the course of the story, or through the dialogue the characters speak, but it should be extremely condensed in a short-short. Your focus is on *now*, not *then*. As David Shields writes, "Short-shorts eschew the furniture-moving, the table-setting typical of the longer story." Instead, "in the best short-shorts, the writer seems to have miraculously figured out a way to stage, in a very compressed space, his own metaphysic: *Life feels like this* or, at least, *Some aspect of life feels like this.*"

Remember that the burden is always on you, the author, to draw your readers in. If you're worried about whether you're off to a strong start, imagine an intelligent, interested, but not entirely patient reader who will give you about half a page to make your story come to life. If you haven't hooked your reader by then, chances are he or she will probably stop reading. Lights out, game over. Begin again.

Our three model authors are very aware of the need to start strong and economically. Let's look at how skillfully they use their first few sentences to create their fictional worlds.

Isaac Babel writes:

The commander of the Sixth Division reported that Novograd-Volynsk was taken at dawn today. The staff is now withdrawing from Krapivno, and our cavalry transport stretches in a noisy rear guard along the high road that goes from Brest to Warsaw, a high road built on the bones of muzhiks by Czar Nicholas I.

Babel could have begun his story during the morning's heated battle. That certainly would have made for some exciting writing. But the heart of his story is the protagonist's encounter with the Jewish girl and her dead father. All that fighting—the explosions and gunfire, the blood and suffering—ultimately would have been wasted words, so much hot air standing between the reader and the story's moment of crisis. Babel's opening has only two sentences, but they are crammed with information. Even if we know nothing at all about the people and places involved, we do know that a battle has taken place, with one side capturing a city or region, and that portions of the army are now on the move to consolidate that victory. The details of the battle, the cause of the war, who's right and who's wrong: none of this material is essential to the story about to be told, so Babel leaves it out.

Here is Barthelme's opening gambit:

> The first thing the baby did wrong was to tear pages out of her books. So we made a rule that each time she tore a page out of a book she had to stay alone in her room for four hours, behind the closed door. She was tearing out about a page a day, in the beginning, and the rule worked fairly well, although the crying and screaming from behind the closed door were unnerving.

In only three sentences, we are brought immediately into the perverse but ultimately comic universe of the story. Sentence 1 gives a hint that something may be wrong with the speaker's parenting style: after all, can a baby really do anything "wrong"? Sentence 2 introduces the first of the many ridiculous punishments the parents mete out to their child: *four hours* behind a closed door for tearing out the page of a book? Now we *know* something is seriously amiss. And sentence 3 heightens the narrator's skewed, even cruel, perspective: despite his baby's "unnerving" crying and screaming, the father sticks with his draconian punishment. It's a testament to how adroitly **Barthe**lme uses exposition in the form of description and action that after only seventy-six words, we sense that we have entered a seriously dysfunctional home. The fun comes when the author abruptly reverses our expectations and leads us on the humorous romp that follows.

Finally, here are Roberta Allen's first two sentences:

> At a crowded party, a pretty girl closes her eyes and bites into a marzipan pear, a look of rapture on her face. "I just love marzipan!" she says to the tipsy young Englishman beside her.

"Marzipan" begins in medias res. Allen could have chosen to start the story at a different point. She could have showed us the preparation for the party: the hosts decorating their home, selecting the music to be played, deciding which food and libations to purchase, welcoming the first guests, and so on. She could have told us whether the girl is a good student, if she has had many boyfriends in the past, why she is sensitive about her weight (Does she have an eating disorder? Has she been overweight in the past?). Did the girl beg a friend to come along, or did someone else drag her there, unwillingly? Did she come alone, and, if so, why? Allen might have thought through all these questions; she might be able to describe the party's preparation, to answer every query we have about the girl. But what would be the point of including all this material in the story? "Marzipan" is about a conversation between a "pretty girl" and a "tipsy young Englishman." Until those two characters take the stage, there is no story.

Every part of a story is important, but the middle—the longest part—is often the most difficult to sustain. Let's say you have managed to pique your readers' interest in the scene and characters. Now what? Once you have begun, you will want to make the central conflict immediately apparent. "Where's the trouble?" James Gordon Bennett used to say in his fiction workshops. Bennett felt that a story didn't really begin until we knew the crisis afflicting the main characters, and most fiction writers would agree: *conflict* in some form is at the center of every good story.

We may all wish for a calmer, gentler life, but fiction is not the place to seek that tranquillity. Your reader will quickly become bored if nothing significant happens to your protagonists. "Do not be nice to your characters," Romelda Shaffer advises. "Slap them with one problem after the other. What is compelling about a nice, smart, handsome, rich man?" The answer in real life is, "Quite a lot." But in fiction, nice guys (and gals) often do finish last.

There is nothing especially nice about the characters in "Crossing the River Zbrucz." The narrator is insensitive at best. His hosts are war-shocked and bedraggled. Trouble is everywhere in this battle-scarred landscape, but the real trouble, we learn in the second half of the story, is located in the repercussions of one particularly loathsome act of torture and cruelty. "Crossing the River Zbrucz" is designed so that we move from the very large to the very small, from history to one family's personal tragedy. We can imagine a cinematic equivalent of the story, beginning with a shot of a map of eastern Poland that dissolves into a long shot of the landscape. The camera follows the army across the river; then we focus in on the narrator as he enters the home of the Jewish family. The closer we get to the action, the more our curiosity grows: What is on the other side of this black and foaming river? What is at the end of this troubling road?

In contrast to Babel's concentration on a single day, Donald Barthelme's "The Baby" covers an indeterminate time span, although it seems to be at minimum a duration of several weeks—from the time we first hear of the baby's "misbehavior," through the many punishments that continue right up until the day the father finally gives up on disciplining his child and joins the baby in smashing the windshields of cars. If Babel's strategy is gradually to close in on his subject, Barthelme keeps us involved by very briefly describing key scenes: the baby tearing out first one page at a time, then two, then swallowing them, then tearing a corner when she thinks her father isn't looking, and so forth. Stuart Dybek believes it is possible to "argue that the art of the short story is the art of transition," and Barthelme has mastered this art. He clearly signals the passage of time, the relation of one action to the next: "The first thing the baby did wrong . . . So we made a rule. . . . She was tearing out about a page a day, in the beginning. . . . But then as her grip improved she got to tearing out two pages at a time. . . . But she wouldn't quit doing it. . . . And then as time went on . . ." We are inside the story because with each transition, we are *shown* events rather than just being told about them.

Allen's strategy for sustaining our interest through the middle of "Marzipan" is to increase the understated sexual tension in the conversation between the young man and woman: their flirtation intensifies with each new piece of unlikely information that he provides about the almond-flavored candy. This accelerating agitation is similar to what Aristotle called **rising action**, the escalation and complication of the central conflict. Short-shorts are normally too brief to have a true rising action, but even the shortest stories transition from moments of lesser to greater tension.

This increase of conflict can be represented as an inverted check mark, with the peak of the check signifying the **climax**, the point of maximum dramatic attention, and the turning point in the narrative:

Traditionally what follows the climax is called the **resolution**—the "falling action," or the working out of the remaining complications. This process is also called the **denouement** (French for "untying")—in this case, untying the knot of the plot. Even in a novel, the resolution is normally quite brief, but in a short story, there is likely to be no resolution at all. We reach the climax, and the story is over. Like someone who has been punched in the stomach by a stranger, we're left gasping *What?* or *Why?*

Isaac Babel is especially good at delivering this final blow in his short fiction, and the concluding sentences of "Crossing the River Zbrucz" make for a superlative twist to his story:

> "Sir," the Jewess says, shaking out the eiderdown, "the Poles were hacking him to death and he kept begging them, 'Kill me in the backyard so my daughter won't see me die!' But they wouldn't inconvenience themselves. He died in this room, thinking of me. . . . And now I want you to tell me," the woman suddenly said with terrible force, "I want you to tell me where one could find another father like my father in all the world!"

We don't know the narrator's response to this sudden, awful revelation (although we can imagine that even he is taken aback). Yet there is no need to show his reaction on the page: we readers have essentially become the narrator at this point, so we respond for him. Babel rightly wants the focus to remain on the woman and her story; if we were to see the narrator speechless and aghast, or hear whatever inadequate response he might mutter, some of the power of that final moment would be diminished.

Although Barthelme's denouement is brief, it is nevertheless more extended than Babel's. Following the climax—when the narrator finally admits that he and his wife have "more or less of an ethical crisis on [their] hands"—the story ends with a resolution of the many complications brought on by the baby's page-tearing proclivities:

> I solved it by declaring that it was all right to tear pages out of books, and moreover, that it was *all right* to have torn pages out of books in the past. That is one of the satisfying things about being a parent—you've got a lot of moves, each one good as gold. The baby and I sit happily on the floor, side by side, tearing pages out of books, and sometimes, just for fun, we go out on the street and smash a windshield together.

The sense of gleeful bad judgment that runs through the story receives one final hallelujah here. If we were at all worried that this was a real story about a real baby, those worries have been banished.

The climax of "Marzipan" comes when the young man unexpectedly reveals that his mother committed suicide:

> "I'm so sorry," says the girl, removing her hand from the candy dish.
>
> "So am I," says the man, who knows he's ruined his performance; he feels the curtain falling on his stage. The scent of the almond-flavored sweet, however, stirs his memory; he suddenly recalls how much his mother loved marzipan. Angry at himself, he avoids the girl's eyes as he thinks about his hours wasted in the library searching for stories to use at parties, where he feels shy, where he rarely meets girls, where he's so afraid someone will see how much he's been hurt. As he turns to walk away, he tosses a piece of marzipan into his mouth, but its taste gives him no pleasure.

There are so many questions we might ask at this point. Why did his mother kill herself? Was she close to her son? What is the young man's relationship with his father? The author tells us that the suicide occurred in 1978, but how long ago was that in the world of the story? Is the young man about to enter a long period of depression, or will he shake off this encounter and go looking for another pretty girl to listen to his mixture of odd anecdotes and flattery? The author's work is accomplished if she can prompt her readers to wonder about these issues; she need not answer the questions herself.

For Russell Banks, the end of the story has an almost mystical significance for the writer. It is "the most exhilarating moment of writing fiction—getting to that point where the stakes are so high that who you are will emerge with those last couple of sentences." Charles Baxter has a somewhat more pragmatic way of deciding whether a story is complete: "If, no matter how many times I have reread it, I can't think of anything else to do to it, it's probably finished." You will need to come up with your own criteria for deciding when your story is over, but in general it is better to stop earlier rather than later. Remember that "flash fiction" is just that: a sudden flame that is gone almost as soon as it appears.

Of course, when we analyze polished, published stories—as we have just been doing—it might seem as though the authors knew exactly what they were up to from the very start. That, however, may be far from the truth. Jill McCorkle admits, "Most of my stories surprise me." For Tobias Wolff, "Stories tend to grow in the writing of them, and to begin to define themselves as I work on them." You will often learn what you really need to know about your story by writing a first draft. If you realize that the structure you thought was inevitable is in fact a maze from which you cannot seem to emerge, knock down the walls that are blocking your way. Redesign your story. Tell it differently. Just because you initially envisioned things happening one way, don't feel bound to that version of events in subsequent drafts.

Even as vigorous a proponent of story structure as Madison Smartt Bell acknowledges that the "experience of imagining and composing any story is much more fluid than any reverse-engineering analysis could convey." In short, while it helps to have a plan in mind as you draft, you should be open to the possibility that an unexpected twist or turn will restructure your story, transforming it into something that surprises even you with the ingenuity of its design.

CHECKLIST Structure and design

- [ ] **Have you begun your story at the most opportune moment?** In very short fiction, there is no room for elaborate preambles. Babel begins his story as the Russian army crosses into Poland. Barthelme drops us directly into the life of his wacky, dysfunctional family. Allen's cocktail party has already begun; the characters are in the midst of their conversation. In general, you will want to start your story as *late* in the narrative as possible. The conflict and tension should already be present in the situation: you just need to put your characters down in the midst of it.

- [ ] **Is the story's conflict immediately clear?** You may think that a story about a man wandering up and down the city streets contemplating the meaning of life will impress your readers with its profundity. Think again. The "navel-gazing narrator" is usually a bore. Too often he or she is simply an excuse to keep you, the author, from delving into more emotionally troubling, but far more interesting, material. Your reader should be able to answer the crucial question "Where's the trouble?" by the end of the first page—at the very latest. It's not impossible to write a story in which a character is in conflict only with his or her environment, but it's much easier to bring two people into conflict. Someone wants something, but a second person is in the way. It is the oldest plot formula in the world—which means that it has been working for millennia.

☐ **Does some significant change occur during the course of your story?** Short-shorts operate on truncated principles, so there isn't time for the extended rising action of a novel or a long story. Still, there must be movement in your story. Maybe your protagonist, like the young man in "Marzipan," suffers a sudden lapse of self-confidence. Perhaps, like the narrator of "The Baby," he significantly modifies his own beliefs. Or maybe, like the narrator of "Crossing the River Zbrucz," he encounters some aspect of the world so chilling that it stuns him into silence. Your characters might succeed, or they might fail, in facing the challenges in front of them, but at the end of the story, they should be different than they were when it began.

☐ **Does your story end at the best possible place?** You may feel that your story requires a sentence or two of tying things up, as in the short-shorts by Barthelme and Allen. Or you may follow the example of Babel and stop at the point of maximum impact. You don't want to end before your conflict has played itself out, but don't hang around too long after the climax. Consider deleting the last paragraph or two of your first draft. Leave it to your reader to puzzle out the meaning of your story.

Creating characters ▶

The convoluted plots of horror tales, romances, and espionage thrillers don't work well in the short-short story. But if your story doesn't re-create the twists and turns of your favorite movie or genre novel, what will be its focus? In all likelihood, the answer is your characters.

If we catch glimpses of real human beings in your main characters, we are more likely to connect with them, to understand and sympathize with them—even if they are engaged in activities that we do not approve of. From Odysseus to Emma Bovary to Holden Caulfield, readers have always cherished the imperfect yet vividly rendered protagonist, and contemporary short stories tend to succeed or fail according to the believability of their fictional inhabitants. Therefore, one of your chief jobs is to create characters that readers will find authentic. But how?

First, experienced readers of fiction will expect your characters to show both their good and bad sides. Since everyone, alas, is flawed, a character who is perfect is also implausible. An imperfect character is more likely to be **round**, or **three-dimensional**. According to E. M. Forster, such a character is someone whom we can credit with actually being alive. "The test of a round character," Forster says, "is that it is capable of surprising in a convincing way." Not only must the character startle us with a behavior or comment we weren't expecting, but she or he must do so "in a convincing way."

The surprise at the end must be prepared for earlier in the story, and we can see this authorial groundwork in "Marzipan." The young man is initially described as "haughty," with a "mocking smile." Yet although he seems somewhat pompous, there are hints that he is unsure of himself: "His every move seems mannered, artificial; he plays a role." If confidence doesn't come naturally to him, there must be some reason. When, at the end of the story, he bursts out with the revelation about his mother's suicide, his shaky attempts at sophistication and savoir-faire are shown to have been nothing more than the empty boasting of an insecure person.

Forster contrasts round characters with **flat**, or **two-dimensional, characters**. Flat characters are caricatures, incapable of surprise or complexity, yet they are often necessary as plot devices that throw the three-dimensional characters into greater relief. Forster says that in "their purest form, they are constructed around a single idea or quality: when there is more than one factor in them, we get the beginning of the curve towards the round." The two red-haired men in "Crossing the River Zbrucz" who help the woman clean up after their home has been ransacked are flat characters. The narrator says that they "hop around in silence, like monkeys, like Japanese acrobats in a circus." Their primary function in the story seems to be to disguise the fact that the third man in the room is dead and to highlight the more three-dimensional daughter, whose passionate denunciation of the men who killed her father is "the beginning of the curve towards the round."

"Fiction is about trouble," says Rick DeMarinis. "Trouble is a direct consequence of desire. Characters are living embodiments of desire. A character without desire is immobilized." Obviously, troubled people are more likely to find themselves in trouble, and as you consider which characters will star in your short-short, you should think first of people whose lives are in turmoil. We may love being in the company of that sunshiny person whose every decision seems blessed and who has a correspondingly optimistic vision of the world. Unfortunately, people like that tend to make poor protagonists for a story. Think instead of individuals you avoid because they make embarrassing comments in restaurants, or have a habit of choosing the wrong partners, or always start fights at family reunions. Memorable characters are often based on people the writer knows who don't always do the right thing and suffer the consequences as a result.

Authors frequently speak of their characters as though they were real human beings rather than just fictional constructs, and in a sense that's understandable. Nearly always, we draw on our own lives or the lives of people we have met to create characters. In fact, the desire to put ourselves in a story, to render friends, relatives, lovers, and acquaintances on paper, is what compels many writers to write in the first place, and, not surprisingly, good fiction writers are usually good people watchers: they remember little tics of speech, characteristic gestures, details of face and dress. If, for instance, you can capture in a story your aunt Consuela's odd scent of rosewater and freshly baked bread and sweat, or your first boyfriend's habit of wetting his little finger before he smoothed down his eyebrows, you are well on your way to creating vividly rendered characters.

One common misperception new writers have is that characters based on real people must be as close to those individuals as the writer can make them. That is not the case, especially if your protagonist resembles yourself. When you create characters, invention is at least as important as including (auto)biographical details. As Grace Paley reminds us, even if your characters are based on real people, once they inhabit your fictional world, "you don't really know them, so you're going to start inventing right away." A piece of dialogue you heard last night will find its way into a character's mouth. A trip you took to the Grand Canyon a year ago suddenly seems just the sort of vacation your character ought to be thinking about at the top of page two. Everything you have ever seen or heard or done is potential material for character development. The well is deeper than you know: dip into it.

Most convincing fictional creations are composites of ourselves and our friends, family, and acquaintances. When you create an amalgamation of several real people, you can bring in the most interesting aspects of each one. If you combine your mother's need to wash and put away every dish before she goes to bed, your father's love of old issues of *National Geographic*, your own fondness for Sonic Youth, and your little sister's habit of beginning every other sentence with "I was all like . . . ," things start to get interesting.

Not only do composite characters make the people in your story more believable, but they also give you license to go beyond "what really happened," to take your characters in more intriguing directions than those normally provided by real life. Moreover, composite characters get you off the hook from the accusation every writer fears hearing from a friend or relative: the person in your story is *exactly* like me!

However your characters come into being, you must be able to see the world through their eyes. "Each character needs to be real to me," says Sue Miller. "I inhabit each of them. I try to give them my sympathy, even the ones I don't like very well: to understand why they are as they are, what they do to make what they do defensible to them." This is crucial: the less appealing a character is, the more she or he requires the *possibility* of redemption. If your protagonist is an unloving stepmother, for example, what is there about her own life that made her that way? You won't have time to give a detailed personal history, but you can hint at the origins of a character's defects. Readers of a short-short won't be expecting characters as nuanced as David Copperfield or Anna Karenina, but they will be looking for a suggestion of complexity: the well-thumbed black-and-white photo of her own mother that the stepmother carries in her purse; the offhand remark she makes about being struck by her father that time she forgot to bring in the clothes from the clothesline before a big storm.

When you begin your story, you may well figure that it's best to get all the characterization out of the way in the first paragraph or two so that you can get down to the story itself. You might, for example, write:

> Jezebel Johnson was five feet seven inches tall, weighed 130 pounds, and had hair dyed the color of ripe peaches. Smart and lively, she had a lacerating wit but crummy taste in men. Jezebel's parents had divorced when she was eight, and she always blamed that traumatic event on her propensity to be either hopelessly romantic or wildly cynical about love. There was no in between as far as Jezebel was concerned: you were either drowning in a sea of hearts and violins, or looking down on the ocean of love from a very high cliff with a bad taste in your mouth. Jezebel's weakness was handsome slackers who reminded her of her father. She was always falling for them at the worst possible time. Sleepy-eyed, unshaven Harvard Koonin was just the latest in a long line of bad choices.

In addition to being a pile-up of clichés, this description tries to do all the work of characterization much too fast. Rather than *showing* us Jezebel in action—letting us hear who she is through her conversations with Harvard, or providing us with a flashback to her parents' divorce—we are given the Cliffs-Notes version of characterization.

Developing a convincing character may take the entire length of your story. You know from watching films that we learn about characters by what they do and say, scene by scene, and Stephen Minot reminds us that "in order to maintain the reader's sense of personal discovery, the writer of fiction has to supply a series of little hints, and they have to be slipped in stealthily." In a short-short story, it's all the more important to dole out that information bit by bit: if your reader knows everything at the beginning, there won't be any room for surprise at the end.

Somerset Maugham said, "You can never know enough about your characters." For many writers, getting to know their characters begins with naming them. Because of the short-short's brevity, characters are less likely to be named than in longer works of fiction, but whether you call someone "the young man" or Edgar, you should have a sound reason for doing so. As you consider names, don't just use the first one that pops into your head. A name's **connotation** is important, and you ignore these associations and related meanings at your peril. Jezebel Johnson, the creation above, has an awful name. It may be memorable, but what contemporary parents would christen their child after the wicked queen in the Bible who was thrown out of a window and eaten by dogs? Simply giving someone the name Jezebel makes her less believable as a character. (Instead, why not call her Jessie, or Jasmine, or Jules?) Make sure, too, that the names of your main characters aren't easily confused with one another. Generally names in a short-short should not begin with the same letter. Joe and John are not as distinguishable from each other as Joe and Ricardo.

Once you have decided what to call your characters, you will realize that there is still quite a lot about them that you don't know. We have mentioned Hemingway's "iceberg theory of character," which Kim Edwards summarizes as "the idea . . . that what's unstated must nonetheless exist clearly in the author's mind for a character to have sufficient depth." Novelists and writers of extended stories frequently write many pages of notes about their characters. They jot down everything from their characters' heights, weights, birthplaces, and dates of birth to their current addresses and their biggest dreams and fears. Short-short stories may reveal only the tip of the iceberg, but that's all the more reason for you to have a clear sense of who your characters are so that you can convey their personalities in just a few well-chosen words.

The following questions will help you think more thoroughly about your main characters. This is just a start, though. To delve more deeply, you'll want to make up your own questions and answer them in some detail.

▶ Where were they born?
▶ How old are they?
▶ What do they look like (for example, their race and ethnicity, height, weight, eye and hair color, and other physical characteristics)?
▶ What type of music and movies do they like?
▶ What jobs do they have?
▶ How do they get to work?
▶ What are their biggest dreams? Greatest fears?
▶ What do they want more than anything else in the world?

Spending fifteen or twenty minutes brainstorming about each of your central characters may save you a great deal of time later on. As you decide whether your protagonist was born in São Paulo, Brazil, or Santa Fe, New Mexico, whether she listens to Bob Marley or Franz Schubert, whether she commutes in a Porsche 911 Carrera S Cabriolet or on the city bus, and whether she works as a corporate lawyer or a salesclerk at The Gap, you begin to make her come alive, to distinguish this *particular* character from all the other people about whom you might have written.

Even though much of this material may never wind up in your story, going through the process helps you gain a clearer sense of who your characters are. As you begin to write, your character profile will serve as a biographical reference point, a summary that will help guide your decisions about a character's appearance, speech, actions, and motivations.

A word of caution: Although it's good to be concrete and detailed when describing your characters, it's also possible to be *too specific*. Suppose Alberto glances at someone he has never seen before and then describes that person as "six feet two and a half inches and 342 pounds." It's much more likely that the character doing the observing would register something along the lines of "over six feet and nearly 350 pounds." Unless Alberto works for the FBI or guesses heights and weights for a carnival, don't give him greater powers of observation than most of us possess.

In general, though, as Dan Chaon remarks, "The more you have [characters] observe things, the more you get to know them." What characters do or don't notice makes them who they are. In the opening paragraph of "Crossing the River Zbrucz," for instance, the narrator seems to have the cool, detached perspective of a military officer, yet he also takes time to describe the natural beauty of the setting in some detail. This appreciation of the region's beauty makes him seem more likable. However, when he enters the home of his hosts later on, he notices only "ransacked closets, torn pieces of women's fur coats on the floor, human excrement, and fragments of the holy Seder plate that the Jews use once a year for Passover." Rather than feeling sympathy for the plight of these people, he becomes furious. "Clean up this mess!" he shouts. "How can you live like this?" Perhaps his anger is a measure of his insensitivity, or maybe he is just masking the guilt he feels at intruding on such a devastated family. Either way, what he doesn't initially register is the corpse on the floor. All he sees is "a third Jew who is sleeping with his face to the wall and a blanket pulled over his head." When that sleeping person is revealed to be a bloody and mutilated body, we understand that the narrator has been psychologically damaged by war: even though he may be able to wax poetic about "flowery hillocks," he is incapable of seeing something horrible right at his own feet.

If Babel's protagonist is ultimately unsympathetic, he nevertheless seems real to us because his observations show him to be a round character. He may act like a tactless bully, but he is not entirely bad. Even the biggest fictional villains normally have some traits that make them seem human, and your job is to find a moment or moments when you can catch those people in a more sympathetic light. Robin Hemley says of "bad, immoral, selfish, mean, or obnoxious" characters: "You must make us care about them. You must make them capable of change, whether they, in fact, *do* change, or at least you should intimate that they were not always as low-down as they appear now."

That possibility of change is crucial. For many readers, the essence of a short story is a notable transformation in one or more main characters, although that alteration doesn't have to be life-changing or even noticeable to a casual observer. Jerome Stern points out that "change usually means psychological change—realization, revelation, revision, epiphany, understanding, decision." In other words, you don't have to shoot your characters to make them realize the error of their ways. In fact, it's usually a bad idea to make something *too* drastic happen to a character in short fiction. Big, dramatic events—explosions and tornadoes and earthquakes—typically require many pages of setup, and you don't have that luxury in a short-short. Instead, think small: it's better to have someone slapped on the cheek than blown away by an Uzi.

The change, modest or otherwise, that occurs in the main characters of two of the three model stories is partially a matter of guesswork on our part, since in a short-short we don't normally see the extended effects of a character's actions or encounters. We don't know how the narrator of "Crossing the River Zbrucz" responds to the revelation that the old man he had thought was sleeping in a corner is actually dead, or what he thinks of the daughter's pronouncement that "I want you to tell me where one could find another father like my father in all the world!" Yet we can surmise that this information has at least as much of an impact on the narrator as it does on us.

Like Babel, Allen knows better than to conclude her story with a pronouncement about how profoundly different her characters are after their encounter with each other. The young man's revelation in "Marzipan" may have taught the young woman how much people hide beneath the surface of their apparently confident exteriors. Or she may quickly forget the awkward moment as she moves on to look for someone else willing to flatter her. Similarly, we can't be sure if the protagonist will be miserable for weeks after his encounter with the girl, or if he will go on the prowl for someone else.

Only the preposterously comic narrator of "The Baby," who decides to smash car windows with his infant daughter rather than punish her, shows a marked change, but the exaggerated nature of his about-face is in keeping with the overall absurdist tone of the story.

Finally, be wary of nonhuman characters, especially nonhuman narrators. You may think that telling a story from the point of view of a housefly or juniper bush is extremely clever, but chances are your instructor won't agree. Of course, great writers have given us everything from a person who has been transformed into an insect, in Franz Kafka's "The Metamorphosis," to the dog who narrates Paul Auster's *Timbuktu*, but the risk of ending up sounding supremely silly is very real. Stick with people when you write your story: unless you are a horse whisperer or have a very clear memory of your previous life as a snail, human beings are what you know best.

CHECKLIST Creating characters

☐ **Do you know your main characters and their desires well?** You should have a strong sense of who your characters are, where they have been, and where they live. You, and your readers, should be able to quickly identify the driving forces that make them act: what they want and what they're prepared to do to get it.

☐ **Does your story show us only the *essential* aspects of your characters?** While it's important that you know your characters thoroughly, you will be revealing only a tiny sliver of that information on the page. Show your characters being themselves, only more so. Whatever conflict they are involved in should bring out a heightened sense of who they really are.

☐ **Can you eliminate any characters? Or can you combine two or more characters into a single character?** In general, a short-short can handle only three main characters. If you need more people to complete the action of your story, try to combine several characters into one. Remember that unless someone serves simply to move things forward, characters should be as complex as possible.

☐ **Is your description of each character appropriate to, and necessary for, that character's function in the story?** You should always have a clear mental picture of your characters. However, because there is so little room to maneuver in the short-short, each piece of description you use in the story must be very carefully chosen. Is it really important for your reader to know that a character is 165 pounds and five feet nine and a half inches tall, or can you just say "medium weight and height"? And do weight and height, or eye and hair color, matter at all in your particular story? Unless some physical aspect of your character is essential to her or his personality as it emerges in your story, leave out the description.

☐ **Are the characters' names appropriate?** In a short story, having too many people with similar-sounding names can be confusing. If Stan wishes Steve would just leave him alone and pick on Stewart or Sterling instead, we're likely to forget who is who. It is better to have Luis square off with Tobias, or have Leticia face down Phuong.

☐ **Do your characters need to be named at all?** One option is to forgo names altogether. None of the characters in any of the three model stories are named, possibly because naming them might distract a reader from the characters' main actions. Whatever you decide to do with your protagonists and **antagonists**—the protagonists' opponents or adversaries—you should avoid naming minor characters in short fiction. For instance, if a busboy at a restaurant comes to clear the table where the two main characters are having a conversation, do we really need to know that his name is Cumbert Wilson-Smith? Especially if Cumbert never makes another appearance in the story, it's better to keep him and other minor characters anonymous so that they don't distract our focus from what is really important.

☐ **Are your main characters different at the end of the story than they were in the beginning?** As Joyce Carol Oates reminds us, in short-shorts, "the smallest, tightest places, experience can only be suggested," but even that suggestion of a character's experience must somehow alter from the first page to the last. Remember that convincing fictional characters are both consistent and surprising. Reread the opening and concluding sections of your story. Do you see a difference in how your protagonist began and how he or she ends?

Writing dialogue ▶

Dialogue is what the people in your story say to one another. Some stories, like "Marzipan," make extensive use of dialogue; others, like "The Baby," contain little or no conversation between characters. Dialogue may not be mandatory, but when it is employed skillfully, it can bring a story to life. Good dialogue contributes to character, introduces backstory, and advances plot. It adds an immediacy to fiction, and crafting it can be a great deal of fun.

Indeed, fiction writers seem to love talking about dialogue almost as much as they love writing it, so there is no shortage of advice on this element of storytelling. "Dialogue should do two things," says Melanie Bishop. "It should sound like people talking minus the *umms* and stumbling, and it should move your story forward." Rick DeMarinis reinforces the idea that although "dialogue must have all the spontaneity of real-life speech, it is in fact nothing like real-life speech. It is a carefully timed give-and-take: a slow dance, a brisk sparring session, or a merciless pummeling. It is carefully and artfully crafted." In other words, dialogue should be an integral part of your story, not just an opportunity for your characters to open their mouths and yap about the weather.

Roberta Allen says that it may be acceptable to use "bad grammar or sentence fragments" to suggest a character's way of speaking but cautions that if the character is long-winded, "you'd do best to make it concise and give the reader the *flavor* of the words without using lengthy sentences. Dialogue must reveal something that the reader needs to know."

The great Irish writer Elizabeth Bowen had this to say about dialogue:

1. Dialogue should be brief.

2. It should add to the reader's knowledge.

3. It should eliminate the routine exchanges of ordinary conversation.

4. It should convey a sense of spontaneity but eliminate the repetitiveness of real talk.

5. It should keep the story moving forward.

6. It should be revelatory to the speaker's character, both directly and indirectly.

7. It should show the relationships among people.

Of course, like any other advice, we can take this with a grain of salt. Writers like Ernest Hemingway, some of whose stories consist almost entirely of dialogue, would be ill served by Bowen's first rule. Still, Bowen was a master of the short story, and overall her advice is sound, particularly for writers of short-shorts, in which everything must be brief. Even when your story is composed *mostly* of dialogue, if that dialogue is to be effective, it should adhere to *most* of Bowen's suggestions.

Fortunately, American students tend to be good writers of dialogue. Ours is such an oral culture that we have an advantage in transcribing the rhythms, the oddities, and the offhanded nature of real speech. Many students find that dialogue comes as naturally to them as it does to Dorothy Allison: "When I hear a character talking, literally, it's like they are dictating and I'm taking it down."

A good way to develop your inborn gift for dialogue is to sit in a crowded place where you don't know anyone—a coffee shop, say, or a mall—and try to write down what you hear people saying. You will quickly notice that people rarely speak in complete, grammatically perfect sentences. We repeat ourselves. We start sentences that we don't finish, and we interrupt other people to finish their sentences. If Amy Bloom is correct in calling good fictional dialogue "conversation's greatest hits," conversation by real people usually consists of outtakes that have no reason to be preserved. Most authors enjoy the process of sifting through the dreck and setting aside the good bits, and writing dialogue can become quite addictive. Once you get the knack for doing it, you will find yourself listening in on all sorts of conversations, extracting those moments that might best serve your creative writing. After all, in many respects, what people say reveals who they are.

If you find that the dialogue on the page doesn't sound the way you imagined it would, that may be because you haven't yet mastered the difference between writing and speaking. The first thing to do is get past the censor in your head telling you that all your characters have to sound as though they just walked out of an English essay, complete with perfect grammar and no contractions. In fact, even highly educated people rarely speak as formally as they write, and our conversations usually sound quite different from written language, especially when we're talking with someone we know well.

What about profanity in dialogue? You should turn to your own instructor for guidelines, but most professors of creative writing would probably agree with Daly Walker that "the language must fit the character. If the character is a soldier likely to speak profanity and harbor prejudice, he must speak and think that way on the page. The reader must understand the author is not condoning profanity or prejudice; he's just trying to bring out the truth in his characters."

One of the most important guidelines to remember is that *context dictates dialogue*. Ask yourself: Who is talking to whom? An older person to a younger person? A more powerful character to someone who is in trouble? And where is their conversation taking place? At a club late Saturday night, or in the pew of a church on Sunday morning? The conversation in "Marzipan" between the young man and woman, who apparently were strangers until just before the story begins, would not unfold as it does if they were sitting in the living room of her house with her parents present. Similarly, the narrator's blunt, rude way of speaking to his hosts in "Crossing the River Zbrucz" would be unthinkable if the conversation were taking place on the veranda of a resort hotel rather than in the midst of a battlefield.

Once you start writing dialogue, you can easily get carried away. If your story seems bogged down by *too much* dialogue, look for passages to cut as well as places to pause so that we can "listen" to the characters think or see them act. Even stories with lots of conversation usually provide periodic breathers. "Marzipan" is dialogue heavy, yet Allen breaks it up with brief internal monologues, descriptions, and actions. Consider this moment of commentary, for instance: "As the girl laughs, licks her sticky fingers, and chooses another marzipan morsel, the poet glances at the other guests." Here we are *shown* what the dialogue has been suggesting—that the girl is interested and flirtatious at this moment, while the young man, in contrast, is still looking around the room for better opportunities.

Jerome Stern is right that "what your characters don't say and the way they don't [say it]" is a vital, if often ignored, consideration: "How characters sit or stand is as significant as their spoken sentences. Make your readers hear the pauses between sentences. Let them see characters lean forward, fidget with their cuticles, avert their eyes, uncross their legs." A thoughtful combination of conversation, thought, and action generally works best in short fiction.

The power of direct dialogue can be highlighted by comparing it with indirect or reported dialogue. "The Baby," for example, contains no direct dialogue; instead, we occasionally hear, secondhand, what has already been said. The narrator tells us:

> My wife said that maybe we were being too rigid and that the baby was losing weight. But I pointed out to her that the baby had a long life to live and had to live in a world with others, had to live in a world where there were many, many rules, and if you couldn't learn to play by the rules you were going to be left out in the cold with no character, shunned and ostracized by everyone.

Reported dialogue is appropriate for this story: the narrator is so disconnected from reality, so unaware of other people, that it makes sense that he wouldn't take the time to quote his wife directly. Nevertheless, the dialogue's impact is diminished considerably by being reported. If you really want your readers to experience your characters speaking, you need to use direct dialogue, which means, among other things, following the conventions of printed dialogue.

Dialogue in stories and novels has a special way of appearing on the page. Each time a different speaker begins talking, you indent that person's speech and start a new paragraph. This is an important point, yet one that new writers forget more often than not, so it's worth repeating: each time a new character speaks, that character gets her or his *own paragraph*. This might seem like an unnecessary convention, but it turns out to be a handy one. If there are only two speakers, you don't need to keep tagging them by name once you identify who's who—for instance:

"I've lost him," Carrie said.

Jonathan's throat went dry. "Who?"

"Who do you *think* I'm talking about?"

"You're telling me that you've lost our *son?*"

The dialogue establishes that only Carrie and Jonathan are present, so our minds can easily toggle back and forth between the two, especially since each has a distinct and conflicting point of view. Indeed, many writers would agree with Russell Banks that readers should be able to tell who is speaking even when there are no dialogue tags. A good writer can capture the tone of his character's voices to such an extent that adding "Jonathan said" or "Carrie shouted" is unnecessary.

There are a few other points to remember about the conventions of fictional dialogue:

▸ Commas and periods go *inside* the quotation marks when you are punctuating dialogue. Jim said, "Hi." *Or:* "Hi," Jim said.

▸ When one character addresses another, you need a comma before, or after, or before *and* after the name of the character who is being addressed. "What are you doing, Lindy?" *Or:* "Lindy, you're making me sick!" *Or:* "Hey, Lindy, what's up?"

▸ Paragraphs are always indented *five spaces,* and the beginnings of sentences are always *capitalized.*

New fiction writers sometimes get carried away with the verbs associated with speaking. Characters will *exclaim* or *remonstrate* or *expostulate* or *admonish* instead of just *saying* something. Often novice writers choose the fancier tags because they mistakenly believe that their readers will be bored by a steady diet of the same word. In fact, though, the word "said" or "say" quickly disappears for most readers. Once in a while you might want to make it clear that a character shouts or whispers a remark, but choose your synonyms for "said" judiciously. (Note: You should never use the word "quoted" as a dialogue tag. For example, in the sentence *"I've lost him," Carrie quoted,* the use of "quoted" is incorrect.)

"Dialogue in fiction should be reserved for the culminating moments," Edith Wharton once remarked, and Isaac Babel seems sympathetic to this idea. In "Crossing the River Zbrucz," there is no dialogue during the march into Poland. We begin to hear characters speak only when the officer enters the commandeered house. Even then, dialogue is used sparingly and strategically, and it always conveys information about the character who is speaking. For instance, when the narrator yells "Clean up this mess! . . . How can you live like this?" at the woman whose home he is occupying, we see that he is insensitive to her plight.

A strong statement early in your story can serve as an attention getter. Not only does the pronouncement "I just love marzipan!" help characterize the young woman speaker, it also announces a main theme—desire—in Allen's story. Similarly, ending your story with a passionate, revelatory outburst can be a sound strategy. Babel takes advantage of this tactic in the closing line spoken by the daughter of the dead man: "I want you to tell me where one could find another father like my father in all the world!"

Finally, wherever, whenever, and however you use dialogue, manage it with as much care as you do the other elements of fiction, for good dialogue is likely to prove one of your most useful tools as a storyteller.

CHECKLIST Writing dialogue

☐ **Do you have enough dialogue?** Although new writers often have an apti-
tude for dialogue, they tend to underuse it. Dialogue is fun to read and generally makes a story move faster. One of the easiest ways to follow the creative
writing mantra of "show, don't tell" is through the use of dialogue. Rather
than writing, "Jim was a very rude person," for example, try, "Jim snarled, 'I'd
rather get my gums cleaned than go out on a date with you!'"

☐ **Do you have too much dialogue?** A less common problem in short-shorts
is too much dialogue, but it does happen. Go through your story and look
for places where the conversations are not moving your story forward or are
introducing irrelevant information about your characters.

☐ **Does your dialogue sound like real speech?** One of the quickest ways
to lose a reader is to write dialogue that doesn't sound like the speech we hear
around us all the time. Unless you're writing a period piece set in a nineteenth-
century drawing room, you wouldn't say: "I am unaware of the nature of your
question. I have not received your postal communication." Instead, use more
realistic dialogue: "What are you talking about? I never got your letter." Read
your dialogue aloud. Have someone else read it to you. If something sounds
phony, delete it or make it less formal. Use contractions and sentence fragments. Rough it up.

☐ **Have you clearly, and unobtrusively, tagged all speakers of dialogue?**
It might be tedious for a reader to be continually reminded which of two
people is speaking, but when three or more characters are involved in a conversation, it's possible for the reader (and writer) to get lost. When you have
finished your first draft, reread your dialogue and make certain your reader
doesn't have to waste time untangling who said what to whom. Also, remember that every time a character "expostulates" or "divulges" something rather
than simply says it, your reader will focus on how that statement is being said
rather than the content of the remark.

Setting the scene ▶

Novelist Richard Russo says, "In the end, the only compelling reason to pay more attention to place, to exterior setting, is the belief, the faith, that place and its people are intertwined, that place is character, and that to know the rhythms, the textures, the feel of a place is to know more deeply and truly its people." Robin Hemley agrees: "Any description of place should . . . be anchored within a character's consciousness, and say as much about the character as it does about the place."

In other words, although setting is important for conveying the atmosphere of a story, its primary function is to highlight the characters and their conflicts. Setting is the place where your story is set (a high school gymnasium in West Texas), as well as the time (late afternoon in the year 1947). As you begin thinking about the setting for your own story, choose a time and place that fit its focus. If, for instance, your story involves two brothers who have always despised and resented each other, it makes more sense to put them in an enclosed atmosphere—for example, at midnight in the cold, damp bedroom they shared as boys rather than in a sunny meadow on a summer day. More than likely, as in the scenario just described, your characters will suggest setting rather than the other way around, and in most stories, as Russo and Hemley advise, the focus will remain on people rather than place.

It *is* important, though, for you to have a strong sense of where and when your story occurs. Does the brothers' old room still contain their childhood dresser, nicked and scraped from some of their battles? Does their window look out on a dreary field? Or a trailer park in the rain? If your story takes place in one or two main locales, you might even sketch out a map or floor plan. Where is the front door located? How long does it take to get there from the kitchen? This may sound trivial, but if it takes a character half an hour to walk across a room, your reader will begin to doubt not just the reality of the setting but also the truth of the rest of your story.

Although you need to have a clear picture of the setting, how much of that information you decide to share with your reader depends on the nature of your story. Some narratives require a great deal of description, while too much setting will grind other stories to a halt. Either way, be wary of piling on any more details than are absolutely necessary for the integrity of your story, especially in the short-short.

Each of the three model stories uses setting appropriately, although in different ways. An extended description of time and place is most crucial to Isaac Babel's "Crossing the River Zbrucz." Unlike Donald Barthelme and Roberta Allen, Babel actually tells us where we are: the border region between Russia and Poland. He doesn't, however, turn the story into a geography lesson. Today's readers of the story, even if they have no footnotes to rely on, can locate

Novograd-Volynsk and Krapivno—the places named in the opening paragraph—with a quick Internet search. Of course, for Babel's first group of readers, Russians in the 1920s, Novograd-Volynsk and Krapivno would have been as familiar as Afghanistan and Baghdad are to Americans at the beginning of the twenty-first century. In addition to establishing the locale for those who are interested, the casual way Babel drops place names into the story establishes the narrator's authority: we believe, especially after reading the rest of the story, that this is someone who has been to the area he describes. In any case, even if we have no idea where the road "from Brest to Warsaw" is, we know the important fact that it was "built on the bones of muzhiks," or peasants.

This rather grim bit of information is followed by a sketch of the countryside that initially seems quite romantic: "Fields of purple poppies are blossoming around us, a noon breeze is frolicking in the yellowing rye, virginal buckwheat is standing on the horizon like the wall of a faraway monastery. Silent Volhynia is turning away, Volhynia is leaving, heading into the pearly white fog of the birch groves, creeping through the flowery hillocks, and with weakened arms entangling itself in the underbrush of hops." *Wow,* the reader may be thinking, *even if Volhynia is an impoverished region in the middle of a war, the place certainly is beautiful.* Of course, that's just what Babel wants us to think because in the following sentence, he gives us a simile that entirely demolishes the bucolic picture he has just been painting: "The orange sun is rolling across the sky like a severed head."

Babel continues this technique of alternately describing the bleak and the beautiful in the second half of the paragraph. While the "gentle light glimmers in the ravines among the clouds," the "stench of yesterday's blood and slaughtered horses drips into the evening chill." The River Zbrucz is itself both lovely and awful. "The majestic moon lies on the waves" created by "the foaming knots of its rapids," yet all the "bridges are destroyed," and the river seems almost to be attacking the people who are trying to wade across it: "Someone sinks, and loudly curses the Mother of God." When Babel describes the stench coming from the Zbrucz and, later, the cold, rushing river, the images of smell and touch offer further evidence about the setting. Normally we think of imagery as referring to vivid visual descriptions, but if you draw on all five of the senses as you write, you will help your reader fully inhabit a scene.

The tiny world of the second paragraph is created in ten sentences. It's an amazing feat of description, and Babel accomplishes it because he uses *specific details* ("fields of purple poppies" and "yellowing rye, virginal buckwheat") rather than generalities (flowers and crops). We see further examples of his descriptive expertise in his account of the home where the narrator is quartered, which has already been plundered by the Polish army: "I find ransacked closets, torn pieces of women's fur coats on the floor, human excrement, and fragments of the holy Seder plate that the Jews use once a year for Passover." Again, the details bring the scene to life. The torn fur coats suggest that the family was well off before the war, yet now their home is covered in excrement. And the detail of the shattered Seder plate is a symbol that indicates something of what has happened to Jewish people in this conflict: they and their religion have come under attack from both sides.

Babel's final descriptive coup comes when he reveals that the man the protagonist thought was sleeping is actually dead: "His gullet has been ripped out, his face hacked in two, and dark blood is clinging to his beard like a clump of lead." It's a gruesome, unforgettable depiction of a brutal murder, one we are unlikely to forget, and it makes a powerful statement: no good can come from war. Yet this sentence of description is far more eloquent and compelling than if the author had come out and baldly declared his opinion. As in poetry, one good image is worth a passel of words.

Donald Barthelme can be quite skilled at describing setting—his well-known story "The Balloon" is just one excellent example—but he apparently decided that emphasizing a specific time and place would detract from the overall effect of "The Baby," so we learn what little we know about the setting of the story through incidental details the narrator lets drop. With no textual assertions in the story to the contrary, a contemporary American audience will probably assume that the time is the present and that the place is somewhere in the United States. The story appears to be set in a home or an apartment, or at least someplace where the baby has a room, but what the place looks like is left mostly to our own imaginations.

The closest thing to a conventional description of setting comes when the narrator tells us why his daughter should be happy spending so many hours in her solitary time-outs: "Her room was very nice, with a nice wooden rocking horse and practically a hundred dolls and stuffed animals. Lots of things to do in that room if you used your time wisely, puzzles and things." Even in this quick sketch, the author *does* provide us with some information about the family's economic status: they must be at least middle class if they are able to afford a wooden rocking horse and all those dolls and stuffed animals for their only child. And while the careless tone of those two sentences may lead us to read through them quickly, they not only give us a glimpse of the baby's room but also tell us a great deal about the narrator's character. For one thing, he doesn't pay much attention to detail. There are "practically a hundred dolls and stuffed animals," but we have no real notion of exactly how many there are or what they look like. His casualness also points to what, in another story, would be an enormous character flaw: he has no idea of how to raise a child. Who could possibly consider locking up his small child an appropriate punishment for tearing out the pages of books? (Incidentally, what in the world is a baby going to do with a puzzle?)

As is the case with "The Baby," setting in Roberta Allen's "Marzipan" is implied more than stated, but it does have a material effect on the characters. After all, a party is a setting in which we too often say things we don't mean to say. Presumably the young man would not have revealed the information about his mother's suicide had he and the young woman been talking at a meeting of the chess club. Yet other than telling us we are at a party where marzipan (as well as alcohol, presumably) is being served, Allen doesn't give us a great deal of information about the setting of her story. Ironically, the few references to the details of a specific setting are found in the young man's anecdotes about Balzac in Paris and the people of Malta eating their domestic animals. He seems to live more vividly through storytelling than he does in his own life.

One of the sharpest descriptions of an event that actually takes place in the time frame of the story occurs when we learn that marzipan was the delicacy his late mother favored. Setting provides the reason for the young man's painful revelation: his mother loved the "almond-flavored sweet," and watching the young woman eat it has reminded him of his mother's death. As Allen evokes both the sharp tang of almonds and the sweetness of candy, we find ourselves connecting, at least through the sense of taste, with the story's characters.

CHECKLIST Setting the scene

- ☐ **Is the description of place and time appropriate to your particular story?** Some stories, such as "Crossing the River Zbrucz," need lots of detail. Others, such as "The Baby," work well without those specifics. Check your story for spots that seem blank or blurry (add more details) or cluttered and jumbled (eliminate unnecessary information). Remember that the simple fact of naming or not naming a location—Walmart versus "a large retail store," or Chicago versus "a large city"—may affect the level of detail you need to include in your story.

- ☐ **Is your description of real places accurate?** Chicago is a great city in which to set a story, but do you really want to put your story there if you have never even visited the place? Be especially wary of using landmarks and details in a way that will strike a false note with people who do know the city. Before heading to London, try looking closer to home for your setting. For readers who have lived their entire lives in large metropolitan areas, Chadron, Nebraska, will be as foreign and exotic as Timbuktu.

- ☐ **If you're certain that your story has to be set in another time or place, have you done sufficient research to make the setting believable?** Novelists usually do a great deal of research when working up background material for their books. Fortunately, as the writer of a short-short, your task is considerably easier. What you're looking for is a handful of details that will be accurate, out of the ordinary, and absolutely right for your story.

- ☐ **If your story is set in an imaginary time and place, are there enough concrete details to make it convincing?** In the introduction to this chapter, we addressed some of the risks of writing genre fiction in a creative writing class; your instructor may have discussed this issue, too.

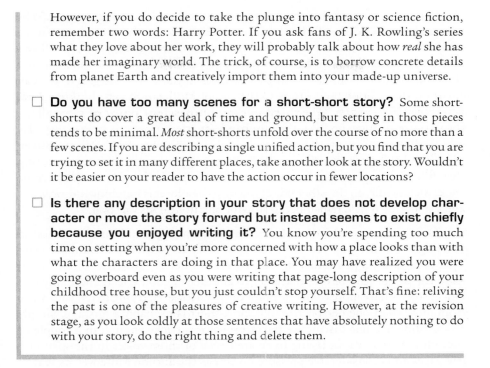

However, if you do decide to take the plunge into fantasy or science fiction, remember two words: Harry Potter. If you ask fans of J. K. Rowling's series what they love about her work, they will probably talk about how *real* she has made her imaginary world. The trick, of course, is to borrow concrete details from planet Earth and creatively import them into your made-up universe.

☐ **Do you have too many scenes for a short-short story?** Some short-shorts do cover a great deal of time and ground, but setting in those pieces tends to be minimal. *Most* short-shorts unfold over the course of no more than a few scenes. If you are describing a single unified action, but you find that you are trying to set it in many different places, take another look at the story. Wouldn't it be easier on your reader to have the action occur in fewer locations?

☐ **Is there any description in your story that does not develop character or move the story forward but instead seems to exist chiefly because you enjoyed writing it?** You know you're spending too much time on setting when you're more concerned with how a place looks than with what the characters are doing in that place. You may have realized you were going overboard even as you were writing that page-long description of your childhood tree house, but you just couldn't stop yourself. That's fine: reliving the past is one of the pleasures of creative writing. However, at the revision stage, as you look coldly at those sentences that have absolutely nothing to do with your story, do the right thing and delete them.

Deciding on point of view, developing tone and style ▶

Antonya Nelson has a test for deciding on the point of view—the narrative perpective from which to tell a story. She asks herself, "Who should be telling the story and why at this particular moment?" Once Nelson has answered those questions, "which sound like simple decisions—but are not at all simple—the stories tend to have their own tone and setting and sense of movement." In short, choosing your narrator is one of the most important decisions you will make about your story.

If you have already begun writing, you may not have consciously realized that you were forced to adopt a point of view the moment you began. Telling your story from one perspective rather than another may seem like a "natural" decision, but it is always worth considering your options, even if you have already completed a draft. Selecting one point of view over another may be the difference between a successful story and a failed one.

There are four main narrative points of view in fiction. The **first-person point of view** is told from the perspective of a character who is participating—sometimes centrally, sometimes more peripherally—in the action of the story:

"I get in the car, turn on the ignition, and drive to the end of Mulligan Street." The **second-person point of view** requires the *reader* to become a character in the story: "You get in the car, turn on the ignition, and drive to the end of Mulligan Street." The **third-person limited point of view** looks over the shoulder, and sometimes into the mind, of a single character in the story: "He gets in the car, turns on the ignition, and drives to the end of Mulligan Street, thinking, *I will never come this way again.*" The **third-person omniscient point of view** allows the narrator to enter, godlike, the mind and situation of anyone in the story. "He gets in the car, turns on the ignition, and drives to the end of Mulligan Street, thinking, *I will never come this way again.* Standing in the driveway, remembering their first night together in that motel near Myrtle Beach, she mutters, 'Don't come back.' Meanwhile, on the other side of town, his new lover is watching *American Idol* and wondering if he'll remember to stop for burritos on his way over."

As we will see, each point of view has its advantages and disadvantages, so you might wonder why you can't tell your story from multiple points of view. That is certainly a possibility in longer works of fiction. Novelists often switch from the perspective of one character to another to good effect, and many fine longer stories have more than one point of view. However, trying to tell your story from more than one perspective in a short-short is probably a mistake. Simply establishing a single distinctive narrative voice is tricky enough in a couple of thousand words or less; trying to create *several* of those voices in the span of a few pages adds considerable pressure on you as the author. Moreover, as Wayne Booth notes in *The Rhetoric of Fiction*, shifting point of view midstory destroys the illusion of a real world and reminds readers that an author is involved in the storytelling process. No less an authority than Flannery O'Connor tells us: "If you violate the point of view you destroy the sense of reality and louse yourself up generally."

First-person point of view

Patricia Hampl believes that "the American consciousness is most congenial in the presence of the first-person voice. Not because we're egotistical, but because, for good or ill, we did predicate this nation based on individuality." And Sue Miller says that "the first person is more propulsive, and more immediately seductive to a reader." Both writers suggest one of the main appeals of the first-person point of view: the energy and urgency of the narrator's voice. First-person narrators are part of the action. Being on the scene gives them a special author-ity to tell the story. "*I* did this . . . ," they can say, or "*I* saw that . . . ," and generally we give credence to such claims.

Of course, not all narrators are reliable. They may declare that they have done or seen something that is a complete fabrication. However, that uncertainty between what's real and what's not sometimes makes first-person narrators all the more interesting. First-person narrators often tell us as much about *themselves* as they do about the story they are relating, and, like police detectives listening to a potentially biased witness, we must decide just how far to trust the narrator.

Both Isaac Babel and Donald Barthelme employ first-person narrators with very subjective points of view. As the biographical note to "Crossing the River Zbrucz" indicates, Babel was Jewish, unlike his pitiless narrator. Yet Babel *did* serve in the Russian army, so he is also drawing on personal experiences to make his story seem authentic. Similarly, Donald Barthelme was indeed the father of a daughter, which means that his story's premise—a child's propensity for tearing up her books—may have come from real life. However, the exaggerated nature of the father's response clearly fictionalizes that real first-person experience.

These examples demonstrate that while you may want to draw on your own life for first-person narration, it's important to remember that you are writing a *story*, not an essay. Don't waste time trying to justify your narrator's behavior; instead, let him or her act in whatever way your story dictates. Seasoned writers will tell you that even when your narrator is based on someone very much like yourself, you still need the freedom to morph that narrator into someone other than the person you really are. Just about any character you create is bound to have elements of you blended in, but when you're beginning to write fiction, it helps to have the extra perspective that comes from stepping outside yourself. There's something liberating about pretending to be someone else, and often it is through "inhabiting" (to use Sue Miller's word) the lives of other people that we really come to understand ourselves.

Frederick Reiken identifies another potential problem of the first-person point of view: "In crossing the line and having a protagonist act essentially as a stand-in for the author, the reader often winds up being asked to become complicit with whatever the character is involved in." If your narrator is doing something readers find particularly loathsome—selling drugs, say, or beating up little kids—those readers will distance themselves from the story in a way that they would not if they were merely looking over the character's shoulder rather than being, as John Gardner puts it, "locked . . . in one character's mind."

Second-person point of view

The second-person point of view is essentially a "command form" of narrative. The writer tells the reader: "You do this" or "You went there." This point of view is relatively rare in fiction writing; however, because the short-short relies so much on surprise, its unusual perspective is an alternative worth considering.

None of the stories in this book are written in the second person, but you can find effective use of this point of view in Lorrie Moore's story collection *Self-Help*. Moore calls her version "second-person, mock imperative," and she uses it, in part, to lampoon self-help books addressed to women. For instance, in "How to Be an Other Woman," a story from that collection, Moore writes: "After four movies, three concerts, and two-and-a-half museums, you sleep with him. It seems the right number of cultural events." This darkly comic touch can also be found in another second-person work of fiction, Jay McInerney's novel *Bright Lights, Big City*, which begins: "You are not the kind of guy who would be at a place like this at this time of the morning. But here you are, and you cannot say that the terrain is entirely unfamiliar, although the details are fuzzy. You are at a nightclub talking to a girl with a shaved head."

Jim Grimsley argues that the second-person voice "gives you exactly the right distance between the narrator and the point-of-view character." Pam Houston, yet another writer who has successfully used the second-person voice, agrees. She believes the second-person narrative point of view has two advantages. It allows the writer to distance herself from her narrator: "The second person takes this layer of shame and washes it over the story without her having to say 'I am ashamed.' It's kind of a diversion—it's not me, it's you." Houston also believes that the second person mimics the way many of us actually speak: "'So, you know, you're in this bar and this guy comes up to you . . .' It's the rhythm of American storytelling."

Given its advantages, you might wonder why the second-person point of view isn't used more often. The answer is that many readers find it annoying and intrusive; they feel as though they are being bossed around or accused of doing something they didn't do. As is the case with an intensely unlikable first-person narrator, your readers may simply stop reading if they can't sympathize with the second-person character they must become in the story.

Third-person limited point of view

Monica Wood has a simple trick for identifying the difference between the third-person omniscient and the third-person limited point of view: "Omniscience works from the outside in: Felix looked like a run-over squirrel. Third-person limited works from the inside out: Felix felt like a run-over squirrel."

Carolyn Chute prefers the third-person limited to the first-person voice because "you can do almost the same stuff . . . but you can get a little bit fancier with the language." Chute believes that the first-person point of view "really limits you in that anything a character wouldn't see you can't talk about, or it will sound too contrived."

Because third-person limited allows you to see both inside the character *and* the world around him or her, this narrative strategy lets the reader make connections before the character does. It's much easier to convey irony with third-person than with first-person, to show how your characters' words and actions don't necessarily correspond with their real desires. The use of third-person limited can be found in most of "Marzipan." Except for a brief excursion into the girl's mind, discussed below, we see the story from the perspective of the male protagonist. We learn that his air of sophistication and casual disinterest is entirely affected: in reality, he is full of self-doubt and haunted by his mother's suicide.

However, with the added flexibility of seeing both through your characters' eyes and over their shoulders comes increased authorial accountability. A first-person narrator who tells his story in a strange way, or leaves out important information, or gets mixed up about details may be doing so because the writer wants the narrator to come across as flaky and confused. Of course, *you* don't want to come across as a flaky and confused writer. Readers are much more forgiving of the eccentricities of a first-person narrator than they are of some-one writing in the third person who appears to have lost control of his story. The third-person limited point of view has distinct advantages as a narrative approach, but using it will test your skills as an author.

Third-person omniscient point of view

The word "omniscient" means "all-knowing," to have infinite awareness of everything. When you write from this point of view, you are able to move, in a godlike fashion, in and out of every character's thoughts. You can jump back and forth in time, and divulge or conceal whatever you please. Sounds tempting, doesn't it?

We get a hint of what the omniscient point of view looks like in "Marzipan" when, in the space of just two sentences, Allen thrusts us straight into the girl's consciousness. The young man has asked her how she stays so thin: "'Metabo-lism I guess. I never gain weight,' she lies. 'What other silly stories can you tell me?' she says to change the subject." It's just a moment, but those two important tags—"she lies" and "she says to change the subject"—give us an insight into this character that we would not have had if the story were being told only from the young man's point of view.

Unfortunately, if you have divine powers as a storyteller, you also have divine responsibilities. In Gustave Flaubert's words: "The artist must be within his work like God within the Creation; invisible and all-powerful; we feel him throughout, but we do not see him." It's quite a daunting task just to maintain a consistent narrative voice—especially if you are a new writer—much less creating a voice that sounds truly "omniscient." Moreover, as Rick DeMarinis warns, the third-person omniscient point of view "is more suited to the novel than it is to the short story." Therefore, third-person omniscience is very rare in the short-short. You don't have the time to go flitting about from one character and scene to another, so it's probably best to avoid this point of view unless you have a truly compelling reason to use it.

Tense

Like choosing a narrative point of view, selecting the verb tense for your story may seem a casual, relatively unimportant decision. The past tense is by far the most common tense for storytelling, and new writers tend to use it as a matter of course. This makes sense: the stories we tell one another have nearly always happened in the past. For most readers, the past tense is "unmarked," that is, they don't notice it one way or the other. Even Barthelme's "The Baby," the least conventional of our three model stories, is told in the past tense, which may suggest how widespread its use is.

For better or worse, the present tense is more conspicuous. It draws readers' attention to the fact that the story is happening *now*, as it is being told. Some writers dislike the present tense because they feel it is too noticeable: it alerts readers to the fact that a narrator is very much behind the telling of the story. Yet the immediacy of the present tense is well suited to the short-short, and both Babel and Allen employ it effectively in their stories.

The future tense is rare, although, as in some of the experimental work of Angus Woodward, it can be used effectively in combination with the second-person point of view. "You will walk down the street and step inside the last phone booth left in the city" is an intriguing way to start a story.

Tone and style

Discussions of point of view and tense inevitably lead to discussions of tone and style. Generally "tone" refers to the mood or atmosphere of a story. "Style" in fiction refers to the author's selection and placement of words in a sentence, sentences in a paragraph, and paragraphs in a story. Stylistic choices are important in creating the tone, and from a writer's perspective, these two elements of fiction writing are practically inseparable.

Each of our three model authors has commented insightfully on style. Isaac Babel wrote, "No iron spike can pierce a human heart as icily as a period in the right place." That's quite a claim, but we see careful attention to every word choice, every mark of punctuation, in "Crossing the River Zbrucz." Donald Barthelme believed that style was "both a response to constraint and a seizing of opportunity. Very often a constraint is an opportunity. . . . Style enables us to speak, to imagine again." We find Barthelme turning a constraint into an opportunity in the way he uses the voice of his narrator. The man is patently unsuitable as a parent, totally unaware of how to care for an infant, yet Barthelme makes the narrator's dim-wittedness the central fun of the story. And Roberta Allen sees effective stylistic choices as vital to the success of the short-short form: "To ensure brevity, short shorts demand greater use of poetic language, words and phrases that connect disparate things, people and events in original and ingenious ways."

"It's all about the sentences," says Rick Moody of Amy Hempel, one of the great contemporary practitioners of the short-short story. "It's about the way the sentences move in the paragraphs. It's about rhythm. It's about ambiguity. It's about the way emotion, in difficult circumstances, gets captured in language." Hempel herself agrees that creating style involves writing good sentences: "Though it's unlikely you'll write something nobody has ever *heard* of, the way you have a chance to compete is in the way you say it."

But how do you write these wonderful sentences? How do you create your own style? The nineteenth-century French novelist Stendahl wrote to his contemporary Honoré de Balzac: "I see but one rule: to be clear. If I am not clear, all my world crumbles to nothing." That's one approach to style—to get things down as close as possible to the way you actually see and imagine them. In the poetry chapter, I advised you to write toward clarity and to revise toward strangeness. That suggestion applies equally well to all creative writing. Your first drafts should be attempts to understand your subject matter, to know your characters and identify their conflicts, to plainly sketch out the world they inhabit. You may be trying to re-create the mind-set of a drug-addled schizophrenic, but if your writing never penetrates beyond your character's haze, it loses clarity. Most literary fiction employs ambiguity in some way, but there is good ambiguity, intentional on the writer's part, and bad ambiguity, which is caused by careless thinking and sloppy writing. Even in a story swirling with doubt about the nature of reality, there will be certain aspects that you *don't* want your reader to misinterpret. At these points, you must be clear so that your world does not "crumble to nothing."

Charles Baxter has this practical stylistic advice: "Cut the adjectives unless you absolutely have to have them. Make sure the verbs are the very best ones you can find. Make them forceful. Make them direct. Make them to the point." Baxter is not alone in his distrust of adjectives. Many creative writing instructors would endorse Mark Twain's famous admonition: "As to the adjective: when in doubt, strike it out." William Zinsser is even more straightforward: "Look for the clutter in your writing and prune it ruthlessly. Be grateful for everything that you can throw away. Re-examine each sentence that you put on paper. Is every word doing new work? Can any thought be expressed with more economy? Is there anything pompous or pretentious or faddish? Are you hanging on to something useless just because you think it's beautiful? Simplify. Simplify."

This need to be precise when revising your work, to evaluate not only every sentence but also every *word,* is a subject writers continually return to when discussing their fiction. Annie Proulx is a big fan of the dictionary: "If I feel a section is limp, [I] take a couple of days and just do dictionary work and recast the sentences so that they have more power because their words aren't overused."

Of course, different stories require different styles. As Richard Lanham says, "A style is a response to a situation." In "Crossing the River Zbrucz," Babel's style moves from the lush passage describing the beauty of the countryside to the curt, brutal sentences about the state of the father's corpse. Even within a single story, style changes when necessary. Barthelme's stylistic emphasis is on the creation of an outrageously memorable narrative voice. Roberta Allen's style, in contrast, is more muted; her language draws less attention to itself, keeping our focus on her characters.

Most writers begin by imitating the work of writers they admire. If you have caught yourself doing this, you may feel a bit guilty. Isn't it wrong to copy? Not necessarily. You have to start somewhere, so imitating writers who seem to be doing something right is a natural first step. If you keep writing long enough, either you will surmount the influence eventually, or you will incorporate elements of the writer's style into your own style. Remember, though, that developing a distinctive individual style is a process that occurs over a long period of time; it generally doesn't happen during a single creative writing course. Once you do find your "voice," you may agree with John Middleton Murry, who says, "The test of a true individuality of style is that we should feel it to be inevitable."

Finally, don't forget that style in fiction means laserlike concentration on every aspect of your writing. "Sloppy style" is an oxymoron, one likely to result in a poor grade for your story. Don't assume that your instructor—or anyone else, for that matter—will do your editing for you. Whether it's your first draft or the finished piece, turn in the very best work you are capable of writing. This means that you must revise, edit, and *proofread*. If you have weak skills in this area, ask a friend who is good at editing to take a look at your story, or consult a tutor in your campus's writing center.

CHECKLIST Deciding on point of view, developing tone and style

- ☐ **Have you given careful thought to the question "Who should be telling this story and why at this particular moment?"** Figuring out when, where, why, and by whom a story is being told influences the story's ultimate success. Even though the first narrative point of view that occurs to you may turn out to be the best for your story, it is possible that an unusual perspective may allow you to do your strongest writing. A story about something painful that actually happened to you might, for instance, be told more easily from the point of view of another character, possibly even set in a different time and place. Similarly, if you find yourself unable to inhabit a story about someone with a very different lifestyle or set of beliefs, it might be useful to try writing in the first person, to "become" the person you are not.

☐ **Have you fully considered which verb tense will most effectively tell your story?** Most stories are told in the past tense, so you will probably want to consider that the "default tense," one that won't arouse much notice in your readers. The present tense is more arresting: it claims that the story is taking place while the reader is reading. As we noted earlier, because very short fiction relies on immediacy and surprise, the present tense is more prevalent here than elsewhere. The future tense is difficult to sustain in a longer work of fiction, but it might be employed successfully in the more experimental realm of the short-short.

☐ **Are the tone and style of your story appropriate to its content?** Obviously, a story about a poker game in a logging camp will require a different tone and style from a story about a bridge game set in a nursing home. Especially when revising your work, think carefully about not only the words you choose but also the construction of your sentences and paragraphs. In literature, the *quality* of your writing ultimately matters at least as much as your subject matter.

Getting started writing the short-short story ▶

In "A Few Words about Revision," at the start of this book, we noted Donald Murray's admonition that "great is the enemy of good," and that advice has equal validity when applied to the efforts of beginning fiction writers. In other words, shoot for something strong but achievable; you can always revise later. In fact, Anne Lamott bluntly advises writers to reconcile themselves to "shitty first drafts." We creative writing instructors assume you will do something about those drafts by the time they reach your final portfolio, but remember that we aren't anticipating a work of genius your first time out. Most of us are more than happy to see good stories rather than fair or bad ones. And as Lamott says, the only way to get started is to jump into the writing process and see what happens: "Very few writers really know what they are doing until they do it."

That's an important point. Throughout this chapter, we have emphasized that you need to make every word count in your *finished* story, but when you're actually sitting down to write, you want to shake free of the demon Expectation and just start writing. Don't worry about grammar. Don't worry about punctuation. Tell yourself that if this story stinks, you can throw it away without ever showing it to a single living soul.

By now, you should have a pretty good idea of what a short-short story is. You have seen some of the ways that different authors structure their pieces, how they create conflict, decide on point of view, set a scene, and shape a character. Ideally, you already have a bit of plot and setting in mind. You know that your opening should make readers want to drop whatever they're doing and read your story instead. You know that something has to change during the course of the story and that there will be a surprise, a *snap* at the end. You may not know exactly what that *snap* is just yet, but that doesn't matter. Start writing. As long as you have a central character who—to paraphrase both Aristotle and Janet Burroway—wants something and wants it very badly, that character's driving motivation will probably be sufficient to ignite your fiction.

So sit down in front of your computer—or notebook or typewriter or voice recorder—and begin.

KICK-STARTS Beginning your story

The material for stories is everywhere. From the anecdote about a party you overheard on the bus this morning, to that old family story about your great-aunt Gladys and her ham radio, to the disastrous Thanksgiving dinner you ate at Denny's last year, the world is full of story ideas. However, if you still have no idea what you want to write about—if your fingers are frozen and your mind is blank—here are some exercises to give you that initial push.

1. Start keeping a journal. Today. Right now. Your journal can be a notebook of lined paper, or a word processing file on your hard drive, or even the notepad on your phone. Write down every possible story idea you can think of, including ideas other writers have already used (you can always tweak the details). Draw pictures of characters and settings. Make lists. Take your journal to a crowded place—your school's cafeteria at lunchtime or the mall on Saturday. Discreetly listen in on several different conversations, and jot down the highlights. In short, just throw everything into the bag. When you're ready to write, raid your journal for ideas.

2. Quickly jot down the names of the five to ten most interesting people you know. Then take a closer look at the list. Which *two* people from that list would make the most sparks fly if they were put into a story together? What would be the nature of their conflict? Set them loose on each other and see what happens.

3. In his excellent book *Turning Life into Fiction*, Robin Hemley recommends the time-honored technique of mixing and matching the most intriguing characteristics from different people to create composite characters. Give it a try, and then look for ways to put those characters at odds with one another.

4. Brainstorm. This is an activity in which you cut loose with your pen or pencil or computer and let the ideas flow. Linda Flower advises: "The purpose of brainstorming is to stimulate creative thought. . . . When you come up with an idea or a phrase that isn't quite right, resist the temptation to throw it out and start again. Just write it down. . . . Don't stop to perfect spelling, grammar, or even phrasing. Keep working at the level of ideas." Flower notes that brainstorming differs from freewriting in that the latter method encourages the writer to spill out *anything* that occurs to him or her, whereas brainstorming "is not free association; it is a goal-directed effort to discover ideas relevant to your problem." Your goal is to write a short story, and your method is to open the floodgates and get everything that is even potentially relevant down on paper.

5. Because literary writing depends so heavily on images, you might want to focus your story around a specific object. Look slowly around the room you're in now until your eye alights on an object that suggests a story, such as those stacks of blank CDs you're waiting to burn. Are they demanding that a story be told about someone obsessed with Bob Marley? What about your stinky running shoes with the holes in the toes or that yearbook with the cover torn off? Why doesn't your protagonist buy a new pair of shoes? Why is he so angry at his senior class?

6. If you have some extra time on your hands, go to a secondhand store. Look around for an object that is begging to be the centerpiece of a story. What is the story behind that peacoat with a big splash of chartreuse paint on the front? Did an artist get in a fight with her lover? Was an elderly man attacked by a paintball gang? Pulitzer Prize–winning novelist Annie Proulx loves poking around among old things and recommends driving down back roads and stopping for yard sales. For Proulx, the attraction is not just the things she buys but also what she hears along the way: "I listen attentively in bars and cafés, while standing in line at the checkout counter, noting particular pronunciations and the rhythms of regional speech, vivid turns of speech and the duller talk of everyday life."

7. The smell and texture of an object can be great triggers for writing, but if you're pressed for time, use the Internet instead. Type a random noun—for example, "pineapple"—into the Google Image Search and see what turns up. A recent search resulted in plenty of photographs of pineapples, as one might expect. However, the search also showed a bare-chested young man holding two pineapple slices over his nipples. On the next page was a photo of the Pineapple Inn in Newport, Rhode Island. It doesn't take much imagination to realize that combining the young man and the inn could produce quite a story!

8. In *Fast Fiction*, Roberta Allen lists pages and pages of writing prompts using the following blueprint: "Write a story about risk. Write a story about a wedding. Write a story about something narrow." And on and on. Scan through the dictionary and make up your own list of writing prompts. Come up with at least ten before you sit down to write. Hint: My students have found that the more specific the prompt, the better the story tends to be. Therefore, "Write a story about pets" is probably less constructive than "Write a story about dogs," which in turn isn't quite as good as "Write a story about a poodle."

9. In a single sitting, write three to five openings for three to five different stories. Then put them aside for a day or two. Reread them, and choose the one that is most likely to make a reader want to keep reading.

▶ **10.** The great short story writer John Cheever once said of his own work: "My favorite stories are those that were written in less than a week and were often composed aloud." Take the "Cheever Challenge": get a digital recorder, or a willing listener, and tell a story aloud. Give yourself less than a week to turn your oral version into a completed story on paper.

▶ **11.** Write a story in which you reveal a secret about yourself, but have that secret apply to a character who is very much unlike you.

▶ **12.** Write a story that could get you into trouble. Expose an uncomfortable truth about someone you know, or reveal a secret you promised never to disclose. Then transform your narrative into fiction by changing the setting and altering the characters' names and appearances.

▶ **13.** Tell the story that only you can tell, the story you have inside that's screaming to get out.

▶ **14.** If you enrolled in this course with a longer story already in mind, go ahead and write it. Once you're finished, let it sit for a few days. Then go back and revise it, cutting out all the extraneous material. Often that merciless revision will result in a much stronger piece of fiction.

▶ **15.** Read before you write. If you find yourself blocked, read the short-shorts in this book's anthology. The excitement of reading a great piece of fiction can often motivate you to try to create one yourself. If you would like to read even more short-shorts, the following full-length anthologies are recommended: *Short Shorts*, edited by Irving Howe; *Micro Fiction*, edited by Jerome Stern; *Crafting the Very Short Story*, edited by Mark Mills; *Flash Fiction*, edited by James Thomas, Denise Thomas, and Tom Hazuka; and *Flash Fiction Forward, Sudden Fiction, Sudden Fiction (Continued)*, and *Sudden Fiction International*, all edited by Robert Shapard and James Thomas.

An Anthology of
Short-Short Stories

Magaret Atwood

An Angel

I know what the angel of suicide looks like. I have seen her several times. She's around.

She's nothing like the pictures of angels you run across here and there, the ones in classical paintings, with their curls and beautiful eyelashes, or the ones on Christmas cards, all cute or white. Much is made, in these pictures, of the feet, which are always bare, I suppose to show that angels do not need shoes: walkers on nails and live coals all of them, aspirin hearts, dandelion-seed heads, air bodies.

Not so the angel of suicide, who is dense, heavy with antimatter, a dark star. But despite the differences, she does have something in common with those others. All angels are messengers, and so is she; which isn't to say that all messages are good. The angels vary according to what they have to say: the angel of blindness, for instance, the angel of lung cancer, the angel of seizures, the destroying angel. The latter is also a mushroom.

(Snow angels, you've seen them: the cold blank shape of yourself, the outline you once filled. They too are messengers, they come from the future. This is what you will be, they say, perhaps what you are: no more than the way light falls across a given space.)

Angels come in two kinds: the others, and those who fell. The angel of suicide is one of those who fell, down through the atmosphere to the earth's surface. Or did she jump? With her you have to ask.

Anyway, it was a long fall. From the friction of the air, her face melted off like the skin of a meteor. That is why the angel of suicide is so smooth. She has no face to speak of. She has the face of a gray egg. Noncommittal; though the shine of the fall still lingers.

They said, the pack of them, I will not serve. The angel of suicide is one of those: a rebellious waitress. Rebellion, that's what she has to offer, to you, when you see her beckoning to you from outside the window, fifty stories up, or the edge of the bridge, or holding something out to you, some emblem of release, soft chemical, quick metal.

Wings, of course. You wouldn't believe a thing she said if it weren't for the wings. ◀

Aimee Bender

Loser

Once there was an orphan who had a knack for finding lost things. Both his parents had been killed when he was eight years old—they were swimming in the ocean when it turned wild with waves, and each had tried to save the other from drowning. The boy woke up from a nap, on the sand, alone. After the tragedy, the community adopted and raised him, and a few years after the deaths of his parents, he began to have a sense of objects even when they weren't visible. This ability continued growing in power through his teens and by his twenties, he was able to actually sniff out lost sunglasses, keys, contact lenses and sweaters.

The neighbors discovered his talent accidentally—he was over at Jenny Sugar's house one evening, picking her up for a date, when Jenny's mother misplaced her hairbrush, and was walking around, complaining about this. The young man's nose twitched and he turned slightly toward the kitchen and pointed to the drawer where the spoons and knives were kept. His date burst into laughter. Now that would be quite a silly place to put the brush, she said, among all that silverware! and she opened the drawer to make her point, to wave with a knife or brush her hair with a spoon, but when she did, boom, there was the hairbrush, matted with gray curls, sitting astride the fork pile.

Jenny's mother kissed the young man on the cheek but Jenny herself looked at him suspiciously all night long.

You planned all that, didn't you, she said, over dinner. You were trying to impress my mother. Well you didn't impress me, she said.

He tried to explain himself but she would hear none of it and when he drove his car up to her house, she fled before he could even finish saying he'd had a nice time, which was a lie anyway. He went home to his tiny room and thought about the word lonely and how it sounded and looked so lonely, with those two l's in it, each standing tall by itself.

As news spread around the neighborhood about the young man's skills, people reacted two ways: there were the deeply appreciative and the skeptics. The appreciative ones called up the young man regularly. He'd stop by on his way to school, find their keys, and they'd give him a homemade muffin. The skeptics called him over too, and watched him like a hawk; he'd still find their lost items but they'd insist it was an elaborate scam and he was doing it all to get attention. Maybe, declared one woman, waving her index finger in the air, Maybe, she said, he steals the thing so we think it's lost, moves the item, and then comes over to save it! How do we know it was really lost in the first place? What is going on?

The young man didn't know himself. All he knew was the feeling of a tug, light but insistent, like a child at his sleeve, and that tug would turn him in the right direction and show him where to look. Each object had its own way of inhabiting space, and therefore messaging its location. The young man could sense, could smell, an object's presence—he did not need to see it to feel where it put its gravity down. As would be expected, items that turned out to be miles away took much harder concentration than the ones that were two feet to the left.

When Mrs. Allen's little boy didn't come home one afternoon, that was the most difficult of all. Leonard Allen was eight years old and usually arrived home from school at 3:05. He had allergies and needed a pill before he went back out to play. That day, by 3:45, a lone Mrs. Allen was a wreck. Her boy rarely got lost—only once had that happened in the supermarket but he'd been found quite easily under the produce tables, crying; this walk home from school was a straight line and Leonard was not a wandering kind.

Mrs. Allen was just a regular neighbor except for one extraordinary fact—through an inheritance, she was the owner of a gargantuan emerald she called the Green Star. It sat, glass-cased, in her kitchen, where everyone could see it because she insisted that it be seen. Sometimes, as a party trick, she'd even cut steak with its beveled edge.

On this day, she removed the case off the Green Star and stuck her palms on it. Where is my boy? she cried. The Green Star was cold and flat. She ran, weeping, to her neighbor, who calmly walked her back home; together, they gave the house a thorough search, and then the neighbor, a believer, recommended calling the young man. Although Mrs. Allen was a skeptic, she thought anything was a worthwhile idea, and when the line picked up, she said, in a trembling voice:

You must find my boy.

The young man had been just about to go play basketball with his friends. He'd located the basketball in the bathtub.

You lost him? said the young man.

Mrs. Allen began to explain and then her phone clicked.

One moment please, she said, and the young man held on.

When her voice returned, it was shaking with rage.

He's been kidnapped! she said. And they want the Green Star!

The young man realized then it was Mrs. Allen he was talking to, and nodded. Oh, he said, I see. Everyone in town was familiar with Mrs. Allen's Green Star. I'll be right over, he said.

The woman's voice was too run with tears to respond.

In his basketball shorts and shirt, the young man jogged over to Mrs. Allen's house. He was amazed at how the Green Star was all exactly the same shade of green. He had a desire to lick it.

By then, Mrs. Allen was in hysterics.

They didn't tell me what to do, she sobbed. Where do I bring my emerald? How do I get my boy back?

The young man tried to feel the scent of the boy. He asked for a photograph and stared at it—a brown-haired kid at his kindergarten graduation—but the young man had only found objects before, and lost objects at that. He'd never found anything, or anybody, stolen. He wasn't a policeman.

Mrs. Allen called the police and one officer showed up at the door.

Oh it's the finding guy, the officer said. The young man dipped his head modestly. He turned to his right; to his left; north; south. He got a glimmer of a feeling toward the north and walked out the back door, through the backyard. Night approached and the sky seemed to grow and deepen in the darkness.

What's his name again? he called back to Mrs. Allen.

Leonard, she said. He heard the policeman pull out a pad and begin to ask basic questions.

He couldn't quite feel him. He felt the air and he felt the tug inside of the Green Star, an object displaced from its original home in Asia. He felt the tug of the tree in the front yard which had been uprooted from Virginia to be replanted here, and he felt the tug of his own watch which was from his uncle; in an attempt to be fatherly, his uncle had insisted he take it but they both knew the gesture was false.

Maybe the boy was too far away by now.

He heard the policeman ask: What is he wearing?

Mrs. Allen described a blue shirt, and the young man focused in on the blue shirt; he turned off his distractions and the blue shirt, like a connecting radio station, came calling from the northwest. The young man went walking and walking and about fourteen houses down he felt the blue shirt shrieking at him and he walked right into the backyard, through the back door, and sure enough, there were four people watching TV including the tear-stained boy with a runny nose eating a candy bar. The young man scooped up the boy while the others watched, so surprised they did nothing, and one even muttered: Sorry, man.

For fourteen houses back, the young man held Leonard in his arms like a bride. Leonard stopped sneezing and looked up at the stars and the young man smelled Leonard's hair, rich with the memory of peanut butter. He hoped Leonard would ask him a question, any question, but Leonard was quiet. The young man answered in his head: Son, he said, and the word rolled around, a marble on a marble floor. Son, he wanted to say.

When he reached Mrs. Allen's door, which was wide open, he walked in with quiet Leonard and Mrs. Allen promptly burst into tears and the policeman slunk out the door.

She thanked the young man a thousand times, even offered him the Green Star, but he refused it. Leonard turned on the TV and curled up on the sofa. The young man walked over and asked him about the program he was watching but Leonard stuck a thumb in his mouth and didn't respond.

Feel better, he said softly. Tucking the basketball beneath his arm, the young man walked home, shoulders low.

In his tiny room, he undressed and lay in bed. Had it been a naked child with nothing on, no shoes, no necklace, no hairbow, no watch, he could not have found it. He lay in bed that night with the trees from other places rustling and he could feel their confusion. No snow here. Not a lot of rain. Where am I? What is wrong with this dirt?

Crossing his hands in front of himself, he held on to his shoulders. Concentrate hard, he thought. Where are you? Everything felt blank and quiet. He couldn't feel a tug. He squeezed his eyes shut and let the question bubble up: Where did you go? Come find me. I'm over here. Come find me.

If he listened hard enough, he thought he could hear the waves hitting. ◄

T. Coraghessan Boyle

The Hit Man

Early Years

The Hit Man's early years are complicated by the black bag that he wears over his head. Teachers correct his pronunciation, the coach criticizes his attitude, the principal dresses him down for branding preschoolers with a lit cigarette. He is a poor student. At lunch he sits alone, feeding bell peppers and salami into the dark slot of his mouth. In the hallways, wiry young athletes snatch at the black hood and slap the back of his head. When he is thirteen he is approached by the captain of the football team, who pins him down and attempts to remove the hood. The Hit Man wastes him. Five years, says the judge.

Back on the Street

The Hit Man is back on the street in two months.

First Date

The girl's name is Cynthia. The Hit Man pulls up in front of her apartment in his father's hearse. (The Hit Man's father, whom he loathes and abominates, is a mortician. At breakfast the Hit Man's father had slapped the cornflakes from his son's bowl. The son threatened to waste his father. He did not, restrained no doubt by considerations of filial loyalty and the deep-seated taboos against patricide that permeate the universal unconscious.)

Cynthia's father has silver sideburns and plays tennis. He responds to the Hit Man's knock, expresses surprise at the Hit Man's appearance. The Hit Man takes Cynthia by the elbow, presses a twenty into her father's palm, and disappears into the night.

Father's Death

At breakfast the Hit Man slaps the cornflakes from his father's bowl. Then wastes him.

Mother's Death

The Hit Man is in his early twenties. He shoots pool, lifts weights and drinks milk from the carton. His mother is in the hospital, dying of cancer or heart disease. The priest wears black. So does the Hit Man.

First Job

Porfirio Buñoz, a Cuban financier, invites the Hit Man to lunch. I hear you're looking for work, says Buñoz.

That's right, says the Hit Man.

Peas

The Hit Man does not like peas. They are too difficult to balance on the fork.

Talk Show

The Hit Man waits in the wings, the white slash of a cigarette scarring the midnight black of his head and upper torso. The makeup girl has done his mouth and eyes, brushed the nap of his hood. He has been briefed. The guest who precedes him is a pediatrician. A planetary glow washes the stage where the host and the pediatrician, separated by a potted palm, cross their legs and discuss the little disturbances of infants and toddlers.

After the station break the Hit Man finds himself squeezed into a director's chair, white lights in his eyes. The talk-show host is a baby-faced man in his early forties. He smiles like God and all His Angels. Well, he says. So you're a hit man. Tell me—I've always wanted to know—what does it feel like to hit someone?

Death of Mateo María Buñoz

The body of Mateo María Buñoz, the cousin and business associate of a prominent financier, is discovered down by the docks on a hot summer morning. Mist rises from the water like steam, there is the smell of fish. A large black bird perches on the dead man's forehead.

Marriage

Cynthia and the Hit Man stand at the altar, side by side. She is wearing a white satin gown and lace veil. The Hit Man has rented a tuxedo, extra-large, and a silk-lined black-velvet hood.

. . . Till death do you part, says the priest.

Moods

The Hit Man is moody, unpredictable. Once, in a luncheonette, the waitress brought him the meatloaf special but forgot to eliminate the peas. There was a spot of gravy on the Hit Man's hood, about where his chin should be. He looked up at the waitress, his eyes like pins behind the triangular slots, and wasted her.

Another time he went to the track with $25, came back with $1,800. He stopped at a cigar shop. As he stepped out of the shop a wino tugged at his sleeve and solicited a quarter. The Hit Man reached into his pocket, extracted the $1,800 and handed it to the wino. Then wasted him.

First Child

A boy. The Hit Man is delighted. He leans over the edge of the playpen and molds the tiny fingers around the grip of a nickel-plated derringer. The gun is loaded with blanks—the Hit Man wants the boy to get used to the noise. By the time he is four the boy has mastered the rudiments of Tae Kwon Do, can stick a knife in the wall from a distance of ten feet and shoot a moving target with either hand. The Hit Man rests his broad palm on the boy's head. You're going to make the Big Leagues, Tiger, he says.

Work

He flies to Cincinnati. To L.A. To Boston. To London. The stewardesses get to know him.

Half an Acre and a Garage

The Hit Man is raking leaves, amassing great brittle piles of them. He is wearing a black T-shirt, cut off at the shoulders, and a cotton work hood, also black. Cynthia is edging the flower bed, his son playing in the grass. The Hit Man waves to his neighbors as they drive by. The neighbors wave back.

When he has scoured the lawn to his satisfaction, the Hit Man draws the smaller leaf-hummocks together in a single mound the size of a pickup truck. Then he bends to ignite it with his lighter. Immediately, flames leap back from the leaves, cut channels through the pile, engulf it in a ball of fire. The Hit Man stands back, hands folded beneath the great meaty biceps. At his side is the three-headed dog. He bends to pat each of the heads, smoke and sparks raging against the sky.

Stalking the Streets of the City

He is stalking the streets of the city, collar up, brim down. It is late at night. He stalks past department stores, small businesses, parks, and gas stations. Past apartments, picket fences, picture windows. Dogs growl in the shadows, then slink away. He could hit any of us.

Retirement

A group of businessman-types—sixtyish, seventyish, portly, diamond rings, cigars, liver spots—throws him a party. Porfirio Buñoz, now in his eighties, makes a speech and presents the Hit Man with a gilded scythe. The Hit Man thanks him, then retires to the lake, where he can be seen in his speedboat, skating out over the blue, hood rippling in the breeze.

Death

He is stricken, shrunken, half his former self. He lies propped against the pillows at Mercy Hospital, a bank of gentians drooping round the bed. Tubes run into the hood at the nostril openings, his eyes are clouded and red, sunk deep behind the triangular slots. The priest wears black. So does the Hit Man.

On the other side of town the Hit Man's son is standing before the mirror of a shop that specializes in Hit Man attire. Trying on his first hood. ◀

Ron Carlson

A Kind of Flying

By our wedding day, Brady had heard the word *luck* two hundred times. Everybody had advice, especially her sister Linda, who claimed to be "wise to me." Linda had wisdom. She was two years older and had wisely married a serviceman,

Butch Kistleburg, whose status as a GI in the army guaranteed them a life of travel and adventure. They were going to see the world. If Brady married me, Linda told everybody, she would see nothing but the inside of my carpet store.

Linda didn't like my plans for the ceremony. She thought that letting my best man, Bobby Thorson, sing "El Paso" was a diabolical mistake. "'El Paso,'" she said. "Why would you sing that at a wedding in Stevens Point, Wisconsin?" I told her: because I liked the song, I'm a sucker for a story, and because it was a love song, and because there *wasn't* a song called "Stevens Point."

"Well," she said that day so long ago, "that is no way to wedded bliss."

I wasn't used to thinking of things in terms of bliss, and I had no response for her. I had been thinking of the great phrase from the song that goes "... maybe tomorrow a bullet may find me..." and I was once again recommitted to the musical part of the program.

What raised *all* the stakes was what Brady did with the cake. She was a photographer even then and had had a show that spring in the Stevens Point Art Barn, a hilarious series of eye-tricks that everyone thought were double exposures: toy soldiers patrolling bathroom sinks and cowboys in refrigerators. Her family was pleased by what they saw as a useful hobby, but the exhibition of photographs had generally confused them.

When Brady picked up the wedding cake the morning we were wed, it stunned her, just the size of it made her grab her camera. She and Linda had taken Clover Lane, by the Gee place, and Brady pictured it all: the cake in the foreground and the church in the background, side by side.

When Brady pulled over near the cottonwoods a quarter mile from the church, Linda was not amused. She stayed in the car. Brady set the wedding cake in the middle of the road, backed up forty feet, lay down on the hardtop there, and in the rangefinder she saw the image she wanted: the bride and the groom on top of the three-tiered cake looking like they were about to step over onto the roof of the First Congregational Church. We still have the photograph. And when you see it, you always hear the next part of the story.

Linda screamed. Brady, her eye to the viewfinder, thought a truck was coming, that she was a second away from being run over on her wedding day. But it wasn't a truck. Linda had screamed at two birds. Two crows, who had been browsing the fenceline, wheeled down and fell upon the cake, amazed to find the sweetest thing in the history of Clover Lane, and before Brady could run forward and prevent it, she saw the groom plucked from his footing, ankle deep in frosting, and rise—in the beak of the shiny black bird—up into the June-blue sky.

"Man oh man oh man," Linda said that day to Brady. "That is a bad deal. That," she said, squinting at the two crows, who were drifting across Old Man Gee's alfalfa, one of them with the groom in his beak, "is a definite message." Then Linda, who had no surplus affection for me, went on to say several other things which Brady has been good enough, all these years, to keep to herself.

When Bobby Thorson and I reached the church, Linda came out as we were unloading his guitar and said smugly, "Glen, we're missing the groom."

Someone called the bakery, but it was too late for a replacement, almost one o'clock. I dug through Brady's car and found some of her guys: an Indian from Fort Apache with his hatchet raised in a non-matrimonial gesture; the Mummy, a translucent yellow; a kneeling green soldier, his eye to his rifle; and a little blue frogman with movable arms and legs. I was getting married in fifteen minutes.

The ceremony was rich. Linda read some Emily Dickinson; my brother read some Robert Service; and then Bobby Thorson sang "El Paso," a song about the intensities of love and a song which seemed to bewilder much of the congregation.

When Brady came up the aisle on her father's arm, she looked like an angel, her face blanched by seriousness and—I found out later—fear of evil omens. At the altar she whispered to me, "Do you believe in symbols?" Thinking she was referring to the rings, I said, "Of course, more than ever!" Her face nearly broke. I can still see her mouth quiver.

Linda didn't let up. During the reception when we were cutting the cake, Brady lifted the frogman from the top and Linda grabbed her hand: "Don't you ever lick frosting from any man's feet."

I wanted to say, "They're flippers, Linda," but I held my tongue.

That was twenty years ago this week. So much has happened. I've spent a thousand hours on my knees carpeting the rooms and halls and stairways of Stevens Point. Brady and I now have three boys who are good boys, but who—I expect—will not go into the carpet business. Brady has worked hard at her art. She is finished with her new book, *Obelisks*, which took her around the world twice photographing monuments. She's a wry woman with a sense of humor as long as a country road. Though she's done the traveling and I've stayed at home, whenever she sees any bird winging away, she says to me: *There you go.*

And she may be kind of right with that one. There have been times when I've ached to drop it all and fly away with Brady. I've cursed the sound of airplanes overhead and then when she comes home with her camera case and dirty laundry, I've flown to her—and she to me. You find out day after day in a good life that your family is the journey.

And now Linda's oldest, Trina, is getting married. We're having a big family party here in Stevens Point. Butch and Linda have all come north for a couple of weeks. Butch has done well; he's a lieutenant colonel. He's stationed at Fort Bliss and they all seem to like El Paso.

Trina came into the store yesterday pretending to look at carpet. People find out you're married for twenty years, they ask advice. What would I know? I'm just her uncle and I've done what I could. For years I laid carpet so my wife could be a photographer, and now she'll be a photographer so I can retire and coach baseball. Life lies before us like some new thing.

It's quiet in the store today. I can count sparrows on the wire across the road. My advice! She smiled yesterday when I told her. Just get married. Have a friend sing your favorite song at the wedding. Marriage, she said, what is it? Well, I said, it's not life on a cake. It's a bird taking your head in his beak and you walk the sky. It's marriage. Sometimes it pinches like a bird's mouth, but it's definitely flying, it's definitely a kind of flying. ◄

Raymond Carver

Popular Mechanics

Early that day the weather turned and the snow was melting into dirty water. Streaks of it ran down from the little shoulder-high window that faced the backyard. Cars slushed by on the street outside, where it was getting dark. But it was getting dark on the inside too.

He was in the bedroom pushing clothes into a suitcase when she came to the door.

I'm glad you're leaving! I'm glad you're leaving! she said. Do you hear?

He kept on putting his things into the suitcase.

Son of a bitch! I'm so glad you're leaving! She began to cry. You can't even look me in the face, can you?

Then she noticed the baby's picture on the bed and picked it up.

He looked at her and she wiped her eyes and stared at him before turning and going back to the living room.

Bring that back, he said.

Just get your things and get out, she said.

He did not answer. He fastened the suitcase, put on his coat, looked around the bedroom before turning off the light. Then he went out to the living room.

She stood in the doorway of the little kitchen, holding the baby.

I want the baby, he said.

Are you crazy?

No, but I want the baby. I'll get someone to come by for his things.

You're not touching this baby, she said.

The baby had begun to cry and she uncovered the blanket from around his head.

Oh, oh, she said, looking at the baby.

He moved toward her.

For God's sake! she said. She took a step back into the kitchen.

I want the baby.

Get out of here!

She turned and tried to hold the baby over in a corner behind the stove.

But he came up. He reached across the stove and tightened his hands on the baby.

Let go of him, he said.

Get away, get away! she cried.

The baby was red-faced and screaming. In the scuffle they knocked down a flowerpot that hung behind the stove.

He crowded her into the wall then, trying to break her grip. He held on to the baby and pushed with all his weight.

Let go of him, he said.

Don't, she said. You're hurting the baby, she said.

I'm not hurting the baby, he said.

The kitchen window gave no light. In the near-dark he worked on her fisted fingers with one hand and with the other hand he gripped the screaming baby up under an arm near the shoulder.

She felt her fingers being forced open. She felt the baby going from her.

No! she screamed just as her hands came loose.

She would have it, this baby. She grabbed for the baby's other arm. She caught the baby around the wrist and leaned back.

But he would not let go. He felt the baby slipping out of his hands and he pulled back very hard.

In this manner, the issue was decided. ◄

John Cheever

Reunion

The last time I saw my father was in Grand Central Station. I was going from my grandmother's in the Adirondacks to a cottage on the Cape that my mother had rented, and I wrote my father that I would be in New York between trains for an hour and a half, and asked if we could have lunch together. His secretary wrote to say that he would meet me at the information booth at noon, and at twelve o'clock sharp I saw him coming through the crowd. He was a stranger to me—my mother divorced him three years ago and I hadn't been with him since—but as soon as I saw him I felt that he was my father, my flesh and blood, my future and my doom. I knew that when I was grown I would be something like him; I would have to plan my campaigns within his limitations. He was a big, good-looking man, and I was terribly happy to see him again. He struck me on the back and shook my hand. "Hi, Charlie," he said. "Hi, boy. I'd like to take you up to my club, but it's in the Sixties, and if you have to catch an early train I guess we'd better get something to eat around here." He put his arm around me, and I smelled my father the way my mother sniffs a rose. It was a rich compound of whiskey, after-shave lotion, shoe polish, woolens, and the rankness of a mature male. I hoped that someone would see us together. I wished that we could be photographed. I wanted some record of our having been together.

We went out of the station and up a side street to a restaurant. It was still early, and the place was empty. The bartender was quarreling with a delivery boy, and there was one very old waiter in a red coat down by the kitchen door. We sat down, and my father hailed the waiter in a loud voice. *"Kellner!"* he shouted. *"Garçon! Cameriere! You!"* His boisterousness in the empty restaurant seemed out of place. "Could we have a little service here!" he shouted. "Chop-chop." Then he clapped his hands. This caught the waiter's attention, and he shuffled over to our table.

"Were you clapping your hands at me?" he asked.

"Calm down, calm down, *sommelier,*" my father said. "If it isn't too much to ask of you—if it wouldn't be too much above and beyond the call of duty, we would like a couple of Beefeater Gibsons."

"I don't like to be clapped at," the waiter said.

"I should have brought my whistle," my father said. "I have a whistle that is audible only to the ears of old waiters. Now, take out your little pad and your little pencil and see if you can get this straight: two Beefeater Gibsons. Repeat after me: two Beefeater Gibsons."

"I think you'd better go somewhere else," the waiter said quietly.

"That," said my father, "is one of the most brilliant suggestions I have ever heard. Come on, Charlie, let's get the hell out of here."

I followed my father out of that restaurant into another. He was not so boisterous this time. Our drinks came, and he cross-questioned me about the baseball season. He then struck the edge of his empty glass with his knife and began shouting again. *"Garçon! Kellner! Cameriere! You!* Could we trouble you to bring us two more of the same."

"How old is the boy?" the waiter asked.

"That," my father said, "is none of your God-damned business."

"I'm sorry, sir," the waiter said, "but I won't serve the boy another drink."

"Well, I have some news for you," my father said. "I have some very interest-ing news for you. This doesn't happen to be the only restaurant in New York. They've opened another on the corner. Come on, Charlie."

He paid the bill, and I followed him out of that restaurant into another. Here the waiters wore pink jackets like hunting coats, and there was a lot of horse tack on the walls. We sat down, and my father began to shout again. "Master of the hounds! Tallyhoo and all that sort of thing. We'd like a little something in the way of a stirrup cup. Namely, two Bibson Geefeaters."

"Two Bibson Geefeaters?" the waiter asked, smiling.

"You know damned well what I want," my father said angrily. "I want two Beefeater Gibsons, and make it snappy. Things have changed in jolly old England. So my friend the duke tells me. Let's see what England can produce in the way of a cocktail."

"This isn't England," the waiter said.

"Don't argue with me," my father said. "Just do as you're told."

"I just thought you might like to know where you are," the waiter said.

"If there is one thing I cannot tolerate," my father said, "it is an impudent domestic. Come on, Charlie."

The fourth place we went to was Italian. "*Buon giorno*," my father said. "*Per favore, possiamo avere due cocktail americani, forti, forti. Molto gin, poco vermut.*"

"I don't understand Italian," the waiter said.

"Oh, come off it," my father said. "You understand Italian, and you know damned well you do. *Vogliamo due cocktail americani. Subito.*"

The waiter left us and spoke with the captain, who came over to our table and said, "I'm sorry, sir, but this table is reserved."

"All right," my father said. "Get us another table."

"All the tables are reserved," the captain said.

"I get it," my father said. "You don't desire our patronage. Is that it? Well, the hell with you. *Vada all' inferno.* Let's go, Charlie."

"I have to get my train," I said.

"I'm sorry, sonny," my father said. "I'm terribly sorry." He put his arm around me and pressed me against him. "I'll walk you back to the station. If there had only been time to go up to my club."

"That's all right, Daddy," I said.

"I'll get you a paper," he said. "I'll get you a paper to read on the train."

Then he went up to a newsstand and said, "Kind sir, will you be good enough to favor me with one of your God-damned, no-good, ten-cent afternoon papers?" The clerk turned away from him and stared at a magazine cover. "Is it asking too much, kind sir," my father said, "is it asking too much for you to sell me one of your disgusting specimens of yellow journalism?"

"I have to go, Daddy," I said. "It's late."

"Now, just wait a second, sonny," he said. "Just wait a second. I want to get a rise out of this chap."

"Goodbye, Daddy," I said, and I went down the stairs and got my train, and that was the last time I saw my father. ◀

Ursula Hegi

Doves

Francine is having a shy day, the kind of day that makes you feel sad when the elevator man says good afternoon, the kind of day that makes you want to buy two doves.

Her raincoat pulled close around herself, Francine walks the twelve blocks to Portland Pet And Plant. She heads past the African violets, past the jade plants and fig trees, past the schnauzers and poodles, past the hamsters and turtles, past the gaudy parrot in the center cage who shrieks: "Oh amigo, oh amigo . . ."

What Francine wants are doves of such a smooth gray that they don't hurt your eyes. With doves like that you don't have to worry about being too quiet. They make soft clucking sounds deep inside their throats and wait for you to notice them instead of clamoring for your attention.

Six of them perch on the bars in the tall cage near the wall, two white with brownish speckles, the others a deep gray tinged with purple. Above the cage hangs a sign: Ring Neck Doves $7.99. Doves like that won't need much; they'll turn their heads toward the door when you push the key into the lock late in the afternoon and wait for you to notice them instead of clamoring for your attention.

"Oh amigo, oh amigo" . . . screeches the parrot. Francine chooses the two smallest gray doves and carries them from the store in white cardboard boxes that look like Chinese takeout containers with air holes. The afternoon has the texture of damp newspaper, but Francine feels light as she walks back to her apartment.

In her kitchen she sets the boxes on top of her counter, opens the tops, and waits for the doves to fly out and roost on the plastic bar where she hangs her kitchen towels. But they crouch inside the white cardboard as if waiting for her to lift them out.

She switches on the radio to the station where she always keeps it, public radio, but instead of Tuesday night opera, a man is asking for donations. Francine has already sent in her contribution, and she doesn't like it when the man says, "None of you would think of going into a store and taking something off the shelves, but you listen to public radio without paying . . ." The doves move their wing feathers forward and pull their heads into their necks as if trying to shield themselves from the fund-raising voice.

Francine turns the dial past rock stations and commercials. At the gaudy twang of a country-western song, the doves raise their heads and peer from the boxes. Their beaks turn to one side, then to the other, completing a nearly full circle. Low velvet sounds rise from their throats. Francine has never listened to country-westerns; she's considered them tacky, but when the husky voice of a woman sings of wanting back the lover who hurt her so, she tilts her head to the side and croons along with the doves.

Before she leaves for her job at K-Mart the next morning, Francine pulls the radio next to the kitchen sink and turns it on for the doves. They sit in the left side of her double sink which she has lined with yellow towels, their claws curved around folds of fabric, their eyes on the flickering light of the tuner that still glows on the country-western station. When she returns after working all day in the footwear department, they swivel their heads toward her and then back to the radio as if they'd been practicing that movement all day.

At K-Mart she finds that more people leave their shoes. It used to be just once or twice a week that she'd discover a worn pair of shoes half pushed under the racks by someone who's walked from the store with stolen footwear. But now she sees them almost every day—sneakers with torn insoles, pumps with imitation leather peeling from the high heels, work shoes with busted seams—as if a legion of shoe thieves had descended on Portland.

Francine keeps the discarded shoes in the store's lost and found crate out back, though no one has ever tried to claim them. But some are still good enough to donate to Goodwill. She murmurs to the doves about the shoes while she refills their water and sprinkles birdseed into the porcelain soap dish. Coming home to them has become familiar. So have the songs of lost love that welcome her every evening. A few times she tried to return to her old station, but as soon as the doves grew listless, she moved the tuner back. And lately she hasn't felt like changing it at all. She knows some of the lines now, knows how the songs end.

Francine has a subscription to the opera, and after feeding the doves, she takes a bubble bath and puts on her black dress. In the back of the cab, she holds her purse with both hands in her lap. Sitting in the darkened balcony, she feels invisible as she listens to *La Traviata*, one of her favorite operas. For the first time it comes to her that it, too, is about lost love and broken hearts.

In the swell of bodies that shifts from the opera house, Francine walks into the mild November night, leaving behind the string of waiting taxicabs, the expensive restaurants across from the opera house, the stores and the bus station, the fast-food places and bars.

A young couple saunters from the Blue Moon Tavern hand in hand, steeped in amber light and the sad lyrics of a slow-moving song for that instant before the door closes again. Francine curves her fingers around the doorhandle, pulls it open, and steps into the smoky light as if she were a woman with red boots who had someone waiting for her. Below the Michelob clock, on the platform, two men play guitars and sing of betrayed love.

On the bar stool, her black dress rides up to her knees. She draws her shoulders around herself and orders a fuzzy navel, a drink she remembers from a late night movie. The summer taste of apricots and oranges soothes her limbs and makes her ease into the space her body fills.

A lean-hipped man with a cowboy hat asks Francine to dance, and as she sways in his arms on the floor that's spun of sawdust and boot prints, she becomes the woman in all the songs that the men on the platform sing about, the woman who leaves them, the woman who keeps breaking their hearts. ◀

Pam Houston

Symphony

Sometimes life is ridiculously simple. I lost fifteen pounds and the men want me again. I can see it in the way they follow my movements, not just with their eyes but with their whole bodies, the way they lean into me until they almost topple over, the way they always seem to have itches on the back of their necks. And I'll admit this: I am collecting them like gold-plated sugar spoons, one from every state.

This is a difficult story to tell because what's right about what I have to say is only as wide as a tightrope, and what's wrong about it yawns wide, beckoning, on either side. I have always said I have no narcotic, smiling sadly at stories of ruined lives, safely remote from the twelve-step program and little red leather booklets that say "One Day at a Time." But there is something so sweet about the first kiss, the first surrender that, like the words "I want you," can never mean precisely the same thing again. It is delicious and addicting. It is, I'm guessing, the most delicious thing of all.

There are a few men who matter, and by writing them down in this story I can make them seem like they have an order, or a sequence, or a priority, because those are the kinds of choices that language forces upon us, but language can't touch the joyful and slightly disconcerting feeling of being very much in love, but not knowing exactly with whom.

First I will tell you about Phillip, who is vast and dangerous, his desires uncontainable and huge. He is far too talented, a grown-up tragedy of a gifted child, massively in demand. He dances, he weaves, he writes a letter that could wring light from a black hole. He has mined gold in the Yukon, bonefished in Belize. He has crossed Iceland on a dogsled, he is the smartest man that all his friends know. His apartment smells like wheat bread, cooling. His body smells like spice. Sensitive and scared scared scared of never becoming a father, he lives in New York City and is very careful about his space. It is easy to confuse what he has learned to do in bed for love or passion or art, but he is simply a master craftsman, and very proud of his good work.

Christopher is innocent. Very young and wide-open. He's had good mothering and no father to make him afraid to talk about his heart. In Nevada he holds hands with middle-aged women while the underground tests explode beneath them. He studies marine biology, acting, and poetry, and is not yet quite aware of his classic good looks. Soon someone will tell him, but it won't be me. A few years ago he said in a few more years he'd be old enough for me, and in a few more years, it will be true. For now we are friends and I tell him my system, how I have learned to get what I want from many sources, and none. He says this: You are a complicated woman. Even when you say you don't want anything, you want more than that.

I have a dream in which a man becomes a wolf. He is sleeping, cocooned, and when he stretches and breaks the parchment there are tufts of hair across his back and shoulders, and on the backs of his hands. It is Christopher, I suspect, though I can't see his face. When I wake up I am in Phillip's bed. My back is to his side and yet we are touching at all the pressure points. In the predawn I can see the line of electricity we make, a glow like neon, the curve of a wooden instrument. As I wake, "Symphony" is the first word that forms in my head.

Jonathan came here from the Okavango Delta in Botswana; he's tall and hairy and clever and strong. In my living room I watch him reach inside his shirt and scratch his shoulder. It is a savage movement, rangy and impatient, lazy too, and without a bit of self-consciousness. He is not altogether human. He has spent the last three years in the bush. I cook him T-bone steaks because he says he won't eat complicated food. He is skeptical of the hibachi, of the barely glowing coals. Where he comes from, they cook everything with fire. He says things against my ear, the names of places: Makgadikgadi Pans, Nxamaseri, Mpandamatenga, Gaborone. Say these words out loud and see what happens to you. Mosi-oa-Toenja, "The Smoke That Thunders." Look at the pictures: a rank of impalas slaking their thirst, giraffes, their necks entwined, a young bull elephant rising from the Chobe River. When I am with Jonathan I have this thought which delights and frightens me: It has been the animals that have attracted me all along. Not the cowboys, but the horses that carried them. Not the hunters, but the caribou and the bighorn. Not Jonathan, in his infinite loveliness, but the hippos, the kudu, and the big African cats. You fall in love with a man's animal spirit, Jonathan tells me, and then when he speaks like a human being, you don't know who he is.

There's one man I won't talk about, not because he is married, but because he is sacred. When he writes love letters to me he addresses them "my dear" and signs them with the first letter of his first name and one long black line. We have only made love one time. I will tell you only the one thing that must be told: After the only part of him I will ever hold collapsed inside me he said, "You are so incredibly gentle." It was the closest I have ever come to touching true love.

Another dream: I am in the house of my childhood, and I see myself, at age five, at the breakfast table; pancakes and sausage, my father in his tennis whites. The me that is dreaming, the older me, kneels down and holds out her arms waiting for the younger me to come and be embraced. Jonathan's arms twitch around me and I am suddenly awake inside a body, inside a world where it has become impossible to kneel down and hold out my arms. Still sleeping, Jonathan pulls my hand across his shoulder, and presses it hard against his face.

I'm afraid of what you might be thinking. That I am a certain kind of person, and that you are the kind of person who knows more about my story than me. But you should know this: I could love any one of them, in an instant and with every piece of my heart, but none of them nor the world will allow it, and so I move between them, on snowy highways and crowded airplanes. I was in New York this morning. I woke up in Phillip's bed. Come here, he's in my hair. You can smell him. ◄

Jamaica Kincaid

Girl

Wash the white clothes on Monday and put them on the stone heap; wash the color clothes on Tuesday and put them on the clothesline to dry; don't walk barehead in the hot sun; cook pumpkin fritters in very hot sweet oil; soak your little cloths right after you take them off; when buying cotton to make yourself a nice blouse, be sure that it doesn't have gum on it, because that way it won't hold up well after a wash; soak salt fish overnight before you cook it; is it true that you sing benna[1] in Sunday school?; always eat your food in such a way that it won't turn someone else's stomach; on Sundays try to walk like a lady and not like the slut you are so bent on becoming; don't sing benna in Sunday school; you mustn't speak to wharf-rat boys, not even to give directions; don't eat fruits on the street—flies will follow you; *but I don't sing benna on Sundays at all and never in Sunday school;* this is how to sew on a button; this is how to make a button-hole for the button you have just sewed on; this is how to hem a dress when you see the hem coming down and so to prevent yourself from looking like the slut I know you are so bent on becoming; this is how you iron your father's khaki shirt so that it doesn't have a crease; this is how you iron your father's khaki pants so that they don't have a crease; this is how you grow okra—far from the house, because okra tree harbors red ants; when you are growing dasheen,[2] make sure it gets plenty of water or else it makes your throat itch when you are eating it; this is how you sweep a corner; this is how you sweep a whole house; this is how you sweep a yard; this is how you smile to someone you don't like too much; this is how you smile to someone you don't like at all; this is how you smile to someone you like completely; this is how you set a table for tea; this is how you set a table for dinner; this is how you set a table for dinner with an important guest; this is how you set a table for lunch; this is how you set a table for breakfast; this is how to behave in the presence of men who don't know you very well, and this

---

1. **benna**: Calypso music.
2. **dasheen**: An edible root.

way they won't recognize immediately the slut I have warned you against becoming; be sure to wash every day, even if it is with your own spit; don't squat down to play marbles—you are not a boy, you know; don't pick people's flowers—you might catch something; don't throw stones at blackbirds, because it might not be a blackbird at all; this is how to make a bread pudding; this is how to make doukona;[3] this is how to make pepper pot; this is how to make a good medicine for a cold; this is how to make a good medicine to throw away a child before it even becomes a child; this is how to catch a fish; this is how to throw back a fish you don't like, and that way something bad won't fall on you; this is how to bully a man; this is how a man bullies you; this is how to love a man, and if this doesn't work there are other ways, and if they don't work don't feel too bad about giving up; this is how to spit up in the air if you feel like it, and this is how to move quick so that it doesn't fall on you; this is how to make ends meet; always squeeze bread to make sure it's fresh; *but what if the baker won't let me feel the bread?;* you mean to say that after all you are really going to be the kind of woman who the baker won't let near the bread? ◄

---

3. **doukona**: A sweet and spicy pudding.

Joyce Carol Oates

Wolf's Head Lake

It's an early dusk at the lake because the sky's marbled with clouds and some of them are dark, heavy, tumescent as skins of flesh ready to burst. It's an early dusk because there's been thunder all afternoon, that laughing-rippling sound at the base of the spine. And heat lightning, quick spasms of nerves, forking in the sky then gone before you can exactly see. Only a few motorboats out on the lake, men fishing, nobody's swimming any longer, this is a day in summer ending early. In my damp puckered two-piece bathing suit I'm leaning in the doorway of the wood-frame cottage, #11, straining the spring of the rusted screen door. You don't realize the screen is rusted until you feel the grit on your fingers, and you touch your face, your lips, needing to feel *I'm here! Alive* and you taste the rust, and the slapping of waves against the pebbled beach is mixed with it, that taste. Along Wolf's Head Lake in the foothills of the Chautauqua Mountains the small cottages of memory, crowded together in a grid of scrupulous plotted rows at the southern edge of the lake that's said to be shaped like a giant wolf's head, sandy rutted driveways and grassless lots and towels and bathing suits hanging on clotheslines chalk-white in the gathering dusk. And radios turned up high. And kids' raised voices, shouting in play. He's driving a car just that color of the storm clouds. He's driving slowly, you could say aimlessly. He's in no hurry to switch on his headlights. Just cruising. On Route 23 the two-lane blacktop highway, cruising down from Port Oriskany maybe, where maybe he lives, or has been living, but he's checked out now, or if he's left some clothes and things behind in the rented room he won't be back to claim them. You have an uncle who'd gotten shot up as he speaks of it, not bitterly, nor even ironically, in the War, and all he's good for now, he says, is managing a cheap hotel in Port Oriskany, and he tells stories of guys like this how they appear, and then they disappear. And no trace unless the cops are looking for them and even then, much of the time, no trace. *Where do they come from, it's like maple seeds blowing.* And you think *What's a maple seed want but to populate the world with its kind.* He's wearing dark glasses, as dark comes on. Circling the cottages hearing kids' shouts, barking dogs. He might have a companion. In the rooms-by-the-week hotel in Port Oriskany, these guys have companions, and the companion is a woman. This is strange to me, yet I begin to see her. She's a hefty big-breasted woman like my mother's older sister. Her hair is bleached, but growing out. She's got a quick wide smile like a knife cutting through something soft. She's the one who'll speak first. Asking if you know where somebody's cottage is, and you don't; or, say you're headed for the lake, in the thundery dusk, or sitting on the steps at the dock where older kids are drinking from beer cans, tossing cigarette butts into the lake, and it's later, and darker, and the air tastes of rain though it hasn't started yet to rain, and she's asking would you like to come for a ride, to Olcott where there's the carnival, the Ferris wheel, it's only a few miles away. Asking what's your name, and you're too shy not to tell. Beneath the front seat of the car, the passenger's seat, there's a length of clothesline. You would never imagine clothesline is so strong. Each of them has a knife. The kind that fold up. From the army-navy supply store. For hunting, fishing. Something they do with these knives, and each other, drawing thin trickles of blood, but I'm not too sure of this, I've never seen it exactly. I'm leaning in the doorway, the spring of the screen door is strained almost to breaking. Mosquitoes are drawn to my hot skin, out of the shadows. I see the headlights on Route 23 above the lake, a mile away. I see the slow passage, he's patient, circling the cottages, looking for the way in. ◄

Guadalupe Valdés

Recuerdo

It was noon. It was dusty. And the sun, blinding in its brightness, shone unmercifully on the narrow dirty street.

It was empty. And to Rosa, walking slowly past the bars and the shops and the curio stands, it seemed as if they all were peering out at her, curiously watching what she did.

She walked on . . . toward the river, toward the narrow, muddy strip of land that was the dry Rio Grande; and she wished suddenly that it were night and that the tourists had come across, making the street noisy and gay and full of life.

But it was noon. And there were no happy or laughing Americanos; no eager girls painted and perfumed and waiting for customers; no blaring horns or booming bongos . . . only here and there a hungry dog, a crippled beggar, or a drunk, thirsty and broke from the night before.

She was almost there. She could see the narrow door and the splintered wooden steps. And instinctively she stopped. Afraid suddenly, feeling the hollow emptiness again, and the tightness when she swallowed.

And yet, it was not as if she did not know why he had wanted her to come, why he had sent for her. It was not as though she were a child. Her reflection in a smudged and dirty window told her that she was no longer even a girl.

And still, it was not as if she were old, she told herself, it was only that her body was rounded and full, and her eyes in the dark smooth face were hard and knowing, mirroring the pain and the disappointment and the tears of thirty-five years . . .

She walked to the narrow door slowly, and up the stairs . . . thumping softly on the creaking swollen wood. At the top, across a dingy hallway, she knocked softly at a door. It was ajar, and Rosa could see the worn chairs and the torn linoleum and the paper-littered desk. But she did not go in. Not until the man came to the door and looked out at her impatiently.

He saw her feet first and the tattered sandals. Then her dress clean but faded, a best dress obviously, because it was not patched. Finally, after what seemed to Rosa an eternity, he looked at her face, at her dark black hair knotted neatly on top of her head; and at last, into her eyes.

"Come in, Rosa," he said slowly, "I am glad that you could come."

"Buenas tardes[1] Don Lorenzo," Rosa said meekly, looking up uneasily at the bulky smelly man. "I am sorry I am late."

"Yes," he said mockingly, and turning, he walked back into the small and dirty room.

Rosa followed him, studying him, while he could not see her, seeing the wrinkled trousers, the sweat-stained shirt, and the overgrown greasy hair on the back of his pudgy neck.

He turned suddenly, his beady eyes surveying his domain smugly; then deliberately, he walked to the window and straightened the sign that said:

DIVORCES . . . LORENZO PEREZ SAUZA . . . ATTORNEY AT LAW

---

1. **buenas tardes:** good afternoon.

It was not as important as the neon blinking sign, of course, but sometimes people came from the side street, and it was good to be prepared.

"Well, Rosa," he said, looking at her again, "and where is Maruca?"

"She is sick, señor."

"Sick?"

"Yes, she has had headaches and she is not well . . . she . . ."

"Has she seen a doctor, Rosa?" The question was mocking again.

"No . . . she . . . it will pass, señor . . . It's only that now . . . I do not think that she should come to work."

"Oh?" He was looking out of the window distractedly, ignoring her.

"I am sorry, I should have come before," she continued meekly . . .

"Maruca is very pretty, Rosa," Don Lorenzo said suddenly.

"Thank you, señor, you are very kind." She was calmer now . . .

"She will make a man very happy, someday," he continued.

"Yes."

"Do you think she will marry soon then?" he asked her, watching her closely.

"No," she hesitated, "that is, I don't know, she . . . there isn't anyone yet."

"Ah!" It was said quietly but somehow triumphantly . . .

And Rosa waited, wondering what he wanted, sensing something and suddenly suspicious.

"Do you think she likes me, Rosa," he asked her deliberately, baiting her.

And she remembered Maruca's face, tear-stained, embarrassed telling her: "I can't go back, Mama. He does not want me to help in his work. He touches me, Mother . . . and smiles. And today, he put his large sweaty hand on my breast, and held it, smiling, like a cow. Ugly!"

"Why, yes, Don Lorenzo," she lied quickly. "She thinks you are very nice." Her heart was racing now, hoping and yet not daring to—

"I am much of a man, Rosa," he went on slowly, "and the girl is pretty . . . I would take care of her . . . if she let me."

"Take care of her?" Rosa was praying now, her fingers crossed behind her back.

"Yes, take care of her," he repeated. "I would be good to her, you would have money. And then, perhaps, if there is a child . . . she would need a house . . ."

"A house," Rosa repeated dully. A house for Maruca. That it might be. That it might be, really, was unbelievable. To think of the security, of the happy future frightened her suddenly, and she could only stare at the fat man, her eyes round and very black.

"Think about it, Rosita," he said smiling benevolently . . . "You know me . . ." And Rosa looked at him angrily, remembering, and suddenly feeling very much like being sick.

The walk home was long; and in the heat Rosa grew tired. She wished that she might come to a tree, so that she could sit in the shade and think. But the hills were bare and dry, and there were no trees. There were only shacks surrounded by hungry crying children.

And Rosa thought about her own, about the little ones. The ones that still depended on her even for something to eat. And she felt it again, the strange despair of wanting to cry out: "Don't, don't depend on me! I can hardly depend on myself."

But they had no one else; and until they could beg or steal a piece of bread and a bowl of beans, they would turn to her, only to her, not ever to Pablo.

And it wasn't because he was drunk and lazy, or even because only the last two children belonged to him. He was kind enough to all of them. It was, though, as if they sensed that he was only temporary.

And still it was not that Pablo was bad. He was better actually than the others. He did not beat her when he drank, or steal food from the children. He was not even too demanding. And it gave them a man, after all, a man to protect them . . . It was enough, really.

True, he had begun to look at Maruca, and it bothered Rosa. But perhaps it *was* really time for Maruca to leave. For the little ones, particularly. Because men are men, she said to herself, and if there is a temptation . . .

But she was not fooling anyone, and when at last she saw the tin and cardboard shack against the side of the hill, with its cluttered front and screaming children, she wanted to turn back.

Maruca saw her first.

"There's Mama," she told the others triumphantly, and at once they took up the shout: "Mama! Mama! Mama!"

The other girl, standing with Maruca, turned to leave as Rosa came closer.

"Buenas tardes," she said uncomfortably, sensing the dislike and wanting to hurry away.

"What did Petra want?" Rosa asked Maruca angrily, even before Petra was out of earshot.

"Mama, por favor, she'll hear you."

"I told you I did not want her in this house."

"We were only talking, Mama. She was telling me about her friends."

"Her friends!" Rosa cut in sharply, "as if we did not know that she goes with the first American that looks at her. Always by the river that one, with one soldier and another, her friends indeed!"

"But she says she has fun, Mama, and they take her to dance and buy her pretty things."

"Yes, yes, and tomorrow, they will give her a baby . . . And where is the fun then . . . eh? She is in the streets . . . no?"

Rosa was shaking with anger. "Is that what you want? Do you?"

"No, Mama," Maruca said meekly, "I was just listening to her talk."

"Well, remember it," Rosa snapped furiously, but then seeing Maruca's face, she stopped suddenly. "There, there, it's alright," she said softly. "We will talk about it later."

And Rosa watched her, then, herding the children into the house gently, gracefully; slim and small, angular still, with something perhaps a little doltish in the way she held herself, impatient, and yet distrusting, not quite daring to go forward.

And she thought of Don Lorenzo, and for a moment, she wished that he were not so fat, or so ugly, and especially, so sweaty.

But it was an irrecoverable chance! Old men with money did not often come into their world, and never to stay.

To Rosa, they had been merely far away gods at whose houses she had worked as a maid or as a cook; faultless beings who were to be obeyed without question; powerful creatures who had commanded her to come when they needed variety or adventure . . .

But only that.

She had never been clever enough, or even pretty enough to make it be more.

But Maruca! Maruca could have the world.

No need for her to marry a poor young bum who could not even get a job. No need for her to have ten children all hungry and crying. No need for her to dread, even, that the bum might leave her. No need at all. ◀

3

Writing Short Creative Nonfiction

▶ A few things you should know about short creative nonfiction

Poetry, fiction, and drama aren't regularly assigned in high school and college courses, but essays certainly are. By the time most students sign up for an introductory creative writing class, they have written position essays, descriptive essays, comparison-and-contrast essays, argumentative essays, and research essays—in every discipline from anthropology to zoology. Midterms and final exams often include an essay-writing component. In fact, you have probably written so many essays in your life that just the thought of writing another one makes you a little queasy.

But before you reach for the Pepto-Bismol, wait just a minute. What you will be writing in this chapter is not the sort of essay you have written in the past—or not *exactly* that sort of essay. You may well use argumentation, comparison and contrast, and description. And it's the rare essayist who doesn't do at least a little research, even if the essay's subject is very personal. However, in this chapter you will be writing in a genre called literary nonfiction or, more frequently, **creative nonfiction**. Most students find that working in this genre is much more fun than traditional essay writing.

So how do we distinguish *creative* nonfiction from the nonfiction you have been writing for so many years? There are almost as many answers to that question as there are creative nonfiction writers, but one way to define this genre is to do two things that essayists love to do: quote from other writers and make lists.

In their groundbreaking book *The Fourth Genre: Contemporary Writers of/ on Creative Nonfiction*, Robert Root and Michael Steinberg identify a number of elements common to this genre. Root and Steinberg believe that creative nonfiction:

▸ **Requires a Personal Presence**   Whether working in formats like the memoir, in which they reveal a great deal about themselves, or in less immediately personal forms like the nature essay, essayists always insert themselves in some fashion in their own essays.

▸ **Demands Self-Discovery and Self-Exploration**   Essays allow, and even encourage, their authors to learn as they go. The essay form "grants writers permission to explore without knowing where they will end up, to be tentative, speculative, reflective."

▸ **Allows Flexibility of Form and Takes a Literary Approach**   Creative nonfiction uses "literary language," borrowing techniques from fiction and poetry. Creative nonfiction experiments with both linear and nonlinear structures; essayists sometimes wander and backtrack a bit or break the text into fragments.

▸ **Insists on Veracity**   The genre "is reliably factual, firmly anchored in real experience, whether the author has lived it or observed and recorded it." Although writers of creative nonfiction may take liberties with the facts— for example, leaving out an unimportant detail to speed up the narrative, or leaving out an important detail to protect someone's privacy—they must nevertheless maintain an "accuracy of interpretation."

▸ **Blurs Boundaries between Genres**   "Creative nonfiction . . . brings artistry to information and actuality to imagination, and it draws upon the expressive aim that lies below the surface in all writing." By "expressive," the authors here mean the personal and the emotional: creative nonfiction tells us what an author *feels*.

Root and Steinberg's *The Fourth Genre*, originally published in 1999, was one of the first college textbooks to deal exclusively and extensively with creative nonfiction. That may give you a sense of how recently this genre of creative writing has become popular, but right now it is a very hot market indeed. Aspiring writers used to turn automatically to the novel to achieve literary renown, but these days they are just as likely to pen nonfiction, which now routinely outsells fiction.

In fact, many essayists come to creative nonfiction from fiction and poetry. For John T. Price, "Personal essays bring together the best of both poetry and fiction, combining lyrical and imagistic language with narrative appeal." Judith Ortiz Cofer also sees a thorough connection between fiction, poetry, and creative nonfiction: "The point is to continue the emphasis on control of language and craft from poem to prose. The poem is as minutely planned as the creative nonfiction, which is nothing more and nothing less than a composite of the narrative poem and the finely crafted plotted story: a story as polished and economically constructed as a poem." As Cofer pictures it, there is a fusion, a synthesis, a symbiosis that comes from crossing genres. Rather than distracting the author from the demands of one type of literature, writing in multiple genres helps the author identify what is best about each one of them.

In the introduction to *The Art of the Personal Essay*, published in 1997, editor Philip Lopate acknowledges that the genre is "notoriously adaptable and flexible"—a comment that essayists make time and again about their field. Nevertheless, Lopate manages to isolate a number of qualities that most personal essays have in common:

- The personal essay is conversational—often ironic, humorous, even cheeky—in tone.
- It values honesty and confession—self-disclosure is a necessary component.
- It has "a taste for littleness," dwelling on the often ignored minutiae of daily life, while at the same time expanding the importance of the writer's self.
- It goes against the grain of popular opinion.
- It wrestles with the "stench of ego," trying to reveal the writer's true self without seeming narcissistic and proud.
- It demonstrates the author's learning while distancing itself from the scholarly treatise.
- Perhaps most important, it is a mode of thinking and being, an attempt "to test, to make a run at something without knowing whether you are going to succeed."

Although Lopate focuses more on the writer and her or his distinctive and idiosyncratic voice, you can see similarities between his definitions and those of Root and Steinberg. They all emphasize the essayist's independence and imagination. Writers of creative nonfiction, in short, are the *opposite* of the uninspired student grinding out a required essay. Instead, they are passionate about their subjects and committed to seeing them from as many angles as possible. Remember this key point as you begin thinking of the subject for your essay: it should be something that you truly want to explore rather than something you feel obliged to write about.

Let's look at one more list by one more expert on the subject. Lee Gutkind has been given, and has embraced, the moniker "the Godfather of Creative Nonfiction." He shares Lopate's focus on the personality and style of the writer, but Gutkind is more concerned with the writer's subject matter. In his journal *Creative Nonfiction* (issue no. 6, 1995), Gutkind describes "the 5 Rs" of creative nonfiction:

1. **Real Life** "The foundation of good writing emerges from personal experience."
2. **Reflection** "Creative nonfiction should reflect a writer's feelings and responses about a subject."

3. **Research** "I want to make myself knowledgeable enough to ask intelligent questions. If I can't display at least a minimal understanding of the subject about which I am writing, I will lose the confidence and the support of the people who must provide access to the experience."

4. **Reading** "Almost all writers have read the best writers in their field and are able to converse in great detail about the stylistic approach and intellectual content."

5. **"Riting"** "This is what art of any form is all about—the passion of the moment and the magic of the muse."

Most essayists would agree with *most* of these characterizations, but item 3 clearly places Gutkind's definition of creative nonfiction closer to journalism than to memoir. In fact, in the first issue of *Creative Nonfiction*, Gutkind claims that *reportage* (the French term for "reporting") is "the anchor and foundation of the highest quality of journalism and of creative nonfiction." In this respect, many of the essays published in *Creative Nonfiction* are in the camp of literary journalism, or New Journalism, which came of age in the 1960s and 1970s. Books such as Truman Capote's *In Cold Blood*, about a gruesome murder in Kansas, and Tom Wolfe's *The Electric Kool-Aid Acid Test*, which details the exploits of Ken Kesey's Merry Pranksters, found the authors either imaginatively re-creating scenes they didn't witness themselves (Capote) or directly participating in the lives of their subjects, which is normally taboo for journalists—Wolfe was "on the bus" and even experimented with LSD to capture the lives of the Pranksters.

Traditional reporting insists on the fiction of the invisible reporter "objectively" collecting facts and passing them on, without comment, to the reader; literary journalism, however, acknowledges the reality that *which* facts reporters choose to write about and *how* they convey those facts makes an enormous difference in what particular version of the truth is being told. Consequently, literary journalists employ many of the elements of fiction. Descriptions of places and people in literary journalism are far more lavish than in conventional reporting. Literary journalists use dialogue extensively. The writer's own point of view, her opinions about what she is witnessing, become part of the story. Because literary journalism is written by an individual writer with personal tastes, style is foregrounded. Nonetheless, as we shall see in the section "Ethics and Edicts," journalists must deal in facts, and readers must believe that what is reported on the page actually happened.

To inform or to entertain: Which should be your primary goal as an essayist? The debate goes back at least as far as the sixteenth century, when two of the masters of the genre were writing. Michel de Montaigne, a Frenchman often considered the father of the personal essay, wrote essays about himself, his friends and family, and on topics as diverse as glory, vanity, drunkenness, cannibals, and thumbs. Composed during the same period as Montaigne's informal pieces, the work of Francis Bacon represents a second strand of essay writing, sometimes known as the "traditional argument." Bacon prized clarity, order, and conciseness: the qualities that, until very recently, have dominated our thinking about what a good college essay should be. Yet from the perspective of creative nonfiction, even though Bacon remains an ideal of succinct, argumentative writing, he appears somewhat naive: he wants to condense his argument into a handful of crystal-hard sentences, to say everything there is about a topic in a few pages, which we now know is an impossible task.

These two essayists are often held up as conflicting models for creative nonfiction, with Montaigne recently having become the clear favorite among those making the comparison. Bacon is authoritative and final in his pronouncements, while Montaigne is open to changing his mind. Bacon has a clear thesis statement and follows it rigorously to its unequivocal conclusion; Montaigne meanders from thought to thought, like a child who is chasing a butterfly and stops to examine the flowers each time the butterfly alights. Bacon dictates; Montaigne suggests. Bacon instructs; Montaigne delights.

A great deal can be said for this contrast, but even Lopate, who clearly prefers Montaigne, believes that the two essayists "should not be viewed as opposites; the distinction between formal and informal essay can be overdone, and most great essayists have crossed the line frequently." Your essay may also cross and recross the line between informal and formal writing, but, like most of the essayists in this book, you should probably err on the side of the Montaignian tradition. Think first of keeping your readers interested before you worry too much about informing them. And don't stand on ceremony. We are accustomed to being on our best behavior in the formal academic essay. Figuratively speaking, we fold our hands in our laps and speak in a moderate tone of voice, making sure not to alienate our audience. As you know, too often the result is a dry piece of writing that puts the reader straight to sleep. But when you write creative nonfiction, you need to do a little bit of shouting and wave your arms around. Show us your most interesting self: beguile, intrigue, and charm us.

The elements of creative nonfiction ▶

The sections in this chapter are as follows:

- ▶ **Organizing Creative Nonfiction** The word "essay" comes from the French word *essai*, which means an "attempt," and indeed the essay form is often flexible and exploratory. However, there's a big difference between wandering with a purpose and writing without one. This section suggests several ways to structure your essay that still allow freedom and experimentation.

- ▶ **Telling the Truth** Perhaps the biggest difference between creative nonfiction and the other three genres discussed in this book is the "non-"

attached to "fiction." Whatever your subject, your reader will expect it to be true. Initially that might not sound like a difficult demand to negotiate; however, the vagaries of memory, competing interpretations of a single event, and our normal desire to portray ourselves in the best possible light all make telling the "truth" much trickier than one might think.

▶ **Creative Nonfiction as Narrative**   Many of the elements of fiction that make an entertaining story work equally well in creative nonfiction. True stories are often the most compelling ones, and the judicious use of dialogue, scene setting, and character development will aid in bringing your reader inside the world of your essay.

▶ **The Poetry of Creative Nonfiction**   Using various elements of poetry can make your creative nonfiction more vivid. From concrete imagery and surprising metaphors to the sounds and rhythms of language itself, many of the aspects of poetry that please readers of verse will also gratify readers of creative nonfiction.

▶ **Writing Yourself into Creative Nonfiction**   In creative nonfiction, it's all about you—really, it is. Even if you're not writing specifically about yourself, your own attitudes and opinions about your subject matter are a crucial component of your essay. Students moving from high school to college often report that their instructors forbid the use of the first-person pronoun. However, when it comes to creative nonfiction, point of view is crucial: you can't avoid the "I."

▶ **Ethics and Edicts**   Sometimes telling the truth can get you in trouble. You may hurt someone's feelings, or breach a confidence, or even make a claim that another person considers libelous. In this section, we discuss both the moral and legal dimensions of creative nonfiction, focusing on the demands of literary journalism.

Short creative nonfiction: Three models ▶

Like the short-short story, the short essay may range anywhere from 200 to 2,000 words. Two thousand words (seven or eight pages, depending on your font) may sound formidable to students who are used to writing brief academic essays, but the freedom of creative nonfiction, where *you* are in control of the subject and the style, tends to open the "wordgates." Once you start writing, you might even find yourself wondering how you will stay within a page count rather than how you will reach one.

Still, as you draft your essay, you need to address what Annie Dillard calls the "two crucial points" in any work of nonfiction: "what to put in and what to leave out." Even though creative nonfiction allows for exploration and asides, this genre is no more tolerant of padding than is any other form of creative writing. In a good short essay, every sentence is necessary and rewards careful consideration by the reader. *"Miniatures encourage attention,"* says Lia Purpura, "in the way whispering requires a listener to quiet down and incline toward the speaker. Sometimes we need binoculars, microscopes, viewmasters, steriopticons to assist our looking, but mediated or not, miniatures suggest there is more there than meets the eye easily. They suggest there is much to miss if we don't look hard at all the spaces, crevices, crannies."

Despite their length, the three model essays do indeed "look hard" at their topics. Rebecca McClanahan's "Liferower" uses the heart as a topic and a metaphor, shifting frequently from present to past and from fact to memory and imagination. Brian Doyle's *"Joyas Voladoras,"* as musical and imagistic as a prose poem, employs a less personal perspective on the subject, exploring the "spaces, crevices, and crannies" of hearts—both tiny and immense, real and figurative. And while comedy predominates in David Sedaris's "Jesus Shaves," the author also slyly scrutinizes the vagaries of language and the nature of spirituality.

The final section in this chapter provides kick-starts to get your creative juices flowing. However, because essay topics can be so wide ranging, you will probably find something worth writing about without too much effort. In fact, Linda Norlen, a former staff member of *Brevity: A Journal of Concise Literary Nonfictions*, says, "Good ideas are common; so are interesting experiences. The challenge is to develop the germ of the piece into something that is complete and resolved, and to do it in very few words." For Norlen, as for most other writers of creative nonfiction, a good idea is an essential starting point, but the writing itself determines the ultimate value of the essay.

Rebecca McClanahan

Liferower

Rebecca McClanahan's tenth book, *The Tribal Knot*, a multigenerational memoir based on hundreds of archival documents, will be published by Indiana University Press in 2013. Other books include *The Riddle Song and Other Rememberings*, and *Deep Light: New and Selected Poems*. The winner of the Glasgow Prize in Nonfiction, she has published her work in *Best American Essays, Best American Poetry, The Kenyon Review, The Gettysburg Review, The Sun,* and numerous anthologies. McClanahan teaches in the MFA programs of Queens University and Rainier Writers Workshop.

"Liferower" is an essay about working out on an exercise machine, but the thoughts that her workout inspire are far ranging, ultimately leading to a meditation on life and death. McClanahan uses the segmented essay form. Each block of text is juxtaposed against the next in mosaic fashion, and with so few traditional transition sentences, we never quite know what's coming next.

There I am on the Liferower screen, the computerized woman in the tiny boat, and the little woman rowing below me is my pacer. We look exactly alike, except she does not get tired. Her strokes are even and unchanging. I aim for thirty-three pulls per minute, but if I rest even a second between strokes, I fall behind. I want to train my heart, to make it stronger.

"Keep up with the pacer," blinks the sign on the screen. "Use your legs. Keep your back straight."

You row with your whole body, not just your arms. There is a leaning into, then a pulling away. The filling and the emptying. Systole, diastole. The iambic lub and dub—and sometimes a murmur, a leak in the heart. My father's valve has been replaced with plastic that clicks when he overexerts himself. Bad hearts run in our family. An infant sister died of a congenital ailment; another sister nearly died from a myocardial infection contracted while she was giving birth to her second child. I have no children. Which is why I am free to come here to the Y and row my heart out three times a week. Aside from a husband who can take care of himself—as most second husbands are able to do—I have no one to worry about. This thought disturbs me, wakes me at night. If I have no one to care for, who will care for me? When I was small I shared a bedroom with an old woman, my mother's childless aunt, who had nowhere else to go. I have fifteen nephews and nieces. Will any of them claim me? Each month from my paycheck I put away more than I can afford, insurance against what time will bring. According to surveys, women fear old age more than men do—the poverty, the loneliness. And the hearts of women beat faster and harder, both waking and sleeping, than the hearts of men.

"Keep up the good work. You are one boat ahead."

From the shoreline a crowd of miniature fans waves me on to victory. Each time I pull the rowing rope, the little woman on the screen moves her cartoon arms. The oar dips and lifts and a ripple of water sloshes across the screen, accompanied by a *whoosh* that's intended to sound like rushing water, but sounds more like the breath of a woman in labor: in through the nose, out through the mouth. Whoosh, whoosh. In the delivery room I smoothed my sister's clenched fist and watched the electrocardiograph as twin waves danced across the screen—the rise and fall of mother and daughter. The heart is a double pump composed of four separate rooms. If I divide my age into four equal chambers, I am eleven again. It is the year I begin to bleed, the year my mother pushes my sister into the world.

I pump my legs and pull the rope. In a large open area beside the rowing machines, a yoga class begins. The instructor greets the sun, breathing in *prana*, the invisible life force: in through the nose, out through the mouth. The other women follow, open their mouths on the first half of the healing mantra *Om*. The yoga master has now become a tree—arms branching into finger leaves high above her head, one leg balanced against a thigh, the other the root sinking her deep into imaginary soil. *You can't learn balance,* she is saying. *You can only allow it.* The heart is controlled by two opposing bundles of nerves, the sympathetic and the parasympathetic. One slows the beat, the other quickens it. Thus, balance is achieved through a back and forth dance, two mutually antagonistic forces pushing simultaneously against and for one another.

On the screen, red buoys bob between me and my pacer, marking off the miles in tenths: one point six, one point seven. The water rolls beneath us, and in the distance a miniature skyline looms. It's the kind of city a child might construct from Lego pieces, chunks of towers and boxy buildings in the shape of bar graphs a math teacher draws on the blackboard. What goes up must come down. My Y locker combination—32-22-32—is easy to remember because those were my measurements half a lifetime ago, when I was being fitted for my first wedding dress. The marriage lasted three years, three years longer than it should have because I was determined not to fail. My mother was my measure, my pacer, and when my husband began turning from me, I rowed faster and faster toward him. I would work harder, cook more of his favorite foods, steam his khakis with a sharper pleat.

"Lean into the stroke. Keep up with the pacer. You are three boats behind."

On the rower beside mine, a young woman pumps with long tanned legs and pulls with lean muscled arms that she probably believes will never soften. Her body is something she counts on—the belly flat, the skin snug and elastic as the Spandex leotard glowing in oranges and greens, the neon parrot hues of one whose life does not yet depend on camouflage. The weight instructor, a short well-built man about my age, bends to speak to her, to comment on her form and technique. He does not see me. When he leaves, she watches her reflection in the floor-to-ceiling mirror as if her body belongs to someone else. Her forehead is prematurely lined with worry; she is not enjoying this. Nearby, the yoga master assumes the lion pose, crouched and ready. She bares her teeth, lifts her mane into the air.

"Use your legs. Keep your back straight. You are five boats behind."

The heart is a hollow muscle housed in a slippery, loose-fitting sac and protected by three layers of membranes. Its size varies from person to person, but is approximately the size of a clenched fist. At five weeks a fetus is barely eight millimeters long, but already its heart is beating on its own. When my sister had her first sonogram, I watched on the screen the undulating blur that would become my niece. The heart cells were already in place, all the cells my niece would need for the rest of her life. Her heartbeat sounded like a train roaring through a tunnel. A child comes into this world hammering its heart out, 160 beats per minute, a Teletype machine tapping its urgent message. And deep in the atrial chamber of each adult there survives a hole, the *foramen ovale*, remnant of the place where blood passed through the fetal heart.

The child I chose against would have been born into the cramped space of my life between marriages. I still ask myself how it could have happened. Things happen. You wake one morning and you know. Your tender breasts tell you and the flush across your cheeks and the feeling of something larger and smaller than yourself moving inside you. Time passes, liquid as a dream, and one morning, because you are alone and your life is a rented room, you make the call. And the next day when it's over and the nurse takes the gauze from between your teeth, the doctor, who is kind and slightly plump, his forehead lined from having seen too much, holds up a glass bottle filled with something bright and red. And then it's over, it's done. But your legs are still trembling and your tongue is bleeding from where you bit down and missed.

Five boats ahead of me, the pacer slides over the finish line, leaving buoys bobbing in her wake. I place my fingertips on my carotid artery and begin the count that will bring me back to myself. Easing up on the rope, I pump slower, slower, my boat cruising past the crowd of bystanders waving from the shoreline. The yoga master begins her descent into this world, shifting from eagle to fish to cat to flower, shape by shape removing herself, moving towards a place that knows no shape. When she reaches it, she bows to the altar of Sadguru, the larger self that dwells within the smallest place. Forehead pressed to the ground, she assumes the child position: shoulders down, knees folded to belly, hands and feet at rest, ears open to the slightest sound. The music of a single heartbeat is actually two-part harmony, a duet sung by opposing valves, the low-pitched *lub* of the atrioventricular and the higher pitched *dub* as the semilunar closes down. The yoga master opens her mouth on "O" and the others follow, float on this communal pond until together their lips close on the hum and, one by one, their single breaths give out. ◄

Brian Doyle

Joyas Voladoras

Brian Doyle is the editor of *Portland Magazine* and the author of *The Wet Engine: Exploring the Mad Wild Miracle of the Heart*, from which this self-contained selection is taken; the essay collection *Grace Notes*; and *The Grail: A Year Spent Ambling and Shambling through an Oregon Vineyard in Pursuit of the Best Pinot Noir Wine in the Whole Wide World*. His essays have appeared in a number of publications, including *The Atlantic Monthly* and *Harper's*.

"*Joyas Voladoras*" originally appeared in the *American Scholar* and was chosen for *The Best American Essays 2005*. Like "Liferower," Doyle's essay contains factual information about the heart, though he is celebratory where McClanahan is full of apprehension and foreboding. Doyle was inspired to compose the piece after his son was born with a missing chamber in his heart and was forced to undergo surgery at the age of five months and again when he was a year and a half old. Yet Doyle never mentions this distressing fact. Instead, he focuses his essay on the wonders and delights—both physical and figurative—of this amazing and indispensable muscle.

Consider the hummingbird for a long moment. A hummingbird's heart beats ten times a second. A hummingbird's heart is the size of a pencil eraser. A hummingbird's heart is a lot of the hummingbird. *Joyas Voladoras*, flying jewels, the first white explorers in the Americas called them, and the white men had never seen such creatures, for hummingbirds came into the world only in the Americas, nowhere else in the universe, more than three hundred species of them whirring and zooming and nectaring in hummer time zones nine times removed from ours, their hearts hammering faster than we could clearly hear if we pressed our elephantine ears to their infinitesimal chests.

Each one visits a thousand flowers a day. They can dive at sixty miles an hour. They can fly backward. They can fly more than five hundred miles without pausing to rest. But when they rest they come close to death: on frigid nights, or when they are starving, they retreat into torpor, their metabolic rate slowing to a fifteenth of their normal sleep rate, their hearts sludging nearly to a halt, barely beating, and if they are not soon warmed, if they do not soon find that which is sweet, their hearts grow cold, and they cease to be. Consider for a moment those hummingbirds who did not open their eyes again today, this very day, in the Americas: bearded helmetcrests and booted racket-tails, violet-tailed sylphs and violet-capped woodnymphs, crimson topazes and purple-crowned fairies, red-tailed comets and amethyst woodstars, rainbow-bearded thornbills and glittering-bellied emeralds, velvet-purple coronets and golden-bellied starfrontlets, fiery-tailed awlbills and Andean hillstars, spatuletails and puff legs, each the most amazing thing you have never seen, each thunderous wild heart the size of an infant's fingernail, each mad heart silent, a brilliant music stilled.

Hummingbirds, like all flying birds but more so, have incredible enormous immense ferocious metabolisms. To drive those metabolisms they have racecar hearts that eat oxygen at an eye-popping rate. Their hearts are built of thinner, leaner fibers than ours. Their arteries are stiffer and more taut. They have more mitochondria in their heart muscles—anything to gulp more oxygen. Their hearts are stripped to the skin for the war against gravity and inertia, the mad search for food, the insane idea of flight. The price of their ambition is a life closer to death; they suffer more heart attacks and aneurysms and ruptures than any other living creature. It's expensive to fly. You burn out. You fry the machine. You melt the engine. Every creature on earth has approximately two billion heartbeats to spend in a lifetime. You can spend them slowly, like a tortoise, and live to be two hundred years old, or you can spend them fast, like a humming-bird, and live to be two years old.

The biggest heart in the world is inside the blue whale. It weighs more than seven tons. It's as big as a room. It *is* a room, with four chambers. A child could walk around in it, head high, bending only to step through the valves. The valves are as big as the swinging doors in a saloon. This house of a heart drives a creature a hundred feet long. When this creature is born it is twenty feet long and weighs four tons. It is waaaaay bigger than your car. It drinks a hundred gallons of milk from its mama every day and gains two hundred pounds a day, and when it is seven or eight years old it endures an unimaginable puberty and then it essen-tially disappears from human ken, for next to nothing is known of the mat-ing habits, travel patterns, diet, social life, language, social structure, diseases, spirituality, wars, stories, despairs and arts of the blue whale. There are perhaps ten thousand blue whales in the world, living in every ocean on earth, and of the largest mammal who ever lived we know nearly nothing. But we know this: the animals with the largest hearts in the world generally travel in pairs, and their penetrating moaning cries, their piercing yearning tongue, can be heard underwater for miles and miles.

Mammals and birds have hearts with four chambers. Reptiles and turtles have hearts with three chambers. Fish have hearts with two chambers. Insects and mollusks have hearts with one chamber. Worms have hearts with one chamber, although they may have as many as eleven single-chambered hearts. Unicellular bacteria have no hearts at all; but even they have fluid eternally in motion, wash-ing from one side of the cell to the other, swirling and whirling. No living being is without interior liquid motion. We all churn inside.

So much held in a heart in a lifetime. So much held in a heart in a day, an hour, a moment. We are utterly open with no one, in the end—not mother and father, not wife or husband, not lover, not child, not friend. We open windows to each but we live alone in the house of the heart. Perhaps we must. Perhaps we could not bear to be so naked, for fear of a constantly harrowed heart. When young we think there will come one person who will savor and sustain us always; when we are older we know this is the dream of a child, that all hearts finally are bruised and scarred, scored and torn, repaired by time and will, patched by forces of character, yet fragile and rickety forevermore, no matter how ferocious the defense and how many bricks you bring to the wall. You can brick up your heart as stout and tight and hard and cold and impregnable as you possibly can and down it comes in an instant, felled by a woman's second glance, a child's apple breath, the shatter of glass in the road, the words "I have something to tell you," a cat with a broken spine dragging itself into the forest to die, the brush of your mother's papery ancient hand in the thicket of your hair, the memory of your father's voice early in the morning echoing from the kitchen where he is making pancakes for his children. ◄

David Sedaris

Jesus Shaves

David Sedaris, whom Whitney Pastorek calls "the preeminent humorist of his generation," was born in Binghamton, New York, and grew up in Raleigh, North Carolina. He came to prominence in 1992 when his essay "Santaland Diaries" aired on National Public Radio. Sedaris's many subsequent appearances on NPR made his speaking voice nearly as famous as his comic memoirs. That voice—nasal, nerdy, and often brutally ironic—is the perfect complement to his acerbic observations on everything from cleaning houses to the meaning of life.

"Jesus Shaves," taken from Sedaris's 1997 essay collection, *Holidays on Ice*, recounts the efforts of a class of beginning French speakers to describe to their professor the meaning of Easter. Although the essay is set in France, it is written entirely in English, and much of the fun comes from the English translations of the wretched French the students attempt to speak. Humorists frequently use exaggeration to generate comedy, and this short piece of creative nonfiction is probably at least as much "creative" as it is "nonfiction." Nevertheless, "Jesus Shaves" demonstrates the elasticity of the genre: sometimes it's okay, Sedaris reminds us, just to make your reader laugh.

"And what does one do on the fourteenth day of July? Does one celebrate Bastille Day?"

It was my second month of French class, and the teacher was leading us in an exercise designed to promote the use of *one*, our latest personal pronoun.

"Might one sing on Bastille Day?" she asked. "Might one dance in the streets? Somebody give me an answer."

Printed in our textbooks was a list of major holidays accompanied by a scattered arrangement of photographs depicting French people in the act of celebration. The object of the lesson was to match the holiday with the corresponding picture. It was simple enough but seemed an exercise better suited to the use of the pronoun *they*. I don't know about the rest of the class, but when Bastille Day eventually rolled around, I planned to stay home and clean my oven.

Normally, when working from the book, it was my habit to tune out my fellow students and scout ahead, concentrating on the question I'd calculated might fall to me, but this afternoon we were veering from the usual format. Questions were answered on a volunteer basis, and I was able to sit back and relax, confident that the same few students would do most of the talking. Today's discussion was dominated by an Italian nanny, two chatty Poles, and a pouty, plump Moroccan woman who had grown up speaking French and had enrolled in the class hoping to improve her spelling. She'd covered these lessons back in the third grade and took every opportunity to demonstrate her superiority. A question would be asked, and she'd race to give the answer, behaving as though this were a game show and, if quick enough, she might go home with a tropical vacation or a side-by-side refrigerator/freezer. A transfer student, by the end of her first day she'd raised her hand so many times that her shoulder had given out. Now she just leaned back and shouted out the answers, her bronzed arms folded across her chest like some great grammar genie.

We'd finished discussing Bastille Day, and the teacher had moved on to Easter, which was represented in our textbooks by a black-and-white photograph of a chocolate bell lying upon a bed of palm fronds.

"And what does one do on Easter?" she asked. "Would anyone like to tell us?"

The Italian nanny was attempting to answer when the Moroccan student interrupted, shouting, "Excuse me, but what's an Easter?"

It would seem that despite having grown up in a Muslim country, she would have heard it mentioned once or twice, but no. "I mean it," she said. "I have no idea what you people are talking about."

Our teacher then called on the rest of us to explain.

The Poles led the charge to the best of their ability. "It is," said one, "a party for the little boy of God who calls his self Jesus and . . . " She faltered and her fellow countryman came to her aid.

"He call his self Jesus and then he die one day on two . . . morsels of . . . lumber."

The rest of the class jumped in, offering bits of information that would have given the pope an aneurysm.

"He die one day and then he go above of my head to live with your father."

"He weared of himself the long hair and after he die, the first day he come back here for to say hello to the peoples."

"He nice, the Jesus."

"He make the good things, and on the Easter we be sad because somebody makes him dead today."

Part of the problem had to do with vocabulary. Simple nouns such as *cross* and *resurrection* were beyond our grasp, let alone such complex reflexive phrases as "to give of yourself your only begotten son." Faced with the challenge of explaining the cornerstone of Christianity, we did what any self-respecting group of people might do. We talked about food instead.

"Easter is a party for to eat of the lamb," the Italian nanny explained. "One too may eat of the chocolate."

"And who brings the chocolate?" the teacher asked.

I knew the word so I raised my hand, saying, "The rabbit of Easter. He bring of the chocolate."

"A rabbit?" The teaching, assuming I had used the wrong word, positioned her index fingers on top of her head, wriggling them as though they were ears. "You mean one of these? A *rabbit* rabbit?"

"Well, sure," I said. "He come in the night when one sleep on a bed. With a hand he have a basket and foods."

The teacher sighed and shook her head. As far as she was concerned, I had just explained everything that was wrong with my country. "No, no," she said. "Here in France the chocolate is brought by a big bell that flies in from Rome."

I called for a time-out. "But how do the bell know where you live?"

"Well," she said, "how does a rabbit?"

It was a decent point, but a least a rabbit has eyes. That's a start. Rabbits move from place to place, while most bells can only go back and forth—they can't even do that on their own power. On top of that, the Easter Bunny has character. He's someone you'd like to meet and shake hands with. A bell has all the personality of a cast-iron skillet. It's like saying that come Christmas, a magic dustpan flies in from the North Pole, led by eight flying cinder blocks. Who wants to stay up all night so they can see a bell? And why fly one in from Rome when they've got more bells than they know what to do with right here in Paris? That's the most implausible aspect of the whole story, as there's no way the bells of France would allow a foreign worker to fly in and take their jobs. That Roman bell would be lucky to get work cleaning up for a French bell's dog—and even then he'd need papers. It just didn't add up.

Nothing we said was of any help to the Moroccan student. A dead man with long hair supposedly living with her father, a leg of lamb served with palm fronds and chocolate; equally confused and disgusted, she shrugged her massive shoulders and turned her attention back to the comic book she kept hidden beneath her binder.

I wondered then if, without the language barrier, my classmates and I could have done a better job making sense of Christianity, an idea that sounds pretty far-fetched to begin with.

In communicating any religious belief, the operative word is *faith*, a concept illustrated by our very presence in that classroom. Why bother struggling with the grammar lessons of a six-year-old if each of us didn't believe that, against all reason, we might eventually improve? If I could hope to one day carry on a fluent conversation, it was a relatively short leap to believing that a rabbit might visit my home in the middle of the night, leaving behind a handful of chocolate kisses and a carton of menthol cigarettes. So why stop there? If I could believe in myself, why not give other improbabilities the benefit of the doubt? I told myself that despite her past behavior, my teacher was a kind and loving person who had only my best interests at heart. I accepted the idea that an omniscient God had cast me in his own image and that he watched over me and guided me from one place to the next. The Virgin Birth, the Resurrection, and the countless miracles—my heart expanded to encompass all the wonders and possibilities of the universe.

A bell, though—that's fucked up. ◀

Organizing creative nonfiction ▶

One of the great pleasures of writing creative nonfiction is the opportunity it gives you to go from thought to thought, and from one place and time to the next. However, if you attended an American high school in the recent past, most likely the essays you had to write were nothing like the three essays you have just read. Instead, you probably encountered a creature sometimes referred to as the five-paragraph theme. The structure of that essay is straightforward: it begins with an introductory paragraph consisting of a hook to draw the reader in and quickly moves to a thesis statement that presents the topic of the essay. Each of the three body paragraphs begins with a topic sentence that is followed by supporting evidence. The concluding paragraph summarizes the essay's three main points and then ends with a slight twist designed to leave the reader thinking further about the material.

There is nothing inherently wrong with this particular type of essay. If he could be transported from the sixteenth to the twenty-first century, Francis Bacon would find it a rather familiar form. And, in fact, the five-paragraph theme serves a clear purpose for high school English teachers who must grade hundreds of papers every semester. If students have a clear structure they are supposed to follow, it's easier to assess whether they have achieved their goals.

You may be surprised to learn, therefore, that most writers of creative nonfiction look at the five-paragraph essay and shake their heads in dismay. The idea of being boxed into such a tight, uncompromising structure seems ridiculous to them. What if the writer has only one main point, instead of three, but she has six different ways to approach and support her argument? What if the essayist wants to make ten very short points? Or what if he doesn't want to make a point at all but instead prefers to explore the topic and come to the conclusion that there is no conclusion? Jonis Agee is fairly typical in her attitude toward essay structure. She writes not to prove a thesis, but because "certain thoughts or perceptions or experiences are pressing on me for attention. My job in writing the essay then is to discover the unique connections that these elements possess and what that connection means."

What true essayists want to do is *essayer* (another French term), "to attempt"; they value the process of investigation, but that doesn't mean their final products have no organizational principle. Often the essayist simply begins writing about those thoughts, perceptions, and experiences that are pressing for her attention; the act of writing helps her discover what she knows about her topic, and before long, a way of organizing the essay becomes evident. In fact, for all their freedom of exploration, each of our three model essayists employs a fairly clear structure.

Philip Lopate points out that "many times the personal essayist will start to explore a subject, then set up a countertheme, and eventually braid the two." We see this skillful interlacing of themes quite clearly in Rebecca McClanahan's essay. She introduces us to the Liferower machine, briefly discusses the heart, and then begins weaving in autobiographical details. McClanahan's braids are generally short units: one or two related sentences. And she introduces a number of thematic elements: working out, her family's heart problems, her marriages, her nieces and nephews, yoga, her abortion. The Liferower itself is the most frequently repeated of these elements, and one might almost think of the essay's structure as a maypole, with references to the rowing machine serving as a kind of post around which McClanahan's other themes are wrapped like colored ribbons.

"Liferower" uses another common organizational tactic: individual blocks of text are juxtaposed against one another without traditional transition sentences. Root and Steinberg call this technique "jump cuts." In fact, the blank spaces between sections serve as a kind of "anti-transition," with the white space suggesting that the writer mistrusts traditional transitions. Life seems to be a series of things happening one after another, without obvious cause and effect; it is with difficulty that we piece together the diverse moments in our lives. To add yet another metaphor into the mix, Root compares the white spaces in the segmented essay to the divisions between layers of sedimentary deposits: "Perhaps this is a geologic essay, then," he says of essays like "Liferower," "or a tectonic essay, where the segments are like plates moving and colliding and rearranging themselves on the crust of the essay."

The idea that the essay can be active, even destructive, jibes with McClanahan's own sense of the form. She says that writing a memoir "requires the most destruction" of any form of creative writing, "particularly in the early stages of the draft. One has to destroy—or at least deconstruct—what happened before one can make a text out of that happening." If you decide to write about your own past, keep in mind McClanahan's advice: at some point, the *writing* of your memoir is going to supersede your own memories, and the life you have lived will become secondary to your expression of it.

Brian Doyle also uses braiding and segmenting to structure his essay. If we use the maypole analogy again, Doyle's discussions of the heart might be compared to the post around which his various comments are wound. Like McClanahan, Doyle uses self-contained blocks of text that also serve as paragraphs. Transitions from one paragraph to the next are less clearly marked than in "Jesus Shaves" but are more evident than in "Liferower." Frequently, Doyle's transitions are implicit rather than explicit, but he does provide us with something resembling a topic sentence in each of his paragraphs: "Each [hummingbird] visits a thousand flowers a day." "Hummingbirds, like all flying birds but more so, have incredible enormous immense ferocious metabolisms." "The biggest heart in the world is inside the blue whale." And so on. Individual segments stray somewhat from what you might guess to be the paragraph's topic, but each paragraph does address the subject in some fashion.

While there are a number of asides in "Jesus Shaves," the essay's organization is basically chronological, moving from the beginning of a French class to its conclusion. Comedy requires clarity, and David Sedaris clearly notes who's speaking, what they're saying, and where we are in each part of the lesson. Shane Borrowman emphasizes the importance of making clear connections among the disparate parts of an essay: "Writing creative nonfiction requires a knack for linking lived experience with echoes of interpretation. It's all about carpentry, about nailing the pieces of narrative together with transitions, about spiking the past to the present to clarify both, about gluing surface events together to add strength and depth and meaning." David Sedaris repeatedly demonstrates his skills as a carpenter of language. Transitions, especially, are handled with aplomb in "Jesus Shaves." Often the opening sentence of a paragraph references the previous paragraph while introducing new material. For instance, "It was a decent point," Sedaris concedes after his teacher wonders how rabbits know where people live; then he shifts to his own point that rabbits are likely to have a better sense of direction than bells because "at least rabbits have eyes."

Like McClanahan, Sedaris juggles a number of repeating subjects: the students' inability to speak proper French, the idiosyncrasies of his fellow students, the ways different cultures celebrate religious holidays. His braiding is perhaps less obvious than that of McClanahan and Doyle, but he's just as preoccupied as they are with weaving the strands of his essay together.

Overall design is obviously important to these authors, and they are particularly concerned with the beginnings and endings of their essays. As editors tell journalists, "Don't bury your lead," meaning journalists should put their strongest material first. Drawing the reader in immediately is probably the most important task of any essayist. Unless readers are intrigued enough to make a commitment to a piece of writing, they will never see whatever glories lie within.

Sedaris's opening sentences are unexpected: "And what does one do on the fourteenth of July? Does one celebrate Bastille Day?" If we live in North America, we might immediately we wonder: Why would we be celebrating Bastille Day? And what is going on with the strange use of the pronoun "one"? The short second paragraph answers our questions, and the third paragraph reinforces the note of absurd humor introduced in the first as we imagine ourselves singing and dancing in the streets. *What strange detail will be next?* we want to know, so we read on.

Doyle's first line asks us to "consider the hummingbird for a long moment." *Why bother?* we might wonder, although there is something engaging about his request that our consideration last a "long" moment. Then right away we learn that the hummingbird deserves extra attention because it is such a fascinating and unusual creature: "A hummingbird's heart beats ten times a second. A hummingbird's heart is the size of a pencil eraser. A hummingbird's heart is a lot of the hummingbird."

McClanahan's initial block of text compares the miniature digital woman portrayed on her exercise machine—someone who never gets exhausted—with her own less flourishing condition: "There I am on the Liferower screen, the computerized woman in the tiny boat, and the little woman rowing below me is my pacer. We look exactly alike, except she does not get tired. Her strokes are even and unchanging. I aim for thirty-three pulls per minute, but if I rest even a second between strokes, I fall behind. I want to train my heart, to make it stronger." Again, the author finds a way to interest us in her situation, to make us wonder: What has happened that she needs to train her heart and make it stronger?

Let's look now at the end of the essay. Knowing how to conclude requires paying attention to the material you have already written so that you can close on a powerful moment. All three writers find such a moment in their essays. McClanahan uses her final paragraph to tie together the many themes she has been working with. Most important, she has made an implicit argument that no matter how much we worry about our past transgressions, no matter how hard we exercise to try to forget them, it will all wind up the same: in death. McClanahan uses the end of the nearby yoga lesson to symbolize our inevitable, "communal" annihilation: "The yoga master opens her mouth on 'O' and the others follow, float on this communal pond until together their lips close on the hum and, one by one, their single breaths give out." Doyle's last sentence includes a long list of poignant things and events: "a woman's second glance, a child's apple breath, the shatter of glass in the road, the words 'I have something to tell you,' a cat with a broken spine dragging itself into the forest to die, the brush of your mother's papery ancient hand in the thicket of your hair, the memory of your father's voice early in the morning echoing from the kitchen where he is making pancakes for his children." And Sedaris, after waxing poetically about how the day's lesson has caused his heart to expand and "encompass all the wonders and possibilities of the universe," suddenly remembers the flying bell of Easter, whereupon he comically undercuts everything he has just been saying.

Finding a strong conclusion is likely to be one of your most demanding tasks as an essayist, yet if you do it well, it will also be one of your most rewarding accomplishments. Lee Martin knows he has come to the end of an essay by listening "closely enough to hear the resonance of something popping into sharp relief—to hear a turn or an irony or a deepening that tells me I've gotten somewhere I had no idea I was going when I set out." Rather than belaboring a point, as you might if you were writing for another class, listen for that moment of resonance, then end your essay quickly, so that your conclusion continues to reverberate in your reader's mind.

CHECKLIST Organizing creative nonfiction

☐ **Is your reader immediately drawn into your essay?** Like any effective piece of creative writing, a good short personal essay needs a strong introduction. Be sure that by the end of the first paragraph there is something about your essay—an unanswered question, a hint of mystery, a promise of the fascinating material still to come—that will make a reader want to continue reading.

☐ **If, like most essayists, you are braiding several topics together, is each thematic strand clear? Are transitions between those strands well marked?** One of the essay's great pleasures, for both writers and readers, is its ability to address multiple topics in a relatively short space. However, readers can easily get confused if themes aren't clear. Transitions, even if they are only the white space between segments of your essay, should aid readers in the sometimes difficult mental process of jumping from one theme to another.

☐ **Does each paragraph have a clear focus?** Granted, you are not composing a traditional academic essay, but that's no excuse for sloppy, imprecise writing. Essay readers expect authors to have complete control of their material. Ensuring that each of your paragraphs concentrates on an easily identifiable cluster of ideas or images will keep readers engaged from beginning to end.

☐ **Does your essay have a strong conclusion?** Make sure you give sufficient attention to your last two or three paragraphs. Short creative nonfiction rarely attempts to tie up everything in a neat package. Instead, conclusions are more often startling and surprising, with the *oomph* one expects from the ending of a good story or poem. Try to avoid the obvious moralizing you may have engaged in when you were in your introductory composition class. Instead, consider ending your essay with a striking image that evokes all that has come before.

Telling the truth ▶

Students in introductory creative writing courses often refer to their nonfiction essays as "stories," and that makes sense inasmuch as telling a good story is typically a key element of a successful piece of creative nonfiction. However, there is one crucial difference: stories are fictional, or made up, whereas essays, in the words of Michael Pearson, have "a genuine obligation to factual truths."

But what is truth? Postmodernists tell us that "The Truth" is an illusion; instead, there are many lowercase "truths." We each inevitably construct our own individual version of reality, and our version can never be *entirely* in accord with the truth perceived by those around us. To an extent, of course, we know that to be the case from the experience of our daily lives. Even people who are very close to one another—best friends, sisters and brothers, husbands and wives—occasionally view things very differently. "Especially when it comes to personal essays and memoirs," say B. Minh Nguyen and Porter Shreve, "the nature of 'truth' is bound so inescapably by personal viewpoints that it can never be charted and pinpointed."

Memory is selective, and writers of creative nonfiction must take this into account. Essayist John Lane says, "I don't make things up, but I work from and trust memory, my memory." Yet Lane acknowledges that different people remembering the same event will not only remember the event differently but also "come to different conclusions about what situations mean."

Most of us will acknowledge that our memories rarely function to perfection. We misremember details. We may even wish things had happened other than they did, so much so that our memory actually begins to transform the past. Yet despite memory's notorious inaccuracy, personal essayists rely on it heavily to help them gauge the truth of an event. For Brett Lott, self-scrutiny is the most effective method of combating our tendency to reshape the past: "Only through rigorous and ruthless questioning of the self can we hope to arrive at any kind of truth."

"Tell the truth," says Laurie Lynn Drummond, "even if it makes you wince." And wince we often do, as we look back on our lives and remember all the things we shouldn't have done. Ironically, of course, the memories that make us most uncomfortable are often the very ones that make the best subject matter for our essays. This is clearly the case for Rebecca McClanahan in "Liferower." Although she mentions her abortion in only one paragraph, the rest of the essay hovers around that painful event. While Brian Doyle never mentions his son's heart problems, we know from biographical material that the genesis of *"Joyas Voladoras"* is a family crisis. And David Sedaris's comic recounting of his French class is full of moments when his lack of fluency in French makes him seem downright ridiculous.

The events we write about may not necessarily be painful; nevertheless, it is still challenging to write about our lives accurately. One way to convince your reader that you are telling the truth is to concentrate on something that happened a short while ago. McClanahan emphasizes the recentness of her experience by writing about it in the present tense. Of course, we know that she is not scribbling away while she works out on an exercise machine. Yet the combination of present tense and clear recall of specific details is enough to convince most readers that these events happened more or less the way she claims.

While David Sedaris writes in the past tense, "Jesus Shaves" is told in a minute-by-minute fashion that mimics the way real life unspools. Sedaris is sitting in a classroom, presumably with a notebook in front of him: we can easily imagine him jotting down his teacher's and classmates' comments, their expressions and gestures, and his own responses to the crazy conversation. Granted, every quote may not be exact—in fact, we know that the dialogue has been translated from the French—but his description of a particularly funny day in French class is close enough to achieve **verisimilitude**, the realistic portrayal of people and their environments.

The trouble, of course, comes when we move further into the past. How do we know we can trust the truth of distant memories? We talk more about the problems in fictionalizing our lives in the next section, but for now it's important to note that one way of anticipating potential reader objections is by suggesting that some of the events occurred on a number of occasions. If someone frequently made the same comment ("Well, I'll be danged"), it's no wonder the author can remember it well. Similarly, we are likely to remember a particularly striking remark—"'The rabbit of Easter. He bring of the chocolate"—long after it is uttered.

Fortunately, readers of creative nonfiction generally don't expect writers to have a *precise* memory of dialogue spoken years earlier. Even a stickler for accuracy like Lee Gutkind admits that when he reads a book of creative nonfiction, he knows that "certain situations are going to be manipulated." Some writers compress material that happened over the course of several weeks into a single day. We inevitably leave out material that doesn't add to the main thrust of our essay. And time blurs the fine lines of details, so writers may employ their imaginations to sharpen the focus.

Nevertheless, readers do expect "truth in advertising." As Gil Allen notes, "If you call something a memoir . . . then you're obliged to respect the facts. You're free to select from them, emphasize them, and reconstruct them according to your own conscience, but you can't write as if they don't exist." Or, as Carol Bly observes, "Readers rightly feel bruised and condescended to when an author lies to them."

This is certainly what happened in the case of James Frey and his book *A Million Little Pieces*. The story made headlines in the national news. After being endorsed by Oprah Winfrey, Frey's "memoir" about his drug and alcohol addiction and recovery became a best seller, until journalists writing for the Smoking Gun Web site revealed that much of what Frey had reported to be true in his book was, in fact, fiction. Frey's national humiliation included Oprah Winfrey's public chastisement and harsh rebukes from creative nonfiction gurus such as Lee Gutkind.

Of course, Frey did have his defenders. They claimed that the *essence* of what he had written about was true for many addicts. Even if Frey hadn't actually been through some of the events he described, he nevertheless captured the pain and suffering and self-loathing that accompany addiction, as well as the break-through that comes when an addict admits he has a problem and begins to face it seriously.

More recently, Jonah Lehrer, a writer for *The New Yorker*, found himself in trouble after he invented quotes by Bob Dylan for a chapter in his best-selling book *Imagine: How Creativity Works*. Michael Moynihan, a journalist and Dylan fan, confronted Lehrer about the fabricated material, and Lehrer ultimately had to admit the quotes "either did not exist, were unintentional misquotations, or represented improper combinations of previously existing quotes." Lehrer's untruthfulness cost him big. He resigned from *The New Yorker*, his publisher pulled *Imagine* from the market, and public opinion ran strongly against him.

Writers of creative nonfiction often issue disclaimers acknowledging that—in order to protect the privacy of others (and avoid potential lawsuits)—the names, places, and descriptions of people have been altered. James Brown's pow-erful book *The Los Angeles Diaries*, also about addiction and recovery, did just that. However, James Frey's book had no such disclaimers, and many people would agree with Sherry Simpson that "there's a place for his kind of writing. It's in the section titled 'Fiction.' " Frey's detractors point out that that is precisely what fiction is for: to *suggest* a higher Truth, not to claim to be something it is not. In the end, Frey and Lehrer, probably would have done well to heed E. B. White's warning that an essayist "cannot indulge himself in deceit or concealment, for he will be found out in no time."

Making an honest attempt to recount what happened in your life is part of telling the truth in a personal essay. However, when the essay contains factual material, something that a reader could actually verify, you must do your home-work. The idea of conducting research for your essay may sound like a chore, but when you are the one deciding what needs to be investigated, you may find that there is a feeling of power and pleasure involved. Some authors enjoy the research as much as—or even more than—the writing itself. Joan Didion, one of our finest essayists, believes that organizing notes and facts is a kind of art form in itself: "Writing nonfiction is more like sculpture, a matter of shaping the research into the finished thing."

Whether or not you like researching, nothing undercuts reader confidence in a piece of creative nonfiction as quickly as a carelessly researched fact or a slipshod statement that a brief check in a reliable database reveals to be false. In contrast, a few well-placed details from even an hour's worth of Internet or library research can bolster your authority considerably. Brian Doyle's research is heavily foregrounded in *"Joyas Voladoras."* Doyle says that the secret of writing good creative nonfiction is working from "a sense of wonder." His essay began because his son was "issued a recalcitrant engine at birth," and Doyle was "absorbed by hearts and their function and misfunction":

> I scoured for fact and information and detail and explanation; and more and more I was knocked out by the sheer miracle of Hearts, tiny and huge, speedy and sluggish, driving their vehicles through oceans of air and water and love and pain. My habit is to follow where nutty curiosity leads me and gather every scrap of story I can find (books, voices, Google, magazines, academic papers, reports, etc., but most of all voices, the key to being a writer is of course the ability to ask a question and then actually shut your trap and listen to the answers spilling out), and then play with my fingers. I never sit down to write anything; I sit down and write up my notes and then a certain driving playfulness takes over and off we go. One of the coolest parts of writing is how you are often surprised by what you write; which might be why writers write. But what do I know?

One hears in Doyle's description of his research process some of the same pleasure that Joan Didion takes in "sculpting" her essays. Curiosity is at work here, and a sense of play, and a desire to get at the truth. What is absent is the sense that research is a boring, laborious process, something that the writer "has to do."

Like Doyle, Rebecca McClanahan is interested in the function of the heart. We learn from her that "the heart is a hollow muscle housed in a slippery, loose-fitting sac and protected by three layers of membranes," that it "is controlled by two opposing bundles of nerves, the sympathetic and the parasympathetic." McClanahan also provides us with information about yoga: the *prana* is "the invisible life force," *Om* is "the healing mantra," and certain yoga positions require that the practitioner imagine herself as a tree. We are given other information as well, right down to the combination to her locker at the YWCA, although everything we learn is in service of the thematic elements of the essay.

Don't let the facts overwhelm you, though. If you find yourself bogged down in research, no longer having fun, perhaps you need to eliminate the research component or rethink your topic altogether. Remember that if you don't enjoy writing your essay, your reader probably isn't going to enjoy reading it. Yet if you write about something that truly matters to you, the truth telling that goes into your essay—even if it's difficult at times—will make all the hard work worthwhile.

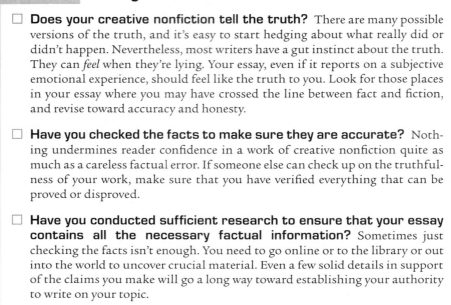

CHECKLIST Telling the truth

☐ **Does your creative nonfiction tell the truth?** There are many possible versions of the truth, and it's easy to start hedging about what really did or didn't happen. Nevertheless, most writers have a gut instinct about the truth. They can *feel* when they're lying. Your essay, even if it reports on a subjective emotional experience, should feel like the truth to you. Look for those places in your essay where you may have crossed the line between fact and fiction, and revise toward accuracy and honesty.

☐ **Have you checked the facts to make sure they are accurate?** Nothing undermines reader confidence in a work of creative nonfiction quite as much as a careless factual error. If someone else can check up on the truthfulness of your work, make sure that you have verified everything that can be proved or disproved.

☐ **Have you conducted sufficient research to ensure that your essay contains all the necessary factual information?** Sometimes just checking the facts isn't enough. You need to go online or to the library or out into the world to uncover crucial material. Even a few solid details in support of the claims you make will go a long way toward establishing your authority to write on your topic.

Creative nonfiction as narrative ▶

We have just seen in the cases of James Frey and Jonah Lehrer how much trouble a writer can get into by claiming that a work of fiction is nonfiction. Nevertheless, authors frequently use the tools of storytelling to create exciting, believable moments and scenes in their essays. How do they fictionalize without turning their writing into fiction? Essayists *re-create* things rather than simply making them up. Their basic material already exists; the author's concern is to make that material interesting to read about.

Judith Kitchen and Mary Paumier Jones believe that even though short creative nonfiction employs "many techniques of fiction—narrative, dialogue, descriptive imagery, point of view, interior voice, etc."—it does so "not to invent imaginary worlds . . . but to make something *of* the facts." That's an important qualification. If a mystery writer, for instance, suddenly decides he needs to change the killer from Joe to Jane, that's just fine. But if a writer of creative nonfiction made the same decision—accusing Jane of murder when Joe had already been convicted of the crime—his or her credibility would be shot, and the possibility of a lawsuit would be very real.

According to Philip Lopate, "So often the 'plot' of a personal essay, its drama, its suspense, consists in watching how far the essayist can drop past his or psychic defenses toward deeper levels of honesty." We have already discussed structure in a previous section, so let's look at three other key elements of fiction writing that can be applied to creative nonfiction: character, dialogue, and scene setting.

Character

Writers of creative nonfiction prize character development almost as much as contemporary writers of fiction do. Of course, the character who is nearly always developed most fully is the writer herself or himself. We discuss how to write yourself into your essay more fully in a later section, but for now let's concentrate specifically on you as a character in your own story.

If an essay focuses on other people or on a particular subject—the way that "*Joyas Voladoras*" discusses hearts—the essayist may hardly mention himself at all, so that other than his authorial voice, he is absent altogether. However, most essayists are fairly prominent in their own work, which means that you will need to be both author and character. The first-person narrator is a common point of view in fiction, but in an essay you are more likely to sharply differentiate between the person talking and the person being talked about. Being the narrator requires that you tell the story of your essay in an interesting and coherent fashion. Yet when you are onstage in your essay as a character, you may act very differently than does the person whose voice is relating the events of your life. According to McClanahan, "If you are a character in your memoir . . . you have to write yourself as that character, not just as the author talking from the 'now' of your life. Literarily, you have to do whatever it takes to frame your experience in another way—to view it from a different angle, for instance, or with a different time frame, or in a different voice or rhythm, or by smacking it up against something that seems totally opposed to it." In short, the "you" represented in your essay will *not* be identical to the voice that is narrating the essay, but your readers will recognize this as a convention of essay writing.

Over the course of McClanahan's essay, her character changes from someone who seems almost as small and distant as "the computerized woman in the tiny boat" on the Liferower's screen, to a real person with real problems in the world. We learn that her family has heart troubles, that she's been divorced, that she loves her nieces and nephews, and that sometimes she is very lonely. It is vital that McClanahan postpones the revelation about her abortion until near the end of the story so that readers who might otherwise be unsympathetic to her action nevertheless can identify with her as a human being.

We create characters in nonfiction the same way we do in fiction: not by making generalities about their lives—"Boy, there's a Moroccan woman in my French class you wouldn't believe"—but by *showing* them interacting with the world. Lee Gutkind advises essayists to be as specific as possible: "Through the use of intimate detail, we can hear and see *how* the people about whom we are writing say what is on their minds; we may note the inflections in their voices, their elaborate hand movements, and any other eccentricities." Sedaris does a wonderful job of using specific details to create the character of the Moroccan woman in "Jesus Shaves." She's "pouty" and "plump" with "massive shoulders." She hurries to answer the teacher's questions "as though this were a game show and, if quick enough, she might go home with a tropical vacation or a side-by-side refrigerator/freezer." She raises her hand so often that "by the end of the first day . . . her shoulder had given out." Even when she's bored—turning "her attention back to the comic book she kept hidden beneath her binder"—Sedaris's use of details continue to make her a vivid character.

As the writer of a *short* essay, you are always searching for those small but unique details that will distinguish your characters from other people. Being unusual is what makes us human. However, Theodore Cheney rightly cautions that it *is* possible to go overboard: "Be careful not to stereotype or even ridicule by emphasizing too many idiosyncrasies of a person's speech; use just enough of these attributes to give the flavor of a person. Too much emphasis, for example, on someone's poor grammar may make the person seem unintelligent when he or she is merely ignorant."

Dialogue

Kim Stafford believes that writers should be "professional eavesdroppers." He writes down snippets of conversations and then holds on to them until he can find the proper place to use them: "By listening to the glories of the conversation around me, I am moved to write." Transcribing conversations is one way to ensure that the dialogue in your essays is accurate. We don't always have a pen and paper (or a smart phone) at the ready when something important is being said, but memorable phrases have a way of hanging around in a writer's head until he or she can jot them down.

We expect dialogue in a play or a story, but dialogue in creative nonfiction stands out—in ways both good and bad. Much of the humor in "Jesus Shaves" comes from the English translations of the bad French spoken by the students. Again, the fact that Sedaris is sitting someplace where he could plausibly transcribe what is being said makes the dialogue more believable, even if we suspect there's some comic exaggeration going on. However, an essay doesn't have to be dialogue-heavy to give it some of the zip of a short story. Just a few spoken words in a direct quote can suddenly transport an audience from a distant perspective to the immediacy of the present. Think of the Liferower's instructions to McClanahan: "Use your legs," "Lean into the stroke." Of course, as editor Daniel Menaker points out, "anytime you are reading about an important incident and you start introducing dialogue and scenes that are virtually impossible to know, you've got a problem."

As a general rule, the more recent the event, the more dialogue you can use. If you overheard or participated in a significant conversation yesterday or this morning, you probably still have good recall of the specific words and phrases that were used, the speaker's tone of voice, and the body language that accompanied the dialogue. In contrast, paragraphs of supposedly verbatim dialogue from a conversation that took place decades earlier will inspire skepticism in most readers. A shrewd way of including the essence of speech without relying on direct quotes is by employing **paraphrase**—putting the speech in your own words—and **summary**—condensing long speeches into a few succinct sentences or words.

Scene setting

One of the most crucial aspects of fiction writing as it applies to creative nonfiction is scene setting. Creating a successful scene requires more than just the judicious use of images, which we consider more fully in the next section. We have to know right away where we are, who is involved, and what is at stake. Theodore Cheney points out that "scenes give vitality, movement, action—life to a story. Scenes show people doing things, saying things, moving right along in life's ongoing stream." Scenes in stories may be pages long, but scenes in essays can be as short as a paragraph or even a sentence. McClanahan specializes in the brief but vivid scene. "When my sister had her first sonogram, I watched on the screen the undulating blur that would become my niece," she writes at one point, sketching in not just a hospital visit but also the outline of a family relationship in only twenty words.

Even more powerful is McClanahan's own visit to a hospital, but for different reasons. The most gripping moment in her essay comes right after the abortion: "When it's over and the nurse takes the gauze from between your teeth, the doctor, who is kind and slightly plump, his forehead lined from having seen too much, holds up a glass bottle filled with something bright and red. And then it's over, it's done. But your legs are still trembling and your tongue is bleeding from where you bit down and missed." The description here is so concise, so poignant, so well chosen that a reader would be hard-pressed not to experience some of the narrator's own complex emotions.

If your scenes, like McClanahan's, contain little or no dialogue, you may feel more confident about the accuracy of your description. Most of us have a better memory for the visual than for the auditory, so we are more reliable in describing a setting than in remembering long-ago conversations. Sometimes we can even return to the places we are writing about and take notes on what they looked and smelled and sounded like, whereas it is impossible to return to conversations that have not been recorded.

Although creative writing instructors preach imagery and specificity, all narrative relies in part on summary. Jeff Gundy advocates "speedy narrative" in creative nonfiction as a way to retain the excitement of scenes while moving the summary forward:

> [Speedy narrative] has two main principles: keep the summary linked firmly to details and concrete language, and keep the scenes as snappy and

brief as possible. The result is writing with a lot of zip and zing, capable of reaching over broad stretches of time without lapsing into blandness ("My high school years were happy ones") or getting lost in the aimless recording of whatever we happen to remember ("Sherri had a pair of blue plaid slacks that she wore every Monday, and a denim jumper that she wore on Tuesdays").

"*Joyas Voladoras*" makes expert use of the "speedy narrative." It contains a number of passages where details and concrete language summarize a key point and also create mini-scenes with "zip and zing": the Spanish explorers coming across hummingbirds for the first time, the image of a child walking through a room-size whale's heart, the author's elderly mother touching his hair, his father making pancakes for him in the early morning.

Other than the ruminations about faith at the very end of the essay, David Sedaris's "Jesus Shaves" takes place during a single scene. Sedaris's scene setting is mostly done by implication. We know that the location is a classroom for second language learners in Paris, yet the room itself is presumably less than scintillating, as Sedaris provides no description of it. We do get a brief glimpse of the textbook the students are using, with its "list of major holidays accompanied by a scattered arrangement of photographs depicting French people in the act of celebration," but the lack of detail in the scene hardly matters: the essay focuses on the characters and their hilarious conversation. Be wary, though. Sedaris is a comic genius; your essay is likely to benefit from a thorough use of physical description.

Ultimately, however, there is more to the essay as narrative than just the judicious use of fictional elements such as character, dialogue, and scene setting. David Romtvedt believes that "almost all writing is fiction in the sense that we shape our experience to suit the needs of what we believe to be a truth greater than chronology or biography." In other words, the moment we sit down to tell a story, even a true one, it becomes a *story*, our version of the truth.

Contemporary fiction opens up possibilities. It allows us to see the world from multiple viewpoints; it makes us question our beliefs rather than simply confirming them. The contemporary essay works in a similar fashion. As Deb Olin Unferth says, "The best personal . . . essays have the same qualities I admire in fiction: they preserve ambiguity and complexity; they unsettle, do not conclude." If you are new to creative nonfiction, not ending your essay with a concise summary of its main points may initially feel irresponsible, just as not ending your short story by reciting the fates of all your characters may seem wrong if you are new to fiction writing. But be assured that a literary approach to your story or essay will embrace possibility and shy away from certainty.

CHECKLIST Creative nonfiction as narrative

☐ **Are the characters believable?** No matter who the main characters in your essay are—and that may well include yourself—they should come across as real and unique people, with believable motivations and emotions. Caricatures don't work any better in creative nonfiction than they do in fiction. If your ex-husband or your estranged mother inspires a great deal of passion in you, it may be difficult to write about them as three-dimensional human beings. Be sure to show both the good and the bad sides of people, the noble and the less-than-admirable.

☐ **If your creative nonfiction contains dialogue, is it short, vivid, and believable?** The more recent the event described, the more dialogue you can probably include. Paraphrase and summary are options for reporting conversations that occurred years ago. In most essays, a little dialogue goes a long way.

☐ **Are the settings of your creative nonfiction vividly rendered?** Short essays rarely linger on a single scene or two the way that short fiction does. However, you can still find ways—from a sentence to a well-chosen noun or verb—to help your reader see, hear, feel, taste, and touch your world. Keep your scenes dynamic and your pacing lively by using concrete and specific details whenever possible.

The poetry of creative nonfiction ▶

If one version of the personal essay—the narrative essay—is concerned primarily with telling a story, the essay that is more like a poem is sometimes called the "lyric essay." The short poetic essay is as compact as a poem. "The compression of the brief form, completely familiar to poets and to those who read poetry," Peggy Schumaker writes, "gains a fine elasticity in nonfiction. Tone can range from somber to whimsical, lament to praise." Brenda Miller and Susan Paola note that poetic essays "favor fragmentation and imagery; they use white space and juxtaposition as structural elements. They're as attuned to silences as they are to utterance."

Even if you don't consider yourself much of a poet, *reading* poetry can help increase your skills as an essayist. Carol Bly argues that "it's a good idea for creative nonfiction writers to read poetry because poets drive exposition inward so much faster than most fiction writers and nonfiction writers do—they have so little space." By "inward exposition," Bly means "not settling for only 'outer' observations," but instead quickly discovering what really matters to the essay and the essayist. Good poets are always delving beyond the obvious toward the mysterious, and good essayists share that restless curiosity.

Aside from its organizational structure and overall tone, essay writing can be said to have a poetic aspect when we pay extra attention to imagery and figurative language, to diction, and to the sound and rhythm of words. Let's look at these elements of poetry as they apply to creative nonfiction.

Imagery and figurative language

Imagery—language that evokes one of the five senses—is as important in the short essay as it is in a poem, and for the same reasons: because you have so little space in which to work, you need to make every word count, and what the mind can see—or smell or hear or taste or feel—leaves a stronger impression than a mere abstraction.

Our model essayists all use imagery to great effect. McClanahan *shows* us whatever she is discussing, even the Liferower's computerized monitor where on "the shoreline a crowd of miniature fans wave [her] on to victory" as "the little woman on the screen moves her cartoon arms." Throughout *"Joyas Voladoras,"* we can *see* not only the exterior but also the interior of hummingbirds and blue whales. Sedaris is similarly adept at evoking visuals, often to humorous effect, as when he invites us to picture the absurdity of the flying French bell: "It's like saying that come Christmas, a magic dustpan flies in from the North Pole, led by eight flying cinder blocks."

You will recall that **metaphors** and **similes** show how two apparently unlike things are similar, and we see these ingenious comparisons throughout our model essays. McClanahan, for example, calls the quick-beating heart of a child "a Teletype machine tapping its urgent message." It is as loud as "a train roaring through a tunnel." She remarks that the woman in the rowing machine next to hers has "skin snug and elastic as the Spandex leotard" she is wearing. The Moroccan woman in "Jesus Shaves" folds her arms "like some great grammar genie." And Doyle uses metaphorical language when describing the short span of the hummingbird's heart. "You fry the machine. You melt the engine," he writes, equating the hummingbird with something man-made and mechanical. Its heart, he says, is as big as "a pencil eraser" or "an infant's fingernail." A blue whale's heart valves are "as big as the swinging doors in a saloon." Even his essay's title draws on a metaphor, the Spanish explorers' name for hummingbirds: *Joyas Voladoras,* or "flying jewels."

Diction

Sedaris, Doyle, and McClanahan are as meticulous as poets about their choice of words, or **diction**. Their precision in choosing the best word or phrase is evident in every paragraph. Nouns are as specific and concrete as possible. Verbs are accurate and sometimes unexpected. Adjectives are evocative and used only when needed. Let's look at just a few random examples of our authors' mastery of language.

In "Jesus Shaves," Sedaris notes that it was his habit to "scout" ahead in his textbook, rather than just simply "look." He's especially good at highlighting the funniest incorrect words when quoting the other students in the French class. When a student is attempting to describe a cross, she calls it two "morsels"—that is, small mouthfuls of food. Then she hesitates and chooses a word that is the opposite of what we would expect someone to be eating: "lumber." Another student describes heaven as "above of my head," and yet another student characterizes Christ's resurrection as "the first day he come back here for to say hello to the peoples." Yes, the language is "wrong," but for the purposes of the essay it is also absolutely right.

Doyle clearly loves everything about words, never compromising for the obvious and mundane. In his first paragraph alone, he selects participles like "whirring" and "zooming" and "hammering" that propel us directly into the hummingbird's high-speed lifestyle. And his adjectives are equally well chosen when he contrasts our size with theirs: we have "elephantine ears," while they have "infinitesimal chests."

Finally, consider McClanahan's description of her attempt to recapture her first husband's interest in their dying marriage: "I would work harder, cook more of his favorite foods, steam his khakis with a sharper pleat." This movement from the general ("work harder") to the more specific ("cook more of his favorite foods") to the very specific ("steam his khakis with a sharper pleat") mirrors the increasing desperation of a wife grasping at *anything* to make her husband stay.

You may have rushed through writing your essays in the past, and sometimes your instructor may have allowed that as long as the content was sufficient to the essay's purpose. In creative nonfiction, however, word choice is at least as important as content, so slow down and consider more than just the first words that come to mind.

Sound and rhythm

Poets write not only for the eye but also for the ear. Similarly, when the best essays are read aloud, they are almost indistinguishable from poetry, so attuned are they to sound and rhythm.

Take, for instance, the explanations of Easter offered by the students in Sedaris's beginning French class. Because they are working with limited vocabulary and grammar, they start their unorthodox sentences with similar constructions: "He call ...," "He die ...," "He weared ...," "He nice ...," He make. ..." Initially, we may think that Sedaris is merely poking fun at the mess the class is making of "proper French," but the overall effect of the passage is to accentuate the surprising music and rhythm made by speakers of a new language.

We hear a kind of wild poetry in Doyle's long, varied, and peculiar list of the names of hummingbird species: "bearded helmetcrests and booted racket-tails, violet-tailed sylphs and violet-capped woodnymphs, crimson topazes and purple-crowned fairies, red-tailed comets and amethyst woodstars, rainbow-bearded thornbills and glittering-bellied emeralds, velvet-purple coronets and golden-bellied star-frontlets, fiery-tailed awlbills and Andean hillstars, spatuletails and puff legs." Clearly, *t* and hard *c* sounds are important to the writer, which makes sense: the sounds mirror the harsh precision of the hummingbird itself. Moreover, as the listing gains momentum, we hear a beat and cadence emerging that is not unlike the rapid firing of the hummingbird's wings.

McClanahan uses **onomatopoeia**, words that sound like what they mean, when she describes heartbeats as "iambic lub and dub" and when she says that the electronic rowing sound generated by the exercise machine "sounds more like the breath of a woman in labor: in through the nose, out through the mouth. Whoosh, whoosh." Birth, of course, turns out to be a key theme in the essay: the fact that the narrator's infant sister died of a congenital ailment, another sister nearly died after giving birth, and, finally, McClanahan's own decision not to give birth are all evoked by the *sound* of computerized oars in the digital water.

The rhythms of poetry writing are akin to those found in strong essays. "Repetition is the most powerful method of creating rhythm," Stephen Minot tells us, and we see that rhythm in Sedaris's intentionally ungrammatical sentences and his variations on the Easter rabbit and the Easter bell, in Doyle's return throughout his essay to the nature and function of the heart, and in McClanahan's use of the Liferower's voice commands as a kind of refrain: "Use your legs. Keep your back straight. You are five boats behind."

As Kristen Iversen says, "Writing prose is like writing music. There is a rhythm and a beat to the language that the reader will enjoy." Iversen recommends tapping into this music by varying sentence structure and the length of sentences and by avoiding repeated words and phrases unless the repetition is done consciously and for a specific effect. She also advocates reading your work aloud so that you can *hear* its rhythms.

As we have seen, our model authors are adroit manipulators of language. They vary, as Iversen recommends, short sentences with long ones, and they combine those sentences in ways that highlight their content. These essayists use commas and periods and dashes correctly and skillfully, and they have a clear sense of grammatical boundaries. For instance, they use sentence fragments for emphasis, not because they forgot to attach a predicate to the subject. In their hands, the rhythm of writing well becomes the rhythm of authority: the ability to stop and start at will, to lull readers, then to suddenly wake them with a "whoosh, whoosh." McClanahan, Doyle, and Sedaris fit Michael Pearson's description of the very best writers of creative nonfiction; they "can use words with the force of poets [and] can shape characters syllable by syllable until we feel that we know them better than we know ourselves." Such authors can, in short, "carve landscapes out of blank space."

CHECKLIST The poetry of creative nonfiction

☐ **Does your creative nonfiction make extensive use of imagery?** Paragraphs of abstractions and extensive philosophizing may be acceptable for some essays, but they will ruin a piece of creative nonfiction. Make sure that your essay, like a good poem, evokes the senses of smell, touch, taste, and hearing. Above all, look for ways to allow your reader to join you in *seeing* whatever you visualize in your mind's eye.

☐ **Do you use metaphors and similes to good effect?** Because they point out similarities between apparently unlike objects and ideas, metaphors and similes are particularly useful tools for essayists, who are themselves always discovering hidden relations between things. A few memorable metaphors and similes will show your reader that you have taken as much time to craft your essay as a poet takes to craft a poem. Be sure, though, that your figurative language is appropriate for your subject and that your metaphors and similes aren't, in fact, clichés.

☐ **Have you paid careful attention to diction, sound, and rhythm?** Be mindful not only of the mood and connotations your word choice suggests but also of how the words sound together. Ideally, if someone were to hear your work read aloud, the sentences would be so eloquent that a listener might mistake what you have written for poetry.

Writing yourself into creative nonfiction ▶

"A modest, truthful man speaks better about himself than he does about anything else," said Alexander Smith, and if we eliminate the nineteenth-century sexist language, most personal essayists would probably agree with this statement. After all, whom do we know better than ourselves? We are the ones who have lived the life and collected the memories and memorabilia. We know the main characters involved and their relationships to one another. *Auto*biography is a version of biography, and essayists often look at who they are and where they have been with the same scrutiny as a historian examining the life of a president or a famous artist.

John T. Price believes that "when someone picks up a collection of personal essays, they will read it differently than a work of fiction. As an essayist I am saying to that person, like Montaigne did: 'Here I am, up front and center, thinking out loud about my life and about the general complexity of being human. You're not alone in this mess.' I think readers turn to personal nonfiction, in part, to experience this sense of companionship." We mentioned Montaigne earlier in this chapter, and it's worth reiterating that his approach to essay writing is currently very much in favor. Skeptical, frank, and curious, by turns sardonic and enthusiastic, Montaigne was never afraid to follow a tangent if he thought it might prove productive, and ultimately his favorite subject was how he might best approach the living of his own life.

But are essayists *always* their own favorite subjects? Judging by our three model authors, the answer would have to be no, although the "I" of the essay is certainly of interest to both Sedaris and McClanahan. And even though Doyle does not mention himself in *"Joyas Voladoras,"* his voice and point of view are present throughout the essay. In fact, the personal perspective is hard to avoid in creative nonfiction, and in their book *Writing True*, Sondra Perl and Mimi Schwartz map out possible positions for the authorial "I" by drawing a diagram that consists of four circles. In the first circle, the "I" is in the center; in the second, the "I" shares the space with others; in the third, the "I" is near the edge; and in the fourth, the "I" is outside the circle altogether. "Wherever the 'I' stands," they argue "its voice must be right for the part."

Being right for the part usually means that the author's voice is appealing and distinctive without being overwhelming. Sedaris is part of the action of his essay, but he does not dominate it. Granted, we see the chaos of the beginning French class from his entertaining perspective, and he does contribute some funny one-liners, but the real star of the show is the outspoken Moroccan woman, and Sedaris's classmates and teacher play just as important a role in the essay as he does himself.

McClanahan's "I" is much closer to the center of her essay's circle. She writes about her life and emotions in some detail, yet we never have the sense that she is conceited in any way. Partly that's because she sees herself with such a cynical eye, and this skepticism about one's own values and decisions is a hallmark of the essayist's voice. Philip Lopate says that "common to the [essay] genre is a taste for littleness. This includes self-belittlement." For all its emphasis on the self, creative nonfiction is not a good genre for egomaniacs. Rather than pointing out, "Look how wonderful I am!" the essayist is more likely to say, "Look at all the mistakes I've made." Lopate warns that the process of self-disclosure can be tricky. We must wrestle with the "stench of ego," trying to reveal our true selves "without seeming narcissistic or proud."

McClanahan achieves this delicate balance by writing about all the ways that others might perceive her to be inadequate. Some of these inadequacies are minor: she can't keep up with the electronic pacesetter on the Liferower's screen. Other insufficiencies are larger but not her fault: her family has a history of "bad hearts." But the crisis at the center of the essay is the fact that she has no children because she has had an abortion. "Crisis" may be too strong a word, though, for while the abortion seems to haunt her, she does not necessarily regret her choice: "The child I chose against would have been born into the cramped space of my life between marriages." For readers who are "pro-life," this decision based on timing may seem immoral; for "pro-choice" readers, it will be entirely justifiable. McClanahan leaves those judgments to her readers. She simply explains how the situation appeared to her, and in this regard "Liferower" does what Judith Kitchen and Mary Paumier

Jones say all good personal essays do. It provides us with "a way of seeing the world, of examining its meanings, of exploring and expressing the interior life. It is intimate without being maudlin. It is private without being secret."

David Sedaris is well-known for his self-deprecating humor, and "Jesus Shaves" admirably demonstrates Lopate's call for "self-belittlement." The narrator makes no attempt to claim his French is any better than that of anyone else in the class; indeed, it may be worse. He admits, "it was my habit to tune out my fellow students," acknowledging that he is far from being a model student and is basically disconnected from the rest of his classmates, who seem to strike him as, at best, amiably incompetent. In short, Sedaris is something of a misfit, even among this group of eccentrics. And yet his willingness to disclose his shortcomings ultimately makes him more, not less, likable as a character in his essay.

Brian Doyle wrestles with the "stench of ego" by leaving the "I" out of his essay altogether. Philip Gerard has warned, "Too often these days, I'm afraid we writers of nonfiction . . . enter the story whether it needs us or not." Doyle appears to have heeded that warning, although something of his self is present even in an essay with a scientific slant. We know about this author not because he agonizes over the fate of his soul, but through his syntax and diction. Doyle is present in every sentence he writes; his "I" is hidden just below the language's surface. A scientist, for instance, when describing the size of a baby blue whale would stop with its length and weight. But Doyle keeps going. "It is waaaaay bigger than your car" is an essayist's humorous touch. Even the arrangement of his material—the movement from the smallest and largest mammals to a discussion of actual and then figurative hearts—bespeaks an essayist's mind. And the final sentence—although the pronoun "your" is used—seems to be a list of memories from the speaker's own life.

Of course, not all essayists are enamored of the idea of exposing everything about themselves in their work. They may not even trust the accuracy of what they are claiming to reveal. "I trust nothing," Terry Tempest Williams writes, "especially myself." Mimi Schwartz's response to that concern is to "gather the facts by all means" and then "go for the emotional truth." When you are not entirely sure of a memory, you should err on the side of what your subconscious *feels* to be the truth. After all, as Peter Ives acknowledges, "We do not perceive or write about things as they are, but, rather, we perceive or write about them as *we* are." As an essayist, it is *your* vision of the world that matters. If others disagree with that vision, let them tell their own versions of the truth.

But no matter where you position the "I" in your essay, your voice will not be right for the part if the writing itself is not worthy of the events being described. Most essayists would agree with Steven Harvey: "Only the text, shed of ourselves and hammered into shape, can redeem us. The enemy of the text, then, is what happened. . . . What happened may matter to us, but it is lost on us if we do not transform it into art." It's not enough simply to report the facts of your life. You need to structure that material effectively, to use the elements of narrative and poetry to craft your life and opinions into literature. In fact, Annie Dillard insists that writing a memoir is the best way *not* to preserve your memories: "You can't put together a memoir without cannibalizing your own life for parts. The work battens on your memories. And it replaces them."

"I am large," said Walt Whitman. "I contain multitudes." That is not just hyperbole. All of us contain these multitudes: crowds of attitudes, mobs of experiences, and throngs of personae. The essayist sifts through these different selves and includes only those that are necessary for the particular essay being written at that moment. Lopate calls it "a subtractive process: You need to cut away the inessentials, and highlight just those features in your personality that lead to the most intense contradictions or ambivalence." While one of your tasks as an essayist is to present a clearly identifiable version of yourself, another equally important one is deciding which aspects of your "multitudes" to leave out.

CHECKLIST Writing yourself into creative nonfiction

☐ **Have you located the "I" in your creative nonfiction in the most effective authorial position?** Sometimes you and your thoughts and actions are the proper focus of a piece of creative nonfiction, but you don't have to be front and center in every essay. Occasionally your voice is better heard offstage, in the background. Don't feel shy about being present in your own work, but make sure that your essay doesn't have "the stench of ego."

☐ **Are you sufficiently candid about yourself?** Readers quickly become suspicious of an essayist who seems intent on hiding or disguising himself or herself. "Face the dragon," as Sondra Perl and Mimi Schwartz put it. "Write toward the tensions of the subject, not away from them." Be sure you have revealed all that your readers need to know about you and your life. If the subject is too emotionally vexing for you at the moment, consider addressing another topic, one you can write about with honesty and candor.

☐ **Have you given at least as much attention to style as you have to content?** Readers want to get a feeling of who you are as an author, but an essay is not a police confession; it is a work of literature. The "I" you present to your reader is shaped at least as much by *how* you write as by what you write about. Once you have made your personal disclosures, return to your essay again and again to make it the best piece of writing it is capable of becoming.

Ethics and edicts ▶

When you write a short story, you are granted a certain amount of freedom. Even if your fictional story is based on a real person and real events, you may exaggerate aspects of a person's character or alter events radically. In fact, by calling your story "a story," you are obliged to move away from the literal truth of "what really happened." If someone feels that an unflattering portrayal in a novel is too close to her real self, she may want to sue the writer. But as long as the author has made clear disclaimers—such as "This is a work of fiction," and "Any resemblance to actual persons or events is coincidental and purely imaginary"—American courts have generally sided with the writer.

That is not the case when you label your work "nonfiction." Suddenly the accuracy of your reporting is an issue, and the more that the people you are writing about have at stake, the more you are bound to a truth that all (or most) reasonable parties can agree on.

Of course, there is a range of situations in which both ethics (moral aspects) and edicts (legal aspects) can come into play. Most students will be writing about personal material that has limited moral and legal dimensions. An essay about an unhappy childhood memory, or about a girlfriend or boyfriend who behaved badly, may get you into trouble with an individual or with family and friends, but it is unlikely to result in a lawsuit.

In fact, before the Internet, when manuscripts could be circulated only in hard copies, it was highly unlikely that anything a student wrote in class would ever be seen by anyone outside that class. Today that's not the case. Students discuss their classes in online forums such as MySpace, or Facebook, or RateYourProfessor.com. Usually it's the professor who is under fire, but occasionally other students and their work can become the subject of classroom gossip. Especially if your class is distributing peer drafts in an electronic format, you never know who is going to read what you have written. The quiet guy who sits two rows over from you may be the third cousin of the best friend of the person you're writing about.

Whereas writing an essay for class is unlikely to result in much more than embarrassment for those you write about, the stakes are significantly higher if you publish your work. In an essay entitled "The Creative Nonfiction Police," Lee Gutkind recommends that in an effort to avoid victimizing the innocent, the characters in an essay be allowed to read what the writer has written or even to offer their perspective on the narrative. Stephen Minot describes this "absolutist's position" as "clear and straightforward: use people's actual names and ask them to sign an approval form." Minot says that "in a surprising number of cases, individuals are willing to do this" because they are flattered to be written about. However, this is not a problem-free solution, and you may face difficult questions if you employ this strategy. What if the people you are writing about decide they don't want you to write about them? Do you take them out of the essay? Change their names? Give up on your essay altogether? And what if they want you to change something you know to be true but they insist is false? If no factual record of the event exists, who gets the last word on its veracity?

In contrast to this almost lawyerly approach to the ethics of nonfiction, other writers believe that they, and they alone, have the right to decide how much truth to tell about their own lives. "What can you decently write about other people?" Mary Clearman Blew asks. "Whose permission do you have to ask?

What can you decently reveal about yourself?" Her answer: "I own my past and present. Only I can decide whether or how to write about it." Rich Cohen takes this attitude one step further, arguing that "if you are a writer, your number one priority is to do your job as a writer. If there is no way to do this job without pissing people off, then go ahead and piss people off." Yet even Cohen acknowledges that you should "always read over what you have written to see where people might get hurt. If you can, and it does not change the story—well, why not *not* hurt someone's feelings?" In other words, even if edicts aren't at stake, ethics may very well be involved.

If your instructor has an interest or a background in journalism, you may find that your essay assignment includes the possibility of "literary journalism," the branch of creative nonfiction that is most involved with ethics and edicts. Normally, as Norman Sims says, literary journalists must commit to a "duration and depth of reporting" for which students in an introductory creative writing class don't have the time. Still, a personal essay with a research base and some personal reporting can be quite engaging. Indeed, Philip Gerard believes that "the best nonfiction writers are first-rate reporters, reliable eyewitnesses focused on the world, not themselves, and relentless researchers with the imagination to understand the implications of their discoveries."

Although writing a short piece of literary journalism requires more research, more investigation, and more *reporting* than the other varieties of creative nonfiction, it could be an option for your essay. Our model essays do not fall into this category, but you can get a sense of this subgenre's parameters from Mark Kramer's eight "breakable rules" for literary journalists:

1. Literary journalists immerse themselves in subjects' worlds and in background research.

2. Literary journalists work out implicit covenants about accuracy and candor with readers and sources.

3. Literary journalists write mostly about routine events; they seek material in places that can be visited and avoid places that can't.

4. Literary journalists write in "intimate voice," informal, frank, human, and ironic.

5. Style counts, and tends to be plain and spare.

6. Literary journalists write from a disengaged and mobile stance, from which they tell stories and also turn and address readers directly; the author is like a host, telling you a good camping tale.

7. Structure counts, mixing primary narrative with tales and digressions to amplify and reframe events; most literary journalism is primarily narrative, telling stories, building scenes.

8. Literary journalists develop meaning by building on the reader's sequential reactions: how a situation came about and what happens next.

As you read through Kramer's list, you will notice that a number of the elements of literary journalism are common to creative nonfiction in general: literary journalism employs an informal voice, uses concrete and detailed description, and is often engaged in storytelling. Nevertheless, there are differences. Clearly, literary journalists are more focused on their subjects than on themselves, and they have a much less ambiguous relationship to the truth. Once again, edicts play a defining role in shaping the writer's ethics.

None of our three model essayists crosses the ethics and edicts boundary. Doyle's focus on animals and people as a general group keeps him at a safe distance from personal disclosure. Sedaris, of course, makes fun of everyone in his class, including his teacher, but provides no names, dates, or specific locations. The closest he comes to identifying someone is the Moroccan woman, but obviously many other people have similar physical traits. Rebecca McClanahan mentions real people—her ex-husband and current husband—though she gives no names and portrays neither man in a negative light. She does reveal that she has had an abortion, but she never identifies her partner, who will not be affected as a result of this revelation. McClanahan's handling of this sensitive material is expert: rather than blaming others for her problems, she shoulders the responsibility herself.

CHECKLIST Ethics and edicts

- ☐ **Have you double-checked the facts in your essay?** Memories can be unreliable, and whether grandma's umbrella was red or orange doesn't really matter. However, if a reader can find information about something mentioned in your essay—whether it is a name, place, or historical fact—be sure that your facts are correct.

- ☐ **Have you reread your creative nonfiction carefully to make sure that nothing is "actionable," that is, subject to a possible lawsuit?** It is highly unlikely that students in a creative writing class will be sued for something they have written, but it is not entirely out of the question. Highlight all the places in your essay where you're worried that you may have invaded someone's privacy. If these concerns are serious, then revise what you have written. Be sure to avoid libeling anyone, that is, "conveying an unjustly unfavorable impression."

- ☐ **If you know that someone you have written about is going to read your creative nonfiction, have you gauged that person's likely response and how you will be affected by it?** Even if what you have written won't result in a lawsuit, you may hurt someone's feelings. Put yourself in the position of the people you are discussing and consider how you would feel if you were the subject of your own essay.

Getting started writing short creative nonfiction ▶

You didn't realize it at the time, of course, but all the essays you have ever written up to this point were good practice for the short creative nonfiction essay you will be writing for this class. Over the years, you have learned a few things about organizing your material. You know that an argument of any sort needs to have evidence to support it. You realize that specifics are more persuasive than generalities. You have played with words, trying to get your sentences to sound just right.

The difference between those other kinds of essays and creative nonfiction is that now you suddenly have much more freedom to write about what really matters to you. For some writers, however, that freedom is frightening. They prefer to be told what to write about, or at least to be nudged in a certain direction. The following list of kick-starts will help you overcome any blocking you may face as you begin your essay.

Whatever you decide to write about, though, your short essay should, in some essential way, be personally important. Your reader will want to come away feeling not only that something worthwhile has been discussed but that something of genuine value was at stake for the writer.

Essayists believe that writing begets writing, so get started on *something*, even if you're not exactly sure of your topic just yet. If you get that *So what?* feeling halfway through the writing process, you can always begin again.

▶ KICK-STARTS Beginning your creative nonfiction

▶ **1.** Write an essay inspired by one or several significant photographs from your own past. Be sure to describe the photographs in detail, and use the five senses to help re-create the world portrayed in the photos. Look for ways to braid separate narrative strands into a coherent whole.

▶ **2.** The "noble art" of walking, to use Henry David Thoreau's phrase, has inspired many essayists. Take a walk around your neighborhood and jot down observations in a notebook. Or you might use your phone to take some pictures or to text yourself. Then write an essay describing what you saw, what it made you remember, and how it made you feel.

▶ **3.** The titles of Michel de Montaigne's essays are intriguing: "On Idleness," "On Liars," "On Friendship," "On Smells," "On Cruelty," "On the Art of Conversation," "On the Custom of Wearing Clothes." His counterpart Francis Bacon also tackled some unusual subjects: "Of Prophecies," "Of Deformity," "Of Superstition," "Of Seeming Wise." Let the titles of these early essays inspire you to write about an uncommon topic of your own.

4. James Baldwin wrote, "I want to be honest and I want to be a good writer." Choose a topic that will allow you to write honestly about something that is important to you as to well as to draw on your individual strengths as a writer.

5. "For nature essayists," Lisa Knopp says, "the subjects of our excavations fall at our feet like bread rained from heaven. A dead possum. A flushed pheasant. An approaching cloud of mayflies. Bare branches studded with white-headed eagles." Follow Knopp's example and look around you for some aspect of the natural world—whether it be a sycamore leaf or a goose feather or a drop of pond water. Examine the object carefully, research it, and then write about it with insight and enthusiasm.

6. Research a topic—*any* topic—that you have always found fascinating. Then write about it in a completely personal way. It helps if you have had some actual contact with your subject, but even if your topic is as distant as the Trojan War, your essay should record your own immediate and individual responses.

7. Write an essay that only you are qualified to write.

8. "Write easily," Donald Murray tells us. "If it doesn't come, don't force it." Write an essay on a subject you know so well that the words flow from your fingertips.

9. "Lower your standards," Donald Murray also said. And William Stafford concurred: "You should be more than willing to forgive yourself. It doesn't really make any difference if you are good or bad today. The *assessment* of the product is something that happens *after* you've done it." Even if you can think of *nothing* to write about, just write. Write about what you did last night. Write about what you plan to do today. Write about why you can't seem to write. Don't expect anything great, but once you have finished, dig around and see if you can find some nuggets among the gravel and fool's gold.

10. If you keep a journal, raid it for ideas. If you don't yet keep a journal, try keeping one for a week. Write down anything of interest that you see, hear, or think. Then sit down in a quiet place with your favorite beverage and comb through the journal for ideas.

11. Take Stephen Minot's advice and "revisit a particular place"; then write an essay about it. According to Minot, "When you select a place you know well you have at your disposal thousands of details that can help to provide a sense of authenticity." Jot down these details while you are at the place. Later on, sort through your notes and select the material that will work best in an essay.

12. Go someplace new. Bring your notebook (or iPad or phone) and take notes on everything you see, hear, smell, touch, taste, or feel. Just as returning to a familiar place can inspire you to write, so visiting someplace new can make a vivid impression.

13. Write about a dwelling you lived in that made a strong impression on you. It could be a house, an apartment, a mobile home, or a yurt. Re-create the dwelling by evoking the five senses and describing specific incidents that happened to you while you lived there.

14. Write about an event in your life that is almost too embarrassing to write about, but not quite.

15. Conduct an interview with someone you find interesting, and write a profile of that person. Learn everything you can about the person beforehand. Prepare a set of questions for the person using the "reporter's questions" of "Who? How? Why? Where? What? When?" These words will help you generate an almost endless variety of queries for your subject. But don't rely only on your written questions. Listen to what your subject is actually saying and ask follow-ups. Use a digital recorder if possible and take notes. Be aware not only of what the person says but of *how* she or he says it.

16. Write an essay about someone who makes you jealous. Don't mention the person's name in the essay, but explore in detail why he or she possesses things or attributes you wish you had.

17. Write an essay about a piece of clothing you own, or once owned, that was involved in several important events in your life.

18. In Chapter 2, you learned James Gordon Bennett's urgent question about any story: "Where's the trouble?" Write an essay in which the trouble is apparent in the opening paragraph.

19. Laura Wexler believes that "creative nonfiction writers are in an ideal position to be one-person 'truth and reconciliation' commissions." She urges writers to avoid the constant temptation to make things up, and instead to seek out "events that have been forgotten or understudied by official histories, and to unearth lives at the margin of bigger events." Do some research about an event that you believe should be better understood but has been largely ignored by those who were more concerned with the major players and the big story.

20. Tracy Kidder argues that in order to write nonfiction that is "as gracefully accomplished as good fiction," the writer must be very conscious of choosing point of view, which he believes "affects everything else, including voice." Place the "I" in your essay in an unusual position—outside the center, when a reader would expect it to be in the center, or vice versa—and see whether an unusual point of view opens up your essay in productive ways.

21. Rebecca McClanahan's Liferower machine seems to be—at least in part—a symbol of the futility of our efforts to outrace death. Write an essay that has as its focus an object with symbolic value. Don't explicitly explain the symbolic element. Instead, let your concrete and detailed description of the object *suggest* its symbolism.

22. Brenda Miller sees in what she calls "the lyric essay a tendency toward fragmentation that invites the reader into those gaps that emphasize what is unknown rather than the already articulated known." Write an essay in blocks of texts that have—like McClanahan's and Doyle's pieces—few or no transitions between those blocks. Focus on the gaps and empty spaces. Write in such a way that your reader must do some of the work of making sense of your essay.

23. "As strange as it may sound," Michael Pearson writes, "all memoir is a process of researching one's own life. By that I mean rethinking, of course. I also mean reimagining and perhaps revising—because to see the past anew is often to view it, even at great distances, more clearly." Talk with family members and friends about your own life. Approach it as a research project. Write a slice of your life story as though you were writing about someone else.

24. According to Theodore Cheney, "One way to convey the sense of authority is to use words that not only *are* accurate and real but that *sound* accurate and real." Choose a topic that interests you, and begin your essay by making a list of words related to that topic that "sound accurate and real." Then think of how those words—and the people, places, events, and things they evoke— might find their way into your essay.

25. Write an opening paragraph so good that everyone will want to read the rest of the essay. Then write the rest of the essay.

26. Write a concluding paragraph so wonderful that you feel compelled to write the essay that precedes it.

27. Thoreau said, "If thou art a writer, write as if thy time were short, for it is indeed short at the longest. Improve each occasion when thy soul is reached. Drain the cup of inspiration to its last dregs." Write the essay you would write if today were your last day on earth.

An Anthology of Short Creative Nonfiction

Diane Ackerman

The Mute Sense

Nothing is more memorable than a smell. One scent can be unexpected, momentary, and fleeting, yet conjure up a childhood summer beside a lake in the Poconos, when wild blueberry bushes teemed with succulent fruit and the opposite sex was as mysterious as space travel; another, hours of passion on a moonlit beach in Florida, while the night-blooming cereus drenched the air with thick curds of perfume and huge sphinx moths visited the cereus in a loud purr of wings; a third, a family dinner of pot roast, noodle pudding, and sweet potatoes, during a myrtle-mad August in a midwestern town, when both of one's parents were alive. Smells detonate softly in our memory like poignant land mines, hidden under the weedy mass of many years and experiences. Hit a tripwire of smell, and memories explode all at once. A complex vision leaps out of the undergrowth.

People of all cultures have always been obsessed with smell, sometimes applying perfumes in Niagaras of extravagance. The Silk Road opened up the Orient to the western world, but the scent road opened up the heart of Nature. Our early ancestors strolled among the fruits of the earth with noses vigilant and precise, following the seasons smell by smell, at home in their brimming larder. We can detect over ten thousand different odors, so many, in fact, that our memories would fail us if we tried to jot down everything they represent. In "The Hound of the Baskervilles," Sherlock Holmes identifies a woman by the smell of her notepaper, pointing out that "There are seventy-five perfumes, which it is very necessary that a criminal expert should be able to distinguish from each other." A low number, surely. After all, anyone "with a nose for" crime should be able to sniff out culprits from their tweed, India ink, talcum powder, Italian leather shoes, and countless other scented paraphernalia. Not to mention the odors, radiant and nameless, which we decipher without even knowing it. The brain is a good stagehand. It gets on with its work while we're busy acting out our scenes. Though most people will swear they couldn't possibly do such a thing, studies show that both children and adults, just by smelling, are able to determine whether a piece of clothing was worn by a male or a female.

Our sense of smell can be extraordinarily precise, yet it's almost impossible to describe how something smells to someone who hasn't smelled it. The smell of the glossy pages of a new book, for example, or the first solvent-damp sheets from a mimeograph machine, or a dead body, or the subtle differences in odors given off by flowers like bee balm, dogwood, or lilac. Smell is the mute sense, the one without words. Lacking a vocabulary, we are left tongue-tied, groping for words in a sea of inarticulate pleasure and exaltation. We see only when there is light enough, taste only when we put things into our mouths, touch only when we make contact with someone or something, hear only sounds that are loud enough. But we smell always and with every breath. Cover your eyes and you will stop seeing, cover your ears and you will stop hearing, but if you cover your nose and try to stop smelling, you will die. Etymologically speaking, a breath is not neutral or bland—it's *cooked air;* we live in a constant simmering. There is a furnace in our cells, and when we breathe we pass the world through our bodies, brew it lightly, and turn it loose again, gently altered for having known us. ◄

James Brown

My Papa's Waltz

We have an old reel-to-reel tape recorder, and when my father gets drunk he puts on Patsy Cline's song "Crazy" and asks me to dance. He has this sloppy smile on his face. I'm six maybe seven years old at the time. He is in his midfifties and his drunken sentimentality annoys me. His palms feel rough and hard when he slips them into mine and tries to lift me from my chair at the kitchen table. But I hold tight to the edge, the chipped green Formica, or one of the slick chrome legs. "Up, up," he says. "Let go. Dance." His breath smells of whiskey, his collar of sawdust and sweat. My father is a building contractor, a good one, a real finish man who charges people according to what he thinks they can afford, and they often take advantage of him.

A few years back I wrote a novel that uses this memory as its heart. I've mined the territory before, if not this particular moment then something like it, and I've done it so often that I find myself confusing what actually happened with how I imagine it. In trying to sort between autobiography and fiction, or invention, and then trying to put the pieces together so that they make some kind of sense, I've come to think that the truth as it occurs isn't of much use to me other than, say, as a catalyst for a story. While I'm figuring this out, I lose a couple of years writing a bad novel. I don't get through it and that's a good thing, because if I hadn't given up I would have lost more time. And I worry about time.

The problem, at least one of them, was that I was being dishonest with myself in the worst, most shameful way. I was writing about people and events and places that I didn't fully understand, and I wasn't good enough at it for it not to show. So I start another book, one that makes me see past what I think actually occurred, to what hasn't but *should have* according to that thing I imagine called plot. And the writer's obsession, as I also come to understand, suggests something other than limitation or theme, that as storytellers we basically spend our lives telling the same story over and over, only we do it from different angles.

The trick is disguising it, so it doesn't seem the same.

The trick is how well you can keep doing it, not once or twice, but hundreds of times, page after page, with one real detail after another. The hardest part is to make it appear seamless and vivid in the end as if it all came naturally.

Like magic.

Like you don't have to think. Like it really couldn't have happened any other way.

I was in college when I encountered "My Papa's Waltz," Theodore Roethke's short dark poem about dancing with his drunken father. I don't know for a fact if Roethke ever danced with his father and I don't believe that it matters. Of course, when I'm six or seven years old, I'd never heard of the poet, and it wouldn't have made any difference if I had. Reading is for sissies, especially poems, and like my old man I consider myself a tough guy. Pound for pound I can kick any kid's ass in the neighborhood, and where we live on the poor side of San Jose I have some serious competition. My mother is in prison at the time, and my father, my brother, and sister and I share a one-bedroom apartment with a kitchenette and a hot plate, a window overlooking the warehouse next door and a sofa bed in the living room. You have to push it back into place in the morning, so you can get to the bathroom.

William Street Park is only a few blocks away, and I spend plenty of hot summer days playing around the creek that passes through it. It was a rough place then and it's no better now, with all the dope and every other kid carrying a piece. The generation has changed. The clothes are different. But the pose is the same. Black kids still hang out on the benches and behind the bathrooms, glossy eyed, getting wasted, and the *pachucos* or *cholos*, what they call *homies* now, are on the other side of the park at the mouth of the old drain storm tunnel that runs under the street. My father buys the old reel-to-reel recorder here, off some older guy who needs a few quick bucks.

I like the tunnel. On the hottest days, when everybody is dragging, I stop about halfway through the tunnel and suck the cool air deep into my lungs. I like to press my cheek against the cool steel and feel the vibrations of the cars and the trucks rumbling past on the street above. I think about my mother. I think about when she's coming home. My old man doesn't like to talk about it and I'm left to wonder, to make up stories. To imagine. I plan the Great Escape in that tunnel and play it over and over in my head.

I need rope.

I need a gun.

I need a guard's uniform and a pair of walkie-talkies, so that my father and I can coordinate our actions, working from the inside and out. The first two items are easily had; the rope I buy, a hundred feet of good nylon five-hundred-pound test, and my father owns a German Luger. We'll steal her away to Mexico in our Chevy stepside. But there's a catch. Finding a guard's uniform to fit a sixty-pound kid will take some doing.

It isn't funny, either.

Every detail has to work or I will fail.

Lives, real or imagined, are at stake.

In that novel I wrote, a father plays a prominent role in a boy's life. His mother disappears years before. The boy, the narrator, can't recall knowing her, because she deserts him before he has the power of memory, and toward the end of the book he decides to pull up stakes and go looking for her. In my own life, when I try to remember exactly what happens the night that my father asks me to dance, I get confused.

Maybe it isn't 1962 in that cramped apartment on the poor side of San Jose. Maybe it's 1963. Maybe I'm closer to eight than seven, and why my mother is sent to prison doesn't really matter because she is never coming back, not the same woman anyway, and what I did know of her—*before*—is little more than imagined.

For dancing, I am too awkward, too timid and full of anger and blindness. But when I write today, when I write now, when I write *this*, the drunken smile on my father's face no longer annoys me. I let him take my hands and guide me across the cracked and yellowed linoleum floor in that kitchenette with Patsy Cline playing on the old reel-to-reel tape recorder that is probably stolen. I feel the warm harsh breath of his whisper in my ear and I smell the whiskey. I smell the sawdust and sweat.

"Smile," he says. "Dance. Your momma's coming home tomorrow."

That's fiction. But, in fact, it doesn't matter.

I let go of the table and dance with my father and the song is always "Crazy." ◀

Edwidge Danticat

Westbury Court

When I was fourteen years old, we lived in a six-story brick building in a cul-de-sac off of Flatbush Avenue, in Brooklyn, called Westbury Court. Beneath the building ran a subway station through which rattled the D, M, and Q trains every fifteen minutes or so. Though there was graffiti on most of the walls of Westbury Court, and hills of trash piled up outside, and though the elevator wasn't always there when we opened the door to step inside and the heat and hot water weren't always on, I never dreamed of leaving Westbury Court until the year of the fire.

I was watching television one afternoon when the fire began. I loved television then, especially the afternoon soap operas, my favorite of which was *General Hospital*. I would bolt out of my last high school class every day, pick up my youngest brother, Karl, from day care, and watch *General Hospital* with him on my lap while doing my homework during the commercials. My other two brothers, André and Kelly, would later join us in the apartment, but they preferred to watch cartoons in the back bedroom.

One afternoon while *General Hospital* and afternoon cartoons were on, a fire started in apartment 6E, across the hall. There in that apartment lived our new neighbors, an African-American mother and her two boys. We didn't know the name of the mother, or the names and ages of her boys, but I venture to guess that they were around five and ten years old.

I didn't know a fire had started until two masked, burly firemen came knocking on our door. My brothers and I rushed out into the hallway filled with smoke and were quickly escorted down to the first floor by some other firemen already on our floor. While we ran by, the door to apartment 6E had already been knocked over by the fire squad and inside was filled with bright flames and murky smoke.

All of the tenants of the building who were home at that time were crowded on the sidewalk outside. My brothers and I, it seemed, were the last to be evacuated. Clutching my brothers' hands, I wondered if I had remembered to lock our apartment door. Was there anything valuable we could have taken?

An ambulance screeched to a stop in front of the building, and the two firemen who had knocked on our door came out carrying the pliant and lifeless bodies of the two children from across the hall. Their mother jumped out of the crowd and ran toward them, screaming, "My babies—not my babies," as the children were lowered into the back of the ambulance and transferred into the arms of the emergency medical personnel. The fire was started by the two boys, after their mother had stepped out to pick up some groceries at the supermarket down the street. They had been playing with matches.

(Later my mother would tell us, "See, this is what happens to children who play with matches. Sometimes it is too late to say, 'I shouldn't have.'" My brother Kelly, who was fascinated with fire and liked to hold up a match to the middle of his palm until the light fizzled out, gave up this party trick after the fire.)

We were quiet that afternoon when both our parents came home. We were the closest to the fire in the building, and the most religious of our parents' friends saw it as a miracle that we had escaped safe and sound. When my mother asked how come I, the oldest one, hadn't heard the children scream or hadn't smelled the smoke coming from across the hall, I confessed that I had been watching *General Hospital* and was too consumed in the intricate plot.

(After the fire, my mother had us stay with a family on the second floor for a few months, after school. I felt better not having to be wholly responsible for myself and my brothers, in case something like that fire should ever happen again.)

The apartment across the hall stayed empty for a long time, and whenever I walked past it, a piece of its inner skeleton would squeak, and occasionally burnt wood that might have been hanging by a fragile singed thread would crash down and cause a domino effect of further ruptures, unleashed like those children's last cries, which I had not heard because I had been so wrapped up in the made-up drama of a world where, even though the adults' lives were often in turmoil, the children came home to the welcoming arms of waiting mommies and nannies who served them freshly baked cookies on porcelain plates and helped them to remove their mud-soaked boots, if it was raining, lest they soil the lily-white carpets. But should their boots accidentally sully the carpet, or should their bright yellow raincoats inadvertently drip on the sparkling linoleum, there would be a remedy for that as well. And if their house should ever catch fire, a smart dog or a good neighbor would rescue them just in time, and the fire trucks would come right quick because some attentive neighbor would call them.

Through the trail of voices that came up to comfort us, I heard that the children's mother would be prosecuted for negligence and child abandonment. I couldn't help but wonder, would our parents have suffered the same fate had it been my brothers and me who were killed in the fire?

When they began to repair the apartment across the hall, I would occasionally sneak out to watch the workmen. They were shelling the inside of the apartment and replacing everything from the bedroom closets to the kitchen floors. I never saw the mother of the dead boys again and never heard anything of her fate.

A year later, after the apartment was well polished and painted, two blind Haitian brothers and their sister moved in. They were all musicians and were part of a group called les Frères Parent, the Parent Brothers. Once my parents allowed my brothers and me to come home from school to our apartment, I would always listen carefully for our new tenants, so I'd be the first to know if anything went awry.

What I heard coming from the apartment soon after they moved in was music, "engagé" music, which the brothers were composing to protest against the dictatorship in Haiti, from which they had fled. The Parent Brothers and their sister, Lydie, did nothing but rehearse a cappella most days when they were not receiving religious and political leaders from Haiti and from the Haitian community in New York.

The same year after the fire, a cabdriver who lived down the hall in 6J was killed on a night shift in Manhattan; a good friend of my father's, a man who gave great Sunday afternoon parties in 6F, died of cirrhosis of the liver. One day while my brothers and I were at school and my parents were at work, someone came into our apartment through our fire escape and stole my father's expensive camera. That same year a Nigerian immigrant was shot and killed in front of the building across the street. To appease us, my mother said, "Nothing like that ever happens out of the blue. He was in a fight with someone." It was too troublesome for her to acknowledge that people could die randomly, senselessly, at Westbury Court or anywhere else.

Every day on my way back from school, I hurried past the flowers and candles piled in front of the spot where the Nigerian, whose name I didn't know, had been murdered. Still I never thought I was living in a violent place. It was an elevated castle above a clattering train tunnel, a blind alley where children from our building and the building across the street had erected a common basketball court for hot summer afternoon games, an urban yellow brick road where hopscotch squares dotted the sidewalk next to burned-out, abandoned cars. It was home.

My family and I moved out of Westbury Court three years after the fire. Every once in a while, though, the place came up in conversation, linked to either a joyous or a painful memory. One of the girls who had scalded her legs while boiling a pot of water for her bath during one of those no-heat days got married last year. After the burglar had broken into the house and taken my father's camera, my father—an amateur photography buff—never took another picture.

My family and I often reminisce about the Parent Brothers when we see them in Haitian newspapers or on television; we brag that we knew them when, before one of the brothers became a senator in Haiti and the sister, Lydie, became mayor of one of the better-off Haitian suburbs, Pétion-Ville. We never talk about the lost children.

Even now, I question what I remember about the children. Did they really die? Or did their mother simply move away with them after the fire? Maybe they were not even boys at all. Maybe they were two girls. Or one boy and one girl. Or maybe I am struggling to phase them out of my memory altogether. Not just them, but the fear that their destiny could have so easily been mine and my brothers'.

A few months ago, I asked my mother, "Do you remember the children and the fire at Westbury Court?"

Without missing a flutter of my breath, my mother replied, "Oh those children, those poor children, their poor mother. Sometimes it is too late to say, 'I shouldn't have.'" ◄

Joan Didion

In Bed

Three, four, sometimes five times a month, I spend the day in bed with a migraine headache, insensible to the world around me. Almost every day of every month, between these attacks, I feel the sudden irrational irritation and the flush of blood into the cerebral arteries which tell me that migraine is on its way, and I take certain drugs to avert its arrival. If I did not take the drugs,

I would be able to function perhaps one day in four. The physiological error called migraine is, in brief, central to the given of my life. When I was 15, 16, even 25, I used to think that I could rid myself of this error by simply denying it, character over chemistry. "Do you have headaches *sometimes? frequently? never?*" the application forms would demand. "Check one." Wary of the trap, wanting whatever it was that the successful circumnavigation of that particular form could bring (a job, a scholarship, the respect of mankind and the grace of God), I would check one. "*Sometimes,*" I would lie. That in fact I spent one or two days a week almost unconscious with pain seemed a shameful secret, evidence not merely of some chemical inferiority but of all my bad attitudes, unpleasant tempers, wrongthink.

For I had no brain tumor, no eyestrain, no high blood pressure, nothing wrong with me at all: I simply had migraine headaches, and migraine headaches were, as everyone who did not have them knew, imaginary. I fought migraine then, ignored the warnings it sent, went to school and later to work in spite of it, sat through lectures in Middle English and presentations to advertisers with involuntary tears running down the right side of my face, threw up in washrooms, stumbled home by instinct, emptied ice trays onto my bed and tried to freeze the pain in my right temple, wished only for a neurosurgeon who would do a lobotomy on house call, and cursed my imagination.

It was a long time before I began thinking mechanistically enough to accept migraine for what it was: something with which I would be living, the way some people live with diabetes. Migraine is something more than the fancy of a neurotic imagination. It is an essentially hereditary complex of symptoms, the most frequently noted but by no means the most unpleasant of which is a vascular headache of blinding severity, suffered by a surprising number of women, a fair number of men (Thomas Jefferson had migraine, and so did Ulysses S. Grant, the day he accepted Lee's surrender), and by some unfortunate children as young as two years old. (I had my first when I was eight. It came on during a fire drill at the Columbia School in Colorado Springs, Colorado. I was taken first home and then to the infirmary at Peterson Field, where my father was stationed. The Air Corps doctor prescribed an enema.) Almost anything can trigger a specific attack of migraine: stress, allergy, fatigue, an abrupt change in barometric pressure, a contretemps over a parking ticket. A flashing light. A fire drill. One inherits, of course, only the predisposition. In other words I spent yesterday in bed with a headache not merely because of my bad attitudes, unpleasant tempers and wrongthink, but because both my grandmothers had migraine, my father has migraine and my mother has migraine.

No one knows precisely what it is that is inherited. The chemistry of migraine, however, seems to have some connection with the nerve hormone named serotonin, which is naturally present in the brain. The amount of serotonin in the blood falls sharply at the onset of migraine, and one migraine drug, methysergide, or Sansert, seems to have some effect on serotonin. Methysergide is a derivative of lysergic acid (in fact Sandoz Pharmaceuticals first synthesized LSD-25 while looking for a migraine cure), and its use is hemmed about with so many contraindications and side effects that most doctors prescribe it only in the most incapacitating cases. Methysergide, when it is prescribed, is taken daily, as a preventive; another preventive which works for some people is old-fashioned ergotamine tartrate, which helps to constrict the swelling blood vessels during the "aura," the period which in most cases precedes the actual headache.

Once an attack is under way, however, no drug touches it. Migraine gives some people mild hallucinations, temporarily blinds others, shows up not only as a headache but as a gastrointestinal disturbance, a painful sensitivity to all sensory stimuli, an abrupt overpowering fatigue, a strokelike aphasia, and a crippling inability to make even the most routine connections. When I am in a migraine aura (for some people the aura lasts fifteen minutes, for others several hours), I will drive through red lights, lose the house keys, spill whatever I am holding, lose the ability to focus my eyes or frame coherent sentences, and generally give the appearance of being on drugs, or drunk. The actual headache, when it comes, brings with it chills, sweating, nausea, a debility that seems to stretch the very limits of endurance. That no one dies of migraine seems, to someone deep into an attack, an ambiguous blessing.

My husband also has migraine, which is unfortunate for him but fortunate for me: perhaps nothing so tends to prolong an attack as the accusing eye of someone who has never had a headache. "Why not take a couple of aspirin," the unafflicted will say from the doorway, or "I'd have a headache, too, spending a beautiful day like this inside with all the shades drawn." All of us who have migraine suffer not only from the attacks themselves but from this common conviction that we are perversely refusing to cure ourselves by taking a couple of aspirin, that we are making ourselves sick, that we "bring it on ourselves." And in the most immediate sense, the sense of why we have a headache this Tuesday and not last Thursday, of course we often do. There certainly is what doctors call a "migraine personality" and that personality tends to be ambitious, inward, intolerant of error, rather rigidly organized, perfectionist. "You don't look like a migraine personality," a doctor once said to me. "Your hair's messy. But I suppose you're a compulsive housekeeper." Actually my house is kept even more negligently than my hair, but the doctor was right nonetheless: perfectionism can also take the form of spending most of a week writing and rewriting and not writing a single paragraph.

But not all perfectionists have migraine, and not all migrainous people have migraine personalities. We do not escape heredity. I have tried in most of the available ways to escape my own migrainous heredity (at one point I learned to give myself two daily injections of histamine with a hypodermic needle, even though the needle so frightened me that I had to close my eyes when I did it), but I still have migraine. And I have learned now to live with it, learned when to expect it, how to outwit it, even how to regard it, when it does come, as more friend than lodger. We have reached a certain understanding, my migraine and I. It never comes when I am in real trouble. Tell me that my house is burned down, my husband has left me, that there is gunfighting in the streets and panic in the banks, and I will not respond by getting a headache. It comes instead when I am fighting not an open but a guerrilla war with my own life, during weeks of small household confusions, lost laundry, unhappy help, canceled appointments, on days when the telephone rings too much and I get no work done and the wind is coming up. On days like that my friend comes uninvited.

And once it comes, now that I am wise in its ways, I no longer fight it. I lie down and let it happen. At first every small apprehension is magnified, every anxiety a pounding terror. Then the pain comes, and I concentrate only on that. Right there is the usefulness of migraine, there in that imposed yoga, the concentration on the pain. For when the pain recedes, ten or twelve hours later, everything goes with it, all the hidden resentments, all the vain anxieties. The migraine has acted as a circuit breaker, and the fuses have emerged intact. There is a pleasant convalescent euphoria. I open the windows and feel the air, eat gracefully, sleep well. I notice the particular nature of a flower in a glass on the stair landing. I count my blessings. ◄

Pico Iyer

In the Dark

It was dark when I set foot on the island, and it felt as if the darkness was chattering. I could see oil lamps flickering at the edges of the forest. I could hear the gamelan coming from somewhere inside the trees, clangorous, jangled, and hypnotic. I could see people by the side of the road as I drove in from the airport, but I couldn't tell how many there were, or what they were doing in the dark. When I woke up, jet-lagged, in the dead of night, and walked down to the beach, figures came out of the shadows to offer me "jig-jig" or some other amenity of Paradise. There was a holy cave on the island, I had read, inhabited only by bats; there was a temple in the sea guarded by a snake.

The bush is burning only for those who are completely foreign to it, I had often thought; in the works of V. S. Naipaul, say, the jungle is seldom a force of magic, and if it is, it speaks for a magic that is only pushing back and down the clear daylight world of reason. Those born to nature seldom have to go back to it. Yet in Bali all these ideas are upended. Bali is a magical world for those who can see its invisible forces and read all the unseen currents in the air (that woman is a *leyak* witch, and that shade of green portends death). Yet for everyone else, it is simple enchantment. We stand at the gates of Eden, looking in, and choose to forget that one central inhabitant of the Garden is a snake.

I walked through the unfallen light my first day in Bali, to the beach, to watch, as foreigners do, the sun sink into the sea. Snake-armed masseuses were putting their things away for the day and boys were kicking a soccer ball into the coloring waves. As the outlines of the place began to fade, and the dark to take over, a woman came up to me and asked if I'd like to take a walk with her.

I couldn't really see her in the dark, and the name she gave me—Wayan—is the same name given to the oldest son or daughter of every family on the island. It was pitch-black as we walked along the sand, and pitch-black when we turned into what I thought was the little lane that led back to my guest house. At night in Bali, the dogs come out, and they are nothing like the serene creatures who sit outside the temples of Tibet, seeming to guard the monks. The dogs in Bali howl and curse and bite. As we walked through the forest on the path back to where I slept, I could feel the dogs very close to us, and everywhere.

We know Bali, those of us who read about it, as a magic island where there are thirty thousand temples in a space not much bigger than a major city; we have heard that it is a forest of the kind you see in *A Midsummer Night's Dream,* where people fall in love with the first Other that they meet. A childhood friend of mine had had her first experience of real transport with a stranger in a thatched hut on Kuta Beach; all around, you can see what look like asses—or rude mechanicals—waiting to be picked up by Titania.

But the stranger by my side did not seem interested only in romance as she led me up into the heart of her island's cosmology of light and dark. We walked along the buzzing lanes of Kuta after dark, dogs growling on every side. We walked along a beach on the other side of the island, where couples are supposed to walk on full-moon nights. We took a ride up into the interior, where whole villages are given over to ritual dance: small girls were fluttering their bare arms in the temple courtyards, and boys were chattering in a trance. Foreigners often awaken in the night in Bali to see ghosts standing by their beds; when a brother needs to communicate with a brother, a Balinese dancer once told me, with no drama in his voice, he finds telepathy easier than the telephone.

I walked through all these spaces with the girl from the beach, and through the skepticism I brought to them, and felt at times we were walking through parallel worlds: she could read everything around us, and I could read nothing. This was the way people were buried on the island, she said; this was why black magicians lived in that forest of monkeys. Part of the excitement of being a foreigner in a place like Bali is that you can't reduce the signs around you to an everyday language.

That is also what is unsettling about being a foreigner in a place like Bali, and after some days I slipped away from the girl, and went to the airport, to fly away. When I got there, she was standing at the gate, come, she said, to say goodbye. We would not meet again, she went on, because she had dreamed the previous night that she would put on a white dress and go across what is the Balinese equivalent of the Styx.

This is the kind of mystery that makes an almost ideal souvenir: something strange and a little spooky that you can take back to your regular life in (as it was for me then) Rockefeller Center. When I chanced to return to Bali, eighteen months later, I took pains not to tell Wayan I was coming, and to make my way discreetly back to the little lane where I'd stayed before. But when I came out of my guest house the first night back, at dusk, there she was, waiting, at the threshold, as if we had made a prior arrangement.

We went out again into the dark, the unlit fields behind the night market, the lanes that seemed, after dark, to be inhabited only by dogs. It was better to meet in broad daylight, I told her, and made a date to get together on the public beach at noon. She was wearing a sky-blue dress when I met her there, not scarlet as before, and her manner was withdrawn. I wasn't here for very long, I said, I didn't know where we were going: all the visitor's easy evasions. She looked at me, and then it was goodbye.

When I went back to my little room, I was unable to move. For days on end, I couldn't stir. I wasn't feverish, and yet something in me was waterlogged, leaden. I couldn't step out of my hut to eat or drink or take a walk; I couldn't sleep. For three days I lay in my bed and listened to the dogs amidst the trees, the gamelan. An Australian was pressing his claim on a local girl in the next room and she, laughing, was dancing away. I saw lizards on the walls of my room, and I awoke one morning to find that the lizard was nothing but a light switch. I went up into the hills, summoning all my strength for the one-hour trip, but something in me was evacuated: a guardian spirit vanished in the night.

It was time to leave the enchanted island, I decided. But before I did, I wanted something to remind me that I had been here, and that all of this had really happened: proof, of a kind. The streets of Bali teem with masks, which hang from the fronts of stores, staring-eyed, with tongues protruding, as talismans of the island's nighttime ceremonies. Knowing that they were too potent to take back home, I looked for something more innocuous, and found an owl.

I took the owl back with me to my small studio apartment in Manhattan and put it up on my wall. Almost instantly the New York night was so full of chatterings and hauntings that I had to get up and rip the thing down, and put it away in a closet where I'd never have to lay eyes on it again. You go into the dark to get away from what you know, and if you go far enough, you realize, suddenly, that you'll never really make it back into the light. ◀

Dinty W. Moore

El Toro Rojo

You've barely managed to distinguish the lean Spaniard in the white suit, Reyes Mendoza, from his *bandilleros,*[1] when the *matador*[2] cinches his hips, centers himself before the horns of the bull, raises the heavy cape. A lunge, a blur, a twist of taurine muscle, and the man is gored. Twice.

Mendoza attempts to rise from the sand, but falls back quickly, sickly, and must be carried away.

Now his second, Tomas Lopez, startling in his athleticism, guides the bull, as if *el toro rojo* were the most beautiful woman at the dance. A sweep and pass, a deft *mariposa,*[3] a swirling *veronica,*[4] all in service of the slaughter. The air flows thick with the language you do not speak; the bull so close you hear his anxious breath. *Olé,* you shout, despite yourself.

The red bull was not expecting to die, but the colorful *bandilleras*[5] are plunged into his thick back, two at a time. Perched oddly on the concrete bench, breath held, you lean forward as the bull crumples. Knees in the sand. The brute thrust of *descabello*[6] into spinal fiber.

In your own life, death has lingered. Your father, for one. All lives end badly. But for now, you are watching the instantaneous moment. The crowd held silent by the matador's lance. You, clutching an empty can of *San Miguel,* whispering *Toro!* as if you don't want the bull to hear. The bull on his knees.

You count to one. ◀

---

1. **bandilleros:** Members of the principal bullfighter's team who are responsible for stabbing the bull with metal tipped spikes.
2. **matador:** The principle bullfighter, whose job is to kill the bull with a sword thrust.
3. **mariposa:** Literally, butterfly, but used in bullfighting to indicate a dazzling pass at the bull with the cape held behind one's back.
4. **veronica:** A maneuver in which the matador stands with both feet planted and slowly swings the cape away from the charging bull.
5. **bandilleras:** Metal-tipped spikes, often decorated, that are thrust into a bull's neck to weaken it.
6. **descabello:** A small sword used for the final kill.

Aimee Nezhukumatathil

The Witching Hour

The Philippine witching hour begins at sundown. While the night is still soft and the rosal blooms fold damp after saying their good-nights, the *aswang* morphs from her day persona as a beautiful young woman with long, silky black hair to a creature of fantastic evil. She discards her lower torso, hiding it in her bedsheets or a dark corner of her house, beside a bookcase, under a rattan table. Anointing her armpits with a musky oil, the aswang smoothes it into the thin skin under her shoulders. Now she can fly at will. Her oil-stiffened hair propels her into the night sky, a terrible helicopter in search of her favorite food: fetus. Claws spring from her fingertips like a Swiss army knife to aid her tongue in its victual catch. If someone happens upon her abandoned lower half and sprinkles any of the following—ashes, salt, vinegar, lemon juice, garlic, or pepper—into the cross-section of the body, reattachment is impossible and the aswang dies fragmented.

For Sunburst Elementary's Endangered Species Week, my teacher, Mrs. Johnson, gave the third graders a list of possible animals to draw in the *"Save the Animals"* poster competition. The blue whale, California condor, American bald eagle, snow leopard, and African rhinoceros—all possible seeds for our blank poster boards. At the very bottom of the list was the phrase, *or any other important animal*. I drew the aswang.

Mrs. Johnson had one of those short, unisex perms of the eighties, very "Conway Twitty." Her large pillow arms swooped over us as she handed out giant posterboard pieces to everyone in the class. As we scribbled furiously on our drawings, she wove in and out of our desks, reminding us of the prizes: first place was a large, one-topping from Pizza Hut, second was to be Line Leader for a whole week, and for third prize, our choice of *one* of her "special" markers—the giant brush pens that she saved for bright and colorful bulletin boards and *Happy Birthday* signs. My knees bobbed up and down as I drew—I couldn't wait for her to walk by my desk. She usually always stopped and remarked on the detail of a face or building that I drew, and sometimes she held my drawing up for the class to see. When Mrs. Johnson came closer, I always looked at my shoes—pink Velcro 'Roos with a zip-up pocket for my lunch money right there above the arch of my foot. I couldn't tell if she was about to yell or if she just found her slip peeking out from under her dress because her face was always red. Her shadow, lavender in the fluorescent light, paused over my drawing.

"And what animal is that, Aimee?"

I responded quietly as possible, "The aswang."

"Speak up, honey, I can barely hear you."

"It's from the Philippines. It flies only at night though, so no one really sees it." The kids around my desk turned around, craning their necks to see my drawing. Some even walked over, mouths open. On my poster: the witch, tongue extended, long hair sweeping around her in the twilight sky, denoted by the half-circle yellow sun I drew sinking behind the green rectangle of countryside. I had not yet begun to draw a little baby. As I began to explain the nature of the aswang and what it eats, Mrs. Johnson narrowed her eyes to slits.

"Aimee, this is *not* an endangered species. You have to start over. And I don't want you to repeat these lies *ever* again. Do I make myself clear?" I stared at my shoes. "Do I make myself CLEAR?" I think I nodded yes, I don't remember. All I know is the two rips of poster board I heard next. Mrs. Johnson ripped fast, as if faster meant erasing the entire episode. She went back to her desk, depositing the four torn squares of my work into the army green wastebasket. The room was silent—all twenty-five third graders stopped their coloring, their cutting. My best friend, Andrea, walked up to the front of the room to the supplies closet and brought a fresh sheet of poster board to my desk for me, giving me a half-smile. I wiped the mix of snot and tears on my sleeve when the other kids finally went back to their posters. Mrs. Johnson saw me wipe my face with my sleeve, and though a box of billowing Kleenex was on her desk, went back to her grading.

I redrew my poster for Endangered Species Week. I had to miss recess to catch up with the others, but I drew an American bald eagle mother on the left, clutching at a branch that jutted out from the side of a cliff, since that's where the 1983 World Book Encyclopedia said bald eagles lived. The mama eagle I drew had a hat with a daisy on it, wearing a purse across her breast. On the edge of the cliff itself, a giant nest with two baby eagles, one stretching its neck towards the mama eagle, the other with musical notes in a balloon from its mouth. On the bottom of the poster, I carefully lettered, "Save Our Planet" in round bubble letters, each colored like Earth—complete with continents and water within each letter.

I won first place in the whole grade, and third in the school competition. But I still felt invisible. Deep down I didn't *really* believe in the aswang, but in our class's story hour, everyone freely talked about Paul Bunyan and Babe the Blue Ox, or Zeus and the gang, as if they lived right there in Phoenix, so why was the very *mention* of an aswang so dangerous, so naughty? In my mother's wild bedtime stories, the aswang came alive, and was more visceral to me than any giant lumberjack that liked to eat flapjacks and had a blue cow. Her voice softened when she told these stories—I'd have my head in her lap and she never acted rushed, even if she had a stack of paperwork to finish before work the next day. We always rushed—to the dentist, to my sister's violin lessons, to find me toy dinosaurs at ten o'clock at night for a diorama due the next morning in Science class—but never when she told me those stories at night. She took her time during these moments and for me that meant that even if these stories and warnings were not all true, that at the very least I should pay attention. No matter if she was on-call the night before or had to get up early for a meeting at the hospital, or had yelled at me for my messy room—at night, she freely laughed and we giggled together. I loved playing with her long and lovely thick hair as she propped herself up on her elbow next to me in bed. Often, her bedtime "stories" consisted of simply trying to describe a favorite fruit from the islands like the *jackfruit,* or recalling a special bread like *pan de sal.* I always went to bed full of her delicious memories, folktales, and legends. If anyone were to check on me later in the night, they surely would have seen a little girl sleeping with a smile on her face. Maybe clutching her stuffed bunny a bit tighter than usual, but with a smile nonetheless.

I didn't want the pizza for my first place award, much to sister's chagrin. Mrs. Johnson shook my hand at the awards ceremony and even hugged me on stage, as if nothing had happened, grinning for the Principal as if *she* had drawn the winning poster. But when we returned to homeroom, I asked that my prize be her famous colored marker set, the expensive ones—barely even used—and coveted by all the students during art class. She looked at the box, still so glossy and new, paused, and to my surprise—she relented. I skipped recess voluntarily the next day and spent the whole period drawing the aswang over and over again—aswang flying, aswang sleeping, even aswang reading a book under a tree. I smiled as I gathered up my new shiny markers and carefully tucked them each into their special case. When recess was over and the students started filing back in, my classmates shuffled by my desk and marveled over the drawings within earshot of Mrs. Johnson. She came over to see what I was drawing, sighed, and hurried the rest of the class inside to get ready for Science. ◀

Reg Saner

Late July, 4:40 a.m.

Plains of western Kansas. Across the pavement, a wheat field now stubble is still giving off the earth smells of night. Miles distant, oncoming headlights from an occasional car or truck flare against a background of dusk. Though the sun's first glint over the horizon is a good half-hour away, that eastern rim is already orange, modulating to indigo overhead—with two or three stars so very faint, I'm not sure the growing light hasn't already dissolved them.

On three sides of the "Kountry Korner Grocery/Restaurant & Truck Stop" a herd of big rigs, some fifteen or twenty, pulses and throbs, motors idling under empty cabs while their drivers order the biscuit and gravy special, or maybe plain eggs, hash browns, and coffee. Walking among those mumbling diesels toward my car, I hear a very American possibility, one we can't remember not having, can't imagine being without: the road's ongoing promise—endless, auspicious.

In terms of waste, of pollution, we know a better way could be found. Just as surely as the bulk and chuff of each mastodon eighteen-wheeler feels already outmoded, we're certain a better way *will*. Because it must. Yet how could we fail to be expressions of what we grew up in? A U.S. of cheap cars, cheap gas, and roads going every which where. Haven't they made us a people most at home when making good time? Whipping past dinky towns like dull habits discarded.

Despite that pack of engines idly burning off foliage of the Carboniferous period, the early air is astonishingly clear, even delicious. In the waning dusk along I-70's westbound lane, headlights from the occasional onrushing trucker reflect off a green-and-white sign placing Salinas and Abilene straight ahead, Colorado beyond them. It's my way, too. Out of Illinois for a thousand miles and more, mountains and desert become my favorite directions. With dawn at my back, a full moon low in the west, well rested, undersides of the eyelids not grainy with fatigue, I ride the adrenaline rush of early hour highway euphoria.

County after county my pickup pours me into a phantasmagoria of phallic silos, ditches where sunflowers flutter like windmills, fields of hay bales rounded like Iroquois lodges. Far below the easy equilibrium of high hawks, the plain rolls as if burrowed by some great, loam-shouldering mole. Sioux place names appear—"Ogallala," for instance, "Oh, Ogallala! Ogallala, oh!" I pronounce aloud and laughingly often. Over miles of interstate, "Ogallala" insists on its syllables: a chant, a sing-song, a mantra.

Oncoming billboards loom, growing in size like imperatives: THREE MILES FROM THE LARGEST PRAIRIE DOG IN THE WORLD. Stuffed or alive, such a creature abides my visit to Rexford, Kansas. Which is the more peculiar specimen, I ask myself, that prairie dog or any animal called *Homo Sapiens* who pulls over to see it? Then farther on, 20 MILES TO 5-LEGGED COW, residence unspecified, yet those miles pour past in no time.

With neither need nor intention to stop, I feel motion itself becoming my truest urge. Motion as essence, as life's very definition. Don't we say "animated" of things that move on their own? Of even drawn lines colored for romping across a movie screen. *Anima*, which we've borrowed to say "animal." *Anima*, which in Latin means "soul"—a gift we confer on the road through connotations in "highway," and which that highway returns by seeming to proffer us, its fastest, traveling vertebrates, more future than anybody can have. Diesel cab after cab, all chrome-glint and smoke, rushes toward and past like an explosion. Going west along with me, great double-trailer rigs high as the Wall of China sway slowly as they overtake my speeding six-cylinder truck. Animation: the soul of all highways? Road itself the Prime Mover?

Kansas dwindles, thins to its own state line, then is gone, as into Colorado I hurtle, scattering crows convened by a damp splat of fur-bearing roadkill. Soon, against a background of pine boards once painted but weathered now to a barn-wood blue-gray, and in faded red or black lettering, hints at quite a story leap from billboard to billboard, with only a sort of meditation space in between: 8 YEARS OF STARVATION HAVE BEEN HARD TO ENDURE. Then a half-mile farther, BETTER TIMES ARE COMING. Another half-mile. MOM DID LET SOME GROW UP TO BE COWBOYS. And another. BEING STARVED ON MY OWN LAND BY MY OWN GOVERNMENT. And another. PRIVATE PROPERTY OR BUREAUCRATIC DICTATORSHIP. Yet another. FROM PRODUCTIVE CITIZEN TO BEGGAR THANKS TO BUREAUCRATS. And so on, to KING BUREAUCRAT VS. CONSTITUTION—thence to—ONE YEAR SINCE KING'S ORDER: "THESE SIGNS MUST BE REMOVED"—till finally, like a return to some opening F-minor chord—8 YEARS COLORADO STARVATION RANCH.

Beyond and behind that lettering, what's the sad upshot? Beats me. To learn more, I'd have to turn aside, wouldn't I, seek out that rancher or one of his neighbors. Impossible. The road's motion won't let me. "On," it says. "Farther." As for Colorado Starvation Ranch, slow adversity can occur only if we stop, settle down. Which is something the road never does. ◄

Alice Walker

Dreads

It has been over ten years since I last combed my hair. When I mention this, friends and family are sometimes scandalized. I am amused by their reaction. During the same ten years they've poured gallons of possibly carcinogenic "relaxer" chemicals on themselves, and their once proud, interestingly crinkled or kinky hair has been forced to lie flat as the slab over a grave. But I understand this, having for many years done the same thing myself.

Bob Marley is the person who taught me to trust the Universe enough to respect my hair; I don't even have to close my eyes to see him dancing his shamanic dance onstage, as he sang his "redemption songs" and consistently poured out his heart to us. If ever anyone truly loved us, it was Bob Marley, and much of that affirmation came out of the way he felt about himself. I remember the first time I saw pictures of Marley, and of that other amazing rebel, Peter Tosh. I couldn't imagine that those black ropes on their heads were hair. And then, because the songs they were singing meant the ropes had to be hair, natural hair to which nothing was added, not even a brushing, I realized they had managed to bring, or to reintroduce, a healthful new look, and way, to the world.

I wondered what such hair felt like, smelled like. What a person dreamed about at night, with hair like that spread across the pillow. And even more intriguing, what would it be like to make love to someone with hair on your head like that, and to be made love to by someone with hair on his or her head like that? It must be like the mating of lions, I thought. Aroused.

It wasn't until the filming of *The Color Purple* in 1985 that I got to explore someone's dreads. By then I had started "baby dreads" of my own, from tiny plaits, and had only blind faith that they'd grow eventually into proper locks. In the film there is a scene in which Sofia's sisters are packing up her things as she prepares to leave her trying-to-be-abusive husband, Harpo. All Sofia's "sisters" were large, good-looking local women ("location" was Monroe, North Carolina), and one of them was explaining why she had to wear a cap in the scene instead of the more acceptable-to-the-period head rag or straw hat. "I have too much hair," she said. "Besides, back then [the 1920s] nobody would have been wearing dreads." Saying this, she swept off her roomy cap, and a cascade of vigorous locks fell way down her back. From a downtrodden, hardworking Southern black woman she was transformed into a free Amazonian Goddess. I laughed in wonder at the transformation, my fingers instantly seeking her hair.

I then asked the question I would find so exasperating myself in years to come. How do you wash it?

She became very serious, as if about to divulge a major secret. "Well," she said, "I use something called shampoo, that you can buy at places like supermarkets and health food stores. I get into something called a shower, wet my hair, and rub this stuff all over it. I stand under the water and I scrub and scrub, working up a mighty lather. Then I rinse." She smiled, suddenly, and I realized how ridiculous my question was. Through the years I would find myself responding to people exactly as she had, delighting in their belated recognition that I am joking with them.

The texture of her hair was somehow both firm and soft, springy, with the clean, fresh scent of almonds. It was a warm black, and sunlight was caught in each kink and crinkle, so that up close there was a lot of purple and blue. I could feel how, miraculously, each lock wove itself into a flat or rounded pattern shortly after it left her scalp—a machine could not have done it with more precision—so that the "matting" I had assumed was characteristic of dreadlocks could more accurately be described as "knitting." How many black people had any idea that, left pretty much to itself, our hair would do this, I wondered. Not very many, I was sure. I had certainly been among the uninformed. It was a moment so satisfying, when I felt my faith in my desire to be natural was so well deserved, that it is not an exaggeration to say I was, in a way, made happy forever. After all, if this major mystery could be discovered right on top of one's head, I thought, what other wonders might not be experienced in the Universe's exuberant, inexhaustible store? ◀

Writing the Ten-Minute Play

▶ A few things you should know about the ten-minute play

Before you enrolled in this class, you almost certainly wrote a number of essays and probably also tried your hand at writing a poem and a story or two (or three or four). However, few students in an introductory creative writing course have ever written a play.

The very idea sounds daunting to many creative writers. How do you work in a form you know nothing about? And by the way, wasn't Shakespeare — the greatest writer of all time, in the opinion of many people — himself a playwright? Who could ever compete with him?

Fortunately, students often find that they have a surprising knack for playwriting. That's partly because we live in such an oral culture. We *hear* people talking all the time — whether it's in person, on television, in the movies, or on cell phones. We will discuss ways of crafting dialogue later in the chapter, but for now you should feel some comfort knowing that you undoubtedly have an untapped gift for mimicking other people's speech.

Indeed, Marsha Norman believes that playwriting is particularly suited to young adults:

There is a kind of inherent struggle in the form that is echoed by the struggle in the lives of young people to say, "Here's who I am, here's what I'm gonna do, and watch out. Here are the things that scare me, here are the things that seem unfair." It's almost a kind of petulance of form: "I insist on telling you this. I'm gonna interrupt your life to tell you this."

Another natural advantage you have as a budding playwright is that you constantly watch people interact. We all do. Even if we don't know the people involved, we can usually tell when someone doesn't mean what he says through tone of voice and gestures, or when someone is furious even though she hasn't said a word. People are born actors, and one aspect of playwriting is simply the process of getting down on paper the things we already know about human nature.

Getting involved in the world of theater can be all-encompassing, and many playwrights believe that their chosen genre is, in the words of Oscar Wilde, "the greatest of all art forms" because it provides "the most immediate way in which a human being can share with another the sense of what it is to be a human being." George Bernard Shaw, no slouch when it came to making big statements, said that the task of "the great dramatist" is "to interpret life." That's a tall order, yet we hear an echo of this grand claim in John Guare's decision to move from fiction to playwriting: "I felt I was betraying a higher calling by writing mere short stories or novels. I believed plays to be on a higher and rarer plane. I still do. Novelists were only a couple hundred years old. Playwrights were thousands of years old. If I was going to be a writer, it had to be plays."

Tina Howe, whose short play *The Divine Fallacy* is reprinted in this book, describes a less ethereal, more pragmatic process in becoming a playwright. Howe originally enrolled in a fiction writing workshop in college, but she felt she was "clearly the worst in the class, and my stories were pretty much of an embarrassment." Almost accidentally, she began writing a one-act play, which, to her genuine surprise, turned out to be a hit. Howe attributes her own success as a playwright in part to the fact that "I'd finally found a form where I could practice my imagination but not be bogged down by all those damn words."

Like poetry, playwriting is a genre that makes maximum use of few words. When students discover that a ten-minute play is generally ten pages long, they tend to panic — until they learn that a standard playscript looks much different in manuscript form than it does in a book. In general, one page of script — a hundred to a few hundred words — equals one minute of stage time. (See the section "Playscript Format: A Model" for an example of a Samuel French–style playscript.)

A few words on etymology: A person who engages in play*writing* is called a play*wright,* not a "playwrite" or a "playwriter." A wright is a worker skilled in the manufacture of objects, such as a wheelwright or a shipwright. From this perspective, the author of a play is a craftsperson, someone who covers the basics. A wheel won't roll if it's not round; a ship will sink if it's not built soundly. Similarly, a play that doesn't incorporate the essentials — conflict, character, dialogue, and stagecraft — will likely falter.

While we're on the subject of words associated with plays, let's look at two more: drama and theater. The word "drama" comes from *dran,* a Greek word meaning "to do or act." By definition, drama is action. It does not consist of people simply standing onstage saying lines. Throughout this chapter, we will be talking about the necessity of creating conflict between your characters, and that's because the clash between opposing actions and forces is so integral to the nature of playmaking. When we tell someone, "You're so dramatic!" we mean that the person is larger than life, that they seem to feel emotions more deeply than most of us. Characters in a play tend to take things very personally. Whatever happens to them, it really, really *happens*.

We might also describe a dramatic person as being very "theatrical," meaning that his or her behavior is "marked by extravagant display or exhibitionism." Being on exhibit is part of what plays are all about. The word "theater" is derived from the Greek *thea*, "to see," and is related to the word *thauma*, meaning "miracle."

Because Greek plays are the earliest surviving complete works of drama we have, playwrights continue to look in their direction for inspiration, but theater has changed a great deal since the days of Aeschylus, Sophocles, and Euripides. All the actors were men, and they all wore versions of the smiling- and sad-face masks we now associate with comedy and tragedy. The real action — the murders, the battles, and so forth — took place offstage. Mostly the actors recounted things that had happened to the gods or to themselves and the people they knew. Singing and dancing were part of the pageantry. It was a rather static spectacle, perhaps similar to something you might see in a modern church, and this makes sense, since the subject of Greek plays was usually the immortals and their relationship to heroes. Greek plays, in short, reenacted the old familiar miracles.

A discussion of the history of theater is outside the scope of this book, but it is worth mentioning a few important developments in drama after the Greeks. Let's fast-forward to the plays of Shakespeare, produced in the late sixteenth and early seventeenth centuries. Shakespeare admired the Greek plays — or at least the *idea* of the Greeks — and the characters in his plays do spend a great deal of time making speeches. However, Shakespeare's plays incorporate considerably more action onstage than do the Greek plays, and his many fans will say that no one else has ever quite approached his ability to depict the range and essence of humanity.

Of course, comparing yourself with Shakespeare is a fruitless exercise. In any case, he's not an especially good model for us because, as far as we know, he never wrote a ten-minute play. There is also something otherworldly about his work that no one has ever been able to emulate. You would be hard-pressed to mistake a Shakespeare play for real life, and in the nineteenth century, writers such as Émile Zola began championing what they called "naturalism," which we tend to think of as "realism." According to Zola, although novelists had managed to master **verisimilitude** — realistic portrayals of people and their environments — playwrights were lagging far behind:

I am waiting for everyone to throw out the tricks of the trade, the contrived formulas, the tears and superficial laughs. I am waiting for a dramatic work void of declamations, majestic speech, and noble sentiments, to have the unimpeachable morality of truth and to teach us the frightening lesson of sincere investigation. I am waiting, finally, until the . . . playwrights return to the source of science and modern arts, to the study of nature, to the anatomy of man, to the painting of life in an exact reproduction more original and powerful than anyone has so far dared to risk on the boards.

Zola's ideas certainly influenced two of the nineteenth century's greatest playwrights, the Russian Anton Chekhov and the Norwegian Henrik Ibsen, and I quote Zola at length because many contemporary playwrights still aspire to the sort of theater he celebrated. They avoid formulaic plots and grandiose speechmaking and try to show people as they truly are, not as the playwrights wish them to be.

Today we might share Zola's distaste for long, pretentious speeches, but in the first half of the twentieth century, realism, naturalism, and the "well-made play" were themselves under attack. Jean-Paul Sartre, for instance, scoffed at "the so-called 'realistic theater' because 'realism' has always offered plays made up of stories of defeat, laissez-faire, and drifting: it has always preferred to show how external forces batter a man to pieces, destroy him bit by bit, and ultimately make of him a weathervane with every change of wind." During the same period, Bertolt Brecht developed a new sort of over-the-top theatricality that he called "epic theater." The actors made no attempt to pretend that they weren't actors. In order to emphasize the fact that it was a play, not real life, being performed before an audience, actors used cast-off clothing and cheap **props**. (Props, short for "properties," include everything from the furniture the actors sit on to the objects they handle.)

Other playwrights took the crusade against realism even further. In plays such as *The Spurt of Blood*, Antonin Artaud's characters, who clearly represent types (a priest, a knight, a judge, and so on), declaim crazy poetry that borders on gibberish and run around the stage like hyperactive children. In his essay "No More Masterpieces," Artaud advocates for a "theater of cruelty." This type of theater thumbs its nose at conventional plots and characters. Instead, it is full of spectacle, with constant noises and sounds, unexpected lighting, and bizarre onstage behavior: "Here the theater, far from copying life, puts itself whenever possible in communication with pure forces."

The "theater of the absurd" has led to great plays such as those by Harold Pinter and Samuel Beckett. The hallmark of this theater, according to critic Martin Esslin, "is its sense that the certitudes and unshakable basic assumptions of former ages have been swept away, that they have been tested and found wanting, that they have been discredited as cheap and somewhat childish illusions."

Esslin wrote this in 1969, yet in many ways the world of doubt and uncertainty he describes is still our own.

In the 1960s and early 1970s, even using a script became passé. Bert Cardullo describes "happenings" in which "each spectator, in becoming the partial creator of a piece, derived any meaning that might be desired from the experience, thus downplaying the artist's intention or even existence." Cardullo points out that in this type of theater "all production elements speak their own language rather than being mere supports for words, and a text need be neither the starting point nor the goal of a production—indeed, a text is not even necessary, and therefore there may be none. In other words, fidelity to the text, that sacred tenet which has so long governed performance, has become irrelevant."

Most creative writing instructors will probably be a bit skeptical if you try to stage a "happening" for your ten-minute play; nevertheless, this brief overview should suggest what a smorgasbord of approaches is available to playwrights. Our model plays are closer to Zola's naturalism than to the theater of cruelty or the theater of the absurd, but they, like most other ten-minute plays, have not only a basis in realism but also a hint of something strange and surreal.

Whatever your own biases as a playwright turn out to be, there is nothing like seeing a play—any play, good or bad, amateur or professional—to help you understand the demands of the theater. If your school has a theater department, it will probably produce a play this academic term. Go see it. If possible, talk to the student actors and directors about what a good play requires. The more you immerse yourself in the world of theater, even if it's only by joining an audience, the clearer will be your sense of how to write your own play.

After seeing just a few plays, you will probably agree with playwriting professor David Rush that a play is *not* "a screenplay or a conversation or a rant or an essay." Most playwriting instructors would concur with Rush, so let's look at his admonishments one at a time:

▶ **A Play Is Not a Screenplay**   Most people go to movies far more often than to plays, so it makes sense that beginning playwrights, especially if they have never attended a play before, will turn to the big screen for models. "Being a playwright is good training for film school," says Stephen Peace, but watching movies isn't necessarily good training for playwrights. A screenplay has many short scenes, often with minimal or no dialogue. In a play, however, scenes tend to be considerably longer, with greater emphasis on the characters' verbal exchanges. Moreover, movie scenes are shot again and again; when the camera is rolling and someone flubs a line, the actors just start over. A play, on the other hand, is *live*. When an actor forgets a line, there are no second takes. A play production has a sense of excitement, tension, and immediacy that is generally missing from the other creative writing genres.

▶ **A Play Is Not a Conversation**   A good conversation may be stimulating, but most conversations meander and falter and never reach heightened intensity. In contrast, dialogue in a play is always driven by the central conflict between the characters.

▶ **A Play Is Not a Rant**   Although it is sometimes entertaining to listen to someone yell and rave, you can do that onstage for only a short while before it gets boring. Plays do have lots of talking—and often some shouting— but *all* of it matters.

▶ **A Play Is Not an Essay**   An essay, as Rush refers to it here, is a document meant to explain things. Its main purpose is to convince an audience that a particular point of view is correct. Plays, in contrast, value ambiguity. Even though plays often address relevant contemporary and universal issues, and even though some characters may be *more right* than others, good playwrights always try to see the world from the perspective of all of their characters.

J. M. Synge said that "drama is made serious . . . not by the degree in which it is taken up with problems that are serious in themselves, but by the degree in which it gives the nourishment, not easy to define, on which our imaginations live. We should go to the theatre . . . as we go to a dinner, where food we need is taken with pleasure and excitement." Indeed, once you begin writing and rehearsing your ten-minute play, you may well be surprised by how much "pleasure and excitement" are involved in the process.

The elements of playwriting ▶

The sections in this chapter are organized as follows:

▶ **Structuring the Ten-Minute Play**   More than any other genre of creative writing, plays need structure to succeed. This section discusses how to create an immediate conflict, how to complicate and reverse the audience's initial expectations, and how to end your play.

▶ **Creating Believable Characters**   As is the case for writers of fiction, characterization and character development are primary concerns for playwrights. You will learn how to decide who should be in your play as well as how to avoid creating characters that come across as two-dimensional **stereotypes**—people with one or two easily recognizable traits or characteristics.

▶ **Writing Convincing Dialogue**   Poets, fiction writers, and essayists can give us background information without resorting to dialogue. They describe scenes and tell us what we need to know. In contrast, playwrights have only dialogue to tell us who the relevant people are, where they have

been, and where they are going. This section shows you how to use dialogue to develop believable characters, introduce backstory in a credible
fashion, and heighten and develop your conflict.

▶ **Crafting a Theme**   Besides being arenas for gripping conflict, satisfying
character development, and convincing dialogue, plays are places to discuss ideas. The themes of your play should arise naturally from the play
itself, and this section discusses ways to highlight and clarify the topics
you address.

▶ **Onstage: The Elements of Production**   Big Broadway productions can
afford elaborate props and costumes and spectacular lighting and effects.
Unfortunately, you probably can't, so this section presents a few ways that
you can use basic production elements and provides an overview of the
people and things involved in putting on a play with limited resources.

The ten-minute play: Three models ▶

A one-act play — that is, a play without an intermission — can range in
length from a couple of minutes to more than an hour; the ten-minute play
is a type of one-act play. Ten minutes is an arbitrary slice of time, but right now
it is a popular length for plays. If creative nonfiction is the hot genre in creative
writing, then the ten-minute play is what's currently hot in playwriting. Edu-
ardo Machado, head of Columbia University's playwriting program, calls the
ten-minute play "a great learning tool. . . . It's so well-suited to the immediacy
of the young playwright's experience." Marc Masterson lauds the "tremendous
potential of ten-minute plays," which he says are "capable of packing a punch
with a deft stroke." And Ellen Lauren says that they "provide as rich a challenge, demand as articulate a portrayal, and contain possibilities as limitless
as any full-length text." In short, according to Gary Garrison, the ten-minute
play brings "an audience through the same cathartic/entertainment experience that a good one-act or full-length play accomplishes — i.e., sympathetic
characters with recognizable needs encompassed within a resolvable dramatic
conflict."

Ten-minute plays generally are produced as a group. Although grouping the
plays dilutes the attention focused on each individual playwright, it does have
a number of benefits. An evening of eight ten-minute plays not only generates
opportunities for eight playwrights and directors and as many as twenty or more
actors but also increases the likelihood of an audience. Attracting an audience
is often the most demanding aspect of a production, but if you can draw on the
friends and family of thirty people, suddenly a theater begins to fill up.

We will talk more about structure in the next section, but it's worth emphasizing that a ten-minute play is not a skit masquerading as a play. Unlike a

comedic play, a skit is something done quickly for cheap laughs. A number of jokes and gestures are bundled together under a single broad topic, but the parts of a skit don't necessarily connect: we usually just get the beginning, middle, or end of a scenario. The characters are stereotypes, and nothing much is at stake; therefore, nothing of any consequence is resolved. A play, in contrast, gives us "resolvable dramatic conflict," and even if it's hilarious, it points to deeper truths about the human condition.

All three of our model plays are interested in who we are as humans and what we want from life, although each playwright uses a different combination of humor and gravity to explore these issues. On the surface, David Ives's *Sure Thing* is pure fun, a farce about a man trying to pick up a woman; however, when we dig deeper, we find that the play also has some serious commentary about how difficult it is for two people to get together. David Henry Hwang's *Trying to Find Chinatown* addresses the critical topic of racial identity, although Hwang too uses humor to investigate the various ways we categorize ourselves and others. Tina Howe's *The Divine Fallacy* begins as a comedy about a brilliant yet painfully shy author and ends as a meditation on the nature of personal, and possibly celestial, revelations.

"By shortening a play you can lengthen it," wrote the German critic Friedrich Hebbel, and our model plays confirm that apparent paradox. When we squeeze an entire world, an entire dramatic action — from beginning to end — into ten minutes, we insist that audience members increase their attention, that they grant this little slip of time the same authority they would give to a full-length play. As you begin to generate ideas for your ten-minute play, try to think of conflicts and characters that are funny enough to keep us laughing the entire time, or that have the weight and heft and consequence necessary to keep us on the edge of our seats.

David Ives

Sure Thing

David Ives is a graduate of the Yale School of Drama and a widely produced playwright. He is best known for *All in the Timing*, his collection of six one-act comedies, which includes *Sure Thing*. *All in the Timing* received the 1993 Outer Critics Circle Playwriting Award, as well as a number of other honors, and it continues to be produced around the country. Ives has taught at Columbia University and the Tisch School for the Arts and has worked in musical theater in various capacities (he adapted David Copperfield's magic show *Dreams and Nightmares* for Broadway). He has also written for *The New Yorker* and *Spy* magazine, and he is the author of the children's book *Monsieur Eek*.

The charm of *Sure Thing* is certainly all in the timing. Not only does the rapid back-and-forth repartee between Bill and Betty require precise timing on the part of the actors, but the stop-and-start structure of the play itself also suggests that getting together with a romantic partner depends on meeting that special someone at just the right moment and saying just the right things. Performed well, *Sure Thing* is hilarious. The play demonstrates just how much you can do with funny, well-crafted lines and the simplest production elements: two chairs, a table, and a bell.

Characters

BILL and BETTY, both in their late 20s

Setting

A café table, with a couple of chairs

Important Note

The bell is not visible, is not onstage, is not on the table or anywhere else in sight. It is rung from the wings and neither Bill nor Betty ever acknowledges the sound of the bell.

Betty is reading at the table. An empty chair opposite her. Bill enters.

BILL: Excuse me. Is this chair taken?

BETTY: Excuse me?

BILL: Is this taken?

BETTY: Yes it is.

BILL: Oh. Sorry.

BETTY: Sure thing. (*A bell rings softly.*)

BILL: Excuse me. Is this chair taken?

BETTY: Excuse me?

BILL: Is this taken?

BETTY: No, but I'm expecting somebody in a minute.

BILL: Oh. Thanks anyway.

BETTY: Sure thing. (*A bell rings softly.*)

BILL: Excuse me. Is this chair taken?

BETTY: No, but I'm expecting somebody very shortly.

BILL: Would you mind if I sit here till he or she or it comes?

BETTY: (*Glances at her watch.*) They do seem to be pretty late. . . .

BILL: You never know who you might be turning down.

BETTY: Sorry. Nice try, though.

BILL: Sure thing. (*Bell.*) Is this seat taken?

BETTY: No it's not.

BILL: Would you mind if I sit here?

BETTY: Yes I would.

BILL: Oh. (*Bell.*) Is this chair taken?

BETTY: No it's not.

BILL: Would you mind if I sit here?

BETTY: No. Go ahead.

BILL: Thanks. (*He sits. She continues reading.*) Every place else seems to be taken.

BETTY: Mm-hm.

BILL: Great place.

BETTY: Mm-hm.

BILL: What's the book?

BETTY: I just wanted to read in quiet, if you don't mind.

BILL: No. Sure thing. (*Bell.*) Every place else seems to be taken.

BETTY: Mm-hm.

BILL: Great place for reading.

BETTY: Yes, I like it.

BILL: What's the book?

BETTY: *The Sound and the Fury.*

BILL: Oh. Hemingway. (*Bell.*) What's the book?

BETTY: *The Sound and the Fury.*

BILL: Oh. Faulkner.

BETTY: Have you read it?

BILL: Not . . . actually. I've sure read *about* it, though. It's supposed to be great.

BETTY: It is great.

BILL: I hear it's great. (*Small pause.*) Waiter? (*Bell.*) What's the book?

BETTY: *The Sound and the Fury.*

BILL: Oh. Faulkner.

BETTY: Have you read it?

BILL: I'm a Mets fan, myself. (*Bell.*)

BETTY: Have you read it?

BILL: Yeah, I read it in college.

BETTY: Where was college?

BILL: I went to Oral Roberts University. (*Bell.*)

BETTY: Where was college?

BILL: I was lying. I never really went to college. I just like to party. (*Bell.*)

BETTY: Where was college?

BILL: Harvard.

BETTY: Do you like Faulkner?

BILL: I love Faulkner. I spent a whole winter reading him once.

BETTY: I've just started.

BILL: I was so excited after ten pages that I went out and bought everything else he wrote. One of the greatest reading experiences of my life. I mean, all that incredible psychological understanding. Page after page of gorgeous prose. His profound grasp of the mystery of time and human existence. The smells of the earth. . . . What do you think?

BETTY: I think it's pretty boring. (*Bell.*)

BILL: What's the book?

BETTY: *The Sound and the Fury.*

BILL: Oh! Faulkner!

BETTY: Do you like Faulkner?

BILL: I love Faulkner.

BETTY: He's incredible.

BILL: I spent a whole winter reading him once.

BETTY: I was so excited after ten pages that I went out and bought everything else he wrote.

BILL: All that incredible psychological understanding.

BETTY: And the prose is so gorgeous.

BILL: And the way he's grasped the mystery of time —

BETTY: —and human existence. I can't believe I've waited this long to read him.

BILL: You never know. You might not have liked him before.

BETTY: That's true.

BILL: You might not have been ready for him. You have to hit these things at the right moment or it's no good.

BETTY: That's happened to me.

BILL: It's all in the timing. (*Small pause.*) My name's Bill, by the way.

BETTY: I'm Betty.

BILL: Hi.

BETTY: Hi. (*Small pause.*)

BILL: Yes I thought reading Faulkner was . . . a great experience.

BETTY: Yes. (*Small pause.*)

BILL: *The Sound and the Fury* . . . (*Another small pause.*)

BETTY: Well. Onwards and upwards. (*She goes back to her book.*)

BILL: Waiter—? (*Bell.*) You have to hit these things at the right moment or it's no good.

BETTY: That's happened to me.

BILL: It's all in the timing. My name's Bill, by the way.

BETTY: I'm Betty.

BILL: Hi.

BETTY: Hi.

BILL: Do you come in here a lot?

BETTY: Actually I'm just in town for two days from Pakistan.

BILL: Oh. Pakistan. (*Bell.*) My name's Bill, by the way.

BETTY: I'm Betty.

BILL: Hi.

BETTY: Hi.

BILL: Do you come in here a lot?

BETTY: Every once in a while. Do you?

BILL: Not so much anymore. Not as much as I used to. Before my nervous breakdown. (*Bell.*) Do you come in here a lot?

BETTY: Why are you asking?

BILL: Just interested.

BETTY: Are you really interested, or do you just want to pick me up?

BILL: No, I'm really interested.

BETTY: Why would you be interested in whether I come in here a lot?

BILL: Just . . . getting acquainted.

BETTY: Maybe you're only interested for the sake of making small talk long enough to ask me back to your place to listen to some music, or because you've just rented some great tape for your VCR, or because you've got some terrific unknown Django Reinhardt record, only all you really want to do is fuck — which you won't do very well — after which you'll go into the bathroom and pee very loudly, then pad into the kitchen and get yourself a beer from the refrigerator without asking me whether I'd like anything, and then you'll proceed to lie back down beside me and confess that you've got a girlfriend named Stephanie who's away at medical school in Belgium for a year, and that you've been involved with her — *off and on* — in what you'll call a very "intricate" relationship, for about *seven YEARS*. None of which *interests* me, mister!

BILL: Okay. (*Bell.*) Do you come in here a lot?

BETTY: Every other day, I think.

BILL: I come in here quite a lot and I don't remember seeing you.

BETTY: I guess we must be on different schedules.

BILL: Missed connections.

BETTY: Yes. Different time zones.

BILL: Amazing how you can live right next door to somebody in this town and never even know it.

BETTY: I know.

BILL: City life.

BETTY: It's crazy.

BILL: We probably pass each other in the street every day. Right in front of this place, probably.

BETTY: Yep.

BILL: (*Looks around.*) Well the waiters here sure seem to be in some different time zone. I can't seem to locate one anywhere. . . . Waiter! (*He looks back.*) So what do you — (*He sees that she's gone back to her book.*)

BETTY: I beg pardon?

BILL: Nothing. Sorry. (*Bell.*)

BETTY: I guess we must be on different schedules.

BILL: Missed connections.

BETTY: Yes. Different time zones.

BILL: Amazing how you can live right next door to somebody in this town and never even know it.

BETTY: I know.

BILL: City life.

BETTY: It's crazy.

BILL: You weren't waiting for somebody when I came in, were you?

BETTY: Actually I was.

BILL: Oh. Boyfriend?

BETTY: Sort of.

BILL: What's a sort-of boyfriend?

BETTY: My husband.

BILL: Ah-ha. (*Bell.*) You weren't waiting for somebody when I came in, were you?

BETTY: Actually I was.

BILL: Oh. Boyfriend?

BETTY: Sort of.

BILL: What's a sort-of boyfriend?

BETTY: We were meeting here to break up.

BILL: Mm-hm . . . (*Bell.*) What's a sort-of boyfriend?

BETTY: My lover. Here she comes right now! (*Bell.*)

BILL: You weren't waiting for somebody when I came in, were you?

BETTY: No, just reading.

BILL: Sort of a sad occupation for a Friday night, isn't it? Reading here, all by yourself?

BETTY: Do you think so?

BILL: Well sure. I mean, what's a good-looking woman like you doing out alone on a Friday night?

BETTY: Trying to keep away from lines like that.

BILL: No, listen — (*Bell.*) You weren't waiting for somebody when I came in, were you?

BETTY: No, just reading.

BILL: Sort of a sad occupation for a Friday night, isn't it? Reading here all by yourself?

BETTY: I guess it is, in a way.

BILL: What's a good-looking woman like you doing out alone on a Friday night anyway? No offense, but . . .

BETTY: I'm out alone on a Friday night for the first time in a very long time.

BILL: Oh.

BETTY: You see, I just recently ended a relationship.

BILL: Oh.

BETTY: Of rather long standing.

BILL: I'm sorry. (*Small pause.*) Well listen, since reading by yourself *is* such a sad occupation for a Friday night, would you like to go elsewhere?

BETTY: No . . .

BILL: Do something else?

BETTY: No thanks.

BILL: I was headed out to the movies in a while anyway.

BETTY: I don't think so.

BILL: Big chance to let Faulkner catch his breath. All those long sentences get him pretty tired.

BETTY: Thanks anyway.

BILL: Okay.

BETTY: I appreciate the invitation.

BILL: Sure thing. (*Bell.*) You weren't waiting for somebody when I came in, were you?

BETTY: No, just reading.

BILL: Sort of a sad occupation for a Friday night, isn't it? Reading here all by yourself?

BETTY: I guess I was trying to think of it as existentially romantic. You know—cappuccino, great literature, rainy night . . .

BILL: That only works in Paris. We *could* hop the late plane to Paris. Get on a Concorde. Find a café . . .

BETTY: I'm a little short on plane fare tonight.

BILL: Darn it, so am I.

BETTY: To tell you the truth, I was headed to the movies after I finished this section. Would you like to come along? Since you can't locate a waiter?

BILL: That's a very nice offer, but . . .

BETTY: Uh-huh. Girlfriend?

BILL: Two, actually. One of them's pregnant, and Stephanie—(*Bell.*)

BETTY: Girlfriend?

BILL: No, I don't have a girlfriend. Not if you mean the castrating bitch I dumped last night. (*Bell.*)

BETTY: Girlfriend?

BILL: Sort of. Sort of.

BETTY: What's a sort-of girlfriend?

BILL: My mother. (*Bell.*) I just ended a relationship, actually.

BETTY: Oh.

BILL: Of rather long standing.

BETTY: I'm sorry to hear it.

BILL: This is my first night out alone in a long time. I feel a little bit at sea, to tell you the truth.

BETTY: So you didn't stop to talk because you're a Moonie, or you have some weird political affiliation—?

BILL: Nope. Straight-down-the-ticket Republican. (*Bell.*) Straight-down-the-ticket Democrat. (*Bell.*) Can I tell you something about politics? (*Bell.*) I like to think of myself as a citizen of the universe. (*Bell.*) I'm unaffiliated.

BETTY: That's a relief. So am I.

BILL: I vote my beliefs.

BETTY: Labels are not important.

BILL: Labels are not important, exactly. Take me, for example. I mean, what does it matter if I had a two-point at— (*Bell.*) —three-point at—(*Bell.*)—four-point at college? Or if I did come from Pittsburgh—(*Bell.*)—Cleveland—(*Bell.*)—Westchester County?

BETTY: Sure.

BILL: I believe that a man is what he is. (*Bell.*) A person is what he is. (*Bell.*) A person is . . . what they are.

BETTY: I think so too.

BILL: So what if I admire Trotsky? (*Bell.*) So what if I once had a total-body liposuction? (*Bell.*) So what if I don't have a penis? (*Bell.*) So what if I once spent a year in the Peace Corps? I was acting on my convictions.

BETTY: Sure.

BILL: You can't just hang a sign on a person.

BETTY: Absolutely. I'll bet you're a Scorpio. (*Many bells ring.*) Listen, I was headed to the movies after I finished this section. Would you like to come along?

BILL: That sounds like fun. What's playing?

BETTY: A couple of the really early Woody Allen movies.

BILL: Oh.

BETTY: You don't like Woody Allen?

BILL: Sure. I like Woody Allen.

BETTY: But you're not crazy about Woody Allen.

BILL: Those early ones kind of get on my nerves.

BETTY: Uh-huh. (*Bell.*)

BILL: (*Simultaneously.*)	BETTY: (*Simultaneously.*)
Y'know I was headed to the—	I was thinking about—

BILL: I'm sorry.

BETTY: No, go ahead.

BILL: I was going to say that I was headed to the movies in a little while, and . . .

BETTY: So was I.

BILL: The Woody Allen festival?

BETTY: Just up the street.

BILL: Do you like the early ones?

BETTY: I think anybody who doesn't ought to be run off the planet.

BILL: How many times have you seen *Bananas*?

BETTY: Eight times.

BILL: Twelve. So are you still interested? (*Long pause.*)

BETTY: Do you like Entenmann's crumb cake . . . ?

BILL: Last night I went out at two in the morning to get one. (*Small pause.*) Did you have an Etch-a-Sketch as a child?

BETTY: Yes! And do you like Brussels sprouts? (*Small pause.*)

BILL: No, I think they're disgusting.

BETTY: They *are* disgusting!

BILL: Do you still believe in marriage in spite of current sentiments against it?

BETTY: Yes.

BILL: And children?

BETTY: Three of them.

BILL: Two girls and a boy.

BETTY: Harvard, Vassar and Brown.

BILL: And will you love me?

BETTY: Yes.

BILL: And cherish me forever?

BETTY: Yes.

BILL: Do you still want to go to the movies?

BETTY: Sure thing.

BILL and BETTY: (*Together.*) *Waiter!* ◀

BLACKOUT

David Henry Hwang

Trying to Find Chinatown

David Henry Hwang was born in Los Angeles to parents who immigrated to the United States from China. As a student at Stanford, Hwang began by studying pre-law, but he soon switched to English and became involved in the theater. His first play, *FOB* (for "fresh off the boat"), won an Obie Award for best new play in 1981. His breakthrough play was *M. Butterfly,* about a French diplomat who falls in love with a Chinese "woman" who turns out to be a man. The play won the Tony Award for best play of the year in 1988 and later was turned into a film starring Jeremy Irons and John Lone. *Chinglish*, first produced in 2011, was named *Time* magazine's "Best American Play of the Year."

Trying to Find Chinatown was originally produced in 1996 by the Actors Theater of Louisville for the prestigious Humana Festival. In much of his work, Hwang is concerned with overturning stereotypes about Asian Americans, and that is certainly the case with this play. Ronnie is a street-smart musician who plays jazz violin. Benjamin is a young white man adopted by Asian American parents; he is looking for his roots by trying to find the tenement where his father grew up. Neither character conforms to received ideas about what it means to be Asian or white, and the play challenges both them, and us, to expand our concept of racial identity.

Characters

BENJAMIN
RONNIE

Setting

A street corner on the Lower East Side, New York City. The present.

Note on Music

Obviously, it would be foolish to require that the actor portraying Ronnie perform the specified violin music live. The score of this play can be played on tape over the house speakers, and the actor can feign playing the violin using a bow treated with soap. However, to effect a convincing illusion, it is desirable that the actor possess some familiarity with the violin, or at least another stringed instrument.

Darkness. Over the house speakers, fade in Hendrix-like virtuoso rock 'n' roll riffs—heavy feedback, distortion, phase shifting, wah-wah—amplified over a tiny Fender pugnose.

Lights fade up to reveal that the music's being played over a solid-body electric violin by Ronnie, a Chinese American male in his mid-twenties, dressed in retro sixties clothing, with a few requisite nineties body mutilations. He's playing on a sidewalk for money, his violin case open before him, change and a few stray bills having been left by previous passers-by.

Enter Benjamin, early twenties, blond, blue-eyed, looking like a midwestern tourist in the big city. He holds a scrap of paper in his hands, scanning street signs for an address. He pauses before Ronnie, listens for a while. With a truly bravura run, Ronnie concludes the number, falls to his knees, gasping. Benjamin applauds.

BENJAMIN: Good. That was really great. (*Pause.*) I didn't . . . I mean, a fiddle . . . I mean, I'd heard them at square dances, on country stations and all, but I never . . . wow, this must really be New York City!

(*He applauds, starts to walk on. Still on his knees Ronnie clears his throat loudly.*)

BENJAMIN: Oh, I . . . you're not just doing this for your health, right?

(*He reaches in his pocket, pulls out a couple of coins. Ronnie clears his throat again.*)

BENJAMIN: Look, I'm not a millionaire, I'm just . . .

(*Benjamin pulls out his wallet, removes a dollar bill. Ronnie nods his head, gestures toward the violin case, as he sits on the sidewalk, takes out a pack of cigarettes, lights one.*)

RONNIE: And don't call it a "fiddle," OK?
BENJAMIN: Oh, well, I didn't mean to—
RONNIE: You sound like a wuss. A hick. A dipshit.
BENJAMIN: It just slipped out. I didn't really—
RONNIE: If this was a fiddle, I'd be sitting here with a cob pipe, stomping my cowboy boots and kicking up hay. Then I'd go home and fuck my cousin.
BENJAMIN: Oh! Well, I don't really think—
RONNIE: Do you see a cob pipe? Am I fucking my cousin?
BENJAMIN: Well, no, not at the moment, but—
RONNIE: All right. Then this is a violin, you hand over the money, and I ignore the insult, herein endeth the lesson. (*Pause.*)
BENJAMIN: Listen, a dollar's more than I've ever given to a . . . to someone asking for money.
RONNIE: Yeah, well, this is New York. Welcome to the cost of living.
BENJAMIN: What I mean is, maybe in exchange, you could help me—?
RONNIE: Jesus Christ! Do you see a sign around my neck reading "Big Apple Fucking Tourist Bureau"?
BENJAMIN: I'm just looking for an address, I don't think it's far from here, maybe you could . . . ?

(*Ronnie snatches the scrap of paper from Benjamin.*)

RONNIE: You're lucky I'm such a goddamn softie. (*He looks at the paper.*) Oh, fuck you. Just suck my dick, you and the cousin you rode in on.
BENJAMIN: I don't get it! What are you—?
RONNIE: Eat me. You know exactly what I—
BENJAMIN: I'm just asking for a little—
RONNIE: 13 Doyers St.? Like you don't know where that is?
BENJAMIN: Of course I don't know! That's why I'm asking—
RONNIE: C'mon, you trailer-park refugee. You don't know that's Chinatown?
BENJAMIN: Sure I know that's Chinatown.
RONNIE: I know you know that's Chinatown.

BENJAMIN: So? That doesn't mean I know where Chinatown—

RONNIE: So why is it that you picked *me*, of all the street musicians in the *city*—to point you in the direction of Chinatown? Lemme guess—is it the earring? No, I don't think so. The Hendrix riffs? Guess again, you fucking moron.

BENJAMIN: Now, wait a minute. I see what you're—

RONNIE: What are you gonna ask me next? Where you can find the best dim sum in the city? Whether I can direct you to a genuine opium den? Or do I know how you can meet Miss Saigon for a night of nookie-nookie followed by a good old-fashioned ritual suicide? (*He picks up his violin.*) Now, get your white ass off my sidewalk. One dollar doesn't even begin to make up for all this aggravation. Why don't you go back home and race bullfrogs, or whatever it is you do for—?

BENJAMIN: Brother, I can absolutely relate to your anger. Righteous rage, I suppose would be a more appropriate term. To be marginalized, as we are, by a white racist patriarchy, to the point where the accomplishments of our people are obliterated from the history books, this is cultural genocide of the first order, leading to the fact that you must do battle with all Euro-America's emasculating and brutal stereotypes of Asians—the opium den, the sexual objectification of the Asian female, the exoticized image of a tourist's Chinatown which ignores the exploitation of workers, the failure to unionize, the high rate of mental illness and tuberculosis—against these, each day, you rage, no, not as a victim, but as a survivor, yes, brother, a glorious warrior survivor!

(*Silence.*)

RONNIE: Say what?

BENJAMIN: So, I hope you can see that my request is not—

RONNIE: Wait, wait.

BENJAMIN: —motivated by sorts of racist assumptions—

RONNIE: But, but where . . . how did you learn all that?

BENJAMIN: All what?

RONNIE: All that—you know—oppression stuff—tuberculosis . . .

BENJAMIN: It's statistically irrefutable. TB occurs in the community at a rate—

RONNIE: Where did *you* learn it?

BENJAMIN: Well . . . I took Asian-American studies. In college.

RONNIE: Where did you go to college?

BENJAMIN: University of Wisconsin. Madison.

RONNIE: Madison, Wisconsin?

BENJAMIN: That's not where the bridges are, by the way.

RONNIE: Huh? Oh, right . . .

BENJAMIN: You wouldn't believe the number of people who—

RONNIE: They have Asian-American studies in Madison, Wisconsin? Since when?

BENJAMIN: Since the last Third World Unity sit-in and hunger strike. (*Pause.*) Why do you look so surprised? We're down.

RONNIE: I dunno. It just never occurred to me, the idea of Asian students in the Midwest going on a hunger strike.

BENJAMIN: Well, a lot of them had midterms that week, so they fasted in shifts. (*Pause.*) The Administration never figured it out. The Asian students put that "they all look alike" stereotype to good use.

RONNIE: OK, so they got Asian-American studies. That still doesn't explain—

BENJAMIN: What?

RONNIE: What *you* were doing taking it?

BENJAMIN: Just like everyone else. I wanted to explore my roots. After a lifetime of assimilation, I wanted to find out who I really am. (*Pause.*)

RONNIE: And did you?

BENJAMIN: Sure. I learned to take pride in my ancestors who built the railroads, my Popo who would make me a hot bowl of jok with thousand-day-old eggs when the white kids chased me home yelling, "Gook! Chink! Slant-eyes!"

RONNIE: OK, OK, that's enough!

BENJAMIN: Painful to listen to, isn't it?

RONNIE: I don't know what kind of bullshit ethnic studies program they're running over in Wisconsin, but did they teach you that in order to find your Asian "roots," it's a good idea first to be Asian? (*Pause.*)

BENJAMIN: Are you speaking metaphorically?

RONNIE: No! Literally! Look at your skin!

(*Ronnie grabs Benjamin's hands, holds them up before his face.*)

BENJAMIN: You know, it's very stereotypical to think that all Asian skin tones conform to a single hue.

RONNIE: You're white! Is this some kind of redneck joke or something? Am I the first person in the world to tell you this?

BENJAMIN: Oh! Oh! Oh!

RONNIE: I know real Asians are scarce in the Midwest, but . . . Jesus!

BENJAMIN: No, of course, I . . . I see where your misunderstanding arises.

RONNIE: Yeah. It's called "You white."

BENJAMIN: It's just that—in my hometown of Tribune, Kansas, and then at school—see, everyone knows me—so this sort of thing never comes up. (*He offers his hand.*) Benjamin Wong. I forget that a society wedded to racial constructs constantly forces me to explain my very existence.

RONNIE: Ronnie Chang. Otherwise known as "The Bowman."

BENJAMIN: You see, I was adopted by Chinese-American parents at birth. So clearly, I'm an Asian American—

RONNIE: Even though they could put a picture of you in the dictionary next to the definition of "WASP."

BENJAMIN: Well, you can't judge my race by my genetic heritage.

RONNIE: If genes don't determine race, what does?

BENJAMIN: Maybe you'd prefer that I continue in denial, masquerading as a white man?

RONNIE: Listen, you can't just wake up and say, "Gee, I *feel* Black today."

BENJAMIN: Brother, I'm just trying to find what you've already got.

RONNIE: What do I got?

BENJAMIN: A home. With your people. Picketing with the laundry workers. Taking refuge from the daily slights against your masculinity in the noble image of Gwan Gung.

RONNIE: Gwan *who*?

BENJAMIN: C'mon — the Chinese God of warriors and — what do you take me for? There're altars to him up all over the community.

RONNIE: I dunno what community you're talking about, but it's sure as hell not mine. (*Pause.*)

BENJAMIN: What do you mean?

RONNIE: I mean, if you wanna call Chinatown *your* community, OK, knock yourself out, learn to use chopsticks. Go ahead, try and find your roots in some dim sum parlor with headless ducks hanging in the window. Those places don't tell you a thing about who *I* am.

BENJAMIN: Oh, I get it.

RONNIE: You get what?

BENJAMIN: You're one of those self-hating, *assimilated* Chinese Americans, aren't you?

RONNIE: Oh, Jesus.

BENJAMIN: You probably call yourself "Oriental," right? Look, maybe I can help you. I have some books I can —

RONNIE: Hey, I read all those Asian identity books when you were still slathering on industrial-strength sunblock. (*Pause.*) Sure, I'm Chinese. But folks like you act like that means something. Like all of a sudden, you know who I am. You think identity's that simple? That you can wrap it all up in a neat package and say, "I have ethnicity, therefore I am?" All you fucking ethnic fundamentalists. Always looking for easy answers. You say you're looking for identity, but you can't begin to face the real mysteries of the search. So instead you go skin-deep, and call it a day.

(*Pause. Ronnie turns away from Benjamin, starts to play his violin — slow and bluesy.*)

BENJAMIN: So what are you? "Just a human being?" That's like saying you *have* no identity. If you asked me to describe my dog, I'd say more than "He's just a dog."

RONNIE: What—you think if I deny the importance of my race, I'm nobody? There're worlds out there, worlds you haven't even begun to understand. Open your eyes. Hear with your ears.

(He holds his violin at chest level, does not attempt to play during the following monologue. As he speaks, a montage of rock and jazz tracks fades in and out over the house speakers, bringing to life the styles of music he describes.)

I concede—it was called a fiddle long ago—but that was even before the birth of jazz. When the hollering in the fields, the rank injustice of human bondage, the struggle of God's children against the plagues of the devil's white man, when all these boiled up into that bittersweet brew, called by later generations, the blues. That's when fiddlers like Son Sims held their chin rests at their chests and sawed away like the hillbillies still do today. And with the coming of ragtime appeared the pioneer Stuff Smith, who sang as he stroked the catgut, with his raspy Louis Armstrong voice—gruff and sweet like the timbre of horsehair riding south below the fingerboard, and who finally sailed for Europe to find ears that would hear. Europe—where Stephane Grapelli initialed a magical French violin, to be passed from generation to generation—first he, to Jean-Luc Ponty, then Ponty to Didier Lockwood. Listening to Grapelli play "A Nightingale Sang in Berkeley Square" is to understand not only the song of birds, but also how they learn to fly, fall in love on the wing, and finally falter one day, to wait for darkness beneath a London street lamp. And Ponty, he showed us how the modern violin man can accompany the shadow of his own lead lines, which cascade, one over another, into some netherworld beyond the range of human hearing. Joe Venuti, Noel Pointer, Svend Asmussen. Even the Kronos Quartet with their arrangement of "Purple Haze." Now, tell me, could any legacy be more rich, more crowded with mythology and heroes to inspire pride? What can I say if the banging of a gong or the clinking of a pickax on the Transcontinental Railroad fails to move me even as much as one note, played through the violin MIDI controller of Michal Urbaniak?

(Ronnie puts his violin to his chin, begins to play a jazz composition of his own invention.)

Does it have to sound like Chinese opera before people like you decide that I know who I am?

(Benjamin stands for a long moment, listening to Ronnie play. Then, he drops his dollar into the case, turns, and exits. Ronnie continues to play a long moment. Then Benjamin enters, illuminated in his own special. He sits on the floor of the stage, his feet dangling off the lip. As he speaks, Ronnie continues playing his tune, which becomes underscoring for Benjamin's monologue. As the music continues, does it slowly begin to reflect the influence of Chinese music?)

BENJAMIN: When I finally found Doyers St., I scanned the buildings for Number 13. Walking down an alley where the scent of freshly steamed char siu bao[1] lingered in the air, I felt immediately that I had entered a world where all things were finally familiar. (*Pause.*) An old woman bumped me with her shopping bag—screaming to her friend in Cantonese, though they walked no more than a few inches apart. Another man—shouting to a vendor in Sze-Yup. A youth, in a white undershirt, perhaps a recent newcomer, bargaining with a grocer in Hokkien. I walked through this ocean of dialects, breathing in the richness with deep gulps, exhilarated by the energy this symphony brought to my step. And when I finally saw the number 13, I nearly wept at my good fortune. An old tenement, paint peeling, inside walls no doubt thick with a century of grease and broken dreams—and yet, to me, a temple—the house where my father was born. I suddenly saw it all: Gung Gung, coming home from his 16-hour days pressing shirts he could never afford to own, bringing with him candies for my father, each sweet wrapped in the hope of a better life. When my father left the ghetto, he swore he would never return. But he had, this day, in the thoughts and memories of his son, just six months after his death. And as I sat on the stoop, I pulled a hua-moi from my pocket, sucked on it, and felt his spirit returning, To the place where his ghost, and the dutiful hearts of all his descendants, would always call home. (*He listens for a long moment.*) And I felt an ache in my heart for all those lost souls, denied this most important of revelations: to know who they truly are.

(*Benjamin sits on the stage, sucking his salted plum and listening to the sounds around him. Ronnie continues to play. The two remain oblivious of one another. Lights fade slowly to black.*) ◄

END OF PLAY

---

1. **Char siu bao:** Steamed buns filled with barbecued pork.

Tina Howe

The Divine Fallacy

Tina Howe's best-known full-length works include *The Art of Dining*, *Painting Churches*, and *Approaching Zanzibar*. She is the winner of an Obie Award for Distinguished Playwriting, an Outer Critics Circle Award, an American Academy of Arts and Letters Award in Literature, and a Guggenheim fellowship. In 1987, her play *Coastal Disturbances* received a Tony nomination for Best Play. *Pride's Crossing* was selected as a finalist for the 1997 Pulitzer Prize and was awarded the 1998 New York Drama Critics Circle Award for Best Play. In 2005, Howe received the William Inge Award for Distinguished Achievement in the American Theater.

    The Divine Fallacy premiered at the Humana Festival in 1999. The play focuses on the brief interaction between two characters, fashion photographer Victor Hugo (the great-great-grandson of the famous French novelist) and Dorothy Kiss, a writer and the sister of a famous model. Victor is supposed to take Dorothy's picture, but despite the fact that she has come to his studio, she goes to great lengths to avoid being photographed. By the end of the play, however, we learn that even though Dorothy is not nearly as physically attractive as her sister, there is something about her that is beautiful, possibly even "divine."

Characters

VICTOR HUGO: A photographer, late thirties.
DOROTHY KISS: A writer, mid-twenties.

Setting

Victor's studio in downtown Manhattan. It's a freezing day in late February.

    Victor's studio in downtown Manhattan. It looks like a surreal garden blooming with white umbrellas and reflective silver screens. As the lights rise we hear the joyful bass-soprano duet, "Mit unser Macht ist nichts getan," from Bach's chorale, Ein feste Burg ist unser Gott, BWV 80. *It's a freezing day in late February. Victor, dressed in black, has been waiting for Dorothy for over an hour. There's a tentative knock at his door.*

VICTOR: Finally! (*Rushing to answer it.*) Dorothy Kiss?

    (*Dorothy steps in, glasses fogged over and very out of breath. She's a mousy woman dressed in layers of mismatched clothes. An enormous coat covers a bulky sweater which covers a gauzy white dress. A tangle of woolen scarves is wrapped around her neck.*)

DOROTHY: (*Rooted to the spot.*) Victor Hugo?
VICTOR: At last.
DOROTHY: I'm sorry, I'm sorry, I got lost.
VICTOR: Come in, come in.
DOROTHY: I reversed the numbers of your address.
VICTOR: We don't have much time.
DOROTHY: (*With a shrill laugh.*) I went to 22 West 17th instead of 17 West 22nd!
VICTOR: I have to leave for Paris in an hour.
DOROTHY: The minute I got there, I knew something was wrong.
VICTOR: (*Looking at his watch.*) No, make that forty-five minutes.
DOROTHY: There were all these naked people milling around. (*Pause.*) With pigeons.
VICTOR: The spring collections open tomorrow.
DOROTHY: They were so beautiful.
VICTOR: It's going to be a mad house . . . Come in, please . . .

    (*He strides back into the studio and starts setting up his equipment.*)

DOROTHY: I didn't realize they came in so many colors.

DOROTHY:	VICTOR:
Red, green, yellow, purple . . . I think they'd been dyed.	A tidal wave of photographers and fashion editors is descending from all over the world.

(*Pause.*)

VICTOR: I swore last year would be my last, but a man's got to make a living, right? (*Turning to look for her.*) Hey, where did you go?

(*Dorothy waves at him from the door.*)

VICTOR: Miss Kiss . . . we've got to hurry if you want me to do this.

(*Dorothy makes a strangled sound.*)

VICTOR: (*Guiding her into the room.*) Come in, come in . . . I won't bite.

DOROTHY: (*With a shrill laugh.*) My glasses are fogged over! I can't see a thing!

(*She takes them off and wipes them with the end of one of her scarves.*)

VICTOR: Here, let me help you off with your coat.

(*They go through a lurching dance as he tries to unwrap all her scarves, making her spin like a top.*)

VICTOR:	DOROTHY:
Hold still . . . easy does it . . . atta girl . . .	Whoops, I was just . . . sorry, sorry, sorry, sorry, sorry, sorry, sorry . . .

(*He finally succeeds. They look at each other and smile, breathing heavily.*)

VICTOR: So *you're* Daphne's sister?!

DOROTHY: Dorothy Kiss, the *writer* . . .

(*Victor struggles to see the resemblance.*)

DOROTHY: I know. It's a shocker.

VICTOR: No, no . . .

DOROTHY: She's the top fashion model in the country, and here I am . . . Miss Muskrat!

VICTOR: The more I look at you, the more I see the resemblance.

DOROTHY: You don't have to do that.

VICTOR: No really. There's something about your forehead . . .

DOROTHY: I take after my father. The rodent side of the family . . . Small, non-descript, close to the ground . . . (*She makes disturbing rodent faces and sounds.*)

VICTOR: You're funny.

DOROTHY: I try.

(*Silence.*)

VICTOR: So . . .

DOROTHY: (*Grabbing her coat and lurching towards the door.*) Goodbye, nice meeting you.

VICTOR: (*Barring her way.*) Hey, hey, just a minute . . .

DOROTHY: I can let myself out.

VICTOR: Daphne said you were coming out with a new novel and needed a
photograph for the back cover.

DOROTHY: Another time . . .

VICTOR: It sounded wild.

DOROTHY: Oh God, oh God . . .

VICTOR: Something about a woman whose head keeps falling off.

DOROTHY: This was *her* idea, not mine! I hate having my picture taken!
(*Struggling to get past him.*) I hate it, hate it, hate it, hate it, hate it, hate it,
hate it, hate it . . .

VICTOR: (*Grabbing her arm.*) She told me you might react like this.

DOROTHY: *Hate it, hate it, hate it, hate it!*

VICTOR: Dorothy, Dorothy . . .

(*Dorothy desperately tries to escape. Victor grabs her in his arms as she continues to
fight him, kicking her legs. He finally plunks her down in a chair. They breathe heavily.
A silence.*)

DOROTHY: Why can't you set up your camera in my brain? Bore a hole in my
skull and let 'er rip. (*She makes lurid sound effects.*) There's no plainness here,
but heaving oceans ringed with pearls and ancient cities rising in the mist . . .
Grab your tripod and activate your zoom, wonders are at hand . . . Holy
men calling the faithful to prayer as women shed their clothes at the river's
edge . . . *Click!* Jeweled elephants drink beside them, their trunks shattering
the surface like breaking glass. *Click!* Their reflections shiver and merge,
woman and elephant becoming one . . . Slender arms dissolving into
rippling tusks, loosened hair spreading into shuddering flanks . . . *Click,
click, click!* Now you see them, now you don't . . . A breast, a tail, a jeweled
eye . . . *Click!* Macaws scream overhead (*Sound effect.*), or is it the laughter of
the women as they drift further and further from the shore, their shouts
becoming hoarse and strange . . . (*Sound effect.*) *Click!* (*Tapping her temple.*)
Aim your camera here, Mr. Hugo. *This* is where beauty lies . . . Mysterious,
inchoate, and out of sight!

(*Silence as Victor stares at her.*)

DOROTHY: (*Suddenly depressed.*) I don't know about you, but I could use a drink.

VICTOR: (*As if in a dream.*) Right, right . . .

DOROTHY: VICTOR?! (*Pause.*) I'd like a drink, if you don't mind!

VICTOR: Coming right up. What's your poison?

DOROTHY: Vodka, neat.

VICTOR: You got it! (*He lurches to a cabinet and fetches a bottle of vodka and a glass.*)

DOROTHY: That's alright, I don't need a glass. (*She grabs the bottle and drinks an enormous amount.*) Thanks, I needed that!

VICTOR: Holy shit!

DOROTHY: (*Wiping her mouth.*) Where are my manners? I forgot about you. (*Passing him the bottle.*) Sorry, sorry . . .

VICTOR: (*Pours a small amount in a glass and tips it towards her.*) Cheers!

(*She raises an imaginary glass.*)

DOROTHY: Could I ask you a personal question?

VICTOR: Shoot.

DOROTHY: Are you really related to Victor Hugo?

VICTOR: Strange but true.

DOROTHY: Really, really?

VICTOR: *Really!* He was my great great grandfather! (*Bowing.*) *A votre service.*

DOROTHY: He's my favorite writer! He's all I read . . . Over and over and over again! I can't believe I'm standing in the same room with you!

(*She suddenly grabs one of his cameras and starts taking pictures of him.*)

VICTOR: Hey, what are you doing? That's a two-thousand-dollar camera you're using!

(*He lunges for it. She runs from him, snapping his picture.*)

DOROTHY: A direct descendant of Victor Hugo . . .

VICTOR: (*Chasing her.*) Put that down!

DOROTHY: (*Snapping him at crazy angles.*) No one will believe me!

VICTOR: Give it here! (*Finally catching her.*) I SAID: GIVE ME THAT CAMERA!

(*They struggle. A torrent of blood gushes from her hand.*)

DOROTHY: Ow! Ow!

VICTOR: (*Frozen to the spot.*) Miss Kiss . . . Miss Kiss . . . Oh my God, my God . . .

(*Dorothy gulps for air.*)

VICTOR: What did I do?

(*Her breathing slowly returns to normal.*)

VICTOR: Are you alright?

DOROTHY: (*Weakly.*) A tourniquet . . . I need a tourniquet.

VICTOR: On the double! (*He races around looking for one.*)

DOROTHY: Wait, my sock . . . (*She kicks off one of her boots and removes a white sock.*)

VICTOR: (*Running to her side.*) Here, let me help.

DOROTHY: No, I can do it. (*She expertly ties it to stop the flow of blood.*)

VICTOR: How are you feeling?

DOROTHY: Better thanks.

VICTOR: I'm so sorry.

DOROTHY: It's not your fault.

VICTOR: I didn't mean to hurt you.

DOROTHY: I have a stigmata.

VICTOR: *What?*

DOROTHY: I said I have a stigmata. It bleeds when I get wrought up.

VICTOR: *You have a stigmata?*

DOROTHY: Several, actually.

VICTOR: Jesus Christ!

DOROTHY: Jesus Christ, indeed.

VICTOR: A *stigmata?* In *my* studio?

>   (*Silence.*)

DOROTHY: I'm afraid you're going to miss your plane to Paris. I'm sorry.
>   (*A silence. She hands him his camera.*) Well, I guess you may as well take my picture.

VICTOR: Right, right . . . your picture.

>   (*She removes her glasses and bulky sweater and looks eerily beautiful in her white gauzy dress.*)

DOROTHY: I'm as ready as I'm ever going to be.

>   (*Victor is stunned, unable to move.*)

DOROTHY: Yoo hoo . . . Mr. Hugo?

VICTOR: You're so beautiful!

DOROTHY: (*Lowering her eyes.*) Please!

VICTOR: You look so sad . . . Like an early Christian martyr.

>   (*A great light starts to emanate from her. Victor races to get his camera and begins taking her picture.*)

VICTOR: (*Breaking down.*) I can't . . . I can't . . . I just . . . can't.

DOROTHY: Victor, Victor, it's alright . . . We all have something . . . You have your eye, Daphne has her beauty and I have this. It's OK. It makes me who I am.

>   (*Victor struggles to control himself.*)

DOROTHY: Listen to me . . . Listen . . . When the Navahos weave a blanket, they leave in a hole to let the soul out — the flaw, the fallacy — call it what you will. It's part of the design, the most important part — faith, surrender, a mysterious tendency to bleed . . .

VICTOR: I'm so ashamed.

DOROTHY: You did your job. You took my picture.

VICTOR: But I didn't see you.

DOROTHY: Shh, shh.

VICTOR: I was blind.

DOROTHY: Shhhhhh . . .

VICTOR: (*Breaking down again.*) Blind, blind, blind . . .

(*Dorothy rises and places her hands over his eyes, and then raises them in a gesture of benediction.*)

DOROTHY: There, there, it's alright. It's over.

(*The lights blaze around them and then fade as the closing measures of Bach's duet swell.*) ◄

END OF PLAY

Structuring the ten-minute play ▶

When it comes to structuring plays, both playwrights and literary scholars have a habit of turning to Aristotle. His *Poetics* has been the starting point for thinking about drama for more than 2,000 years, and it discusses issues that are still relevant to us today, including character, language, and theme. Above all, as Jacques Barzun notes, for Aristotle, "The action, the plot, is all-important, not the persons in the conflict. To be effective, this action must be single and straightforward—no subplots." According to Aristotle, what is most important is not so much the story being told as "the arrangement of the incidents" in the most effective order so that "what follows should be the necessary or probable result of the preceding action."

Today character development is considered at least as important as plot (if not more important), but plot—or structure—is even more crucial in a play than in the other genres we have discussed. Contemporary full-length plays can successfully juggle several different subplots, but in the ten-minute play, Aristotle's "single and straightforward" action makes good sense. A ten-minute play is not simply a scene from a larger work. It is, as Aristotle said a full-length play should be, a self-contained whole, with a beginning, a middle, and an end. In order for your plot to function effectively in such a short time span, you need to focus on one main action and to make sure that what happens during the play is a result of something significant that happens onstage, or which the characters tell us happened prior to the play.

But what "incidents" should you write about? What should be the plot of your play? "Violence is what happens in plays," says Suzan-Lori Parks. That may be an exaggeration, but Parks implies a truth about theater: the conflict symbolized by violence is essential to good plays. Right away we need to know that one character wants something very badly, and that another character (or characters) is intent on blocking the first character from achieving his or her goal. The object of the person's desire may be another person, an idea, an admission, an apology, or, in a comedy, a cup of coffee and a cheese Danish. What's important is that the protagonist keeps butting heads with one or more antagonists.

Interestingly, the fewer the characters in a play, the more likely it is that each character will serve as both protagonist *and* antagonist. In two of our three model plays, the characters have a dual protagonist/antagonist role. At times, Bill's quest to date Betty and her refusal to go out with him make Bill seem the protagonist of *Sure Thing*. At other times, Betty's desire to avoid a bad relationship focuses our interest on her. Similarly, in *Trying to Find Chinatown*, Ronnie and Benjamin trade protagonist and antagonist roles. From Ronnie's perspective, Benjamin's midwestern naiveté is just the sort of attitude that will keep Ronnie from ever truly expressing himself. But from Benjamin's point of view, foul-mouthed, close-minded Ronnie is the chief obstacle between himself and "finding Chinatown." Only in *The Divine Fallacy* does the richer, more complex character of Dorothy clearly assume the role of protagonist to Victor's less fully developed antagonist.

However you identify the protagonist or antagonist, a good, strong conflict results in a **dramatic question**, a problem at the core of the play that must be answered by the play's end. In *Sure Thing*, the dramatic question is whether Bill and Betty will get together. After numerous false starts, the answer—despite all odds—is yes. Hwang's title announces his dramatic question: Will Benjamin find Chinatown? With some inadvertent help from Ronnie, the answer turns out to be yes. *The Divine Fallacy* asks, Will Dorothy allow her picture to be taken and thereby reveal her inner beauty? The answer, as she blazes with light at the play's end, is another affirmative. Of course, the answer to whether your characters will achieve their goals is as often no as it is yes; it will be determined by the intensity of the characters' desire and the strength of the obstacles they must overcome.

In his excellent book *Writing and Producing the 10-Minute Play*, Gary Garrison advises playwrights to be very aware of what they do on each page of their script. After reading hundreds of examples of the form, Garrison found that ten-minute plays work best when they follow a fairly consistent structure. (Remember that playscripts have a special format; see "Playscript Format: A Model" for an example. The following page numbers refer to a typed playscript and don't necessarily correspond to how the pages appear in the plays reprinted in this book.)

Pages 1–2: Set up the world we're in, introduce your central character(s), and make sure we understand what they need/want/desire in the journey of the story.

Pages 2–3: Illuminate the central conflict—a dramatic question that will be answered by the play's end.

Pages 3–8: Complicate the story two or three times.

Pages 9–10: Resolve the conflict, even if that creates an unhappy ending.

You may bristle at the idea of having to follow a "formula," but the structure that Garrison outlines works very well, especially for beginning playwrights. Moreover, within this design, there is a great deal of freedom. Our three model playwrights, for instance, all work inventive variations on this basic configuration.

Sure Thing has an unusual stop-start-replay structure. It compresses some aspects of the traditional form and extends others; nevertheless, it basically follows Garrison's outline. The first section establishes both the world we are in—two strangers meet in a café in the evening—and the central conflict of the play: Bill wants to get together with Betty, but she doesn't seem to be interested. Complications and reversals continue for the next several pages of the script, with Bill and Betty gradually getting more and more compatible, only to be repeatedly foiled in their incipient love affair when one of them says the wrong thing. Toward the end of the play, right after the cue *"Many bells ring,"* the resolution finally occurs, with Bill and Betty turning out to be ridiculously perfect for each other, right down to their mutual love of Entenmann's crumb cake and their desire to send their children to Harvard, Vassar, and Brown.

The opening pages of Hwang's play introduce us to the two characters and tell us that Benjamin is seeking directions to an address in Chinatown, which Ronnie seems reluctant to provide. The first reversal comes when Benjamin turns out to know a great deal about "Euro-America's emasculating and brutal stereotypes of Asians." Next, we learn that even though he is white, Benjamin considers himself to be Chinese American. Finally, Ronnie's **monologue**—his long solo speech—shows him to be truly and unexpectedly knowledgeable about the history of the jazz violin. Resolution comes in the form of Benjamin's description of his poignant but successful visit to his father's old home at 13 Doyers Street.

The Divine Fallacy begins with Dorothy arriving, discombobulated, at Victor's studio. We quickly learn that she is a writer and that he is a photographer who has agreed to take her picture. Almost as quickly, the central conflict becomes apparent: Dorothy doesn't really want her picture taken because, unlike her beautiful sister, she takes after "the rodent side of the family." Complications ensue as Victor keeps attempting to take her photograph while Dorothy repeatedly resists his attempts. At one point she tries to run away with the camera, he chases her, and suddenly blood spurts from her palms, a disquieting turn of events. Finally, when she sits down for the shooting, *"a great light starts to emanate from her."* The conflict is resolved as Dorothy relaxes and Victor comes to appreciate her glowing "inner" beauty.

The first couple of minutes of each model play provide us with succinct **exposition**—an explanation of the backstory that has led up to the present situation—and then the plays quickly plunge us into the central conflict. In these three plays, it's easy for the characters to convey meaningful facts about themselves when they are meeting for the first time. (We'll talk more about how dialogue can effectively serve as exposition in the section "Writing Convincing Dialogue.") Moreover, the setting itself presents significant clues about the world we are entering. Within moments from the time the lights come up in *Sure Thing*, we know that Betty is sitting alone at a table in a café or restaurant and that she does not know Bill. In *The Divine Fallacy*, the "surreal garden" of photography equipment tells us where we are before Victor even speaks a word. And in *Trying to Find Chinatown*, Ronnie's open violin case, containing "change and a few stray bills," immediately announces that he is a street musician.

The energy of your play increases when you move from those opening gestures—which are not unlike the "establishing shots" in a film that tell us where we are and who is involved—to the central conflict. Jeffrey Hatcher points out that "*most* flawed plays fail because nothing happens in the middle. The characters run out of goals too quickly. They run out of obstacles. They run out of ideas and strategies. Opportunities don't arise." Hatcher is referring to full-length plays—one and a half to three hours' worth of material—and you might not think that introducing enough obstacles, goals, and ideas would be a problem in the ten-minute play. However, new playwrights do sometimes find their plays ending after five or six minutes rather than ten. You can avoid weak middles in your play by employing the following strategies:

▶ **Allow the Onstage Interactions between Characters to Develop at a Believable Pace** People who are meeting for the first time take a while to get to know each other. People who have known each other for a long time are likely to have a complicated history that will take a while to emerge through their dialogue. Don't rush your characters' interactions simply to get to the next plot point.

▶ **On the Other Hand, Don't Waste Time** While rushing through character interactions makes us feel as though we're watching a speeded-up film of the life and death of a flower, it's equally disconcerting to have characters discussing the weather or what they ate for dinner last night. Every exchange between your characters should tell us something vital about who they are, while also moving the action forward.

▶ **Make Sure That There Are at Least Two or Three Significant Complications or Reversals That Keep the Protagonist from Getting What He or She Wants** This is the single most important tactic you will need to learn. Imagine a football player trying to get from one end of the field to the other. There is no straight line down the middle; instead, his opponents come at him from all sides. He dashes this way, then that, backtracks for a moment, then makes one last burst for the end zone. Your play should cut and juke and surprise us even as it moves inevitably from its beginning to its end.

Scene construction is an integral element of the ten-minute play. If you have ever written a screenplay, you know it's not unusual to spend less than a minute on a single scene. The theater doesn't work that way. Actors operate in real time, with the ten minutes onstage generally corresponding to ten minutes in real time; ideally, you should be able to fit your conflict and its resolution into a single scene. It looks silly if characters are constantly coming and going, and if the scene keeps changing every few minutes. Even two or three scenes in a ten-minute play can feel rushed, and multiple scenes often indicate that the playwright hasn't yet found the ideal ten minutes in which to set the play. *Trying to Find Chinatown* is the only model play with more than one scene, and even then there is no real break between Ronnie's last monologue and Benjamin's final speech. Ronnie keeps playing his violin and the lights never fully go down during Benjamin's brief exit and reentrance.

Janet Neipris advises that when we are thinking about the endings of our plays, "we should look to fairytales as models. In the fairytale there is generally a problem that has to be solved. . . . When that problem, or the evil, is confronted, the story can come to its own conclusion, which means a change of circumstances and therefore, closure." Neipris is not suggesting that plays take the form of fairy tales, but rather that the central conflict in a fairy tale—something is wrong and needs to be made right—is similar to the problem that protagonists in plays face. In a contemporary play, the main character is just as likely to fail as he or she is to succeed, but once we know whether that failure or success has occurred, the play itself (like a fairy tale) is over.

Jeffrey Hatcher suggests that playwrights, when deciding on either an optimistic or a pessimistic ending, look closely at their material and ask, "Was there hope for a happy ending?" Nothing is cornier than two heated antagonists suddenly falling in love, or a pot of gold literally or figuratively dropping from the sky to solve everyone's problems. Remember, too, that whether the ending is happy or sad, the middle of the play should suggest that the final outcome is always in doubt.

Ultimately, every page of your script must count. There should be no bad pages, no dead moments. "A playwright must be his own audience," says Terrence Rattigan. "A novelist may lose his readers for a few pages; a playwright never dares lose his for a minute." If nothing else, think about the poor actors up there onstage. You wouldn't want to come across as silly or boring or lost if you were in their place, so give them a play to perform that hooks the audience immediately, seems to whiz by before we know it, surprises us with its twists and turns, and finishes with an ending that somehow we both expected and yet never actually saw coming.

CHECKLIST Structuring the ten-minute play

- ☐ **Does your play have a clear and immediate conflict?** Plays without a conflict quickly sink under the weight of their own tedium. Make sure you have at least one unmistakable confrontation between protagonist and antagonist. And get to that conflict fast: every minute is precious in a ten-minute play.

☐ **Does the middle of your play contain several complications and reversals that upset our expectations?** If your protagonist glides through his or her ten minutes without any impediments, your audience will fall asleep. Create an obstacle course. Consider letting both your protagonist *and* antagonist be blindsided at least once during the play by a disquieting revelation or turn of events.

☐ **Is your ending both surprising and satisfying?** Nothing is worse than an ending the audience can see coming after the first couple of minutes. On the other hand, a last-minute twist that has no relation to the previous nine minutes of action is almost as bad. Finding just the right ending isn't easy, but holding out for something special is often the difference between a passable play and one that is truly outstanding.

Creating believable characters ▶

Having a sound structure is essential for a successful play. It's equally crucial for you to create believable characters. Fortunately, developing strong characters is intimately connected with the process of structuring your play. Once you have a clear sense of your structure, you will already know the basic outline of your characters, and vice versa.

If you're still searching for characters and conflicts, here are a few well-tested plot structures and accompanying dramatic questions:

▶ A needs something from B, but B doesn't want to part with it. Will A succeed?

▶ A wants B to do something that will hurt B. Will A convince B to do it anyway?

▶ A wants to be with B, but B doesn't want to be with A. Will A and B get together?

▶ A is with B but wants to be with C. Is A successful in getting B out of the picture?

▶ A and B are very happy together, but their happiness makes C insanely jealous. Will C destroy A and B's relationship?

▶ D is in a position of power over A, B, and C, each of whom wants to replace D. Who will prevail?

There are many variations on these themes. The important thing to remember when deciding on your own combination of character and structure is Aristotle's compelling formula, which has been useful to countless playwrights over the centuries: "Character is action." In his classic book *The Art of the Playwright*, William Packard continually returns to this credo, emphasizing that "every character has to have an action, an objective, something that he wants very much. . . . Action is what makes every character dramatic, because it is each character's entire reason for being there on stage." Packard goes on to argue that even Hamlet, one of the most complex characters in the history of world drama, "*is* his desire to avenge his murdered father. . . . Hamlet is his action, no more, and no less."

Many literary critics would say that Packard is overstating his point, but the argument is worth considering. Every character in your play *must* have a goal that from the outset is clear to him or her. Otherwise you will find yourself with characters who chat or squabble or meander or tell jokes or cry, but who never really make us care about what happens to them. If there's nothing at stake for the characters, there will be *less* than nothing at stake for the audience.

"Characters in a drama should be in opposition to the situation," says Janet Neipris. "Don't make it easy for anyone. That's boring. And choose the unexpected: the little man, not the general, leading the troops into battle; the conservative opting for the largest risk; the doctor who is not so humanitarian." Unusual characters make it easier to introduce surprising conflicts, as we see in all three of our model plays.

Neither character in *Trying to Find Chinatown* fits the stereotype of the person he *ought* to be, and their unconventional identities fuel the conflict at the center of the play. Ronnie is a Chinese American man who loves jazz and blues violin music. He wants respect for his music, and he becomes furious when Benjamin, who initially seems to represent midwestern America in all its blandness, refers to Ronnie's violin as a "fiddle." Benjamin, in turn, is frustrated in his quest to find his Chinese American roots because Ronnie cannot see beyond the color of Benjamin's skin.

In *The Divine Fallacy*, camera-shy Dorothy Kiss is "in opposition to the situation" from the moment she appears onstage. Not only is she introverted, awkward, and self-deprecating, but she also appears to be an alcoholic who bleeds spontaneously from the palms of her hands. Even for a writer, that is a pretty unexpected combination. And although Victor seems like a typical fashion photographer, his thwarted attempts to take Dorothy's picture lead to his surprising self-assessment at the end of the play that he has been "blind, blind, blind."

While comedy often flirts with stereotypes, the flawless person with perfect teeth is just as boring—and just as unbelievable—in drama as he or she is in fiction. The characters of Bill and Betty are constantly in flux; that's part of the fun of *Sure Thing*. Yet in their whirlwind of metamorphoses, Bill and Betty reveal a number of odd and unexpected details about themselves. One moment Bill is a Mets fan; the next he is a Harvard grad who loves the novels of William Faulkner. One moment Betty prefers the "existentially romantic" pastime of reading alone in a café on a rainy night; a few minutes later she is inviting Bill to a Woody Allen film festival. Again, specificity, as in every other genre of creative writing, creates interest.

Once you have identified your characters, you will want to learn more about them, although that can become an extended process. Henrik Ibsen wrote, "When I am writing I must be alone; if I have eight characters . . . I have society enough; they keep me busy; I must learn to know them." Ibsen's experience is a common one: as they begin to take shape, characters often seem real to their creators. August Wilson felt that creating believable characters was the easiest aspect of playwriting because "the characters want to explain, as most people do, their entire history and philosophy, their take on the world and the vagaries of life." Janet Neipris wants to imagine how her characters walk and talk, where they grew up, and how they felt about their neighborhood: "I always look for roots, because people carry the past on their backs."

One way to learn about the pasts of fictional characters is to ask questions of them and "listen" to their answers. William Packard uses interrogatory words—who, what, where, why, and when—to generate a list of six questions that playwrights should be able to answer about their characters:

1. Who am I?

2. What do I want?

3. Where am I right now?

4. Why am I here?

5. When is all this taking place?

6. What is my physical life? What kind of clothes am I wearing? What is in my pocket or purse? and so on.

Take a few minutes to see whether you can answer those questions about your characters. If you know the characters well, you will probably be writing for some time. If however, you can't generate much material, you will need to go back and rethink your cast. Do you have the right people for the play? Are you writing the play that is best suited to who you are just at this moment?

Once you have decided on your cast, you will want to continue to explore your characters. You can probably imagine many more questions they might ask of themselves:

▶ Why is my objective so important to me?

▶ Do I have contrasting goals that might get in the way?

▶ What are the chances I will achieve my main goal?

▶ How do I plan to get there?

▶ Who are my allies and my enemies?

▶ What am I willing to do to get what I want?

Naturally, every character you write, even if she or he is based on someone you know well, will also contain elements of yourself. Yet Wendy Wasserstein said that although "you're always writing different aspects of yourself into your characters," you are never simply "writing yourself." For Wasserstein, putting her own words into the mouths of characters who were very unlike herself seemed "less inhibiting." Many playwrights share this feeling: it is liberating, if not downright exhilarating, to have a fictional character say the things you are thinking but dare not utter aloud.

In keeping with the "wright" or "maker" metaphor we discussed earlier, Lajos Egri says, "A shipbuilder knows the material he is working with, knows how well it can withstand the ravages of time, how much weight it can carry." Similarly, Egri argues, "A dramatist should know the material he is working with: his characters. He should know how much weight they can carry, how well they can support his construction: the play."

How do we know "how much weight" our characters can carry? How do we know who they are, or even if they are the best ones for our play? Edward Albee has a test to see whether the characters he has been thinking about are "ready" to become part of a play: "I'll improvise and try them out in a situation that I'm fairly sure *won't* be in the play. And if they behave quite naturally, in this improvisatory situation, and create their own dialogue, and behave according to what I consider their natures, then I suppose I have the play far enough along to sit down and write it."

You can see from Albee's remark that part of the experience of creating believable characters is thinking of them not only "outside" your play but also before and after they come onstage for their ten minutes of glory. Knowing the arc of their transformation is crucial because *the conflict of the play must result in the characters becoming different than they were when the play began.* Once again, we can turn to Aristotle as our guide: "The sequence of events, according to the law of probability or necessity, will admit of a change from bad fortune to good, or from good fortune to bad."

We have been discussing some of the deeper issues of character development, but as you create characters, you will also confront more prosaic matters. For instance, how many characters should you include in your play?

One-person plays usually aren't plays in the sense that we have been discussing, but are something closer to monologues. They can be quite entertaining, and celebrities with salacious tales to relate often make a big hit with one-person shows. A real play, however, must somehow bring the conflict with other, absent characters offstage. With no one to interact with onstage, the lone actor too often ends up "monologuing" in the negative sense of that word: droning on and on about herself or himself without much structure or spark. Unless your instructor says otherwise, you should probably avoid one-person plays for this assignment.

Each of our model plays has only two characters, and many playwrights would say that is ideal for a ten-minute play. Two characters concentrate the conflict and allow for maximum development of each character. No one is superfluous, and you, the playwright, are forced to fully imagine each person onstage. Begin with the assumption that your play will have two characters, and add others only if your conflict requires them.

Sometimes you will feel that the fireworks could be increased considerably if another person were onstage, and inserting a third character can allow a fascinating triangle to emerge. If all three characters have clear goals, the conflicts and complications quickly multiply. But be wary of making the third character someone of minimal importance. A waiter or a cashier or a passerby may initially seem vital to your play, but look for ways to make the play happen without that person actually appearing. Too often these characters spend a lot of time either standing around with nothing to do or entering and exiting with such frequency that they become distractions from the central conflict.

Adding a fourth character increases the number of ways that people can team up against and align with one another. Couples can form, and then re-form with different partners. Characters can switch allegiances. But remember your time constraint. And be wary of thin, two-dimensional characters. Providing the beginnings, middles, and endings of four people's stories requires deft work on your part. You need to clarify, and in some fashion resolve, the combination of conflicts you have created—and you have to do this in far less time than it takes most of us to get to work or class.

Inevitably, the more characters you have in your cast, the less each one will be developed, and the greater the chance a character will be a stereotype. Some successful ten-minute plays have five or more characters, but as with your short story, you should always look for ways to fold two similar characters into one. Let's say Ronda is battling with her three best friends: Noelle, Anya, and Asha. Noelle feels some sympathy for Ronda, but Anya and Asha are both out to get the protagonist. In fact, Anya and Asha have pretty much the same opinion on everything. Merging them into a single character, Aisha, not only focuses their combined energy but also addresses the practical issue of keeping the number of actors at a reasonable level. We'll talk more about this later, but one of the things that differentiates plays from other forms of creative writing is the need for actual people to be onstage. Although you can employ **doubling**—having one actor play more than one character when those characters aren't onstage at the same time—in general, the more characters you have, the more actors you will need. As you enlarge your cast, you have to coordinate more actors with rehearsal time, and you increase the chance that someone will drop out or something will go wrong. Bad things tend to happen when you overcast a short play.

And what about nonadult or nonhuman characters? For your first ten-minute play, it's probably a good idea to write about characters who are at least teenagers. Why? An old adage from the theater world says, "Never work with children or dogs." Actors feel that children and animals always steal the show, although you should avoid them for different reasons. Children have bedtimes and temper tantrums and stage fright. On opening night, little Johnny's mother may decide he shouldn't be in a play after all. And it's difficult to get a dog, much less a cat, to do something on cue in a play. Of course, you might try casting an adult actor to play a child, but this nearly always comes across as broadly comic. Similarly, a person acting like an animal is going to get laughs whether he or she wants them or not.

CHECKLIST Creating believable characters

☐ **Does each of your characters have a clear goal that he or she wants badly to attain?** "Character is action": characters *are* what they want. Make sure that every person onstage is always actively pursuing a goal and that every character's goal differs markedly from the goals of the other characters.

☐ **Are your characters distinctive and unusual?** Bland characters make for a bland play. Find ways to make each character unique. Give them unexpected backgrounds (a white person adopted by Chinese American parents) and unusual gifts (a writer who glows when she is photographed). Make your characters worthy of our attention.

☐ **Are your characters believable as human beings?** Characters in a play are often larger than life, but nevertheless they should be recognizable as human beings. Ask questions about their motivations and fears, their backgrounds and idiosyncrasies. Get to know them so that you can make them come alive for your audience. As in all other genres of creative writing, the more specific, detailed, and concrete you are in your character development, the more convincing your characters will be.

☐ **Do you have too many, or too few, characters?** Normally, new playwrights have too many characters in their plays. If you read over the first draft of your script and find that one or more characters are not doing much, consider eliminating them or merging the most crucial aspects of these characters into a single character. On the other hand, if your play feels bogged down, if you don't feel the spark of conflict, it may be that you need to add a character to act as an antagonist.

Writing convincing dialogue ▶

You may associate dialogue in plays with the high-flown Elizabethan English of Shakespeare — "We pray you throw to earth / This unprevailing woe," and so on — but for a long time now, playwrights have tended to tone things down, so the words coming from the actors' mouths sound much closer to actual speech.

Anton Chekhov, who was a champion of naturalistic dialogue, said that playwrights should "avoid choice diction. The language should be simple and forceful. The lackeys should speak simply, without elegance." We would no longer use the word "lackeys" — a demeaning word for "servants" — but twentieth- and twenty-first-century playwrights, such as Sam Shepherd, Neil LaBute, David Mamet, August Wilson, Tracy Letts, and Suzan-Lori Parks, have been committed to dialogue that is "simple and forceful" and appropriate to the characters' station in life.

As we noted at the beginning of the chapter, students tend to have a natural ear for writing dialogue, even if they aren't yet aware of that talent. Once you have established your conflict and characters, probably the best thing to do is to just start writing. Let your characters say what they have to say. If they're not talking, then you probably don't know them well enough, or you haven't placed them in a situation that is sufficiently charged to make them talk. If you are committed to your play, go back and add to your characters' history, or see if you can put your characters in a different setting.

When you do get on a roll, you may feel, like many playwrights before you, as though you are in a trance, merely writing down — as fast as possible — what you hear your characters saying. If you find yourself in that space, write until you are "written out." Don't censor anything. Get it down on the page, and later, after the inspiration has cooled down, look at what you have written with a cold eye and decide what stays and what goes.

When you do go back to revise your dialogue, evaluate it using generally accepted criteria. Different playwrights have different strengths, but most would agree that good dialogue

- ▶ is believable;
- ▶ adds to character development;
- ▶ introduces backstory in a credible way; and
- ▶ heightens conflict and moves the action forward.

Good dialogue is believable. This doesn't mean that dialogue exactly mimics what you would hear in the real world, but it does mean that you should try to capture the *rhythms* of real speech, the stops and starts, the hesitations, the sudden monologues and quick exchanges.

If you sit in a public place and eavesdrop on conversations, you will quickly realize that most people, even highly educated people, don't talk very formally. Instead, people in conversation

- normally use contractions ("isn't" and "won't" rather than "is not" and "will not");
- frequently use sentence fragments rather than grammatically complete sentences;
- pause often;
- interrupt one another;
- lose their train of thought;
- contradict themselves; and
- usually aren't very original.

Playwrights try to capture the essence of speech, but if it was as simple as transcribing conversations verbatim, everyone could become a playwright. That's not the way it happens, unfortunately. As you practice the playwright's habit of listening in on conversations, you will notice that the average exchange not only is informal but also is too chaotic, too repetitive, and too *boring* to make for very interesting theatrical dialogue. Here it might be useful to recall Amy Bloom's definition of good dialogue in fiction: "conversation's greatest hits." The best dialogue *sounds* realistic, until we go back and see how perfectly crafted it is. "The essence of good dialogue" in a play, according to Michael Wright, "is allowing the fewest words to say or imply the most, or—as with silence or pauses—to allow the audience to infer the most." As you write your ten-minute play, one of your primary goals will be to find the fewest words that will say the most.

In *Sure Thing*, David Ives shows himself to be a master of the halting, truncated patterns of contemporary speech. Let's take just one passage, in the middle of the play, as an example:

BETTY: I guess we must be on different schedules.
BILL: Missed connections.
BETTY: Yes. Different time zones.
BILL: Amazing how you can live right next door to somebody in this town and never even know it.
BETTY: I know.
BILL: City life.
BETTY: It's crazy.
BILL: You weren't waiting for somebody when I came in, were you?
BETTY: Actually I was.
BILL: Oh. Boyfriend?
BETTY: Sort of.
BILL: What's a sort-of boyfriend?
BETTY: My husband.
BILL: Ah-ha.

This exchange reproduces the short sentences and sentence fragments of real speech: "City life." "Sort of." "My husband." The characters also use clichés, which are normally taboo in creative writing. Bill tells Betty that people don't meet because of "missed connections," that "you can live right next door to somebody in this town and never even know it," and they both agree that city life is crazy. The conversation is banal, but that's appropriate to the setting. The characters are making the sort of mindless conversation anyone might engage in under the circumstances. What redeems this passage, and all the other passages in the play, is that Ives turns banality on its head and ends each **beat**—that is, each separate movement in the play—with a punch line. "What's a sort-of boyfriend?" Bill asks. "My husband," Betty replies.

Another thing real people do in real conversations is to curse. In high school courses, profanity is usually frowned on. However, although some instructors and institutions may have different policies, in college it is generally acceptable to let your characters swear if the situation requires it. It's not unusual for the characters onstage, who are often in a heightened state of agitation, to let their language reflect the fact that they are upset, afraid, or outraged. In *Trying to Find Chinatown*, we see this agitation in Ronnie when he first meets Benjamin. And in *Sure Thing*, when Betty imagines an unsatisfying sexual rendezvous with Bill, she, too, uses profanity to dismiss her potential partner.

Playwright Terrence McNally, when asked by an interviewer if "we have to have that kind of language" in plays, responded:

> Do we have to? I think it implies that, when you come to see a play, I'm not going to do anything that upsets you, or my characters won't. That traditional notion of theater I . . . reject. I go to the theater to be appalled, to be stimulated, to be upset. I can't imagine four-letter words today being offensive to anyone. The theater to me is not a sanctuary from the language . . . you hear on the subway and in the streets. . . . I don't expect the theater to be comfortable.

Whether or not you find four-letter words offensive, you should remember that today's theater is one of the last strongholds of free speech in America. Even if you choose not to have your characters swear, try not to be upset if your classmates do.

A related issue in theatrical dialogue is the use of **dialect**—nonstandard language associated with a particular group, culture, or region. Most playwrights would say that you don't have to live in and be part of a culture in order to create characters from that culture. Nevertheless, you should be extremely careful about using dialect if you are not a member of the group that speaks that dialect. Say, for instance, that you are a young white man from the suburbs who feels you have mastered the intricacies of African American speech patterns because of all the gangsta rap you have listened to over the years. Or maybe you live in northern Michigan and have never visited the South, but you are writing southern dialect based on your love of *Dukes of Hazzard* reruns. Obviously, even if you're writing with respect and admiration for your characters, you are likely to miss the nuances that a real speaker of dialect would recognize. A greater worry for a playwright would be sounding as though you were mocking or condescending to the characters who speak in dialect. If you do decide to write in dialect, "be moderate," Raymond Hull wisely advises. "Don't try to express the full strength of a broad dialect with all its peculiarity of accent and its wealth of uncommon words." Instead, give us a hint, a suggestion, and let our imaginations do the rest.

The fundamental test of whether your dialogue is believable is to read it aloud. Playwrights tend to say their dialogue to themselves as they write, although you may find, like Lillian Hellman, that until you hear it spoken by others, you won't know if you have it right or wrong: "I usually know in the first few days of rehearsals what I have made the actors stumble over, and what can or cannot be cured." Most likely, your play won't have days of rehearsals; if your class is a big one, you may be lucky to have it read aloud a single time in front of your fellow students. But you can always draft friends and family into the roles of actors and let them do the necessary work for you.

Good dialogue adds to character development. What your characters say tells you who they are. August Wilson believed that the most important thing about writing dialogue is not to censor your characters: "What they are talking about may not seem to have anything to do with what you as a writer are writing about, but it does. Let them talk and it will connect because you as a writer will make it connect."

Characters often talk "against" one another, as though they are unaware that someone else is even there. The fact that no real communication is taking place is part of the point: often people don't listen to one another, or they hear only what they want to hear, not what the other person is actually saying. We see this "talking against" at the beginning of *The Divine Fallacy*, after Dorothy has arrived for a photo shoot that neither she nor Victor really wants to do. She talks about getting lost on the way to his studio; he talks about having to catch a plane very soon. At several points, they even talk *over* each other simultaneously, as though they cannot wait to let the other person speak.

Often dialogue tells us something about a character when he or she says one thing but clearly believes something else. Janet Neipris points out that even if it is not obvious to the audience or the other characters, there is always a conflict between a character's exterior dialogue—"the actual words that come out of their mouths"—and the interior dialogue—"what the character is actually thinking or feeling." This is what Jeffrey Hatcher calls "dialogue as subtext," with speech serving as a kind of camouflage for the speaker's real emotions and desires: "Subtext means, for example, trying to find ways of saying 'I love you' without having the words 'I love you' at your disposal. The 'I love you' is *under* the text — *below* the line."

In *The Divine Fallacy*, we see an example of a character saying one thing and meaning another when Victor tries, not very successfully, to detect the resemblance between Dorothy and her beautiful sister. "I know. It's a shocker," Dorothy says. "No, no . . . ," Victor replies, but apparently he cannot even finish his sentence because Dorothy is so unlike Daphne.

Another method of character development through speech comes when a character delivers a monologue. Monologues in the midst of plays might be compared to flashbacks in movies, with the forward action halting so that we can go back and catch up on important missing information. However, while filmmakers have the advantage of the visual element to do much of their work for them, the playwright must conjure up entire scenes with words alone. Monologues may involve characters speaking at greater length than they would in real life, but that is theatrically justifiable because a long speech often provides us far more information about the character than could be elicited through dialogue alone. Such is the case with Dorothy's extended monologue:

> Why can't you set up your camera in my brain? Bore a hole in my skull and let 'er rip. (*She makes lurid sound effects.*) There's no plainness here, but heaving oceans ringed with pearls and ancient cities rising in the mist . . . Grab your tripod and activate your zoom, wonders are at hand . . . Holy men calling the faithful to prayer as women shed their clothes at the river's edge . . . *Click!* Jeweled elephants drink beside them, their trunks shattering the surface like breaking glass. *Click!* Their reflections shiver and merge, woman and elephant becoming one . . . Slender arms dissolving into rippling tusks, loosened hair spreading into shuddering flanks . . . *Click, click, click!* Now you see them, now you don't . . . A breast, a tail, a jeweled eye . . . *Click!* Macaws scream overhead (*Sound effect.*), or is it the laughter of the women as they drift further and further from the shore, their shouts becoming hoarse and strange . . . (*Sound effect.*) *Click!* (*Tapping her temple.*) Aim your camera here, Mr. Hugo. *This* is where beauty lies . . . Mysterious, inchoate, and out of sight! (*Silence as Victor stares at her.*)

Monologues stand out, especially when most of the dialogue before and after them is brief, so we in the audience are inclined to pay them extra notice. That attention is repaid here because we learn a great deal about Dorothy: that she is extremely sensitive, that she is imaginative, that she is angry, that she is drawn to religion, and that she is skeptical that anyone will be capable of seeing her real beauty.

As is often the case with this form of dramatic speech, the monologue serves several other functions:

▶ **It Sums Up the Main Themes of the Play**   Dorothy's monologue demonstrates that our interior life can be far richer than our exteriors might indicate.

▶ **It Tells a Story**   The story in this monologue is metaphorical, suggesting that beauty can quickly transform and disappear.

▶ **It Contains an Element of Poetry**   Eloquent speech and concrete imagery are frequently found in monologues, and Dorothy uses both of these poetic devices in phrases such as "slender arms dissolving into rippling tusks, loosened hair spreading into shuddering flanks."

Some plays work well with dialogue alone, but if you feel your characters need a minute to stretch out and become more of who they really are, the monologue is worth considering.

Good dialogue introduces backstory in a credible way. William Packard contends that "the best way of approaching the problem of exposition is not to see it so much as 'information' that has to be passed on to an audience, but to see it as a way of introducing the major actions of the play as quickly as possible . . . prior actions, offstage actions, and given circumstances." Offstage actions are likely to be limited in a ten-minute play, but dialogue about prior actions and given circumstances can go a long way toward introducing backstory.

All three model plays take advantage of the fact that the characters are meeting each other for the first time as a way to bring in background information. Naturally enough, the people onstage need to explain who they are and what they want from each other, and we in the audience overhear that information. The premise of *Sure Thing* is especially easy to follow because the setting itself is so clear — a woman reading alone at a table is interrupted by a stranger wanting to join her. In *The Divine Fallacy*, Victor reveals his occupation when he tells Dorothy that he needs to go to Paris to photograph "the spring collections." Dorothy announces to the audience her own occupation after Victor marvels at the difference between her and her beautiful sister; she tells him, and us, that she is "Dorothy Kiss, the *writer*." The play that requires the most complex exposition is *Trying to Find Chinatown*; consequently, the dialogue between Ronnie and Benjamin contains the most detailed explanations of who they are and how they come to find themselves on the same street corner in Lower Manhattan.

Of course, not all plays involve strangers meeting for the first time. There are wonderful short plays about family members, close friends, casual acquaintances, and business associates. If you are writing a play in which the characters already know one another, you will need to provide exposition in a way that doesn't call attention to itself. Here is a particularly clumsy and heavy-handed example of exposition:

> JACQUES: Wow, June, the last time I saw you was just last night at the Hendersons' party.
>
> JUNE: I know. That was so crazy when my mother, who is your stepmother, told us the story of finding that antique diamond ring in an old trunk. How do you think it got there?
>
> JACQUES: I'm not sure, but it could have happened when my father, who also happens to be your uncle, returned home from his recent voyage to Tanzania.
>
> JUNE: Yes, that trip to Tanzania was an important milestone in our family history. Uncle told us that while he was in Tanzania he learned that . . .

You get the idea. Instead of hitting your audience over the head with explanations of the characters' lives before the play begins, try to introduce exposition in more subtle ways.

  ▶ The central conflict causes characters to reminisce about a significant shared memory: "That morning you left us . . ."

  ▶ Characters argue over competing interpretations of an event or situation: "Dad was only trying to . . . ," to which another character responds, "No, it was Mom who . . ."

  ▶ A character who knows more about a significant situation or event explains that knowledge to the other characters: "What you don't realize is . . . ," or, "They didn't know I was watching, but I saw . . ."

Revise any awkward passages of exposition so that instead of coming across as a mini–history lesson, your backstory is an engrossing and important part of your play.

Good dialogue heightens conflict and moves the action forward. "Active and vital dialogue thrusts your play forward as much as active and vital character and plot give the play forward momentum," Louis Catron reminds us. "Passive or inactive dialogue slows the play's pace no less than passive or inactive character and plot." Catron is right to equate dialogue with character and structure. When one of those links is weak, the others suffer; but when all three elements are working well, a synergy develops that is the hallmark of gripping theater.

If you find your characters discussing the weather or similar topics, you need to rewrite their conversation. Redirect the dialogue so that it focuses on who they are and, more important, *what they want.* When one character says something particularly cutting or kind or outrageous to another character, your play will begin to heat up.

This happens in all our model plays; let's take just one example. In *Trying to Find Chinatown,* Benjamin has just shown Ronnie an address written on a slip of paper and has asked him if he knows where the place is. Ronnie responds with fury:

BENJAMIN: I don't get it! What are you —?
RONNIE: Eat me. You know exactly what I —
BENJAMIN: I'm just asking for a little —
RONNIE: 13 Doyers St.? Like you don't know where that is?
BENJAMIN: Of course I don't know! That's why I'm asking —
RONNIE: C'mon, you trailer-park refugee. You don't know that's Chinatown?
BENJAMIN: Sure I know that's Chinatown.
RONNIE: I know you know that's Chinatown.
BENJAMIN: So? That doesn't mean I know where Chinatown —
RONNIE: So why is it that you picked *me*, of all the street musicians in the city — to point you in the direction of Chinatown? Lemme guess — is it the earring? No, I don't think so.

Ronnie then goes on to list several racist assumptions he assumes Benjamin is making, and Benjamin, in turn, comes right back with the speech beginning "Brother, I can absolutely relate to your anger."

When people are arguing about something that matters a great deal to them, we can't help but listen in and focus on what they are saying. The dialogue here is charged with Ronnie's indignation and Benjamin's bewilderment. Indeed, the conflict is so heightened that half the time one character cannot finish his sentence before the other one interrupts him.

This passage also serves to move the plot forward. Hwang needs a way to introduce the fact that Benjamin, despite being white, sees himself as Asian. Ronnie's rage at Benjamin's apparent insensitivity gives Benjamin the opportunity to show that, contrary to Ronnie's — and probably our own — expectations, he is knowledgeable about and sympathetic to the concerns of Chinese Americans.

As you work on your dialogue, be open to the possibility that your characters will rewrite your play for you. Arthur Miller once said, "I plan something for weeks or months and suddenly begin writing dialogue which begins in relation to what I had planned and veers off into something I hadn't even thought about."

Ultimately, your characters will call the shots, and if you don't place their desires at the center of everything they say, you may find that they begin talking in ways you never anticipated or, far worse, that they refuse to come alive at all.

CHECKLIST Writing convincing dialogue

☐ **Is your dialogue believable?** Listen to your dialogue as other people read it aloud. Be sure that it resembles real speech, not writing. People speak much less formally than they write. Use contractions and sentence fragments. Have your characters pause and interrupt and talk over one another. When in doubt, rough it up.

☐ **Does your dialogue add to character development?** Dialogue reveals your characters' fears and dreams and goals. It may also suggest what they are thinking but not actually saying. Dialogue allows your characters to tell the stories of who they really are.

☐ **Does your dialogue introduce backstory in a credible way?** Your audience learns important background information about your characters through their dialogue. However, make sure that your exposition sounds natural and is integral to the central conflict of the play. Give us the essentials, but don't tell us more than we need to know. It's only natural if some gaps remain here and there.

☐ **Does your dialogue heighten the conflict and move the action forward?** In good plays, dialogue, character, and structure are intertwined. Use dialogue to introduce necessary plot points and to intensify audience interest in what's taking place onstage. If "character is action," then make sure your characters are talking about the things that really matter to them.

Crafting a theme ▶

A good play has a solid structure, believable characters, and convincing dialogue. These elements nearly always result in a discernible **theme**, which Peter Schakel and Jack Ridl define as "the central idea or concept conveyed by a literary work . . . what it is about in the sense of 'what it all adds up to.'" More technically, M. H. Abrams defines theme as "an abstract claim, or doctrine, whether implicit or asserted, which an imaginative work is designed to incorporate and make persuasive to the reader [or viewer]." Your theme, in other words, is the way a set of beliefs or principles manifests itself in your play.

For all their conflict with one another, characters in plays also frequently discuss ideas. It's no coincidence that after a night out at the theater, many audience members love having extended conversations about what they have just witnessed. Good plays energize us intellectually and make us want to explore the subjects that they have raised.

As is the case with most contemporary drama, all three of our model plays are topical, full of ideas and issues. Indeed, plays have always been a particularly good forum for discussing our views and theories of the world. Even when they were explicitly concerned with heroes and gods, the early Greek plays were still implicitly commenting on the current political scene. And playwrights such as Aristophanes used their plays to openly remark on topics of the day, such as men's irrational propensity for war (*Lysistrata*), the justice system (*The Wasps*), and fraudulent academics (*The Clouds*). Shakespeare, of course, has provided literary critics with a virtual industry of thematic material for centuries. In the nineteenth century, Ibsen's plays took on the issues of women's rights (*Hedda Gabler* and *A Doll's House*) and various forms of hypocrisy among members of the middle class (*An Enemy of the People, Pillars of Society*, and *The Master Builder*). In twentieth-century plays such as *No Exit* and *The Flies* (a reworking of the *Oresteia*, by the ancient Greek playwright Aeschylus), the philosopher Jean-Paul Sartre discovered ways to make discussions of complex ideas comprehensible, and sometimes even funny, to the average audience member.

Often ideas in plays are political—they are about the news of the world, about injustice and repression and revolution. Yet the South African playwright Athol Fugard, one of the most insistently political playwrights of the past century, believes that we shouldn't have "instant-coffee" expectations about art's immediate power to change people's actions: "It doesn't work that way. I like that image of art dropping down through the various layers of the individual's psyche, into dreams, stirring around there and resurfacing later in action." Arthur Miller, another frequently political playwright, also warned against maintaining "a schematic point of view." For Miller, this too often led to one of the ultimate sins for a playwright: predictability.

Literary critics look at themes in literature as part of the final product. However, as a playwright, you are likely to find your themes emerging, and changing, as you write your play. A character, for instance, is inspired by the conflict that obsesses her, and she makes a remark. Another character responds. Later, they return to comment on and modify what they have said earlier. Before you know it, you have a theme on your hands.

As you look at the three model plays, notice how *themes arise from who the characters are and the conflicts in which they find themselves.* The playwrights very likely had issues that they wanted to address in their plays, but those issues are never more important than the characters and their conflicts.

One main theme of *Sure Thing* seems to be that romantic relationships are far more likely to fail than they are to succeed. The potential for something to go wrong exists every time we learn some new piece of information about our partner. The play's structure reinforces this theme, as does its title. Each time the bell rings, we are reminded that nothing is a "sure thing." In fact, the play seems to argue, it's extraordinarily unlikely that any two people are ever going to connect on all levels. The coincidences listed in the final scene are preposterous. Not only do Bill and Betty share the same political viewpoints and want their children to attend the same three colleges, but they also love early Woody Allen movies and Entenmann's crumb cake, hate brussels sprouts, and had Etch-a-Sketches as children. How likely are any of us to find so many matching traits in those we love?

And here is where the play's more explicit theme blends into those that are more implicit. For if the chances of two people sharing every single trait are highly remote, then maybe people involved in relationships should set their sights somewhat lower and be willing to forgive their partners for not being quite what they expected. Maybe it is *difference*, not similarity, that is the true spark for romantic passion.

Branching off still further, we might ask ourselves: If circumstances are always conspiring against successful relationships, does that mean most, or all, human endeavor is also likely to fail? Should we adjust our life expectations so that we assume failure rather than success? These ideas are not actually *stated* in the play; rather, they are triggered by our thinking about what occurs onstage.

The notion that most romances are doomed isn't a very cheerful one, so it's interesting to see how much merriment Ives gets out of his theme. He does this by using an arsenal of funny one-liners to keep his audience entertained: "Where was college?" "I was lying. I never really went to college. I just like to party." Themes emerge from the witty dialogue, but they are always subservient to it. Remember: no matter how brilliant your ideas are, your audience won't pay attention if they are not engaged and entertained by the characters and their conflicts.

Like Ives, Tina Howe makes use of comedy to craft her themes, although to a lesser degree. One central motif of *The Divine Fallacy* is that it is very difficult for us to see other people as they really are, and vice versa. As a fashion photographer, Victor is trained to observe and record external beauty, but he has no training in how to see Dorothy's inner loveliness. Again, the play's title is an important tool in announcing the overall theme. According to the European Society for General Semantics, "The divine fallacy is a species of non sequitur reasoning which explains something one does not understand by conjecturing the existence of some unknown force." Robert Todd Carroll, in *The Skeptic's Dictionary,* calls it "a variation of the alien fallacy: *I can't figure this out, so aliens must have done it.*" Howe's title may suggest that both we, and Victor, ascribe Dorothy's sudden radiance at the end of the play to God — or something supernatural — when in fact that luminescence was inside her all along; we were just incapable of seeing it.

Whatever interpretation we give to the title, religion is clearly an important subject in *The Divine Fallacy.* If our ability to perceive, or not perceive, beauty is one theme, another seems to be that faith can be an aid in stripping away "the veil of perception" that keeps us from seeing the truth. In addition to the title's allusion to God, we have Dorothy's monologue about the "holy men calling the faithful to prayer as women shed their clothes at the river's edge," which evokes a world where heavenly mysteries are made evident. Then there is the fact that Dorothy has stigmata, wounds in her hands that bleed the way Jesus's hands did when he was nailed to the cross. This connection is emphasized when Victor sees Dorothy bleeding and yelps, "Jesus Christ!" "Jesus Christ, indeed," she replies. Later she refers to the holes Navajos leave in their blankets as "part of the design, the most important part—faith, surrender, a mysterious tendency to bleed." Finally, of course, the lights blazing around her at the end of the play make her seem like a goddess.

In both the beauty and the divinity themes, Howe does not make the connections for us. Instead, to return to the blanket metaphor, the playwright provides us with the materials, but we must weave them into something useful ourselves.

In *Trying to Find Chinatown*, the title once more hints at the play's themes. One of these is the need for people to go on quests to discover their roots. Because he is adopted and evidently doesn't know his birth parents, Benjamin believes that he can learn more about himself by making a journey into his adopted father's past. Initially, finding Chinatown—which, for Benjamin, has the status of an almost mythical place—proves to be difficult. Benjamin's "guide," Ronnie, isn't at all helpful. According to Ronnie, a white man like Benjamin will never be able to truly understand the lives of Asian Americans. Yet it turns out that Ronnie is wrong. After seeing the place where his father grew up, Benjamin says, "I felt an ache in my heart for all those lost souls, denied this most important of revelations: to know who they truly are."

Hwang's play is the most outspokenly political of the three. Midway through it, Ronnie brings up another crucial thematic question: "If genes don't determine race, what does?" The answer may be that it depends on how we see ourselves. Benjamin *really* believes himself to be Asian, so, in his mind, that is his identity. Or race may be determined by how others perceive us. Benjamin says, "It's just that—in my hometown of Tribune, Kansas, and then at school—see, everyone knows me—so this sort of thing never comes up." Or we may take our racial identity from the family in which we are raised. Benjamin's parents raised him as Asian; therefore, he feels Asian.

Yet Ronnie cannot accept the idea that racial identity is as straightforward as Benjamin presents it. He tells Benjamin: "You think identity's that simple? That you can wrap it all up in a neat package and say, 'I have ethnicity, therefore I am?'" Both characters end up expanding our notions of identity, and the play strongly suggests that stereotyping people based on race is wrong for all sorts of reasons.

Another important theme in *Trying to Find Chinatown* is the ability of art to transcend racial boundaries. Ronnie tells Benjamin, "There're worlds out there, worlds you haven't even begun to understand. Open your eyes. Hear with your ears." In his long final monologue, Ronnie explains how being Asian does not preclude him from loving, appreciating, and participating in a musical tradition that is primarily associated with black and, to a lesser degree, white artists.

No matter how we approach the themes that emerge in our plays, ultimately, as Jeffrey Hatcher tells us, "It is not the quality of the idea that matters most, but rather the quality of the ideas as depicted by the actions of the play." Plays are *not* stories or essays or poems. They are meant to be acted out onstage, and dialogue that loses sight of the conflicts and characters that inspired them will quickly bore an audience. However, if you are attentive to your themes as they emerge, if you highlight your ideas without turning them into mere lectures and lesson plans, your play will be stronger as a result.

CHECKLIST Crafting a theme

☐ **Does your play have at least one clear theme?** Dialogue between characters inevitably generates ideas, but those ideas aren't necessarily coherent. As you revise your play, look for ways to underscore the connections between related thoughts and topics.

☐ **Does your theme emerge as a result of the play's conflict and characters?** A play is not a sermon, and plays that "speechify" tend to put audiences to sleep or send them running for the exits. Make sure that the ideas your play raises result from the central conflict between the characters.

☐ **Does your title subtly, but unmistakably, point your audience in the direction of your play's theme?** Too often new playwrights give little thought to the title: it's the last thing they type, if they even remember to title the play at all. Give your play the title it deserves. Audience members will assume that the title encapsulates the play's message in some important way.

☐ **Is your theme likely to inspire further thought and discussion after the performance is over?** Just as an obvious topic sentence — "War is bad," "Family is important" — will probably result in an uninteresting expository essay, so themes that are predictable and inarguable will deaden a play. Push yourself, and your characters, to think beyond ideas that are so self-evident they aren't worth exploring. Themes such as "War may be justified at times" or "Families can be crippling" are much more likely to invite the sort of postperformance debate that is integral to the theatergoing experience.

Onstage: The elements of production ▶

Throughout our discussion of playwriting, we have been considering how plays differ from other creative writing genres, but everything comes back to one simple fact: no matter how much care playwrights take with their scripts, a play does not truly exist until it is *performed* onstage. "A play is not only paper," Lillian Hellman wrote. "It is there to share with actors, directors, scene designers, electricians." And audiences, she surely would have added.

More than any of the other genres discussed in this book, playwriting is a *collaborative* art form. It takes only one person to write a play, but for the play to come alive, you need, at the very least, actors, some sort of stage, and an audience. Director Elia Kazan echoes Hellman's sentiment: "The theater is not an exclusively literary form. Although the playscript is the essentially important element, after that is finished, actors, designers, directors, technicians 'write' the play together."

In this section, we cover the most important elements of theatrical performance, issues you aren't likely to think about unless you yourself have been an actor in a play. In a bare-bones production, not all of these elements will be applicable. However, if you continue writing plays, eventually you will come across each of these aspects of the theater.

Stage

The most common type of stage is the **proscenium**. In ancient Greek theater, the *proskenion* was the front of the building that formed the background for a theatrical performance. (Incidentally, this is where we get the English word "scene.") "Proscenium" has come to mean that part of the stage that is in front of the curtains, sometimes also called the apron. A proscenium stage, which you may recognize from your high school auditorium, looks like this:

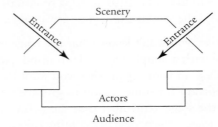

A **thrust stage** takes the apron and pushes it farther out into the theater, so that the actors are surrounded on three sides by the audience:

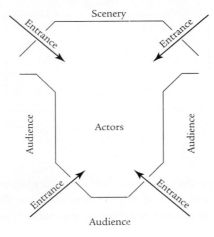

A third type of stage is the **arena theater**, which is also called **theater in the round** or theater in the square. In this variation, the audience surrounds the stage, with actors typically making their entrances and exits in diagonals between the seats:

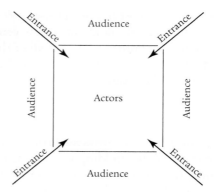

Sometimes, especially if you are a well-known playwright, or if you have been asked to do a play by a particular theater company, you will know in advance what the stage is going to look like. If so, it helps to visualize the placement of any scenery or props and the movement of your actors on- and offstage.

Most often, however, you won't know what the stage will look like, so it's probably best to write with a simple rectangle in mind. Normally, you merely indicate "Enter" or "Exit" in your script when you want the actors to arrive or depart, but if it's important for some reason to give your actors directions on how to move around the stage, remember that these directions are given from the perspective of the *actors* — the people performing the play — not the audience watching it. Thus, you will reverse the way you normally think of left and right, and up and down, like this:

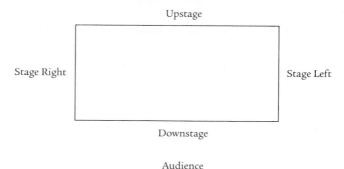

Even if you can't predict the exact look of your play or the space in which it will be performed, you should nevertheless imagine the movement of the actors onstage. If you have Larry cowering on one side of the stage, and the next moment he is punching Lorenzo, who happens to be on the opposite side, you have a problem. Some playwrights make rough sketches of the action as they imagine it. Others move around toy figures, just to see who is where at any given point in the play. One playwright uses coins—a quarter for one character, a dime for another, a nickel for a third—to help him visualize his characters. This positioning of the actors is called **blocking**, an essential element of theatrical performance.

As you write, be sure to think about blocking, but don't give excessive directions in your script. Directors and actors usually prefer to work out stage movement themselves.

Sets

The stage is the empty space on which your play is performed; the **set** (short for "setting") can refer to anything from an elaborately reproduced house or building or even an entire street or town, to the doors and windows and walls of those buildings, to nothing more than a painted backdrop. The set designer is responsible for creating the play's environment. Something of an architect and an interior decorator, the set designer is integral to the overall look of a play.

Even a very low-budget full-length film is likely to have a set designer and to spend tens of thousands of dollars for the set's production, but the theater has different conventions than do movies. The imagination's ability to transform and to people empty space has allowed many small theaters with skeletal sets to produce powerful plays. Compared to small theaters, regional theaters spend more time and money on sets, but the focus normally remains on the acting and the script. Even multimillion-dollar Broadway spectaculars—the closest thing to movies that theater can offer—don't have film's ability to quick-cut from one breathtaking scene to the next. Plays necessarily happen in real time, during which props must be moved and actors must make their way on and off the stage. As Harold Pinter notes, in television or a film, "if you get tired of a scene you just drop it and go on to another one," but in a play, characters are "stuck on the stage, [and] you've got to live with them and deal with them." Playwrights know this, so they shift scenes with care. Every time a new scene is required, they are acutely aware that a certain amount of energy, time, and ingenuity is needed to relocate not just the actors and their props but also the action and momentum of the play.

The presence of a set designer indicates that some money is involved in a production. Major theaters keep set designers on staff or hire them for individual productions, but if you are a beginning playwright, set design is probably going to fall to you or your director. Moreover, most ten-minute plays are presented in an evening of short works. Several playwrights are involved in the production, so settings need to be assembled and taken down in the one- or two-minute interval between plays. Therefore, when it comes to sets for your ten-minute play, think simple. You can't expect a small theater company to build an airplane interior, for instance. You will probably have to settle for a few chairs and lots of audience imagination.

Props, costumes, and effects

Props are part of the setting and can include everything from furniture (set props), like the table and two chairs in *Sure Thing*, to props actually handled by the actors (hand props), such as Ronnie's violin and Benjamin's salty plum in *Trying to Find Chinatown*. In fact, props include everything the actors need to act out the play. If a character needs to write a note, for instance, someone needs to be sure that the actor has a pencil and a piece of paper.

The model play with the most elaborate props and set is *The Divine Fallacy*. According to the stage directions, Victor's studio "looks like a surreal garden blooming with white umbrellas and reflective silver screens." Tina Howe is a famous playwright, so theaters that produce her plays have the resources to borrow or rent the extensive (and expensive) props necessary to re-create a photographer's studio.

The props for your play, however, are likely to be your own possessions or items borrowed from friends and family. Fortunately, in the words of William Packard, "One good onstage visual is worth a thousand oratorical speeches." Packard believes that "a playwright must train himself to present things that are seen, things that can be looked at, things that will show what is happening onstage." As you write your play, try to incorporate at least one object that is representative of the characters' major conflict. A single prop—a wilted rose, an empty bottle, a letter torn in half—can do a lot of work. Props like these are free, or inexpensive, and easy to obtain. Indeed, one of the most famous scenes in twentieth-century drama is centered on such a prop: the tiny glass unicorn with the broken horn that symbolizes Laura Wingfield's stunted emotional growth in Tennessee Williams's *The Glass Menagerie*.

One important rule of props: Don't bring anything onstage that you don't plan to use. Chekhov famously wrote, "If in the first act you have hung a pistol on the wall, then in the following one it should be fired. Otherwise don't put it there." Your actors will have enough to think about without having to worry about handling a prop that is never actually mentioned in your script. And your audience will assume that a skilled playwright wouldn't clutter up the set with unnecessary props.

In a working theater, the stage manager usually handles props, while costumes are under the supervision of the costume mistress or master. When you are writing your script, costumes probably won't be at the forefront of your mind, but they can be a crucial element in your play. That's the case in *The Divine Fallacy*: Dorothy, we are told, is "dressed in layers of mismatched clothes. An enormous coat covers a bulky sweater which covers a gauzy white dress. A tangle of woolen scarves is wrapped around her neck." Costuming emphasizes Dorothy's basic insecurity. She believes herself to be unattractive, so she hides from the world beneath heaps of clothing. The process of unwrapping herself at the end represents how incandescent she is beneath her protective covering.

Established theaters working on a show with a large cast may spend tens of thousands of dollars on costumes and have an entire staff working on them. Costume fittings for actors in these shows often take days. In contrast, if your play receives a staged reading in class, chances are that the actors will wear their street clothes. Even so, you may want to bring in some piece of costuming—an odd-looking hat or a T-shirt with a specific logo on it—to emphasize a particular aspect of your characters' personalities.

Once your play is produced onstage, costuming will become a significant issue for the director and the actors. If your play is set in the present, it will probably be easy enough for the actors to acquire the clothes they need. But if your play is set in Ye Olde England or on a spaceship in the twenty-ninth century, watch out. Unless you have the resources to borrow or rent appropriate costumes, your actors may end up looking silly wearing your little sister's Burger King crown or a space suit made out of tinfoil.

As viewers of films and television shows, we are accustomed to seeing professional sets, props, and costumes as well as first-rate special effects. In the ten minutes between commercials on a TV police drama, for example, we might see a murder, a car crash, and an explosion. We hardly even register how different that is from our actual daily experience because we are so accustomed to the conventions of TV shows, which allow—or require—so many special effects.

Such effects are rare in serious drama. The only notable effect in our three model plays is Dorothy's stigmata, which causes "a torrent of blood [to gush] from her hand." In a large theater, this effect might be handled by a technician or a makeup artist. In a small production, it would probably be the stage manager's responsibility to figure something out. As the author of a limited-budget ten-minute play, you probably should avoid effects like this unless you know someone who can do them well. An amateurish gushing of dyed water or ketchup from Dorothy's palms could easily turn silly, reversing the impact that the effect was supposed to make.

Lights

Good onstage visuals can include not just sets and props but also lighting. In the words of Tennessee Williams, "Sometimes it would take page after tedious page of exposition to put across an idea that can be said with . . . the lighted stage."

If your play is being produced indoors, or outdoors at night, you will probably have at your service at least some of the wonders of modern theatrical lighting. Contemporary theaters have complex digital lighting boards that, in the hands of expert lighting designers, create true magic. These designers can quickly turn day into gloomy night; they can create storms and fires and glowing sunsets. Gels and stencils can produce everything from the shadows of trees to the outlines of cathedral windows.

However, ten-minute plays tend to have limited lighting cues because they are usually produced in a group and on a limited budget. In *Sure Thing*, for example, the lights come up at the beginning of the play, and they go off at the end. The cue "**Blackout**" at the end of Ives's script is a common one and means that all the lights go off at once.

The effect of a blackout—quick and immediate—is quite different from a slow fade, which is what we get in *The Divine Fallacy*. Without lighting, the conclusion of this play would be considerably diminished because the "great light" that emanates from Dorothy is necessary to emphasize her sudden metamorphosis from mousy neurotic to radiant goddess. Fortunately, this effect can easily be created by an experienced lighting operator.

The lighting cues in *Trying to Find Chinatown* are fairly simple yet also important in establishing mood. The play begins in darkness with Ronnie's music being played, and the lights "fade up" to reveal the actors. At the end, Benjamin is "illuminated in his own special"; that is, he has a spotlight on him as he delivers his final monologue. When he is finished, the poignancy of what he has said and the beauty of Ronnie's music linger with us an extra few moments as the "lights fade slowly to black."

Sounds

Each of our model plays includes important sound cues. Ronnie's violin music must be expert and edgy and inventive, and although the actor playing Ronnie doesn't need to actually make the music, hiring and recording a real musician would likely be required for this play. The music cue in *The Divine Fallacy* is even more specific. At the beginning and at the very end of the play, "we hear the joyful bass-soprano duet, 'Mit unser Macht ist nichts getan,' from Bach's chorale, *Ein feste Burg ist unser Gott, BWV 80*."

Hwang and Howe have very specific pieces of music in mind, and you too may know the perfect song that will accent the mood of your play in just the right way. Be practical, though. Don't insist that the script use music you can't provide. Copyright issues can be a problem in larger theaters, and many directors and producers like to have some leeway in this area. They would probably prefer general musical directions, such as "surf music" or "country tune," rather than a specific song and artist.

Sounds can include more than just music, of course. The bell ringing in *Sure Thing* is part of the comedy, and the person in charge of ringing it (or playing the recording) needs to pay careful attention to the script. As with the other technical production elements, be wary of relying too much on sound effects. One gunshot will make a big impact. A thirty-second offstage machine-gun battle will probably end up sounding ridiculous.

Actors

We have been talking about actors throughout this chapter, and as long as you are a playwright, you will want to *keep* talking about and to and with them. Playwrights who don't consider the human dimension of their plays don't last very long in the theater: without actors, there is no play. You may write for yourself, but you must also write for an audience, and the only way to reach that audience is through your actors.

We have seen that "character is action," and of course it is equally true that "actors are action." To act doesn't just mean "to mimic, impersonate, or pretend"; it also means "to do." Actors do things. They cry, they yell, they get in each other's faces, they fling themselves around, and they stalk off the stage, slamming the door behind them. They pick up objects and put them down. Sometimes they throw things. They talk to each other and sometimes to the audience and sometimes to themselves. Everything onstage happens to and for them.

Students who have only read plays, and have never seen them, are often astonished by the impact that even a classroom performance can bring to a script. For example, consider the scene in *The Divine Fallacy* when Victor is chasing Dorothy around his studio as she "makes disturbing rodent faces and sounds." On the page, the play may not read like a romp, but in performance it has almost as many funny, manic, physical antics as a Marx Brothers movie.

The simple act of witnessing human contact can also be powerful for an audience. In *Trying to Find Chinatown*, after Ronnie says, "I don't know what kind of bullshit ethnic studies program they're running over in Wisconsin, but did they teach you that in order to find your Asian 'roots,' it's a good idea first to be Asian?" Hwang gives the following stage direction: "Ronnie grabs Benjamin's hands, holds them up before his face." A minute later, after explaining himself once more, Benjamin offers his hand for Ronnie to shake, and when Ronnie takes it, we know—purely through the physicality of this gesture—that they have, at least for a moment, come to some sort of understanding.

Even when actors aren't moving around the stage, they are still "acting." A good actor playing Ronnie will be able to convey just as much rage with his face and posture as he does with his angry words. Director Peter Brook notes that finding the emotion in the language is an actor's job, not a playwright's;

therefore, a good playwright, according to Brook, doesn't waste time trying to write emotional cues into his script: "He recognizes that however long his description, it doesn't begin to touch what an actor can make crystal clear in a flash. An actor is all the time entering these infinitesimal gaps between the most compact words."

Actors in a play have a physical presence as long as they remain onstage. That may sound obvious, but beginning playwrights often forget to think of what every character will be doing all the time — yet another reason to keep your cast size small. When characters in a work of fiction aren't talking or doing something, they basically disappear from view. Actors don't have that luxury. If, as happens in each of our model plays, one actor delivers an extended monologue, the other actors can listen intently, they can fiddle with a prop, they can move around, or they can even pointedly ignore what the character is saying, but they must do *something*. The actor who is listening to a long monologue may need to engage in some **stage business** — apparently incidental actions done for dramatic effect — when he or she is not the focus of our attention.

As you look over your script, think about all the areas in which actor involvement might affect it. On the positive side, actors can

- ▶ put poetry into ordinary language,
- ▶ bring a dull character to life,
- ▶ make a bad joke funny, or
- ▶ bring tears to the eyes of an audience.

On the negative side, actors can

- ▶ ruin your best speeches,
- ▶ drain the life out of a fascinating character,
- ▶ butcher a hilarious punch line, or
- ▶ turn a tragic moment into low comedy.

You never know what's going to happen onstage. The actor who in rehearsal was wonderful may suddenly freeze before an audience, while the buffoon who missed half the rehearsals is a gamer who suddenly comes alive on opening night. Acting is a craft, but it's also a crapshoot, which is part of the fun of live theater.

Probably the best solution is to attempt to write what William Packard calls an "actor-proof play" — one in which the characters' actions and motivations are so clear that no actor can mistake them for something other than what the playwright intended.

Audience

Actors sometimes refer to the audience as the "fourth wall." This comes from the convention that the three "walls" of the stage are like a room, and the audience is looking in on the play through an invisible fourth wall. "Breaking the fourth wall" means acknowledging that there is an audience out there watching the play. In "realistic" plays, that is taboo, but in more experimental fare — Luigi Pirandello's *Six Characters in Search of an Author* is a famous example — actors sometimes engage the audience directly.

Thornton Wilder said that a play's need for an audience was more than just "economic necessity" and "the fact that the temperament of actors is proverbially dependent on group attention." Instead, Wilder believed that "the pretense, the fiction, on the stage would fall to pieces and absurdity without the support accorded to it by a crowd, and the excitement induced by pretending a fragment of life is such that it partakes of ritual and festival, and requires a throng."

People in crowds — the "throng" — pick up on cues from one another. If your play is a comedy, you'll want it to be funny early on. Once a couple of people laugh, everyone else will know that it's okay to laugh, too. Similarly, for a tragic play, once you have established a tone — that it's *not* okay to laugh — audience members will rarely break the group taboo.

The importance of an audience's spontaneous reaction to your material is yet another way in which drama differs from the other creative writing genres. You may write a poem that nineteen people don't like; however, if one intelligent and insightful person loves and understands your poem, you might well count it a success. That success ratio doesn't work in the theater. If you have an audience of twenty people and nineteen — or even ten or twelve — of them are bored, your play will be a disaster.

Because the response of the crowd is so crucial, playwrights are more likely than other writers to revise their work based on audience response. Plays in the midst of drafting and revision often have audience feedback sessions with the playwright. Audience members offer suggestions and ask questions about the author's intentions, with the playwright responding and asking questions of her or his own. Your class workshop is likely to serve this role for your play. In this process, be open to change and transformation. "You start out with an idea," as David Mamet says, "it becomes something else, and part of the wisdom is learning to listen to the material itself."

CHECKLIST Onstage: The elements of production

☐ **Is your play written so that it can be performed on a theatrical stage and set?** Even though you may not have final say over what your performance space looks like, you can at least think in terms of the *possibilities* of stage and set. Look through your script again, and be sure your play can be acted in a confined area, using a modest and inexpensive set.

☐ **Have you made use of theatrical lighting and sounds, props, costumes, and effects?** Not every ten-minute play will be able to take advantage of elaborate lighting and sound cues. Nevertheless, you can probably count on basic lighting effects such as "fade up," "fade down," or "blackout." Similarly, low-tech sound effects like the bell in *Sure Thing* require little effort but can make a big impression on an audience. Finally, look for ways to incorporate easily acquired props (a Bible for a religious character, a carpenter's tape for a carpenter) and costumes (a red scarf for a liberated character, a black scarf for one who is in mourning) that will help bring your script to life.

☐ **Does your play always reflect the fact that it will be performed by stage actors?** When your actors talk, give them lines that are meant to be said aloud, and provide them with actions that are motivated by their characters' desires. Superheroes and film actors can perform all sorts of amazing feats, but stage actors are real people working in real time, obeying the laws of physics. Don't ask them to do impossible deeds, and don't have unreasonable expectations of the people who will be performing your play. You may think it's crucial that your lead be a six-foot-tall red-headed woman who can sing opera and do handstands, but your actors will rarely possess all the traits that you envisioned. That's okay: that's why it's called *acting*.

☐ **Have you taken into account your audience's response to the play?** You may be wild about your play, but if you receive a lukewarm—or worse— response, you should consider revising the script. Of course, you cannot write, or revise, a play by committee, but don't discount the insights of audience members, especially if many of them have similar questions, comments, or critiques.

Getting started writing the ten-minute play ▶

In all likelihood, the three model plays, our discussion of them, and the plays in the anthology will provide you with an idea for your own ten-minute play. If not, the following kick-starts will help you get going.

As with all other forms of writing, feel free in the early stages of the process to change, to experiment, to give up and start over again. Sometimes, after writing a few pages, new playwrights realize that their play would make a better story or essay or poem. That's fine. One of the advantages of working in all four genres explored in this book is that your ideas have a much broader field in which to germinate.

Once you have settled on an idea for your play, remember that it should make its premise and conflict clear in the first minute or two. It should have several significant reversals and complications, and it should end with a twist that is surprising yet satisfying. And when you have finished your draft, be honest with yourself. As you listen to others read it aloud, try to gauge how you would react if you were an audience member with no particular stake in the play. Would you be bored and confused, or would you be completely absorbed by what was happening onstage?

KICK-STARTS Beginning your play

1. Write a play with two characters who are based on two people you know very well but who have never met each other. These characters should be natural antagonists who are in direct and immediate conflict with each other.

2. Write a play with a protagonist who is about to go over the edge. Introduce another character who is the perfect antagonist to do the pushing.

3. Plays are often topical. Choose a story from the news that has a clear conflict and interesting, compelling characters. Change the names and the circumstances enough so that you feel free to alter the facts of the case for dramatic impact. Then write a play centered around the news item.

4. Fiction writers work extremely hard to "bring their characters to life," but as a playwright, your characters are already alive. Take advantage of the fact that you have people—breathing, moving, talking human beings—on the stage. Write a play that benefits from the proximity of your actors to their audience.

5. Maria Irene Fornes observes, "Work is part of everyone's life. Except in plays." Write a play that is set at work, or one in which work plays an integral role in the dramatic conflict.

6. Luis Valdez says, "The racial issue [in theater] is always just swept aside. It deserves to be swept aside only after it's been dealt with. We cannot begin to approach a real solution to our social ills—a solution like integration, for instance, or assimilation—without dealing with all our underlying feelings about each other." Write a play that deals with a significant issue involving race.

7. Choose an interesting and unusual prop—a shoehorn, a cardboard box of discarded auto parts, a teddy bear with one arm torn off—and write the play that goes with that object.

8. The sound of a bell ringing is a crucial element in David Ives's *Sure Thing*. Choose another sound effect—for example, the ringing of a cell phone, or the shattering of a piece of glass, or a muted cough—and write a play in which that sound features prominently.

▶ **9.** If your play seems too boring or static, ask a couple of actors (they can be friends or relatives) to act out the action of your play silently, without any dialogue at all. If they are just standing around or sitting the entire time, start over with a new play, or rethink your conflict and characters so that the struggle between them is more dynamic, more direct, and more physical.

▶ **10.** Playwrights such as Harold Pinter and Samuel Beckett may be almost as famous for what their characters *don't* say as what they do say. Write a play in which pauses and silences are crucial elements of the script.

▶ **11.** Look back at the stories, essays, and poems you have written in the past — whether they were for this class, another one, or simply yourself. See if you have written something that might have worked better onstage. Using what you have learned in this section, rethink and rewrite your earlier idea so that it is suitable as a play.

▶ **12.** David Rabe says that he begins a play "with an impulse or a situation or some-times just a fragment of dialogue that begins to expand once you work on it. Something sticks in my mind — it could be a real person or a real exchange of dialogue or a fragment that just pops into my head." Write a play that starts from something that, for whatever reason, "sticks in your mind."

▶ **13.** Write a play that combines two or three of the previous kick-starts.

Playscript Format: A Model

HOW TO FORMAT A PLAY

A Play

by

Your Name Here

Your Name

Instructor's Name

Class

The Date

<u>Characters</u>
PROFESSOR MARGUERITE LU, A creative writing instructor in her 30s or 40s

BRYER, A creative writing student in his
early 20s

<u>Setting</u>
Her office. The present.

> Lights up to reveal MARGUERITE, a creative writing instructor, sitting at her office desk, intently typing a play. Off to one side is a chair.
>
> There is a knock at the door.
>
> MARGUERITE frowns as she looks up from her work.

MARGUERITE

(*After a moment*) Come in.

> (Enter BRYER, her student, with a back-pack slung over his shoulder.)

MARGUERITE (CONT.)

Hi, Bryer. Come in. Sit down.

BRYER

Thanks, Professor Lu.

> (BRYER sits down, dropping his backpack on the floor with a thud.)

MARGUERITE

How can I help you?

                    BRYER
(Very frustrated) It's just . . . I don't know.
I'm having trouble figuring out how to do the
playscript you showed us in class. It's weird.

                  MARGUERITE
It's different.

                    BRYER
Like I said: it's weird.

                  MARGUERITE
Weird isn't necessarily different. Come on
now, Bryer.

                    BRYER
Okay. But if you could just show me how to
do it right, I'd really appreciate it.

                  MARGUERITE
No problem. In fact, I can turn this little
scene we're performing right now into a
script.

                              (BRYER pulls his
                              chair closer to her
                              computer.)

                    BRYER
Cool.

                  MARGUERITE
Let's start with the title page. You can see
that the title of your play is 10 spaces from
the top, is centered, and is in all capital
letters. Just below that are the words "A
play by" and then your name also centered.

                    BRYER
And the lower right-hand corner is where my
name, my instructor's name, the class, and
the date go.

MARGUERITE
That's right. If you were sending your play off to a theater company or a potential pro-ducer, that's where you'd include your contact information: address, phone, e-mail.

BRYER
Everything's in, like, 12-point Courier font.

MARGUERITE
That's a convention that comes to us from manual typewriters. Some people have started using Times Roman 12-point font, but I prefer Courier. It's generally pretty accu-rate in translating one page of script into one minute of stage time.

BRYER
What if you have a really long speech--like a full page of somebody just talking?

MARGUERITE
Clearly, that's going to take more than just a minute. In contrast, if you have rapid-fire dialogue where each character only says a few words before the next one starts talking, that page will go more quickly than one minute. Still, on balance, it comes out about right.

BRYER
I see on the next page you have "Charac-ters" and "Setting."

MARGUERITE
Yep. The characters' names are in all caps, wherever they appear in the play.

(BRYER sits back for a moment, looking puzzled.)

                    BRYER
I don't get it: why is that?

                  MARGUERITE
That's so the actors can find their parts
easily. It helps them know when they have to
say or do something in the script.

                    BRYER
The description you have of them is pretty
general.

                  MARGUERITE
That's intentional. Directors want to have
the freedom to cast whoever's right for the
part. All we need to know is that the person playing you is a male in his 20s. Why
say, for instance, that the actor must be
five feet ten inches tall, blond, with blue
eyes, when that doesn't really matter to the
play? And there's even more latitude in age
for the female actor playing me.

                    BRYER
You said "female actor."

                  MARGUERITE
We generally don't say "actress" in the theater anymore. It's considered sexist.

                    BRYER
No comment on that.

                              (MARGUERITE gives him
                              a look. BRYER pauses
                              for a moment to col-
                              lect his thoughts.)

                 BRYER (CONT.)
I see the setting is just as simple.

MARGUERITE

Once again, you don't want to burden the people putting on your play with unnecessary details that may interfere with the production.

BRYER

Fair enough. Could I put the characters and setting on the title page? Just for our class? To save paper, I mean.

MARGUERITE

(*Smiling wryly*) Anything for the environment.

BRYER

So then we get to the actual script itself. It looks like the scene description is moved over to the right half of the page.

MARGUERITE

Yes. The space between margins on this particular page is six inches total from the left to the right margins, so the stage directions begin three inches to the right of the left margin. This helps distinguish stage directions from the dialogue. As I said, it's all about making it easier for the actors. This helps them distinguish between when they should *do* something and when they need to *speak*.

BRYER

So that's why the characters' names are centered, and their dialogue is left margin justified? But stage directions, movement, and so on are all on the right half of the page.

MARGUERITE

That's exactly right. Notice, too, that while the dialogue itself is single-spaced, there is an extra space between the dialogue and the name of the character making the next speech. It opens up the page a bit.

BRYER

I see you have parentheses and italics in front of a couple of speeches, like you're telling the actor how to talk.

MARGUERITE

This is a cue for how to say a particular sentence or phrase, when it might be mis-interpreted. I've tried to go easy on those instructions, though, because actors tend to resent being told how to deliver their lines.

BRYER

So: characters' names are centered, dialogue goes across the page, and stage directions start on the right half of the page.

MARGUERITE

That's correct. You'll notice, too, that after the scene is established at the very beginning, stage directions are in parentheses.

> (BRYER leans over again to take a closer look.)

BRYER

They sure are. A couple of times you've written "(CONT.)." What does that mean?

MARGUERITE

That indicates the character who was speak-ing earlier "continues" talking, even though some action or cue or a page break in the script interrupted him or her.

> (BRYER pushes his chair back to where it was, shoulders his backpack, and gets ready to leave.)

BRYER
Okay. I think I've got it.

MARGUERITE
Take it easy, Bryer.

(BRYER nods and is on
his way out when he
suddenly thinks of
something else.)

BRYER
Is this the way *all* playscripts look? The
way you just showed me?

MARGUERITE
Not exactly. Unlike screenwr,iters, who have
one very specific way to lay out *everything*
in their screenplays, from dialogue to
action, playwrights tend to pick and choose
from several formats. For the purposes of
your play, you'll want to follow this format
as closely as possible. It's not the *only*
way, but anyone who sees it will recognize
that you're following the major conventions
of a playscript, which we've just discussed.

(BRYER gives her a
thumbs-up.)

BRYER
Thanks, Professor Lu. I'll see you later.

MARGUERITE
No doubt you will, Bryer. No doubt you will.

(Exit BRYER.
Lights fade as MAR-
GUERITE returns to
typing her play.)

END OF PLAY.

An Anthology of Ten-Minute Plays

Dan Dietz

Trash Anthem

Characters

WOMAN
BOOTS

Setting

Little house, Big South

Little house. Big South. A pair of men's cowboy boots. Woman stands dressed in cheap but professional clothing. She holds a shovel. Her body is streaked with dirt. She stomps the shovel to the floor three times, then turns to the boots and approaches them in a slow march, stomping a rhythm with the shovel.

WOMAN: *(Sings under her breath.)*
I am earthy
I am raw
My man's in pieces
Down in the soggy soggy

(She stands next to the boots in silence. Drops the shovel. Raises her hands above her head, screams, and thrusts her hands into the boots. Woman pulls out her hands — they are covered in rich black soil. She's got fistfuls of it.)

(New start. A pair of men's cowboy boots. Woman slowly approaches them. She stops, considers them for a moment, then shifts the boots so the left boot is on the right side and the right boot on the left. She smiles to herself, walks off. Pause. The boots talk to the audience.)

BOOTS: Ow. Goddammit. Hey. Scuse me. Y'all in the seats there. Yeah, could one of you, uh, come down here and move these back? Please? I'm serious, this hurts. Come on. One of you men take pity on me. I'm twisted up genital-wise. Please?

(New start. Woman stands by Boots.)

WOMAN: My man ain't a cowboy. 'Cept at his feet. Cowboy feet, leather-wrapped and stinky. My man ain't a cowboy.

　　　My man ain't a talker. 'Cept with his hands. Talking hands, reach out and touch someone, long distance cellular kinda hands, still feel 'em back of my neck, gripping in a man way, slipping in that same man way, you know, down. Ain't a talker, nope.

　　　So I fell in love with his hands and his feet. We'd go dancing, and I'd spend the whole time looking down at his boots. Felt like as long as I kept my eyes locked on them, we could dance across the Gulf of Mexico and never fall in. I loved them hard, those feet, those hands. Listened hard to the heartbeats at the tips of his fingers and toes. Tried to decipher. Unravel the code in bloodflow. Find the secret that binds forever.

WOMAN: Failed.

(Woman raises her hands, screams, thrusts them into the boots, pulls out fistfuls of earth. The boots scream back. The Woman smiles.)

BOOTS: What do you want from me?

WOMAN: Talk.

BOOTS: I don't talk, you know that.

WOMAN: I know. You use your hands. Crack open peanuts when I'm talking to you. Stare at the wall.

BOOTS: I communicate through peanuts, like all men do. I pop the little buggers out of their shells like mussels, like mollusks, like deep-sea snails. I dip them behind my lips, shake the half-shell, rattle 'em into my mouth. And then I crunch. And this combination of pop, rattle, crunch is a language. Sweeter'n English.

WOMAN: You ain't gonna be popping peanuts no more.

BOOTS: Nope. Got myself popped instead.

WOMAN: Your own fault.

BOOTS: Hardly deserving of an execution.

WOMAN: I was pissed off.

BOOTS: Oh. Well. In that case fire away.

WOMAN: I did! *(Pause.)* I hope it didn't hurt.

BOOTS: Course it hurt! Jesus.

WOMAN: Sorry.

BOOTS: Me too.

WOMAN: But you deserved it.

　　　Wish to god this story was more original, folks, but it ain't. I swore when I started paralegal classes I wasn't gonna live the stereotype no more. But here I am, stuck back in that same old same old white trash anthem: Woman finds her man with his dick inside the neighbor. Woman grabs the rifle off the rack. Blah-de-blah-de-blah. It ain't fair. I drive a Jetta.

BOOTS: Well, there is a twist.

WOMAN: Ain't no twist.

BOOTS: Oh, there's a twist all right.

WOMAN: Shut up.

BOOTS: See, folks, what Genevieve ain't saying . . .

WOMAN: Don't you say another word!

BOOTS: What Genevieve ain't exactly being forthcoming about is the fact that . . .

WOMAN: I said, shut it!

(*She grips the boots at the top, squeezes them shut. Boots continues talking, muffled and incomprehensible.*)

WOMAN: (*Sings.*)
> I am earthy
> I am raw
> My man's in pieces
> Down in the soggy soggy (*Boots is silent.*)

WOMAN: Hey. You gonna behave? (*No answer.*) You ain't gonna make me regret this are you? (*No answer.*) Okay.

(*Woman releases Boots.*)

BOOTS: The neighbor was a man.

WOMAN: GODDAMMIT!

BOOTS: Sorry, babe, they got a right to know. It was a man, folks. The dick she is referring to was deep inside a—

WOMAN: PLEASE! Shit.

BOOTS: Jesus, you can be so stone age. Twenty-first century, Jenny. Wake up and smell the tolerance.

WOMAN: I just don't get it. You were so butch.

(*Pause.*)

BOOTS: Did you get Jeff, too?

WOMAN: Nope. He's fast.

BOOTS: More ways'n one.

WOMAN: You mighta got away too, if you hadn't had your boots on. Stuck in the sheets like a drowning man. Boots in bed. Walking on water.

BOOTS: He's got the police headed your way right now.

WOMAN: Probably. How long you been like this?

BOOTS: I don't know. How old are my veins?

WOMAN: I loved you. I gave you a home. We danced. You ever dance with Jeff?

BOOTS: In this town? We'd get our asses kicked.

WOMAN: I'd pay money to see that.

BOOTS: Look. You shot me, okay? You buried me in the backyard, you win. What more do you want?

WOMAN: I don't know.

BOOTS: Well then, woman, LET ME IN PEACE.

(*Woman screams at Boots. Boots screams back. Silence.*)

WOMAN: How many?

BOOTS: Besides Jeff?

WOMAN: How many *times*? (*Pause.*) I never cheated on you.

BOOTS: Okay. Thanks.

WOMAN: (*Stomps the toe of a boot.*) FUCK YOU.

BOOTS: Ow! Goddamn, Jenny, these are my dancing boots. (*Pause.*) You gonna turn yourself in?

WOMAN: Nope.

BOOTS: They're gonna find out.

WOMAN: Maybe.

BOOTS: No maybe about it. You're going down. They're gonna slice your eyes open with them flashing blue lights. Till you tell 'em all your secrets.

WOMAN: Wish I could work that kinda magic on you. Man flows to your doorstep. You let him in. Man flows over the house, his smell washes everything in your home, a weird kinda clean. Saltwater clean. Let him in. Makes life a mystery. Confusion. The bed a place of foreign noises. Muffled sounds. And you can't for the life of you get the water outta your ears.

BOOTS: I didn't mean to get everything in a snarl.

WOMAN: Two years, you and me. When was Jeff?

BOOTS: June. Four months.

WOMAN: He's got a sunken chest.

BOOTS: Nothing makes sense, you know that.

WOMAN: More peanut talk.

(*Sirens in the distance, getting closer.*)

BOOTS: They're coming.

WOMAN: Yep. Listen. I turned my pockets inside out for you. I turned my self inside out. Can't you give me something? Something real, something I can hold in my hands for just a second?

BOOTS: Like what?

WOMAN: When you said you loved me, what did that mean?

BOOTS: There's a mole on your back, the one shaped like the Statue of Liberty.

WOMAN: Bullshit.

BOOTS: Well, like the torch part anyway. I loved that mole.

WOMAN: Not good enough.

(*Sirens are getting closer.*)

BOOTS: There was a way you dug your fingers into me when we made love.
Like you were gonna leave your prints on my bones. Like some kinda fossil.

WOMAN: You loved that?

BOOTS: Scared me.

WOMAN: Not good enough.

BOOTS: Baby, I used you, I'm sorry, you're here, I'm not, you're up on the
ground and walking around, I'm dead and bleeding and sinking into the
soggy soil right beneath your feet! NOW WHAT THE HELL I GOT YOU
WANT?

(*Woman screams. Boots scream. Sirens outside scream. Woman thrusts her hands into
the boots, still screaming. Suddenly, Woman and Boots aren't screaming — they're singing. As they sing, the Woman dances on all fours, her hands in the boots.*)

BOOTS:	WOMAN:
Sea-water body	*I am earthy*
These boots can't hold me	*I am raw*
Salt-fingers touching to your lips	*My man's in pieces*
Still we danced	*Down in the soggy soggy*
Always you drink me	*I am earthy*
Always you thirsty	*I am raw*
Can't get the water past your lips	*My man's in pieces*
Still we danced	*Still we danced*

(*Blue lights flow around the room. It looks like they're surrounded by an ocean of
water. Sound of waves crashing. Then pounding on the door. The blue lights speed
up — police lights. Woman rises, removes her hands from the boots. She picks up the
shovel. Pounding on the door. Woman stares defiantly out to the audience and stomps
the shovel to the floor. Blackout.*) ◄

END OF PLAY

Kristina Halvorson

Now We're Really Getting Somewhere

Characters

JEN, mid 20s. Cynical, unhappy.
BETHANY, mid 20s. Unhappy, trying hard not to be.
ELAINE, late 20s. Jen and Bethany's supervisor, trying hard in general.
JACK, late 20s. Sales guy. Nice enough.

Setting

At work.

Time

Today.

> *Lights up on a conference table. Jen is waiting for someone. Bethany walks in and proceeds to pile tons of office crap on the table — files, legal pads, water bottle, Diet Coke, coffee — is she here for a three-day summit? They barely look at each other, having already gone through their morning greetings earlier. They are waiting. Waiting.*

JEN: This sucks.
BETHANY: You always say that.
JEN: This always sucks.
BETHANY: You just need to adjust your expectations.
JEN: I don't think it's unreasonable to expect that the person who schedules these meetings would actually show up on time.
BETHANY: But she never does.
JEN: And, it sucks.
BETHANY: It could be worse.
JEN: That's how I should adjust my expectations? By thinking it could be worse?
BETHANY: Why not? Look. Elaine is late. And while she's late, I'm sitting here, happily chatting with my friend Jen and getting paid to do it. You, on the other hand, are all worked up over something that happens every single time we have our weekly meeting. Who's better off? Me. Why? Very low expectations.
JEN: Amazing.

BETHANY: You just need an attitude adjustment.

JEN: I need to have my attitude surgically removed.

(Elaine enters the room with her pile of meeting files.)

ELAINE: Good morning! Sorry I'm late.

BETHANY: No problem!

JEN: No problem.

ELAINE: So, how were your weekends?

BETHANY: SO great.

ELAINE: Great! Jen, how was yours?

JEN: Exhausting, short, awful.

ELAINE: *(Wasn't listening.)* Great.

BETHANY: Did you do anything fun?

ELAINE: Nope! So! Let's go ahead and get started.

BETHANY: *(Peeling an orange.)* Anybody want an orange? I have like twelve of them in my bag.

ELAINE: You know, before we begin, I should let you both know that I've asked Jack to join us for a few quick moments this morning.

JEN: *(Pause.)* Jack?

BETHANY: Sales Jack?

ELAINE: Well, of course sales Jack.

JEN: Sales Jack is coming here? Now?

BETHANY: But, this is our Monday morning meeting. OUR Monday morning meeting. I mean, this is supposed to be our safe place.

ELAINE: Well, you two brought up what I consider to be some very important issues last week, and I thought it would be beneficial for the four of us to begin a mutual dialogue.

BETHANY: But, Elaine, we hate him.

ELAINE: Oh, you do not.

BETHANY: Oh, yes. We do.

JEN: You just need to adjust your expectations.

BETHANY: I did. I can't adjust any lower with him.

ELAINE: So, while we're waiting for Jack, let's look at what's on everybody's plate this week.

JEN: Wait, what are we supposed to say to Jack?

ELAINE: Whatever you think will help.

JEN: Help what?

ELAINE: The situation.

JEN: Elaine, I'm sorry, but the situation is that he's totally incompetent, he makes our jobs impossible, and he should be fired.

ELAINE: I don't think that will help the situation.

BETHANY: I don't care if he's incompetent. I just hate him.

ELAINE: But what's behind that?

BETHANY: Yesterday, I had this really important question? So I e-mailed him, and I left him about twelve voice mails, and he never called me back. Just totally ignored me. He always does that.

JEN: He does.

BETHANY: I mean, he's sales, and we're customer support, right, but he never tells us anything that's going on until suddenly somebody calls with this out-of-control problem, and they're like, "Oh, Jack said I should just call you." Hello, I don't know what's going on, I've never even heard of them before, and obviously, I look like a total idiot. Oh, and the way he always calls us his "girls" — I mean, I'm not a feminist or anything, but that totally bugs. "Just call my girls, they'll take care of you." God! He makes me want to, I don't know, throw things, or, or shoot somebody.

JEN: Awesome. (*Pause.*) Sorry.

ELAINE: Well. It seems that perhaps the core issue here is actually a simple personality conflict.

JEN: Um. I like him OK.

ELAINE: Great!

JEN: He doesn't mean to be insensitive. I think he has a good heart.

ELAINE: Yes, I think he does.

JEN: I just think he's utterly incompetent and should be fired.

BETHANY: Or shot. (*Oops — puts her hands over her mouth.*)

ELAINE: OK. Let's talk facts. Jack is the sales specialist for our region, agreed. We are his assigned customer support specialists, agreed. Clearly we need to be able to work as a team, together. Agreed? I'm not asking you to *like* Jack . . . I'm just asking you to treat him with the respect he deserves, as a person who is doing his best. Right? You said it yourself, he has a good heart. He's doing the best that he can.

(*Bethany and Jen consider this. She's probably right.*)

ELAINE: We are all doing the best that we can.

BETHANY: I will do my best to be nice to Jack.

JEN: But we still need to talk about the stuff you were saying. Elaine, you're the team leader . . . just, please be sure to bring that stuff up, OK?

ELAINE: Absolutely.

(*Jack enters.*)

JACK: Good morning, ladies!

ELAINE: Jack! Good morning. Thanks for stopping by.

BETHANY AND JEN: Hey.

JACK: No problem. So, what I miss?

ELAINE: Oh, nothing, really, we've just been chatting about our weekends.

JACK: And how were they?

BETHANY: SO great.

ELAINE: Thanks for asking.

JACK: Jen, how was yours?

JEN: Fabulous. Thanks.

JACK: Great.

ELAINE: (*Pause.*) So. Jack. We thought it would be helpful for the four of us to talk this morning about a few different issues that have come up.

JACK: You have some issues.

ELAINE: Well, not ISSUES, issues.

JACK: Great.

ELAINE: Great. So, Jack. I've asked you here today because the three of us would like to chat about what it is we can do to help make your job easier. That is to say, what could we do to help make you as effective as possible at what you do?

JACK: That's awfully nice.

ELAINE: We're all on the same team. Your team.

JACK: Right.

BETHANY: (*Pause.*) I think what we kind of want to know is, is there anything we could be doing to *partner* with you, with the customers. It just seems like maybe, I don't know, maybe we should be working more closely together.

JACK: I'm not sure I'm following.

(*Bethany looks to Elaine for help. Elaine smiles blankly.*)

BETHANY: Um, well. Like when a customer has a problem, do you think that, I don't know, maybe you could tell us what's going on, you know, before they call us?

JACK: Sure!

BETHANY: Oh. Great.

JACK: Anything else?

JEN: (*Giving it a try.*) Jack. I guess maybe we're feeling like we should be more closely involved with the sales process from the start. And that way we can be more familiar with the customers and the specific issues they're facing . . .

JACK: (*Interrupts Jen after "customers."*) You know, no offense meant here, but after nearly ten years in professional sales, I think I can handle my customers. I just don't think your department really understands what all is involved in pre-sales, which is fine. That's why I'm in sales and you're in support, right? Sales is a multi-layered process that can't always be predicted or precisely measured. I really don't see where it is you feel you need to be "brought in."

BETHANY: But when you're working with the customers and they have a problem and you give them our number . . .

JACK: Exactly. It's great to know I can count on your team no matter what. Really, if I need anything, I'll let you know.

ELAINE: Perfect. Great.

JEN: I don't, um, I don't really feel like this exactly resolves what Bethany is getting at.

ELAINE: What else do you need to hear, Jen?

JEN: Well, Jack (*She's going to go for it.*) . . . do you like your job?

JACK: Sure. Sure, I like my job.

JEN: Because, well, we try really hard to help your customers, and well, I guess I don't see you trying very hard. At anything. Ever.

ELAINE: Now, Jen, let's not . . .

JEN: What I want to say here, Jack, is that what we don't, I don't really see in you is passion. For what you do.

JACK: I don't think passion was in my job description.

JEN: Well, obviously, but . . .

JACK: I sell telecommunications equipment to companies with two hundred and fifty employees or less. There's only so much to get excited about there.

ELAINE: Jack, Jen is certainly not questioning your commitment . . .

JEN: Let's take Bethany, here. Bethany is a customer support specialist for a telecommunications company. When people ask her what she does, and she tells them, they say, "That's great!" But they might be thinking, it would be within their rights to think, "Well, this person isn't exactly changing the world with that, now is she?" But the thing is, I think in Bethany's mind, she *is* changing something, doing some good for somebody. Let's say there's this one guy who's in, I don't know, Kenosha or something . . . this one guy is out there, trying his best daily to accomplish some stupid set of menial tasks, and every day he is absolutely counting on being able to pick up the phone that you sold him and knowing he can make a call. And one day, his phone, our phone, fails him. And that day, maybe Bethany talks to him, answers his questions, and fixes the problem. Now the phone works, and she's made one of the 10 million problems this guy has just because he's a human being go away. And knowing Bethany? She'll be grateful that she was given the opportunity to help.

  That kind of thinking. That's passion. That's what makes Bethany a great person — no, a great woman — to work with. Commitment. Cooperation. Common courtesy. That's what we want from our team members.

(*No one knows what to say. In the silence, Bethany chugs her entire Diet Coke and crushes the can with one hand.*)

ELAINE: Jack, we're on your team.

JACK: Right.

ELAINE: Aren't we, girls?

JEN: That's it? "Girls"?

ELAINE: Thanks so much for coming by this morning, Jack.

JEN: We're not going to talk about this?

ELAINE: We just did, and it's late, and Jack needs to get going.

JACK: Thanks, Elaine.

JEN: Amazing. Absolutely amazing.

ELAINE: Jen, we can continue this conversation . . .

JEN: You know, we always talk, and shit always comes up, and everyone is nice, and no one ever says anything because we don't want anything to disrupt this illusion we have of forward movement. Which, what does that mean anyway? What exactly are we measuring to determine movement? Do you even know?

ELAINE: We're all done here.

JEN: We are not done.

ELAINE: We're done, I say we're done.

JEN: You know, Bethany is convinced that Jack is the problem because he's so clued out 98 percent of the time, but it's really you. It's the way you just smile and nod and say we're all doing our best, we're all on the same team, we all need to respect each other —

ELAINE: Jen, let's try to keep our emotions under control . . .

JEN: You say, "We need to be patient, we need to stick together," and then nothing ever changes because you're so worried about pissing somebody off, like somehow that would move us backward if there were tension or conflict or God *forbid* someone got angry . . .

ELAINE: You know, don't blame me because you're an unhappy person. I like my job here. I like coming in to a place every day where I know everyone is nice, and professional, and respectful, and we all like each other.

JEN: And nothing ever changes, does it, Elaine?

ELAINE: What is so wrong with things the way they are? Why does anything need to change?

JEN: Oh, you're right. Shitty sales, fucked-up nonexistent communication, general mediocrity everywhere you turn, what's wrong with that?

ELAINE: Oh, and you are so much better than that.

JEN: No, Elaine, I'm not. I'm shitty and I'm mediocre. But I don't want to be. I want to be passionate. I want to be inspired. I want to know that what I do means something, that there is an effect, a shift, even a goddamn ripple . . .

ELAINE: But listen to me, Jen. As your team leader, I'm telling you, there is. You contribute. You make a difference. I'm telling you, you matter.

JEN: But I don't respect you.

(*Stunned silence. Elaine musters what little remaining dignity she can, picks up her pile of files and legal pads, and walks out.*)

JACK: Hey, 9:30 already? Whoa, time flies when you're having fun. So. I guess I'll just see you around. Jen? For what it's worth . . . I think you're doing a great job. (*Jack exits. Bethany and Jen sit together. Finally, Bethany gathers up her crap and simply exits. Jen sits at the table and begins to recite to herself, perhaps adding movement or volume as it builds.*)

JEN: I'm doing the best that I can. I'm doing the best that I can. I'm doing the best that I can. I'm doing the best that I can. ◄

END OF PLAY

Adam Kraar

Love on the B-Line

Characters

MARIE, 28
ROBBIE, 28

Place

An elevated subway station in Brooklyn

Time

The present. Late summer.

> [*A deserted, elevated train station. Enter* MARIE, *28, and* ROBBIE, *28.*]

ROBBIE: Here we are again. My home away from home.
MARIE: Look, over the water tower: Mars!

> [*Pause.*]

> Robbie.

ROBBIE: What?
MARIE: [*Kindly.*]

> When the train comes, you stay.

ROBBIE: It's 2 A.M. You think I'm going to let you go home alone?
MARIE: You're such a gentleman. And you're very sweet. Your neck drives me crazy.

> [MARIE *starts to kiss* ROBBIE'S *neck.*]

ROBBIE: ... Let me be.

MARIE: [*Gently.*]

Don't be like that.

ROBBIE: It's just ... I mean ... This ... situation—

MARIE: [*For the fourth time tonight*]

I can't stay over your house.

ROBBIE: Why not?

MARIE: I told you.

ROBBIE: Why can't your father feed the cat?

MARIE: Because he only eats if I feed him.

[ROBBIE *shakes his head in disbelief.*]

Hey. Don't you love that breeze?

ROBBIE: It smells up here.

MARIE: You didn't think it smelled when you wrote me that poem.

ROBBIE: That was in April. Over a hundred subway rides ago.

MARIE: So you don't think I'm the brightest star in Brooklyn anymore?

ROBBIE: I do! I just—

MARIE: You once loved riding the train with me. I have it in writing.

[MARIE *crosses to an advertising poster on which* ROBBIE *had once written her a poem.*]

See?

[*She reads the poem.*]

"When I ride with you, I'm not riding through Brooklyn
I'm on an open-air streetcar, gliding past the palazzi of Sicily
With the brightest star of the Mediterranean Sea: Marie."

ROBBIE: You are, but—

MARIE: And when the lights went out between 36th Street and Pacific?
Was that so bad?

ROBBIE: It was great.

[MARIE *kisses him passionately.* ROBBIE *responds for a couple of moments, but then:*]
I just don't understand how one night Fluffball can't skip dinner.

He's not a thin cat.

MARIE: He depends on me.

ROBBIE: I do too.

MARIE: You do?

ROBBIE: Yes!

[*Pause.*]

MARIE: [*Changing the subject.*]

I remember taking this line out to Coney Island, when I was a kid, and when the train came out the tunnel, you could look right inside the windows of people's houses. I felt like we'd come up out of the ground into another planet. My brothers would open the windows of the train, and you could smell every kitchen and every parlor in South Brooklyn. Like, garlic and hot sugar . . . dough, Old Spice . . .

ROBBIE: How old were you?

MARIE: It was before my mother passed, so I musta been four. The ride seemed to go on for days.

ROBBIE: I know what that's like. . . . That ride home, after dropping you off. Seems to go on forever. There's no one on the train, and I start to think there's no motorman, no conductor, no stops. The clacking gets louder and louder. I try to remember the smell of your hair, of your shoulder. But it seems like a dream. Like a foolish dream.

MARIE: Aw, Robbie.

ROBBIE: Stay.

MARIE: Aww.

ROBBIE: Stay.

MARIE: I wanna stay . . .

ROBBIE: Then?

MARIE: I can't.

ROBBIE: I don't believe it's 'cause of your cat.

MARIE: Oh?

ROBBIE: There's obviously some issue we're not dealing with. Your father doesn't like me. He gave your brothers this look, when I was talking about my job—

MARIE: They don't understand what you do. To them, you're like E.T. They never met anybody from Virginia before. Who cares? I love hearing about the Historical Society.

   [*Beat.*]

ROBBIE: Maybe you don't respect me enough to stay over. You have your way with me, get a second helping of scalloped potatoes, and then you leave.

MARIE: You're the only man I ever knew who makes such a big deal about stayin' over.

ROBBIE: I'm so tired. There's a sleep I've been imagining for three months, when the night goes on and on and on, and there's nobody else in the world. The dreams I dream of having—but I never do.

MARIE: [*Sympathetically.*]
   Robbie . . .

ROBBIE: My whole life I've been dreaming of that kind of sleep. If only you'd just stay tonight.

MARIE: I'm sorry.

ROBBIE: Why?! . . . Because your father thinks I'm not good enough for you, so you don't really want to be with me, in a fundamental way—

MARIE: Come here.

[MARIE *takes him over to the bench, makes him sit down, sits next to him, and then pushes his head onto her shoulder.*]

ROBBIE: It's not the same.

MARIE: Shhh.

ROBBIE: This bench is going to give me sciatica—

MARIE: Shut up and close your eyes. Shut 'em—or I'll shut 'em for you.

[*Slight pause. He closes his eyes. She sings.*]

"Hush, bambino, close your eyes
Stardust's falling from the skies
The birds have all said good night—"

ROBBIE: Marie—

MARIE: [*Sings.*]
"Close your eyes, bambino, dormi."

ROBBIE: Marie: I love you.

MARIE: Aw, Robbie . . .

ROBBIE: Am I always going to be waiting for the next train?

MARIE: Close your eyes.—God, you're handsome.—Now just pretend we're in your bed. You can smell the garlic, the crisp new curtains, the Minwax . . . and us. And that Coney Island air. And you're lying on my shoulder, on the beach, on a cloud.

ROBBIE: [*Half-asleep.*] There's no one else?

MARIE: Just us.

[*After a moment,* Robbie *starts snoring.*]

Robbie? . . . You really asleep? . . . Wow . . . What am I gonna do with you? Don't you know I love you too? I would crawl into bed with you and sleep with you forever, if only . . .

ROBBIE: . . . Mom?

MARIE: Sure, it's Mom. Now sleep.

[*Pause.* Robbie *wakes with a start.*]

ROBBIE: Ah!!!

MARIE: It's okay.

ROBBIE: No. It's not.

MARIE: What were you dreaming?

ROBBIE: The train. Always the train.

MARIE: Oh.

ROBBIE: Come home with me. You're spending the night.

MARIE: No, I'm not.

ROBBIE: Either come home with me, or . . .

MARIE: Or what?

ROBBIE: Or give me a credible explanation. Not Fluffball.

MARIE: I don't do ultimatums, Robbie.

ROBBIE: Okay. Okay. Okay.

MARIE: What's that s'posed to mean?

ROBBIE: I can't do this anymore.

MARIE: I can ride the subway alone. I'm a big girl.

> [ROBBIE *shakes his head.*]

ROBBIE: I just can't.

> [ROBBIE *crosses away from her.*]

MARIE: What? What?

ROBBIE: I'll take you home tonight, but then . . . that's it.

MARIE: You're dumping me. On 25th Avenue. I really—! . . . Just go home.
      I don't need you.

> [ROBBIE *goes to a bench and sits down to wait for the train. Beat.* MARIE *takes out a
> cigarette and lights it.*]

ROBBIE: You told me you gave it up.

MARIE: You told me you loved me.

ROBBIE: I do. But it seems like . . . the train only goes in one direction.

> [*She smokes.*]

When you smoke . . .

MARIE: What?

ROBBIE: It's not attractive.

> [MARIE *angrily puts several cigarettes in her mouth, and one up each of her nostrils,
> then goes to* ROBBIE *and starts to light them.*]

Stop that.

> [Robbie *grabs the cigarettes out of her mouth and nose, and throws them away.*]

MARIE: Hey!

> [*She slaps his face.*]

God!

> [*Slaps him again.*]

You're impossible! Do you realize how freakin' impossible you are? And you
look at me with those eyes, what am I s'posed to do?

ROBBIE: Well . . .

MARIE: If I stayed over your house . . .

ROBBIE: Yes, things would change. We'd learn things about each other. God knows what could happen. But it would be better. It has to be.

MARIE: I been seeing you five months and four days. And you wanna . . .

ROBBIE: Could we at least have a time-table?

MARIE: No!

ROBBIE: Give me a hint. A sign? A light at the end of the tunnel.

MARIE: I thought I was your light.

ROBBIE: Am I yours? Do I do anything more for you than drive you crazy?

MARIE: God. You're gonna make me say it, aren't you? But if I say it, I can't ever get it back. I'm not gonna say it, not yet.

ROBBIE: Why not??!

MARIE: I don't ever . . . wanna live in a cage.

ROBBIE: Of course not! I know you're a wild bird, I love that. I just want to be with you.

MARIE: One year ago I was . . . You wouldn'ta recognized me.

ROBBIE: What do you mean?

MARIE: . . . I locked myself in a cage. Lost the key, and forgot I was in a cage. Smoked two packs a day, ate ravioli out of the can. Drank wine right from the box, and had conversations with Chef Boyardee. I wasn't livin' at my father's; I was on Lorimer Street, a very dark place. With rusty bars on the windows. I had been waitin' for someone . . . who was obviously never coming back, except it wasn't obvious to me.

[*Beat.*]

It was only when I started seeing you. . . . I felt free again. I love ridin' the train with you. The ride out here, the elevated tracks, the breeze. The way you look at me.

[*Beat.*]

I have this way . . . of losing myself, of taking care of guys so good — and I love taking care of you — but . . . I can't — I won't — go back to Lorimer Street. Or any place where I lose myself that way again.

. . . I can't stay over your house. And I can't say when I'm gonna.

I'm just . . .

ROBBIE: It's okay.

MARIE: It's okay?

ROBBIE: Yeah.

[*They go to each other.* MARIE *sprinkles his face with kisses.*]

MARIE: I never touched a cigarette for the past three months. I swear.

[MARIE *throws away her pack of cigarettes.*]

ROBBIE: Tell me about the time you got caught smoking in school.

[Marie *sits next to* Robbie *on the bench, and pushes his head onto her shoulder.*]

MARIE: It was second period. Williamsburg Middle School. People had been smokin' in that girls' room for thirty-five years — the windows were actually yellow from all the nicotine. And there was this new vice principal, Mr. Ventolieri, who'd lost his sense of smell during Vietnam. So we're in there, puffin' away, when there's this loud knock on the door . . .

[*We hear a train slowly screeching towards the station.* ROBBIE *turns to look at the oncoming train and, after a moment, stands up.* MARIE *looks at* ROBBIE *and then also gets up and stands next to him, taking his hand, as they wait for the train to pull into the station. Blackout.*] ◄

END OF PLAY

K. Alexa Mavromatis

Bone China

Characters

MARY: twenty-seven
LAINIE: Mary's sister, twenty-nine

Setting

The attic of Mary and Lainie's childhood home, filled with boxes, random items on shelves, old furniture, clothing racks, etc.

Time

Saturday, mid-afternoon

As the lights come up, we see Mary upstage center, standing in the doorway of the attic. She is watching Lainie, who sits upstage centre right, surrounded by boxes of random items from storage and assorted remnants of their childhood: Barbie dolls, stuffed animals, Sassy *magazines, popsicle-stick art projects, neckties, paperback books, etc. Lainie is repeatedly tapping a Magic Eight Ball on the floor to remove the bubbles from the ball, and flipping it over to "answer" her questions. Lainie wears a scarf on her head.*

MARY: What are you doing?

LAINIE: Just going through all this freaky stuff.

MARY: (*Crossing to Lainie, then kneeling.*) What's that?

LAINIE: (*Holding up a misshapen furry lump.*) I think it was a stuffed animal . . . once.

MARY: I don't remember him.

LAINIE: Well, he was either mine or yours.

MARY: What is . . . *was* he?

LAINIE: I have no idea, poor thing.

MARY: Why would Mom hang on to that?

LAINIE: Mom kept everything—c'mon. Put him over there. That's the "go" pile.

MARY: (*Throwing the animal on the pile, downstage center left.*) You don't have to do this.

LAINIE: I know.

(*Handing Mary a small china teacup—the kind from a child's play set—from a box.*)

Do you remember these?

MARY: Oh yeah. It says "Bone China" on here . . . Isn't that really good?

LAINIE: It's the strongest . . .

MARY: (*Digging through box.*) That's kind of fancy for little kids . . .

LAINIE: That was Mom.

MARY: There aren't any more cups in here. But here's the sugar . . .

LAINIE: *Someone* broke them.

MARY: Me? No!

LAINIE: Yes.

MARY: I did not.

LAINIE: (*Placing cup on top of an unopened box, center.*) And now this one's the sole survivor.

MARY: How many were there?

LAINIE: Like six or something.

MARY: There were not.

LAINIE: Yes . . .

MARY: Really?

LAINIE: (*Crossing downstage right to small stack of boxes, and grabbing another box to sort.*) I remember when Laurie Jennings was over one time you kept running into my room and grabbing them one by one and running away. I thought you were hiding them.

MARY: I do *not* remember that.

LAINIE: You were probably throwing them off the roof or something.

MARY: OK, enough. Are you going to be up here the whole weekend?

LAINIE: I dunno.

MARY: You shouldn't spend your whole weekend this way.

LAINIE: It's kind of fun. It kind of gives you a snapshot of Mom's head.

MARY: Scary place.

LAINIE: Mary . . .

MARY: I know. I'm kidding. You know I loved Mom.

LAINIE: I know.

> (*Slight pause.*)

MARY: I can't believe that was two years ago.

LAINIE: Yeah. I'm really glad you've been able to be here with Dad.

MARY: Me too.

LAINIE: I mean it. He's glad you're here. It's been hard for him.

MARY: I know.

LAINIE: I can't help but feel a little bad . . .

MARY: Why?

LAINIE: You haven't had a chance to lead your own life. I got sick right after you graduated college. Then Mom. Now . . .

MARY: I don't even want to talk about this, Lainie, really . . .

LAINIE: But I worry about you.

MARY: (*Standing.*) Do you want to go for a walk or something?

LAINIE: No, I'm good.

MARY: A movie?

LAINIE: Seriously, Mary, I'm having a good time . . . It's fine.

MARY: I just . . .

LAINIE: You should help me.

MARY: I don't think . . .

LAINIE: I know—you don't think I should waste a weekend this way.

MARY: No, I don't.

LAINIE: Especially now that my weekends are numbered.

MARY: Lainie!

LAINIE: I know you were thinking that. What if I want to spend my weekend going through stuff in the attic? Because I'm glad to have a chance to do it?

MARY: OK, OK.

LAINIE: You should help me . . .

MARY: OK.

LAINIE: . . . and stop giving me a hard time.

MARY: OK.

LAINIE: I'm fine.

MARY: Alright. Jeez. Have you seen my blue coat up here?

> (*Crosses upstage to the door, and shuts it to look behind it.*)

The last time I saw it, it was behind . . .

LAINIE: (*Jumping up.*) Wait!

MARY: What?

LAINIE: Can you open the door?

MARY: (*Frozen.*) Oh shit!

LAINIE: That's why we always leave this door open.

MARY: I know—fuck, I forgot.

LAINIE: Can you open the door?

MARY: (*Trying to open the door.*) No.

LAINIE: We'll have to wait until Dad gets home, then—unless the screwdriver's still on top of the molding . . .

(*Mary feels the frame above the door.*)

MARY: Nope.

LAINIE: Crap.

MARY: Sorry. I remember that day Dad got shut up here and had to wait for us to get back from shopping. Now.

LAINIE: It's OK.

(*Mary crosses right to a small pile of items Lainie has sorted and has decided to keep. Lainie surveys the room and crosses to a small sofa covered by a sheet, left. She sits and takes a few items out of a box that has been sitting on the sofa—a book, a toy rocket, a purse. Lost in thought, she mumbles something.*)

MARY: What?

LAINIE: Nothing.

MARY: What were you going to say?

LAINIE: Just going through all this stuff . . . I was thinking I'm glad Mom's dead.

MARY: Lainie!

LAINIE: No, I mean, I'm not actually glad Mom is dead—you know that. I'm just . . . I'm just glad she didn't have to see me go through surgery this time.

MARY: Yeah.

LAINIE: I remember, one time at the hospital . . .

(*Shifting to sit on the arm of the sofa.*)

I just think it's hard for parents to watch their kids go through stuff like that. Especially since the prognosis isn't, uh, so good now . . . Of course, that means Sarah won't grow up knowing her mother or her grandmother.

MARY: (*Crossing to Lainie and sitting on a small stool right of the sofa.*) But she'll have Nathan, and Dad . . .

LAINIE: And you.

MARY: Yeah.

LAINIE: It's weird. I mean we lost Mom, and we didn't plan for it. We *couldn't* plan for it—a drunk guy crossed over the center line and that was it. Now, we get to plan. I get to think about places I want to go to, people I want to see . . . stuff that's supposed to be fun to think about. Do you know what I mean? It's fucked up.

MARY: Do you know what you're going to tell Sarah?

LAINIE: She's too young, really. To understand. That's something Nathan's going to have to deal with later.

MARY: He'll do great.

LAINIE: I know. He's an amazing dad. Listen, just don't ever tell Sarah "Your Mommy went to sleep" or anything weird like that, OK? You're not supposed to do that.

MARY: I won't.

LAINIE: It'll mess her up—she'll need a night-light until she's twenty-five or something. Tell her . . . just tell her that mommy went to heaven and is looking out for her or something . . . But don't say I'm *watching* her—that sounds creepy.

(*Slight pause.*)

MARY: Do you believe in heaven?

LAINIE: I dunno. You know, to tell you the truth: I'm twenty-nine years old, I'm leaving a husband I thought I'd get old with, a two-year-old daughter . . . Heaven is about the last thing I want to spend time thinking about now.

MARY: Yeah.

LAINIE: In fact, it kind of makes me mad that it's what I'm *expected* to think about now

(*Pause, as Lainie crosses downstage right to boxes, pulls out a poster and throws it on the "go" pile. She continues to look through the box, distracted.*) She won't remember me, you know.

MARY: Don't say that! Of course . . .

LAINIE: No, she won't. And I'm not trying to be humble or melodramatic or whatever. I read this big thing about it online. The average age of your first memory is three-and-a-half.

MARY: Really?

LAINIE: What's your first memory?

MARY: (*Shifting from the stool to the sofa.*) Grandpa Jack's funeral.

LAINIE: See? I was six, so you were four-ish.

MARY: What's yours?

LAINIE: I was trying to think of that when I was reading. It's not a memory, exactly . . . well, it is, but it's not a specific event or anything. I think the first thing I remember is standing outside in the backyard, with the tulips. I remember thinking they were really tall.

(*Slight pause.*)

Anyway, it was this whole study . . . It's a lack of autobiographical memory. At that age. Sometimes, very young children will remember major life events—like Grandpa jack's funeral—but some best-case scenario for a first memory of your mom, huh?

MARY: You just have to make every day a major life event.

LAINIE: (*Laughing slightly.*) Yeah, no pressure. You're such an optimist. You want to hear something funny?

MARY: What?

LAINIE: My tumor — the one with the long-ass name I still can't pronounce right — can take three to five years to grow to the size it was when they removed it. That means I had it when I was pregnant with Sarah. I was growing life and death at the same time. Crazy, huh?

MARY: Yeah. Crazy.

LAINIE: I've been thinking too much. They should have taken out my entire brain. No more reading, though. I was telling Nathan the other day I'm declaring a moratorium on research. *That's* what wears you down. (*Slight pause.*) I have to ask you something.

MARY: Anything.

LAINIE: Did you ever make out with Tommy Marcum?

MARY: What?!

LAINIE: Did you?

MARY: He was your boyfriend!

LAINIE: (*Crossing toward the sofa.*) I know. Did you ever make out with him?

MARY: (*Turning away.*) No.

LAINIE: (*Crossing behind sofa.*) Are you sure?

MARY: I would never do that while you were seeing him.

LAINIE: Aha — but you did when I went to away to college, didn't you?

MARY: (*Standing up and crossing right.*) Why are you asking me that?

LAINIE: (*Following Mary, grabbing a necktie from the "go" pile and wrapping it around her hands, threatening.*) Sonia told me the truth, but I didn't believe her.

MARY: What business was it of hers?

LAINIE: When I die, I'll automatically know the truth, you know, so you may as well tell me now . . .

(*Lainie "catches" Mary around the waist with the tie upstage center, and laughs maniacally.*)

MARY: (*Trying to free herself.*) Stop it! Besides, I was only sixteen.

LAINIE: (*Not letting Mary go, pulling the tie tighter.*) Ah — confession!

MARY: God, he was a creep anyway. He told all his stupid friends I wouldn't let him stick his hand down my pants . . .

LAINIE: Mary!

MARY: . . . *after* I slept with him.

LAINIE: (*Releasing the tie.*) You *slept* with him?!

MARY: Kidding!

LAINIE: Thank God.

MARY: Not even close. (*Pause.*) What made you think of that?

(*Lainie crosses to her "keep" pile and holds up their high school yearbook.*)

MARY: God, no!

LAINIE: Yes!

MARY: (*Reaching for the book.*) Give me that!

LAINIE: No!

MARY: That was the worst picture ever taken of me, ever!

LAINIE: (*Sitting down by her "keep" pile, right, and thumbing through the yearbook.*) What page? Let me see . . .

(*Something in an open box catches Mary's eye as she moves toward Lainie to grab the yearbook.*)

MARY: Oh my God, you're going to like what I just found better.

LAINIE: What?

(*Mary holds up the screwdriver.*)

LAINIE: No way!

MARY: And look what else.

(*Mary holds up a small teacup, the mate of the other, and, kneeling, places it on the box next to the first cup, center.*)

It's a tea party after all.

(*Lights fade to black.*) ◀

END OF PLAY

A Few Words about Getting Your Work Published and Produced

Chances are that sooner or later—and often after much frustration and revision—you are going to feel as though you've written something that deserves a wider audience than your teacher and classmates, your family and friends. If the time comes when you want to share your work with the world, you'll be looking to get published, either in print or online.

Publishing your poems, stories, and essays ▶

If you have a strong poem, story, or essay, and your school has a literary magazine, that's often a good place for a first publication. Many school literary journals and online magazines are handsomely designed, and obviously the competition among potential contributors is much less than if you were competing against writers from all over the country.

While you may think the logical first step on the road to publication is securing the services of a literary agent, that's not the case. Unless you have an incredibly sensational story to tell, or you've secretly been honing your craft for a long time, most agents want you to have a track record of publication before they even *think* of representing you. They get paid a percentage of the money their writers make, and they will be uninterested in taking on clients who are likely to be minimal earners in their early years.

Instead, if you decide to go beyond the boundaries of your institution of higher learning, start by consulting a directory of literary journal listings to find out which magazines print creative writing. In the long-ago days before the Internet, writers turned to print sources like *Poet's Market* and the *Novel and Short Story Writer's Market* (Writers Digest Books) and *The International Directory of Little Magazines and Small Presses* (Dustbooks). These books provide solid and detailed advice about the process of submitting literary work, and they remain valid ways of checking out potential markets: the listings explain editorial biases, describe the physical appearance of a journal, provide circulation numbers and reporting time, and let the writer know the percentage of manuscripts accepted each year.

Online listings, however, have made these books less necessary than they once were. Obviously Web sites may disappear overnight, but among the most reliable online directories of publishing venues are the "Literary Magazines" listings in *Poets and Writers Magazine* (pw.org/literary_magazines), *Duotrope's Digest* (duotrope.com), and the Council of Literary Magazines and Presses (clmp.org). The advantages of Web-based directories are their cost (free), the currency of their listings, and the immediate access they provide through hyperlinks to the publishers' Web sites.

One question you're likely to ask early on is whether to seek online or print publication, but there's no need to stick to just one, and literary writers now often submit to a combination of Web and paper journals.

Each format has advantages and disadvantages. Producing a good-looking digital journal is far cheaper than printing a comparable hard-copy issue, and the best Webzines often have a polished appearance that their print counterparts can only envy. Online journals are also available to everyone with an Internet connection, so the potential audience for your writing is much greater than it would be in even a large-circulation print magazine. That said, most online literary journals aren't read any more widely than their print counterparts. Moreover, the ephemeral nature of online publishing means that a publisher may decide to close up shop without notice, and everything published in the e-zine suddenly vanishes. When that happens, writers may wonder if they can still consider themselves "published" now that their work no longer appears on the Internet.

That problem doesn't exist with print magazines. Your poem or story may appear in an edition of just 500 copies, but those copies aren't going to disappear if the publisher goes out of business. You'll always have a paper souvenir of your publication. And because even a small run of a print journal generally costs at least a few thousand dollars to produce, there is a certain prestige attached to print publication that may still be lacking from online sources. Most print journals now have a Web site, which — in addition to providing current submission guidelines — typically also posts at least a few sample pieces from the current and past issues of the journal, one of which may be yours.

Fortunately, for beginning writers, there are thousands of places to publish work. Indeed, the sheer number of possibilities may initially appear overwhelming. Don't let that scare you off. Once you've found a directory that suits you, take your time and browse. Not every magazine is for every writer, and you'll soon discover that there are some very specialized publishers, from those that want work from writers only in certain regions of the country, to others that focus solely on writing about specific subject matter, to magazines that specialize in particular literary forms. This market research is particularly important for beginning writers, although, as George Core, the editor of the *Sewanee Review*, acknowledges, "anything good enough is likely to be accepted, even if it should violate various sacred guidelines."

As you decide whether to submit to a journal, look for the percentage of submitted manuscripts that are actually published. The editors of long-established magazines like *The New Yorker* and the *Atlantic*, for example, accept only a fraction of 1 percent of the poems and stories sent to them. If you were to send your work only to these first-tier journals, you would probably be in for a world of discouragement. Granted, an acceptance by an exclusive magazine would represent a phenomenal start to your career. However, when you are just starting out, you shouldn't expect to become famous overnight. Choose newer journals that don't receive a flood of submissions and that do indicate they are actively seeking to publish new writers.

The process of submission varies from journal to journal — one more reason to pay careful attention to the listings for the magazines to which you are submitting. Generally, though, you will write a *short* cover letter introducing yourself and stating that the work you are enclosing has not been published before. The work itself should include your name and address in a prominent place on the first page of a story or essay and on every individual poem. Many writers also include their phone numbers and e-mail addresses. Nearly all magazines provide a maximum number of poems — usually three to six — that can be submitted or a maximum word or page count for prose. Take this number seriously if you want your submission to be taken seriously.

If the journal asks for a print submission, you usually need to include a self-addressed stamped, envelope (SASE), which is folded and slipped inside the original envelope. Be aware of how much a postal submission weighs. You can usually mail a cover letter, an SASE, and two or three poems for the price of a first class-stamp. After that, you'll need to pay more. If your submission arrives with insufficient postage, chances are strong that it will never be read.

Editors requesting e-mail submissions typically indicate whether they prefer the work to be sent as an attachment or pasted into the body of the message. Editors can be quite persnickety about such things, so, again, it is essential that you read the journal's listing carefully before submitting your work.

One way of maximizing your chances of publication is to simultaneously submit the same piece to a number of journals. If you do that, make certain that the publisher condones this practice — nearly always this will be stated explicitly in the submission guidelines — and if you have a piece accepted by one journal, be sure to contact the others immediately by e-mail to withdraw the piece that was accepted elsewhere. Publishing the same work in two different journals is considered a serious breach of trust by most editors; there are even rumors of a "blacklist" circulating among editors with the names of writers who have tried to double up on a publication without the editors' permission. If a magazine refuses to accept simultaneous submissions, honor that policy.

Recently, both electronic and print journals have begun turning to online submission managers. These managers allow writers to post their work on a Web site where it can be evaluated by the editors without their ever having to print out copies or meet together in the same physical space. Usually you will be required to register for each new journal, although once you are registered, subsequent submissions to that journal are much quicker. One of these online managers, Submittable.com, requires you to register only once; then all submissions to journals subscribing to this service access the same personal information.

Some journals charge for the convenience of online submissions, but many writers and teachers of writing, and I am one of them, maintain that writers should not have to pay to have their work considered by the editor of a magazine. Most print journals pay only with "contributor's copies" of the issue in which your work has appeared. Cash payment at the beginning level, whether in print or online, is rare. Why should writers pay for the chance to be published when they won't be compensated even if their work is accepted?

That said, journals nearly always operate on a shoestring budget, and you should do what you can to support them. Editors of print journals often ask that potential contributors purchase a sample copy before submitting. This serves the dual purpose of boosting the magazine's sales and giving the submitter an idea of the type of work that the magazine publishes. Online journals will naturally want you to read through a few of their recent issues to be certain your aesthetic matches theirs.

After you've taken the time and trouble to submit your thoroughly revised and carefully proofread work, you'll inevitably want an immediate response. Regrettably, that rarely happens. The best literary magazines receive thousands of submissions a month, and it takes even a large and dedicated staff a good deal of time to read through all that work. Be patient, and *don't* pester publishers with questions about how soon they'll be making a decision on your work. Remember that most of them are working for free and are doing the best they can: they resent your implying otherwise.

When you finally do hear back from a journal, you'll need to be prepared for the most likely outcome of any submission: rejection. Often that takes the form of a brief e-mail or a generic photocopied note on a small slip of paper informing you that while the editors appreciate your submission, they cannot use it a this time. There may be no indication that your work has been read by a living human being other than the word "Sorry" someone has scribbled at the bottom of a note or typed at the end of an e-mail.

Don't let rejection get you down. Every writer gets rejected, and every writer who believes in himself or herself turns around and submits again. Quitting isn't an option if you want to be published.

Indeed, rejection is the dark door at the center of creative writing through which all who hope to survive must pass. Even the most successful writers have been rejected many times, and developing a healthy attitude toward rejection is essential to every writer. "Success is distant and illusory," Joyce Carol Oates points out, "failure one's loyal companion, one's stimulus for imagining the next book will be better, for, otherwise, why write?"

Rejection notices run the gamut from the very brief—like the one described above—to elaborate apologies and explanations about why, this time, the writer's piece could not be printed. Interestingly, many letters of rejection are longer than letters of acceptance, and if you receive the former, consider how much time an editor has invested in commenting on your work. Often these encouraging letters of rejection ask you to submit again and mark the beginning of a writer-editor relationship that ultimately leads to publication. Some writers save their rejection letters in a box, some burn them, some even paper their walls with them. This last act, a fascinating combination of despair (Everyone hates me!) and chutzpah (But I don't care!), suggests something of the difficult balance a working writer must adopt toward publication. At one time there was even a literary journal that accepted only manuscripts that had already been rejected (a rejection notice had to accompany all submissions).

The lesson here is that there are different levels of rejection, and experienced writers come to distinguish among them. They learn to recognize the important fact that not everyone will be a fan of their work; that race, class, gender, artistic predilections, and whether an editor is having a bad day all affect the likelihood of publication. As writer Sue Lick puts it, "I try to tell myself manuscripts are like shoes. If I were selling shoes, I would expect a lot of people to walk by without buying them or even trying them on. Writing is the same way. It usually takes more than one submission to find the publication for which the manuscript fits perfectly." The smartest writers also use rejection letters as an opportunity to meditate on their writing. Does a pattern of editorial commentary emerge over time? Perhaps editors keep remarking, *Your characters are unconvincing*, or, *You need to tighten the lines of your poems*. If so, how much of this commentary is the editors' inability to recognize your individual style, and how much does the criticism reflect real problems you need to address?

Ultimately, it is how one handles rejection that determines whether one will continue on as a creative writer. The initial impulse may be to retreat. However, experienced writers learn to disconnect criticism of the work from criticism of the writer: rejection of the work is not equivalent to rejection of one*self*. Poet Michael Dennis Browne lauds the work of psychotherapist Thomas Moore in helping writers overcome their sense of failure. Moore writes:

> Ordinary failures in work are an inevitable part of the descent of the spirit into human limitation. Failure is a mystery, not a problem. Of course this means not that we should try to fail, or to take masochistic delight

in mistakes, but that we should see the mystery of incarnation at play whenever our work doesn't measure up to our expectations. If we could understand the feelings of inferiority and humbling occasioned by failure as meaningful in their own right, then we might incorporate failure into our work so that it doesn't literally devastate us.

Discovering how to deal with rejection gracefully, to *learn* from it, makes us more human. And since all writers get rejected, at least in this one instance we're all in it together.

Producing your ten-minute play ▶

Dramatists nearly always seek a production of their play before they even consider publication. A play, after all, doesn't really come alive unless it's on the stage, and, in any case, most theatrical publishers won't consider a play unless it's been produced. Luckily, many small theaters are actively looking for new plays and are willing to read unagented scripts. Since most theaters have a Web page, playwrights may find it easiest to get in touch with artistic directors by e-mail, which should include a short description of the play, a brief statement of the playwright's credentials, and possibly the script itself. *Dramatists Sourcebook* (Theatre Communications Group) remains a fount of good information for playwrights, although much more current theaters' calls for scripts can be found online at sites like NYCPlaywrights (nycp.blogspot.com), the Burry Man Writers Center (burryman.com/submissons), the Loop (thelooponline.net), the American Association of Community Theatre (aact.org), and elsewhere.

The most prestigious festival of ten-minute plays is at the annual Humana Festival of New American Plays, produced by the Actors Theatre of Louisville, Kentucky. Anyone can submit a play, regardless of whether it has been produced, although the company stops accepting scripts once they have reached 500. A production here would guarantee a playwright instant recognition, but Humana isn't the only venue for ten-minute plays. Every year there are dozens and dozens of such festivals held throughout Canada and the United States.

If you are fortunate enough to find someone interested in producing your play, you'll need to face the inevitability of losing some, or all, control over that production. Ten-minute play festivals are generally organized by theater companies—that is, by a collaboration of enthusiastic individuals, who may or may not hope to do more than break even financially. These companies take on the role of producers, the people who invest in a play and take ultimate responsibility for—as their name implies—ensuring that an actual production takes place. Generally producers have quite a lot of power. They are likely to be responsible for hiring a director. They may push for certain actors to get certain parts. They probably have a say in everything from the lighting to the set design.

If you're lucky, the company will match you with a director who shares your vision of your script. Traditionally, the director is the mediator among the playwright, the production company, and the actors. Once your script leaves your hands, it will immediately become something other than what you intended it to be — perhaps something better, perhaps something worse. "The thrilling experience for the writer," according to Wallace Shawn, is that the director and actors come up with "something that you never could have imagined." Another playwright, Maria Irene Fornes, echoes this sentiment. She advises directors of her work to "read the play, listen to the play and let the play tell them what it's all about." Once they have done so, she loves "being surprised as long as what they are doing is good."

Ideally, staging a play is a collaborative process among the playwright, the director, and the actors, with each serving, in Stuart Spencer's words, as a "humble servant" of the play. In this model, the director helps the playwright realize the potential of her or his play by maximizing the available resources — the stage, set, lighting and sound effects, props, costumes — and working closely and intensely with the actors to bring out the best performance each of them is capable of giving. The director is like a midwife helping the playwright give birth to the play.

This process can also be confrontational. One book on the subject, edited by Jeane Lueve, is entitled *Playwright versus Director*. In this version of the relationship, both parties claim to know what's best for the script, and each of them seriously doubts the ability of the other to see its true merits. Both the playwright and the director fight constantly for control, with the rehearsal and production process becoming essentially a battleground between two adversaries.

Although the first model is clearly preferable, playwrights quickly learn that the theater is a place of few certainties. If there is a tussle, whose vision will predominate: the playwright's or the director's? In film, the director has the final word on just about everything, and he or she receives the final credit, or blame, for the film's reception. The screenwriter in movies is almost an afterthought. A director who doesn't like the script can change it, or hire another writer to revise it, or start all over from scratch.

In the theater, however, it is still usually considered a director's job to *interpret* the script but never to *modify* it without the playwright's permission. In serious theater, the playwright remains the star. Look at the advertisements for any Broadway play. The playwright's name is likely to be printed as large as (or larger than) any of the actors' names, while the director often appears third in the hierarchy.

Yet any playwright will admit that there is no substitute for a talented director. Especially when you're starting out and don't yet know the conventions of the stage, it is crucial to have the guidance of an experienced director, someone who can see the strengths and limitations of your script in a way that you probably can't.

If your play is part of an evening of ten-minute plays and a director has been assigned to it, how much interaction will you have with that person? Obviously, that depends to a large extent on how close you live to the theater. If you're nearby, some directors like to have the playwright at the rehearsals; others don't. Some directors want the playwright to talk with the actors about each character's goals and motivations; others don't want the playwright to say a word to the cast. Ultimately playwrights need to be prepared to let the director take over, for in the end actors can take only one set of directions.

"Let's put on a show!" Mickey Rooney famously said to Judy Garland in their 1939 film *Babes in Arms*, and that spirit of do-it-yourself verve remains alive and well in the theater. If you're intent on seeing your play produced and you can't find a company willing to take it on, there is a long theatrical tradition of self-production. For beginning playwrights, therefore, the producer may simply be a financially solvent family member or friend. Or, depending on how much it costs to put on the show, the producer might be you. If so, you will find that the major expenses of producing your own play include renting a space for the performance and hiring a director. You might also need to pay for the technical assistance of a stage manager and a lighting person. Then you must rent or buy or borrow the costumes and props, and of course you'll need tickets. Little expenses mount up, but fortunately for playwrights, good actors, the heart of your show, often work for free.

A Few Words of Farewell

Coming to the end of an introductory creative writing class is a bittersweet time. Students are gratified to finish a job well done, but they also sense that there is so much more for them to discover. Still, most students will have learned a great deal—from their instructor and their classmates, from their readings in the genre, and, I hope, from their textbook as well. As I noted in the introduction, *Creative Writing: Four Genres in Brief* is meant to supplement, but never replace, what happens in the classroom, and most of what you take away from your class will be memories of your fellow writers.

Nevertheless, it has been my pleasure to pass on in print what I have learned over the years, not only from my own teachers and the writers I have admired but also from the thousands of creative writing students I have taught, all of them—like you—bringing a fresh perspective and boundless energy to the world of literature.

So let me offer a few final words of advice:

▸ **Keep in touch with the friends you have made** Look for opportunities outside class to share work with people who have been constructive critics of your work. Talk about recent books you have read and loved. Start a writing group. Hang out.

▸ **Keep in touch with your instructor** Drop by next term and say thanks. Take the time to write an e-mail recalling the highlights of your class. Especially if you have had a literary success, she or he will be glad to know about it.

▸ **Take another creative writing class** Attend a writers' conference (you will find many of them listed on the Association of Writers and Writing Programs' Web site). Learn more about the world of creative writing by reading journals such as *Poets & Writers Magazine* and *The Writer's Chronicle* or books such as *Keywords in Creative Writing*.

▸ **When you feel confident enough to do so, submit your work for publication** Reread the previous section on getting published and produced, and don't be discouraged by rejection notices. All writers get them (I have received hundreds of them over the years). Rejection is part of the business of being a writer.

▸ **Most important, keep writing** Even if you never publish a word, the ability to animate the creatures of your imagination is a special gift, one you should cherish all your life.

Glossary

aesthetic A theory or conception of beauty and taste in art.

alliteration The repetition of initial consonant sounds.

allusion A reference to a specific person, place, or thing; literary allusions refer to incidents, images, or passages in previous works of literature.

anapest A metrical foot consisting of two unstressed syllables followed by one stressed syllable.

antagonist A character who serves as another character's opponent or adversary.

archaic language Language that evokes an earlier place and time and is now obsolete.

arena theater A type of stage in which the audience surrounds the actors, who make their entrances and exits in diagonals between the seats; also called theater in the round or theater in the square.

assonance The repetition of vowel sounds without the repetition of similar end consonants.

backstory The narrative of events leading up to the current moment in a work of fiction; also called exposition.

ballad A narrative poem in quatrains rhyming *abcb*, with alternating lines of four and three metrical feet.

beat A distinct movement, whether of action, dialogue, or conflict, in a play. Also refers to the pause following the end of that movement.

blackout A lighting cue in a playscript indicating that all the lights go off at once.

blocking The positioning and movement of actors onstage.

chapbook A short book of poetry, usually fewer than thirty-two pages.

characters The people in a work of creative writing.

chronology An account of the way time actually moves, from past to present to future.

cinquain A poetic form named after the French word *cinq*, meaning "five." In the broadest sense, a cinquain is simply a five-line stanza, although it now usually refers to a five-line form with a specific syllable count in each line.

cliché A trite, overused expression.

climax The turning point in a narrative; the point of maximum dramatic attention.

connotation The meanings a word *suggests* rather than what it specifically names or describes.

consonance The recurrence of consonant sounds, especially at the end of stressed syllables, but without similar-sounding vowels.

couplet Two consecutive lines of verse that are connected in some significant way.

creative nonfiction Literary writing that claims to be true.

dactyl A metrical foot consisting of one stressed syllable followed by two unstressed syllables.

denouement The French word for "untying," in this case referring to untying the knot of a narrative plot.

dialect Nonstandard language associated with a particular group, culture, or region.

dialogue Conversation between characters.

diction A writer's or speaker's choice of words.

dimeter A poetic line consisting of two feet.

double rhyme Words with the same vowel sound in the final two syllables.

doubling Having one actor play more than one character when those characters aren't onstage at the same time.

drama A composition intended for theatrical performance, in which actors perform the designated action and speak the written dialogue.

dramatic monologue A literary work (usually a poem) in which the author adopts a persona and writes as if speaking to another character.

dramatic question A problem at the core of a play that must be answered by the play's end.

elegy A poem expressing sadness and nostalgia for someone who has died or something that has vanished or substantially changed.

end rhyme The agreement of two metrically accented syllables and their terminal consonants.

end-stopped A line of poetry that concludes with any sort of punctuation (a period, semicolon, comma, or dash).

enjambment The act of running a sentence across one or more lines of poetry so that the line of verse does not end with a mark of punctuation.

epithalamium A poem written to celebrate a marriage.

etymology The origin and derivation of a word; its "word history."

exposition An explanation of the history or "backstory" leading up to the present moment in a narrative.

falling rhyme A two-syllable rhyme; formerly called a "feminine rhyme" in which the final syllable or syllables are unstressed.

fiction Something that is invented or made up.

figurative language Language that departs from what speakers or writers ordinarily use in order to achieve a special meaning or effect.

first-person point of view Told from the perspective of a character who is — sometimes centrally, sometimes more peripherally — participating in the action of the narrative.

flashback The sudden intrusion of past events in the middle of a description of current action.

flash forward The sudden intrusion of future events in the middle of a description of current action.

flat (or two-dimensional) character A caricature; a character lacking complexity or incapable of generating surprise.

foot The basic metrical unit in poetry, usually consisting of one stressed and one or two unstressed syllables.

free verse A poetic composition that is not in metrical writing.

genre A particular category of literary work; in this book, refers to poetry, fiction, creative nonfiction, and drama.

ghazal A poetic form derived from Persian and Urdu sources. Ghazals traditionally consist of five to twelve loosely related but self-contained couplets of approximately the same length; have a melancholy subject, often the hopelessness of an unsatisfied romantic attachment; and repeat the final word or words of the second line at the end of all the second lines.

heptameter A poetic line consisting of seven feet.

hexameter A poetic line consisting of six feet.

iamb A metrical foot consisting of one unstressed syllable followed by one stressed syllable.

imagery Mental pictures or impressions that evoke one of the five senses.

in medias res From the Latin phrase meaning "in the middle of things"; refers to beginning a work of literature in the midst of the main action.

internal rhyme A rhyme that occurs within a single line of poetry.

irony The incongruity between the way things appear and the way they actually are.

irregular meter Poetic meter in which not all the feet are identical.

light verse Poetry, usually rhymed, that treats its subject in a comic or good-natured manner.

line A unit of poetry consisting of a word or words, usually beginning on the left side of the page and ending where the poet decides to "break" or wrap the unit, usually before the right-hand margin.

logline A one-sentence summary of a script, usually twenty-five words or less.

lyric poem A short, nonnarrative poem.

metaphor A figure of speech in which a word or phrase that ordinarily denotes one thing is applied to something else in order to suggest an analogy or likeness between the two things.

meter The arrangement of words in a poem based on the relative stress of their syllables.

metonymy A type of figurative language in which the name of something is substituted with the name of something else closely associated with it.

monologue An extended speech by a character.

monometer A poetic line consisting of one foot.

narrative A story.

octameter A poetic line consisting of eight feet.

octave The first eight lines of a Petrarchan sonnet.

octet A stanza of eight lines.

ode A lyric poem often commemorating an important event.

one-act play A play without an intermission.

onomatopoeia A words that sounds like what it means.

pantoum A poetic form that originated in Malaysia consisting of any number of quatrains that rhyme *abab*, with the second and fourth lines of one quatrain repeating as the first and third lines of the following quatrain.

paraphrase Restating something in one's own words.

pedagogy The art or theory of teaching.

pentameter A poetic line consisting of five feet.

perfect rhyme A rhyme in which the correspondence between the two sounds is exact.

personification The awarding of human attributes to an abstraction or nonhuman thing.

Petrarchan sonnet A sonnet named after the Italian poet Francesco Petrarch consisting of an octave and sestet that rhyme *abbaabba cdecde*.

plot A narrative of events, with an emphasis on causality.

poetry Concentrated, vivid, rhythmic, and musical language.

point of view The narrative perspective from which a work of literature is told.

post modern In creative writing, a style that is ironic, skeptical, experimental, and extremely self-aware.

polysyllabic rhymes Rhymes of more than one syllable.

prop Short for stage "property" in a play; can include both larger "set props" and smaller "hand props."

proscenium The most common type of theatrical stage, in which part of the stage extends beyond the curtains toward the audience to form an "apron."

prose The ordinary language of writing and speaking.

prose poem A composition in prose that has all the heightened, compressed, and figurative language found in poetry.

prosody The study of metrical structure in poetry.

protagonist The principal character in a work of literature.

pun A play on the multiple meanings of a word or its relation to other words that sound like it.

pyrrhic A metrical foot consisting of two unstressed syllables.

quatrain A stanza of four lines.

quintet A stanza of five lines.

refrain A repeating line or phrase.

resolution The "falling action" that follows the climax of a work of literature.

revision The act of reconsidering and altering a piece of writing.

rhyme A correspondence of sound in two or more words.

rhyme scheme A purposeful arrangement of rhyming words at the end of each line.

rhythm The recurrent alteration of pronounced and softer elements in poetry or prose.

rising action The escalation and complication of a work's central conflict.

rondeau A French poetic form heavily reliant on repetition, with a total of fifteen lines in three stanzas: a quintet, a quatrain, and a sestet. Two rhyme sounds repeat themselves throughout the poem. The opening words of the first line reappear as a refrain at the end of the second and third stanzas.

round (or **three-dimensional**) **character** A character who is imperfect, resembles a real human being, and is capable of surprising in a convincing way.

scansion The process of counting the number of stressed and unstressed syllables and analyzing their patterns.

second-person point of view A narrative perspective that requires the reader to become a character in the literary work.

septet A stanza of seven lines.

sestet A stanza of six lines; also the concluding six lines of a Petrarchan sonnet.

sestina An Italian poetic form consisting of six sestets followed by a tercet, which constitutes the envoi, the concluding remarks of the poem. The final words in each line repeat themselves in a specific pattern, with the envoi including all six words in its three lines.

set Short for the "setting" of a play; includes stage constructions and painted backdrops.

setting The time, place, and circumstances in which a work of literature occurs.

Shakespearean sonnet A sonnet with three quatrains rhyming *abab cdcd efef,* followed by a final couplet that rhymes *gg.*

sight rhymes Words that look as though they should rhyme, but don't rhyme when they are said aloud.

simile A figure of speech that states a likeness between two unlike things, normally using words such as "like," "as," or "seems."

single rhyme A rhyme between single stressed syllables; formerly called a "masculine rhyme."

situational irony Irony resulting from the fact that a situation is distinctly at odds from what one might reasonably expect.

slant rhyme A rhyme in which vowel sounds may be either similar or significantly dissimilar and in which the rhymed consonants may themselves be similar rather than identical.

sonnet Fourteen lines of rhymed iambic pentameter, with varying rhyme schemes.

spondee A metrical foot consisting of two stressed syllables.

stage business Apparently incidental actions performed by actors for dramatic effect.

stanza A grouping of poetic lines.

stereotype A person with one or two easily recognizable characteristics.

story A narrative of events arranged in their time sequence.

style An author's individual and characteristic use of language.

summary A synopsis that covers the main points succinctly.

suspense Anxiety about the outcome of an event.

symbol Something concrete and specific that stands for something general and abstract.

synecdoche A kind of metonymy in which a part is used to describe the whole.

syntax The arrangement of words to form phrases in a sentence.

tenor The subject to which a metaphor is applied.

tercet A stanza of three lines.

terza rima A poem in three-line stanzas, in which the end words of the first and third lines rhyme and the end word of the second line becomes the rhyming word in the following stanza.

tetrameter A poetic line consisting of four feet.

theater in the round *See* **arena theater**.

theme The central idea or concept conveyed by a literary work.

third-person limited point of view A storytelling perspective in which the narrator looks over the shoulder, and sometimes into the mind, of a single character in the story.

third-person omniscient point of view A storytelling perspective that allows the narrator to enter, godlike, the mind and situation of anyone in the story.

three-dimensional character *See* **round character**.

thrust stage A type of stage in which the proscenium or apron is surrounded on three sides by the audience.

tone A writer's style and manner of expression.

trimeter A poetic line consisting of three feet.

triolet An eight-line poem in iambic tetrameter, with two refrains—A and B—and with the following rhyme scheme: *ABaAabAB*.

triple rhyme Words with the same vowel sound in the final three syllables.

trochee A metrical foot consisting of one stressed syllable followed by one unstressed syllable.

two-dimensional character *See* **flat character**.

vehicle In a metaphor, the metaphoric term itself (as opposed to the tenor).

verbal irony A type of irony that occurs when someone says one thing but means another.

verisimilitude Having the appearance of truth; a realistic portrayal of the world.

villanelle A poetic form consisting of five tercets and a final quatrain. The first and third lines of the first stanza alternately repeat as the third line in the subsequent tercets.

volta Italian for "turn"; refers to the point in a sonnet where the argument changes direction or tone.

Acknowledgments

Diane Ackerman, "The Mute Sense." From *A Natural History of the Senses* by Diane Ackerman. Copyright © 1990 by Diane Ackerman. Used by permission of Random House, Inc.

Elizabeth Alexander, "House Party Sonnet:'66." From *Crave Radiance: New And Selected Poems* 1990–2010. Copyright © 2011 by Elizabeth Alexander. Reprinted with the permission of The Permissions Company, Inc. on behalf of Graywolf Press, Minneapolis Minnesota (www.graywolfpress.org.).

Sherman Alexie, "Baseball." Reprinted from *The Business Of Fancydancing.* Copyright © 1992 by Sherman Alexie. Used by permission of Hanging Loose Press.

Agha Shahid Ali, "Postcard from Kashmir." From *The Half-Inch Himalayas.* Reprinted by permission of Wesleyan University Press.

Roberta Allen, "Marzipan." From *Certain People & Other Stories* by Roberta Allen. Copyright © 1997 by Roberta Allen.

Rae Armantrout, "Duration." From *Money Shot.* Copyright © 2011 by Rae Armantrout. Reprinted by permission of Wesleyan University Press.

Margaret Atwood, "An Angel." From *Good Bones and Simple Murders.* Copyright © 1983, 1992, 1994 by O.W. Toad Ltd. A Nan A. Talese Book. Used by permission of Doubleday, a division of Random House, Inc., the author, and McClelland & Stewart.

Isaac Babel, "Crossing the River Zbrucz." From *Complete Works Of Isaac Babel* by Isaac Babel with Introduction by Cynthia Ozick, edited by Nathalie Babel, translated by Peter Constantine. Copyright © 2002 by Peter Constantine. Used by permission of W. W. Norton & Company, Inc.

Donald Barthelme, "The First Thing Baby Did Wrong." Copyright © 1987 by Donald Barthelme, permission of The Wylie Agency LLC.

Aimee Bender, "Loser." From *The Girl in The Flammable Skirt.* Copyright © 1998 by Aimee Bender. Used by permission of Doubleday, a division of Random House, Inc.

T. Coraghessan Boyle, "The Hit Man." From *T.C. Boyle Stories: The Collected Stories of T. Coraghessan Boyle.* Copyright © 1998 by T. Coraghessan Boyle. Used by permission of Viking Penguin, a division of Penguin Group (USA) Inc.

James Brown, "My Papa's Waltz." From *The Los Angeles Diaries.* Copyright © 2010 by James Brown. Reprinted by permission of Counterpoint.

Ron Carlson, "A Kind of Flying." From *A Kind of Flying: Selected Stories.* Copyright © 2003, 1997, 1992, 1987 by Ron Carlson. Reprinted by permission of W.W. Norton & Company, Inc.

Raymond Carver, "Popular Mechanics." From *What We Talk About When We Talk About Love: Stories* by Raymond Carver. Copyright © 1974, 1976, 1978, 1980, 1981 by Raymond Carver. Reprinted by permission of Alfred A. Knopf, a division of Random House, Inc. Electronic rights by permission of The Wylie Agency LLC.

David Case, "Hideous Towns." Reprinted by permission of the Estate of David Case.

Lorna Dee Cervantes, "Poem for the Young White Man Who Asked Me How I, An Intelligent, Well-Read Person, Could Believe in the War Between the Races." From *Emplumada* by Lorna Dee Cervantes. Copyright © 1982. Reprinted by permission of the University of Pittsburgh Press.

John Cheever, "Reunion." From *The Stories of John Cheever.* Copyright © 1978 by John Cheever. Reprinted by permission of Alfred A. Knopf, a division of Random House, Inc.

Marilyn Chin, "Repulse Bay." Originally published in *Dwarf Bamboo* (Greenfield Review Press, 1987), is reprinted by permission of the author.

Wanda Coleman, "Brute Strength." From *Heavy Daughter Blues: Poems and Stories 1968–1986* by Wanda Coleman. Reprinted by permission of the author.

Billy Collins, "Nostalgia." From *Questions About Angels*. Copyright © 1991. Reprinted by permission of the University of Pittsburgh Press.

Edwidge Danticat, "Westbury Court." First published in *New Letters*, Volume 65, #4. Copyright © 1999 by Edwidge Danticat. Reprinted by permission of the author and Aragi Inc.

Joan Didion, "In Bed." From *The White Album* by Joan Didion. Copyright (C) 1979 by Joan Didion. Reprinted by permission of Farrar, Straus and Giroux, LLC.

Dan Dietz, "Trash Anthem." Copyright © 2001 by Dan Dietz. All rights reserved. Reprinted by permission of Bret Adams Ltd.

Brian Doyle, "Joyas Voladoras." Reprinted from *The American Scholar*, vol. 73, no.4, Autumn 2004, by permission of the publisher. Copyright © 2004 by Brian Doyle.

Elaine Equi, "A Quiet Poem." From *Ripple Effect: New and Selected Poems*. Copyright © 2007 Elaine Equi. Reprinted with the permission of The Permissions company, Inc. on behalf of Coffee House Press, www.coffeehousepress.com.

Kristina Halvorson, "Now We're Really Getting Somewhere." Copyright © 2003 by Kristina Halvorson. All rights reserved. Reprinted by permission of the author.

Joy Harjo, "Santa Fe." From *In Mad Love and War*. Copyright © 1990 by Joy Harjo. Reprinted by permission of Wesleyan University Press.

Ursula Hegi, "Doves." Originally published in *Prairie Schooner*, 65, No.4, Winter 1992. Copyright © 1991 by University of Nebraska Press. Copyright © renewed 1999 by Ursula Hegi. Reprinted by permission of Brandt & Brandt Literary Agents, Inc. All rights reserved.

Geoffrey Hill, "September Song." From *Selected Poems*. Copyright © 2006 by Geoffrey Hill. Reprinted by permission of the publisher Yale University Press.

Brenda Hillman, "Shadows in Snow." From *Practical Water*. Copyright © 2009 by Brenda Hillman. Reprinted by permission of Wesleyan University Press.

Pam Houston, "Symphony." From *Cowboys Are My Weakness* by Pam Houston. Copyright © 1992 by Pam Houston. Used by permission of W.W. Norton & Company, Inc.

Tina Howe, "The Divine Fallacy." Copyright © 1999 by Tina Howe. From the collection of plays by Tina Howe entitled *Shrinking Violets and Towering Tiger Lilies: Six Short Plays About Women In Distress*. Reprinted by permission of William Morris Endeavor Entertainment, LLC on behalf of the author.

David Henry Hwang, "Trying to Find Chinatown." Copyright © 1996 by David Henry Hwang. All rights reserved. Reprinted by permission of Paradigm Talent Agency.

David Ives, "Sure Thing." Copyright © 1989, 1990, 1992 by David Ives from *All in the Timing: Fourteen Plays* by David Ives. Used by permission of Vintage Books, a division of Random House, Inc.

Pico Iyer, "In the Dark." From *Sun After Dark*. Copyright © 2004 by Pico Iyer. Used by permission of Alfred A. Knopf, a division of Random House, Inc.

Allison Joseph, "On Being Told I Don't Speak Like a Black Person." From *Imitation of Life* by Allison Joseph. Copyright © 2003 by Allison Joseph. Reprinted with the permission of The Permissions Company, Inc. on behalf of Carnegie Mellon University Press, www.cmu.edu/universitypress.

Jane Kenyon, "The Blue Bowl." From *Collected Poems*. Copyright © 2005 by The Estate of Jane Kenyon. Reprinted with the permission of The Permissions Company, Inc. on behalf of Graywolf Press, Minneapolis, MN, www.graywolfpress.org.

Jamaica Kincaid, "Girl." From *At the Bottom of the River* by Jamaica Kincaid. Copyright © 1983 by Jamaica Kincaid. Reprinted by permission of Farrar, Straus, and Giroux, LLC. Electronic rights by permission of The Wylie Agency LLC.

Galway Kinnell, "That Silent Evening." From *The Past*. Copyright © 1985 by Galway Kinnell. Reprinted by permission of Houghton Mifflin Harcourt Publishing Company. All rights reserved.

Lois Klein, "Braids," from *A Soldier's Daughter* by Lois Klein. Copyright © 2008 Turning Point Books. Used by permission of WordTech Communications LLC.

Adam Kraar, "Love on the B-Line." Reprinted by permission of the author. Copyright © 2005 by Adam Kraar. All inquiries concerning rights should be addressed to Elaine Devlin Literary, Inc., 20 West 23 St., Suite 3, New York, NY 10010, email: edevlinlit@aol.com

Ben Lerner, "We Have Assembled." From *Angle of Yaw*. Copyright © 2006 by Ben Lerner. Reprinted with the permission of The Permissions Company, Inc. on behalf of Copper Canyon Press, www.coppercanyonpress.org

Perie Longo, "A Way of Healing." Reprinted by permission of the author.

Glenna Luschei, "Cinquain," "Amber," and "Dissertation." Reprinted by permission of the author.

K. Alexa Mavromatis, "Bone China." Copyright © 2007 by K. Alexa Mavromatis. Reprinted by permission of the author. For performance rights, contact Smith and Kraus, Inc., www.smithandkraus.com

Rebecca McClanahan, "Liferower." Reprinted by permission of the author.

Dinty Moore, "El Toro Rojo." Reprinted by permission of the author.

Aimee Nezhukumatathil, "The Witching Hour." Reprinted by permission of the author.

D. Nurkse, "Left Field." From *The Fall*, copyright © 2002 by D. Nurkse. Used by permission of Alfred A. Knopf, a division of Random House, Inc.

Naomi Shihab Nye, "I Feel Sorry for Jesus." From *You & Yours*. Copyright © 2005 by Naomi Shihab Nye. Reprinted with the permission of The Permissions Company, Inc. on behalf of BOA Editions Ltd., www.boaeditions.org.

Joyce Carol Oates, "Wolf's Head Lake." From *I Am No One You Know: Stories* by Joyce Carol Oates. Copyright © 2004 by The Ontario Review, Inc. Reprinted by permission of HarperCollins Publishers.

Mary Oliver, "Crossing the Swamp." From *American Primitive*. Copyright © 1978, 1979, 1980, 1981, 1982, 1983 by Mary Oliver. By permission of Little, Brown and Company. All rights reserved.

David O'Meara, "The Game." From *Noble Gas, Penny Black* (Brick Books 2008). Reprinted by permission of the publisher.

Deborah Paredez, "Bustillo Drive Grocery." First published in *This Side of Skin* by Deborah Paredez (Wings Press, 2002). Reprinted by permission of the publisher.

Linda Pastan, "November." Copyright © 1981 by Linda Pastan from *Carnival Evening: New and Selected Poems* 1968–1998 by Linda Pastan. Used by permission of W.W. Norton & Company, Inc. Electronic rights by permission of the author in care of Jean Naggar Lierary Agency, Inc. email: permissions@jvnla.com.

Bradley Paul, "Short Ends." From *The Animals All Are Gathering*. Copyright © 2010. Reprinted by permission of the University of Pittsburgh Press.

Molly Peacock, "Instead of Her Own." Copyright © 1989 by Molly Peacock, from *Cornucopia: New and Selected Poems* by Molly Peacock. Used by permission of W.W. Norton & Company, Inc.

Jim Peterson, "The Empty Bowl." Reprinted by permission of the author.

John M. Ridland, "After the Holidays." Reprinted by permission of the author. Copyright © 2009 by John M. Ridland.

Reg Saner, "Late July, 4:40 A.M." From *Reaching Keet Seel*. Originally published in *American Literary Review* (Fall 1994). Copyright © 1998 by Reg Saner. Reprinted with the permission of the University of Utah Press.

David Sedaris, "Jesus Shaves." From *Holidays on Ice* by David Sedaris. Copyright © 2008 by David Sedaris. By permission of Little, Brown and Company. All rights reserved. Originally published in *Esquire* magazine. Electronic use by permission of Don Congdon Associates, Inc., collected in *Me Talk Pretty One Day*. Copyright © 2000 by David Sedaris.

Patricia Smith, "Listening at the Door." From *Teahouse of The Almighty*. Copyright © 2006 by Patricia Smith. Reprinted with the permission of The Permissions Company, Inc. on behalf of Coffee House Press, www.coffeehousepress.com.

Gary Snyder, "I Went into the Maverick Bar." From *Turtle Island* by Gary Snyder. Copyright © 1974 by Gary Snyder. Reprinted by permission of New Directions Publishing Corp.

Gary Soto, "What is Your Major?" From *Junior College*. Copyright © 1997 by Gary Soto. Used by permission of the author.

Barry Spacks, "Sestina on Sestinas" and "Satie Playing." Reprinted by permission of the author.

Ruth Stone, "Winter." From *What Love Comes To: New and Selected Poems*. Copyright © 1987 by Ruth Stone. Reprinted with the permission of The Permissions Company, Inc. on behalf of Copper Canyon Press, www.coppercanyonpress.org.

James Tate, "Teaching the Ape to Write Poems." From *Selected Poems*. Copyright © 1991 by James Tate. Reprinted by permission of Wesleyan University Press.

Guadalupe Valdes, "Recuerdo." First published in *De Colores Journal* 2, No. 3 (1976) is reprinted by permission of the author.

Gloria Vando, "new shoes and an old flame." Reprinted with permission of the publisher of *Shadows & Supposes* by Gloria Vando. Copyright © 2002 by Arte Publico Press-University of Houston.

Alma Luz Villanueva, "bitch bitch bitch bitch." Reprinted by permission of the author.

Alice Walker, "Dreads." From *Anything We Love Can Be Saved*. Copyright © 1997 by Alice Walker. Used by permission of Random House, Inc.

Gail White, "My Personal Recollections of Not Being Asked to the Prom." From *The Price Of Everything* (2002). Reprinted by permission of the author.

Paul Willis, "Foothill Road." First appeared in *Christian Century*, 1997. Reprinted by permission of the author.

David Wojahn, "The Assassination of John Lennon as Depicted by the Madame Tussaud Wax Museum, Niagara Falls, Ontario, 1987." From *Interrogation Palace: New and Selected Poems* 1982–2004. Copyright © 2006. Reprinted by permission of the University of Pittsburgh Press.

Matthew Zapruder, "Automated Regret Machine." From *Come On All You Ghosts*. Copyright © 2010 by Matthew Zapruder. Reprinted with the permission of The Permissions Company, Inc. on behalf of Copper Canyon Press, www.coppercanyonpress.org.

Index

REVISION CHECKLIST Creative Nonfiction

▶ **Organizing Creative Nonfiction**

☐ Does your essay begin with an attention-grabbing hook and end in a way that is both surprising and compelling?

☐ If you are braiding together several different topics, are those segments clearly focused and connected by well-marked transitions?

▶ **Telling the Truth**

☐ Do you, to the best of your ability, tell the truth in your essay?

▶ **Creative Nonfiction as Narrative**

☐ Are the people in your essay, including yourself, three-dimensional characters rather than two-dimensional caricatures?

☐ If your creative nonfiction contains dialogue, is it short, vivid, and believable?

☐ Are the settings briefly yet vividly rendered?

▶ **The Poetry of Creative Nonfiction**

☐ Does your creative nonfiction make compelling use of imagery, metaphors, and similes?

☐ Have you paid careful attention to the diction, sound, and rhythm of your sentences?

▶ **Writing Yourself Into Creative Nonfiction**

☐ Have you located the "I" in your creative nonfiction in the most effective and candid authorial position?

▶ **Ethics and Edicts**

☐ Have you double-checked the facts in your essay and steered clear of any unjustified disparagement of people and institutions?

☐ If you know that someone you have written about is going to read your creative nonfiction, have you gauged that person's likely response and how you will be affected by it?